Educational Innovation in Economics and Business V

Educational Innovation in Economics and Business

Volume 5

The titles published in this series are listed at the end of this volume.

Educational Innovation in Economics and Business V

Business Education for the Changing Workplace

Edited by

Lex Borghans
*University of Maastricht,
The Netherlands*

Wim H. Gijselaers
*University of Maastricht,
The Netherlands*

Richard G. Milter
*Ohio University,
Athens, Ohio, U.S.A.*

and

John E. Stinson
*Ohio University,
Athens, Ohio, U.S.A.*

KLUWER ACADEMIC PUBLISHERS
DORDRECHT / BOSTON / LONDON

A C.I.P. Catalogue record for this book is available from the Library of Congress.

ISBN 0-7923-6550-X

Published by Kluwer Academic Publishers,
P.O. Box 17, 3300 AA Dordrecht, The Netherlands.

Sold and distributed in North, Central and South America
by Kluwer Academic Publishers,
101 Philip Drive, Norwell, MA 02061, U.S.A.

In all other countries, sold and distributed
by Kluwer Academic Publishers,
P.O. Box 322, 3300 AH Dordrecht, The Netherlands.

Printed on acid-free paper

All Rights Reserved
© 2000 Kluwer Academic Publishers
No part of the material protected by this copyright notice may be reproduced or
utilized in any form or by any means, electronic or mechanical,
including photocopying, recording or by any information storage and
retrieval system, without written permission from the copyright owner.

Printed in the Netherlands.

Contents

Contributors	ix
Preface	xv
Acknowledgements	xix
The Editors	xxi

Part I: Learning in a Changing Workplace	1
Developing Added Value Skills Within an Academic Program Through Work Based Learning STEWART FALCONER & MALCOLM PETTIGREW	3
Leadership Education in a Changing Workplace JENNIFER FREDERICK & CAROL DALGLISH	17
New Training Methods: A Giant Leap of Faith? DES MONK	31
The Economics of the Learning Organization and the Role of Economics in the Organization of Learning JOSEPH G. NELLIS & STEPHEN REGAN	57

Part II: Technology and Innovation — 69

The IS Department Defines the Future of the College of Business — 71
JAMES PEROTTI

Informatics Engineering and Business Informatics in the Ict Society: Substitutes Or Complements? — 85
HANS HEIJKE & GER RAMAEKERS

An Innovative Approach to Teaching Investments Using Information Technology — 111
RICHARD J. CURCIO

People, Knowledge, and the Internet: Redefining Categories, Concepts, and Models — 129
TATYANA DUMOVA

Integration of Groupware Into a MIS Curriculum — 149
GAIL CORBITT, BEN MARTZ & LAUREN WRIGHT

Part III: Innovative Learning Methods — 167

Innovative Business Education: 'Problem-oriented Learning' – Some Results — 169
NIENKE BASTIAANS & LOUK PAUL

Competitions and Problem-Based Learning: The Effect of an Externally Set Competition on a Cross-Curricular Project in Marketing and Design — 187
FRANCES BRASSINGTON & ALAN SMITH

A Problem-Based Learning Approach to Business Software Skills — 209
VICTOR PEROTTI, PATRICIA SORCE & BEN ISSELHARDT

Some Evidence on the Use of Writing Intensive Methods in the Principles of Macroeconomics Courses — 221
MARTIN MILKMAN, EDWIN CHILDERS, JR. & WILLIAM PAYNE

Designing Assignments and Classroom Discussions to Foster Critical Thinking at Different Levels in the Curriculum — 231
SUSAN K. WOLCOTT

Part IV: Curriculum Issues — 253

Distance Learning: Paradigm Shift or Pedagogical Drift? — 255
THOMAS A. CREAHAN & BETTY HOGE

The Integration Of Service Management Principles In A Business School Curriculum — 275
KLAES ERINGA & HANS OTTING

Promoting the Human Element in Resource Based Learning for Undergraduate Business Education Programs — 291
NEIL HARRIS, ROGER OTTEWILL & ADAM PALMER

Non-Prescriptive Guidelines For More Effective Learning About High Quality Leadership, In Management Education And Development — 307
ERWIN RAUSCH & JOHN B. WASHBUSH

Cross-cultural Learning Practices for Business Education — 321
KARINA R. JENSEN

Lessons Learned: The Implementation of an Innovative Core Curriculum in Business — 345
VALERIE S. PEROTTI

Part V: New Assessment Procedures — 363

Who Am I, What Do I Want, What Can I Do? An Assessment Centre as Part of the HBO Curriculum — 365
VERONICA BRUIJNS & ELISABETH PIEKÉ

The Assessment Center: Global Issues and Local Responses — 383
MICHAEL K. MCCUDDY, WENDY L. PIRIE, MARY YORK CHRIST, LARRY E. MAINSTONE, DAVID L. SCHROEDER & SANDRA E. STRASSER

Assessment & Development Centers in a Problem-based Learning Environment — 399
WICHARD ZWAAL & KLAES ERINGA

Part VI: Cognition and Learning — 417

What Should We Expect to be Different about How Expert Business Economists Solve Problems? — 419
BRENDAN K. O'ROURKE

Tracking Down the Knowledge Structure of Students — 437
FONS VERNOOIJ

Index — 451

Contributors

Nienke Bastiaans, *Faculty of Management and Organization, University of Groningen, PO Box 800, 9700 AV Groningen, The Netherlands.* n.bastiaans@bdk.rug.nl

Lex Borghans, *Research Centre for Education and the Labour Market (ROA), Maastricht University, PO Box 616, 6200 MD Maastricht, the Netherlands.* l.borghans@roa.unimaas.nl

Frances Brassington, *Marketing, The Business School, Buckinghamshire Chilterns University College, Newland Park, Chalfont St Giles, Buckinghamshire, HP8 4AD, UK.* fbrass01@buckscol.ac.uk

Veronica Bruijns, *Co-op HEAO, Hogeschool van Amsterdam, Amsterdam.* v.m.h.bruijns@osb.hva.nl

Edwin Childers, Jr. *Department of English, Murray State University Murray, Kentucky 42071-0009, USA.* archangel@mursuky.campus.mci.net

Gail Corbitt, *College of Business, California State University, Chico California 95929-0295, USA.* gcorbitt@csuchico.edu

Thomas A. Creahan, *Morehead State University, Morehead Kentucky 40351, USA.* t.creaha@morehead-st.edu.

Richard J. Curcio, *Department of Finance, College of Business Administration, Kent State University, Ohio 44242-0001, USA.* prof100m@aol.com

Carol Dalglish, *Graduate School of Business, Queensland University of Technology, Brisbane Qld 4001, Australia.* c.dalglish@qut.edu.au

Tatyana Dumova, *School of Communication Studies, Bowling Green State University, Bowling Green Ohio 43403, USA.*

Klaes Eringa, *Christelijke Hogeschool Noord-Nederland, PO Box 1298, 8900 CG Leeuwarden, the Netherlands.* k.eringa@chn.nl

Stewart Falconer, *Department of Economics, Napier University, EH11 4BN Edinburgh, Scotland.* s.falconer@napier.ac.uk

Jenifer Frederick, *Administrative Services, Queensland Audit Office, Brisbane Qld 4001, Australia.* jfreder@hotmail.com

Wim Gijselaers, *Department of Educational Development and Educational Research, Maastricht University, PO Box 616, 6200 MD Maastricht, the Netherlands.* w. gijselaers@educ.unimaas.nl

Neil Harris, *Business Finance Faculty, Southampton Business School, East Park Terrace, Southampton SO14 0YN, England, UK.* neil.harris@solent.ac.uk

Hans Heijke, *Research Centre for Education and the Labour Market (ROA), Maastricht University, PO Box 616, 6200 MD Maastricht, the Netherlands.* h.heijke@roa.unimaas.nl

Betty Hoge, *Morehead State University, Morehead Kentucky, USA.*

Ben Isselhardt, *College of Business, Rochester Institute of Technology, Rochester New York 14623, USA.*

Karina R. Jensen, *International Communication & Development, ENPC Graduate School of International Business, 75343 Paris Cedex 07, France.*

Ben Martz, *College of Business, California State University, Chico, California 95929-0295, USA.* bmartz@csuchico.edu

Michael K. McCuddy, *College of Business Administration, Valparaiso University, Valparaiso Indiana 46383-6493, USA.* mikemccuddy@valpo.edu

Larry E. Mainstone, *College of Business Administration, Valparaiso University, Valparaiso Indiana 46383-6493, USA*. larry.mainstone@valpo.edu

Martin Milkman, *Department of Economics and Finance, Murray State University Murray, KY 42071-0009, USA*. martin.milkman@murraystate.edu

Richard G. Milter, *College of Business, Ohio University, Athens Ohio 45701, USA*. milter@ohiou.edu

Des Monk, *Department Of International Business, University Of Central Lancashire, Preston PR1 2HE, UK*. d.monk@uclan.ac.uk

Joseph G. Nellis, *Cranfield School of Management, Cranfield University, Cranfield, Bedfordshire MK43 OAL, UK*.

Roger Ottewill, *Sheffield Business School, Sheffield Hallam University, Pond Street, Sheffield S1 1WB, UK*. r.m.ottewill@shu.ac.uk

Brendan K. O'Rourke, *School of Business & Management, Dublin Institute of Technology, Mountjoy Square, Dublin 1, Ireland*. borourke@dit.ie

Hans Otting, *Christelijke Hogeschool Noord-Nederland, Leeuwarden, the Netherlands*. hotting@chn.nl

Adam Palmer, *Human Resource Service, Southampton Institute, East Park Terrace, Southampton SO14 0YN, England, UK*. adam.palmer@solent.ac.uk

Louk Paul, *Faculty of Management and Organization, University of Groningen, Groningen, The Netherlands*.

William Payne, *Department of Economics and Finance, Murray State University Murray, KY 42071-0009, USA*. bill.payne@murraystate.edu

Malcolm Pettigrew, *Department of Economics, Napier University, Edinburgh, Scotland*. m.pettigrew@napier.ac.uk

James Perotti, *College of Business, Ohio University, Athens Ohio 45701, USA*. perotti@oak.cats.ohiou.edu

Valerie Perotti, *College of Business, Ohio University, Athens Ohio 45701, USA.* valerie.perotti@ohio.edu

Victor Perotti, *College of Business, Rochester Institute of Technology, Rochester New York 14623, USA.* vjpbbu@ritvax.isc.rit.edu

Elisabeth Pieké, *Co-op HEAO, Hogeschool van Amsterdam, Amsterdam.* epieke@worldonline.nl

Wendy L. Pirie, *College of Business Administration, Valparaiso University, Valparaiso Indiana 46383-6493, USA.* wendy.pirie@valpo.edu

Ger Ramaekers, *Research Centre for Education and the Labour Market (ROA), PO Box 616, 6200 MD Maastricht, Maastricht University, the Netherlands.* g.ramaekers@roa.unimaas.nl

Erwin Rausch, *Didactic Systems, INC. PO BOX 457, Cranford, New Jersey 07016; USA.* didacticra@aol.com

Stephen Regan, *Economics, Cranfield School of Management, Cranfield University, Cranfield, Bedfordshire MK43 OAL, UK.* S.regan@cranfield.ac.uk

Alan Smith, *Marketing, School of Business and Management, University of Teesside, Borough Road, Middlesbrough, Cleveland, TS1 3BA, UK.* alan.smith@tees.ac.uk

David L. Schroeder, *College of Business Administration, Valparaiso University, Valparaiso Indiana 46383-6493, USA.* dave.schroeder@valpo.edu

Patricia Sorce, *College of Business, Rochester Institute of Technology, Rochester New York 14623, USA.*

John E. Stinson, *College of Business, Ohio University, Athens Ohio 45701, USA and SARANTHER, Albany Ohio 45710, USA.* stinson@sarhanther.com

Sandra E. Strasser, *College of Business Administration, Valparaiso University, Valparaiso Indiana 46383-6493, USA.* sandy.strasser@valpo.edu

Fons Vernooij, *Graduate School of Teaching and Learning University of Amsterdam, Amsterdam, the Netherlands.* vernooij@ilo.uva.nl

John B. Washbush, *University of Wisconsin, Madison, USA.*

Susan K. Wolcott, *School of Accountancy, Daniels College of Business, University of Denver, Denver, Colorado 80208, USA.* swolcott@du.edu

Lauren Wright, *College of Business, California State University, Chico, California 95929-0295, USA.* lkwright@csuchico.edu

Mary York Christ, *College of Business Administration, Valparaiso University, Valparaiso Indiana 46383-6493, USA.* mary.christ@valpo.edu

Preface

The workplace is changing drastically these days. As a consequence of the Information and Communication Technology (ICT) revolution, new economic activities emerge, the production process changes, people use different communication tools, and organizational structures are adjusted. All these changes relate to the heart of business and economics, and there is no doubt that they will also influence education in these areas. Of course ICT provides new technologies to facilitate learning, but a changing workplace also requires a renewed focus within the curriculum of economics and business education.

If ICT is leading to profound change in the workplace, is innovation then only a matter of introducing more technology in education? Unfortunately, this is not necessarily true. The translation of changes in the workplace into an improved curriculum requires serious analysis of the essence of the changes at the work place, and the way technology may enable student learning.

For example, relevant knowledge is changing faster and faster. Does this mean that we have to adopt the curriculum faster and faster? Perhaps not, as students will have a labor market career of 30 or 40 years. Focusing on today's knowledge – even if it is very up-to-date – loses more and more value if the life cycle of knowledge becomes shorter. Increased speed of change also implies a decrease in the value of knowing all these things. Skills that are timeless will therefore increase in their relative value. More distance between what is taught at universities and used in actual work practices could be a rational response. Perhaps these skills might help students adopt new knowledge in the workplace.

It is often argued that students should be trained in using technology to avoid a gap between education and labor market. Many economists have shown that people working with computers earn more than people who don't use a computer! Does this mean that computer skills are rewarded? Perhaps not. Computers take over many tasks we had to perform previously, and to be honest, even we were able to learn Word, PowerPoint, and Excel without much effort. While the computer facilitates our communication, administration and formal analyses, we can spend more time on all those things a computer is still not good at: talking with people, creating new ideas, being friendly to customers etc. So perhaps we could trust that students will pick up computer skills later and focus more on all these "soft skills."

Although the relationships between a changing workplace and the curriculum are not always as linear as one might think or hope, it is evident that change is taking place and some skills are becoming more valuable than others. Does this mean that we should look for a renewed curriculum that takes care of all the things we learned ten years ago plus all these new skills? It is very likely the answer is no! We could regard people responsible for the curriculum as engineers. If they claim to be able to create a new machine that is able to meet new demands without diminishing attention for the old skills, these innovations should of course be implemented. But there is no reason to wait with these innovations until the labor market is changed. Producing more of a certain skill without offering other skills is always a gain. A changing working place requires a reevaluation of skills and, without doubt, means that while some skills increase in value, others become less important. As long as learning resources are scarce, choices have to be made.

Innovation is an important concept in economic theory and widely regarded as a major force behind economic growth and welfare. What's true for society as a whole will also hold for different kinds of activities within society, of which business and economics education are two. This strong belief that investments in educational innovations in this field are worthwhile drives the people who are contributing to the EDINEB network. EDINEB stands for "Educational Innovation in Economics and Business" and is a network organization that aims to encourage and stimulate innovation in business and economics education (visit the EDINEB website: http://www.edineb.com or http://www.edineb.net). This book offers many contributions that deal with the struggle about how to implement changes at the workplace into a renewed curriculum. It is the fifth volume in the EDINEB book series.

Like all products educational innovation in business and economics has a product life cycle. Within six years about 400 papers have been presented, most of which provided new and creative solutions to improve the way we teach, the way we organize the curriculum, the technology we use, and the cooperation with the organizations that recruit our students. The number of papers has grown from 65 for the first conference in 1993 to 120 for the fifth conference in 1998. It is evident that EDINEB has established a position in the field of innovative education in business and economics.

As is true for any product, innovation has to start with creative thought. EDINEB has brought together these creative ideas. After six years in the existence of EDINEB, two new challenges emerge. Both challenges seem to point in the same direction. The first challenge is to convince people of the need for change. Many chapters in this and previous volumes mention the resistance to change among teachers and administrators. "Nobody likes change, except wet babies" has become an important metaphor in the EDINEB discussion. But many experienced parents know that even wet babies prefer to continue playing. In the world of education, administrators and teachers sense that changes in the outside world are affecting the world of education. But it is one thing to notice change is needed, it is quite another to develop appropriate answers to different needs. EDINEB provides a platform for exchange of ideas and knowledge to work out new approaches for changing needs.

The second challenge is about evaluation and educational measurement to facilitate change. After six years of sharing creative approaches to innovation, it is about time to evaluate how far EDINEB has come. It looks like the EDINEB network planted many seeds in the fields of business and economics education. Today there are signals that these seeds have turned into crops ready for harvesting. Over the past six years, many contributors have presented their approaches to educational innovation. But it looks like we lacked sufficient time to develop a research agenda that addresses the issue what the effects of innovations are. Further progress in educational innovation in business and economics requires that we learn about what works and what is less effective. After six years of innovation the product life cycle requires that we turn from pure creativity into developing a research agenda resulting in more insights about the innovations that work. Educational innovations are always born in practice and therefore research will always be hampered by practicalities, but the only way in which we can discover the effectiveness of new ways of learning still remains with conducting educational research. From an economic point of view, this measurement should also include both the costs and the benefits.

The contributions in this volume reflect the central theme of this book: business education for the changing workplace. Part I contains contributions about what education can learn from new developments in business: learning and the changing work place. Part II – technology and innovation - explicitly puts forward the role of technology in learning. Part III contains papers about innovative learning methods.

To complement these thematic parts two smaller sections have been added which are especially interesting from the measurement point of view. Part IV is about assessment, which is a promising way to bring together as much as possible what we measure with the goals of education in business and economics. Part V focuses on cognition and learning and will contribute to our knowledge about the way in which students acquire knowledge and skills.

Finally, we want to make clear that this book is not just a book containing reprints of conference papers. The editors selected papers out of more than one hundred conference submissions based on clarity, relevance to the conference theme, quality, and scope of the innovation described. We then applied a full editorial process, requiring authors to revise their papers in such a way that we could deliver a book containing chapters that addressed the central theme from various perspectives. This is a process that takes time from both the editors as the authors. The time and energy placed in these activities has provided what follows. We trust you will reap the benefits.

Lex Borghans,
Wim H. Gijselaers
Richard G. Milter
John E. Stinson

Acknowledgements

This book is the result of the work of many. It not only required critical examination, selection and revision of conference papers by the editors. But in addition many people provided important background work for realizing a successful conference. We thank all who have made this book possible: the EDINEB Network, the College of Business, Ohio University, Athens Ohio, USA, and the Faculty of Economics and Business Administration, Maastricht University, the Netherlands.

A particular thanks to Ellen Nelissen (office manager of the EDINEB Network) and Henny Dankers (secretary of the Department of Educational Development and Research, Maastricht University) for all the background work making this book possible. Ellen Nelissen took care that the EDINEB conference ran smoothly once again. Henny Dankers wrestled the words through the computer and delivered excellent work by producing this book. We also thank Susan Neylon (Westlake Travel, Cleveland Ohio) and the conference staff of the Marriott Hotel at Key Center (Cleveland Ohio) for their support in dealing with many conference logistics. The final thanks go to the authors who have contributed their experiences, thoughts and reflections in the book.

Lex Borghans
Wim H. Gijselaers
Richard G. Milter
John E. Stinson

The Editors

Lex Borghans (Ph.D., Maastricht University, the Netherlands) works as a principal researcher at the Research Centre for Education and the Labour Market (ROA), Maastricht University. In 1988 he received master degrees in econometrics and philosophy at Tilburg University. In 1993 he finished his Ph.D.-thesis "Educational Choice and Labour Market Information." This thesis is a micro-economic study of the effects of public labor market forecasts on the educational choice of students, and thereby on the functioning of the labor market. Since 1992 he has been involved in several research projects concerning education and the labor market, especially about forecasting the employment structure by occupation and type of education and adjustment processes due to the flexibility of the labor market. Since 1998 he coordinates a research program concerning the production of human capital and the utilization of these competencies on the labor market. His research topics in this program are the measurements of skills, the way in which the learning context influences the production of skills and the economic significance of human capital.

Wim H. Gijselaers (Ph.D., Maastricht University, the Netherlands) is full professor of education at Maastricht University, the Netherlands. He is interested in various aspects of problem-based learning, cognition and instruction, and educational measurement. His current research focuses on the instructional design of powerful learning environments, instructional processes in problem-based curricula, and expertise development in management education. His professional career started at the problem-based medical school of Maastricht University. Over the past 15 years, he was involved with the implementation of problem-based learning in the economics and business programs at this University. He has served as consultant for several institutions in higher education who adopted problem-based learning as leading educational principle. He is chairman of the executive board of EDINEB, an international network of innovative educators. He has presented workshops and directed conferences on curriculum reform across the US, Austria, Scotland, Sweden, and Norway.

Richard G. Milter (Ph.D., University at Albany, SUNY) is associate professor of management and Director of the "MBA Without Boundaries" program (College of Business, Ohio University). His personal management experiences include positions in the construction, retail, education, housing, and consulting industries. He has consulted or served as a training facilitator, organization effectiveness specialist, or learning adviser to dozens of corporations and government agencies across the U.S., Europe, and Asia. His research and publications have paralleled his consulting activity in the areas of executive judgment, group decision-making processes, management information systems, negotiation strategies, managerial ethics, leadership, and innovative learning platforms. He serves on the executive board of EDINEB, and has presented workshops to educators on action-learning strategies across the U.S., Sweden, the Netherlands, Russia, Japan, and Malaysia. He is also an executive board member of the Ohio University Institute for Applied and Professional Ethics.

John E. Stinson (Ph.D., Ohio State University) focuses on corporate-level leadership, strategic transformation, and design of educational systems, with particular emphasis on virtual education and action learning in executive education. He is Professor emeritus and former Dean of the College of Business at Ohio University and he served as Director of Management Development for two Divisions of Litton Industries. Currently he is a consultant with several major companies. He is the author of six books and more than 100 journal articles, professional papers, and grants.

PART I

LEARNING IN A CHANGING WORKPLACE

Developing Added Value Skills Within an Academic Program Through Work Based Learning

Stewart Falconer & Malcolm Pettigrew
Department of Economics, Napier University, Edinburgh, Scotland

1. INTRODUCTION

Charles Handy argued in 'The Age of Unreason' (1989) that there were fundamental changes taking place in organizational life. His suggestion was that organizations were evolving into what he termed the 'shamrock' model with three groups of workers – core, contract and temporary or flexible. While university graduates of the future may see a preference for employment in the 'core' group where the attraction of at least perceived permanency of tenure is available, the likelihood is that these graduates can expect to fill roles in any of the three categories at different times in their working life. They need to be prepared for the challenges inherent in this and Harvey et al (1997) anticipate this through their references to the emergence of the 'portfolio worker' who has accumulated a portfolio of skills and experience to enable him or her to obtain and undertake the temporary, flexible, contract, consultancy or core work at different times. In general terms, Handy (1989) and Harvey (1997) subscribe to the view shared by Guirdham (1995) that the nature of work, the nature of organizations and the structure of the workforce have all changed and will continue to change.

In contrast to this perception of change, it can certainly be argued that perhaps working life is not changing that much in terms of permanency of employment and, for many years, workers have moved between jobs. At the same time, a considerable proportion of the are very likely to remain with the same employer for a major part of their working life. However, there is a view that people can no longer expect to work for the whole of their lives in one occupation and for one employer. As Harvey et al (1997) say "a guarantee of lifetime employment is increasingly unrealistic in many organizations and ... matching the lack of organizational loyalty to the individual, mobile workers are unlikely to be loyal to the organization." Many aspects of working life have become more flexible and Handy (1989) has referred to the need for a 'portfolio of activities' based on professional and technical knowledge but also on more personal skills which individuals can offer to a number of different organizations. People need to accumulate their portfolios of experience and expertise incorporating skills which can be transferred to all of these different organizations. Pugh and Hickson (1996) mention Mckinsey's estimate that by the year 2000, 80% of all jobs will require cerebral rather than manual skills, a complete reversal from half a century ago and, while a proportion of these cerebral skills will be seen as technical or professional, it seems reasonable to anticipate that a substantial number will be transferable.

This paper will focus on ways in which higher education can assist undergraduates to prepare themselves for what seems from the above views to be a changing workplace culture. Specifically, it will examine the potential of work based learning, through the experience of a work placement incorporated in an undergraduate program, to assist students in the acquisition of what are commonly known as transferable skills or competencies and which are so vital in the workplace today. Those skills which, once acquired, can be used to enable individuals to develop their careers in the flexible employment market.

2. BACKGROUND AND RESEARCH

In an effort to demonstrate the potential benefits of work based learning in the acquisition of transferable skills, we shall review our practical experience in the Department of Economics at Napier University through the inclusion of work placements as part of an undergraduate program. However, prior to doing so, it is worth spending some time examining recent developments in and attitudes towards work based learning and transferable skills.

2.1 Work Based Learning

Harvey, Moon, Geall and Bower (1997) have systematically explored the views of a wide range of employers and recent graduates to identify the nature and extent of the knowledge, abilities and skills that graduates will need in the twenty-first century if they are to be successful at work. Respondents overwhelmingly endorsed work-based placements as a means of helping students develop the attributes necessary for that success. Their conclusions included the view that placements were seen by employers and graduates as the single most significant element of the majority of degree programs; that students who have experienced a work placement are in the main better prepared for work; that placements can offer real opportunities for students to decide on a future career path; and, that there is considerable support for work placements to provide students with opportunities to develop an awareness of organizational culture and opportunities for skills development. The authors concluded that younger, full-time students, other than those who had had a significant placement experience on their course, left university with little idea of the nature and culture of the workplace and initially found it difficult to adjust to working life. 'Work placements were one of the most regularly mentioned suggestions by the respondents for helping students towards success at work, improving links and bridging the 'skills gap'. Work experience helped to develop a culture of adaptation to the real world of work'. It is perhaps reasonable to speculate that there would have been an adverse effect, at least in the early stages, on the ability of those students without the placement experience to contribute productively within the work environment but this is outside the scope of the research undertaken to date.

This endorsement of placements by Harvey et al (1997) comes some time into the life cycle of work based learning. In the UK, the concept began to take on a prominent role in the 1950s through the introduction of 'Sandwich' courses, initially in areas such as engineering, but with a rapid extension into a wider range of fields, notably and perhaps not surprisingly, business studies (Brennan and Little, 1996). However, going back further than that, it can perhaps be argued that the integration of education and training or practical experience into a unified learning experience has always been very much a part of University courses in medicine and related subject areas. At the other end of the spectrum, there is no reason why work based learning need only be a component of what we might term the 'vocational' courses. Hamm (1998) puts forward the proposal that students of arts and social sciences would be just as able to bring creativity, initiative and enthusiasm to a work placement and, in terms of broadening out their career horizons, we could speculate that they would be just as keen to do so.

While work based learning is an important component of many undergraduate programs, particularly in the newer, vocational Universities in the UK (which includes Napier University), the Dearing Report (1997) on higher education in the UK has placed more emphasis on the need to make students more familiar with the world of work. According to a recent survey at Warwick University (Purcell & Pilcher, 1996), students themselves point to placements as being one of the most rewarding elements of their courses. The decision to incorporate a work based placement in the B.A. (Honours) degree in Financial Services at Napier University was based on the expectation that a vocational placement which related directly to the degree course had the potential to enable the student to gain experience which augmented theoretical studies. Our experience, which will be demonstrated in the latter part of this paper, is that the placement can broaden out knowledge and understanding of an organization and also of working life, not least through providing the opportunity to acquire transferable skills, enabling the student to demonstrate that they can apply in a practical environment what they have learned at university.

2.2 Transferable Skills

If then, work based learning is already seen as an increasingly significant component of undergraduate programs, it is worth looking at the value it adds in the development of student skills. A useful point of reference in this is the report prepared by Davies (1990) for the UK Council for National Academic Awards on Experience Based Learning in the Curriculum. Davies examined the development of work based learning in terms of how placements are developed and managed, the nature of the experiential learning which occurs within the placements, the different perceptions of academic staff, students and employers and, not surprisingly, the costs and benefits. He also looked at governmental and quasi-governmental attitudes to the development of work based learning ranging across the statement from the Royal Society of Arts (1979) that "learning is to be by active involvement and related to experience ... to provide an appropriately skilled workforce for the future", to the Secretary of State for Education (1988).

> "The curriculum should bring out ... relevance to and links with students' own experience and background and their practical application and continuing value to adult and working life ... the development of general, personal qualities and competencies ... for example, self-reliance, self-discipline, enterprise, social responsibility ... the ability to work harmoniously with others, an ability to apply knowledge and use it to solve practical, real-life problems."

More recently, Harvey and Knight (1996) refer to the Quality in Higher Education (QHE) project undertaken in 1992 which suggested that university staff, students and employers all regarded the development of transferable skills as an important outcome of higher education with employers seeking a range and balance of these skills in their recruits. A considerable list of these skills could be compiled, skills which will in many cases not be an intrinsic part of the study program. Harvey and Knight (1996) list willingness to learn, team work, communication, problem-solving, analytic ability, logical argument and ability to summarize key issues along with a range of more personal attributes such as commitment and energy. Greenwood, Edge and Hodgetts (1987), who have undertaken three research studies across a period of some thirteen years into the characteristics or skills which managers expected of business graduates, identified three groups, knowledge, skills and traits or attributes. The knowledge category included the technical or academic skills while traits consisted of more personal attributes such as Harvey and Knight's commitment and energy. What we have regarded as transferable skills come under Greenwood et al's heading of 'skills' and, across the three studies completed in 1973, 1983 and 1986, the same four groups of skills were most popular amongst the managers who responded:
– communication;
– analyze data, propose solutions, make decisions;
– plan, develop, organize, co-ordinate;
– work with others, motivate.

Their conclusion was that the results followed a continuum which emphasized people-orientated skills and, consequently, their view was that universities should focus on these people-orientated aspects in business education.

In support of these latter two studies, Guirdham (1995) concluded that across the five year period from the beginning of the decade, the value and need for inter-personal skills development had been widely recognized. Changes in organizational life had increased the demands on the inter-personal skills of people at work, partly through a reduction in the degree to which work is organized through procedures, rules, authority and supervision. To take decisions, people at work need information and, despite the increasing use of information technology, a lot of information continues to be obtained through contact with other people, resulting in a demand for communication skills. In addition, she concluded that, since team work is an integral component of the workplace, the need for people to be able to 'gel' is vital. These views are supported by Harvey et al (1997) who say that "team working, communication and inter-personal skills are inextricably interlinked in the delayered organization. For instance, it is highly unlikely that someone with underdeveloped inter-personal skills would be able to engage effectively with colleagues and clients, let alone inspire a team."

2.3 Acquiring the Skills Through Work Based Learning

So, a body of opinion which says that work has changed and that university graduates must be prepared for the new work environment. A substantial part of this preparation is the acquisition of the transferable skills which employers are seeking in their graduate recruits. Additionally, it has been acknowledged that work experience through work based learning can be very beneficial in preparing students for the world of work. It seems fair to suggest, then, that, if work based learning through the medium of work placements incorporated into an undergraduate program can assist in the development of transferable skills, it could take on a substantial weight of responsibility for the future development of the workforce and the economy.

This, of course, is a substantial claim and we recognize this. It is not our intention here to examine the more general and perhaps wide-ranging benefits of work based learning but rather to look specifically at the extent to which work based learning or experience of work can help efforts within the undergraduate program in facilitating the development of transferable skills. The result should be benefits to the student in terms of an easier integration into the world of work and, even more specifically, an easier passage through the prospective employer's assessment process. At the same time the employer should obtain an employee who will adapt more readily to the work environment, require less training and induction and operate effectively and productively more quickly. According to the Washington State Work Based Learning Resource Center, in 1991, 3,000 employers identified attitude, communication skills and previous work experience as the three most desirable qualities sought in a new employee. Since that time assessment methods have become increasingly sophisticated in the area of graduate recruitment and this tends to point towards an increasing demand for transferable skills and work experience.

In an effort to emphasize the points made so far, and highlight the need for and desirability of these transferable skills and, of course, to make the case further for work based learning in the acquisition of these skills, Lane and Robinson (1994) emphasized the need for partnerships between business and education if employers were to keep their workforce skilled and at the forefront of change. They saw the challenge for academics in devising learning opportunities which achieve a natural balance between knowledge and understanding and the ability to perform competently in real world situations. Being successful at work is not just about carrying out the various technical tasks competently. The very fact that organizations are designed and structured creates a need to work with others, often in teams. In fact, it is very much the exception to find someone who is not involved in a team of some sort at work, even in academia! It is essential to be able to communicate well with others both on a social and professional level in addition to being able to perform the technical functions specific to the job. As Lane and Robinson (1994) say "... it is often these less tangible aspects of competence, rather than the technical skills, that distinguish between successful and less successful individuals."

It would also be interesting to examine how best to assess the acquisition of these skills and the various ways in which students should be required to demonstrate their acquisition - what evidence should they produce and what evidence can they produce. It is also very much the case that undergraduates require to take on substantial responsibility for their own learning in the work based learning environment - much more than they have traditionally been used to doing. However, these issues are not the direct concern of this paper albeit that they are critical parts of the work based learning experience. The focus here is on the extent to which transferable skills, which will be of value to employer and employee, can be acquired through the work based content of an undergraduate program. In the Department of Economics at Napier University, three years experience of work based learning has been accumulated. This takes the form of a six month work placement with an organization within the financial services sector and it is undertaken by the students on the full-time BA (Honours) Degree in Financial Services in the semester prior to the commencement of their final year of study.

So, having set the scene in terms of some background, the discussion will now move on to examine practical experience in this area and draw some conclusions on the effectiveness of the work based learning content of our undergraduate program in providing students with the opportunity to acquire transferable skills.

3. SURVEY

3.1 Methodology

The study was conducted by means of a non-attributable questionnaire. This was distributed to the three cohorts of students who had completed the Work Based learning module within the Financial Services honours degree program, and for whom current addresses were held. The total sample was 40; consisting of 13 current students and 27 graduates (10 graduates[98], 17 graduates[97]). The overall response rate was 65%, consisting of current students, 10 (77%), graduates[98], 6 (60%), graduates[97], 10(59%).

3.2 Findings

The survey asked two principal questions. Firstly we investigated the skills that the students considered were most important in the workplace. The range of skills listed were based on those considered important by both students and employers for professionals in the workplace. (Eraut, 1994; Hanson et al., 1996).

The findings for this first question are shown in table 1. The expected mean was 5.5, on the basis that the student ranking of the individual skills would not be consistent, but that each individual would have an individual preference. The first column shows the average ranking for the total population for which we had 24 useable responses (60%). Oral communication and Team Working were very highly significant in terms of importance of the skill, whereas negotiation and innovativeness were very highly insignificant in terms of importance.

When examining the responses of the sub-groups, it can be seen that only oral communication is highly significant and innovativeness very highly insignificant across all the sub-groups. The results are generally mixed, although three skills show a trend over time, with a further one skill showing an improvement to the first graduate group.

Table 1. Student's ranking of the importance of skills for the workplace

	All	Students	Graduates	Graduates97	Graduates98
Teamworking	3.83***	2.60***	4.71*	5.78	2.80***
Oral comm.	3.79***	3.80***	3.79***	3.67***	4.00**
Written comm.	5.08	6.10	4.36**	4.00***	5.00
Problem solving	6.04	6.10	6.00	6.22*	5.60
Information handling	5.25	4.50**	5.79	5.78	5.80
Negotiation	7.33***	9.00***	6.14	5.44	7.40***
Listening	5.08	5.00	5.14	5.56	4.40**
Planning	4.79	5.50	4.29**	5.00	3.00***
Resourcefulness	6.21*	5.10	7.00***	6.11	8.60***
Innovativeness	7.58***	7.30***	7.79***	7.44***	8.40***

All n=24. Students n=10, Graduates n=14. Graduates97 n=9, Graduates98, n=5.
*** significant at 99%, ** significant at 95%, * significant at 90%. Expected mean = 5.5

It is noted that the average ranking for the graduate group shows a much narrower variance with the trend continuing through the sub-groups, the longer the group has been away from university. Thus reflecting that different respondents rate different skills more highly than do others. This may be an indication that all the skills are important but at different stages of their careers and different job characteristics, the importance of each skill will vary. However, this needs further investigation as the current study is limited by a small sample size and all the respondents studied on the same degree program.

The second part of the study asked the respondents to rank statements regarding their experience on the work placement as to whether they agreed or disagreed with the statement based on a four-point scale. They were asked to give their response to 14 statements related to skills developed on the placement:

1. The placement module better equipped me to work as part of a team.
2. The placement enabled me to participate in group problem solving.
3. The placement developed my skills in seeking out innovative solutions to problems.
4. It improved my skills in handling information.
5. It developed my skills in finding resolutions to different types of situation.
6. It enabled me to identify the critical issues with regard to problems.
7. It enabled me to develop my skills in diagnosing the exact nature of problems.
8. It enabled me to plan my work more efficiently and effectively.
9. It developed my negotiation skills.
10. It developed my skills in researching information.
11. It improved my written communication skills.
12. It developed my listening skills.
13. It developed my resourcefulness in obtaining information.
14. It helped the clarity of my communication skills both oral and written to improve.

Table 2 provides a summary of the results for which all 26 respondents provided useable data. It is significant to note that sample as a whole perceived the Work Based Learning to be beneficial. Furthermore with the exception of team working and listening skills, the graduate group ranked all the skills more important than the student group. Moreover it is only within the student group that any skills (innovative solutions and negotiation) score higher than the expected mean of 2.5, albeit not at a significant level.

Table 2. Student's perception of work placement to skill development

	All	Students	Graduates	Graduates97	Graduates98
Teamworking	1.81*	1.80*	1.81*	2.00	1.50*
Problem solving	2.08	2.20	2.00	2.30	1.50*
Innovative solutions	2.12	2.60	1.81*	1.80*	1.83
Information handling	1.46**	1.50**	1.44**	1.40**	1.50*
Finding resolutions to different situations	1.81*	1.90	1.75*	1.80*	1.67*
Identify critical issues	1.85	2.10	1.69*	1.90	1.33**
Diagnose nature of problem	2.08	2.30	1.94	1.90	2.00
Plan work more efficiently	1.69*	1.90	1.56**	1.50**	1.67*
Negotiation skills	2.31	2.60	2.13	2.40	1.67*
Researching information	1.92	2.30	1.69*	1.80*	1.50*
Written communication skills	1.88	2.10	1.75*	1.60*	2.00
Listening skills	1.85	1.80*	1.88	1.80*	2.00
Resourcefulness in obtaining information	2.00	2.10	1.94	2.10	1.67*
Clarity of oral & written communication	1.77*	1.90	1.69*	1.80*	1.50*

All, n=26. Students n=10, Graduates n=16. Graduates97, n=10, Graduates98, n=6.
*** significant at 99%, ** significant at 95%, * significant at 90%. Expected mean = 2.5.

The results for the graduate group as a whole, show that more than half of the skills were perceived positively at the 90% significance level. Furthermore in examining the sub-groups for the graduates, 6 skills:
- innovative solutions
- handling information
- diagnosis of problems
- planning
- written communication
- listening

become more positive with the graduate97 group. This suggests an appreciation of the skills developed in the module increases over time. However a caveat should be added that we are comparing different groups of students and therefore the differences may be due to this and not an appreciation of the skills and also again that we are dealing with relatively small groups.

The skills that were ranked important in table 1 also tend to show a positive perception from the student in relation to the development of that skill on the work placement. Team working and oral communication are very highly important in table 1 and are significant in table 2 whereas negotiation and innovativeness are very highly unimportant in table 1 and are not significant in the development of skills with both having an average ranking in excess of 2.

4. CONCLUSIONS AND RECOMMENDATIONS

This preliminary study, whilst acknowledging the limitations placed upon the results due to the narrow experience and small size of the sample does suggest that Work Based Learning is both a valuable and useful experience from the student's point of view. It appears to offer the opportunity to develop the transferable skills demanded by employers in the 1990s. The conclusions drawn can only be tentative as comparisons are being made between different groups of students.

This study, in order to substantiate the findings, requires to be developed in a number of ways. Firstly a much larger study requires to be conducted to eliminate any small sample bias. Furthermore we would require to be sure that it is in fact the Work Based learning module that provides the positive experience suggested in the study and that this is not a result of the university experience in general. Accordingly a larger study should include students and graduates that have studied a more traditional curriculum without the benefit of a work placement. It should include students from a wider number of institutions to exclude any institutional bias and also a wider spectrum of programs to allow for any bias related to the type of degree program. This wider study would add validity to the generalizability of the findings and also would eliminate any bias due to the self selective nature of narrow programs. Further improvements could be made by stratifying the sample by age at commencement of the program of study and also ascertaining those students that have prior work experience.

Secondly, a larger study should be conducted on a longitudinal basis tracking the same group of graduates over a period of say five years. This would ascertain if the graduate's perception of Work Based Learning does change as their experience of the labor market increases.

Lastly, it would be helpful to be able to measure the input into the development of these skills made by employers. This could perhaps be established by funds expended on graduate training programs or even time spent in training by graduates. This would allow an analysis to be conducted to establish if the benefits perceived by graduates are solely related to Work Based Learning by examining the different inputs provided by the employers.

Overall this would enable an evaluation to be made of the real benefits of programs including Work Based Learning as against the more traditional programs. The results would provide a basis for potential employers as to the suitability and cost of recruiting graduates from the different backgrounds of study. The universities can then evaluate whether the Work Based Learning truly enhances the student's learning and whether the resources employed in this type of program are justified.

REFERENCES

Brennan, J., & Little, B. (1996). *A review of work based learning in higher education.* Department for Education and Employment.

Davies, L. (1990). *Experience based learning within the curriculum - a synthesis study.* Council for National Academic Awards.

Eraut, M. (1994). *Developing professional knowledge and competences.* London: Falmer Press.

Greenwood, R.G., Edge, A.G., & Hodgetts, R.M. (1987). How managers rank the characteristics expected of business graduates. *Business Education, 8, no.3*, 30-34.

Guirdham, M. (1995). *Interpersonal skills at work.* Prentice Hall.

Hamm, S. (1998). Everyone wins with work placements. *Personnel Today,* June.

Handy, C. (1989). *The age of unreason.* London: Pan Books.

Hanson, W.L., Berkely, R.A., Kaplan, D.M., Yu, Q., Craig, C.J., Fitzpatrick, J.A., Seiler, M.R., Derby, D.R., Gheis, P., Ruelle, D.J., & Voss, L.A. (1996). *Needed skills for human resource professionals: A pilot study.* Proceedings of 1996 Spring Meeting, 524-534. Madison W.I.: Industrial Relations Research Association.

Harvey, L., & Knight, P.T. (1996). *Transforming higher education.* Open University Press.

Harvey, L., Moon, S., Geall, V., & Bower, R. (1997). *Graduates' work: Organizational change and students' attributes.* Center for Research into Quality, University of Central England.

Hilton, P. (1993). An accelerated route to the top for graduates. *Personnel Management, 25,* 7, July, 36-39.

Lane, G., & Robinson, A. (1994). *Learning through work: Developing competence through work based learning.* Working Paper, Henley Management College.

Pugh, D.S., & Hickson, D.J. (1996). *Writers on organizations.* London: Penguin Books.

Purcell, K., & Pitcher, J. (1996). *Great expectations: What do students really think about the benefits of a degree in today's graduate job market?* University of Warwick: Institute for Employment Research.
Washington State Work Based Learning Resource Center (1991). Internet.

Leadership Education in a Changing Workplace

Jennifer Frederick[1] & Carol Dalglish[2]
[1]*Administrative Services Queensland Audit Office, Brisbane Qld, Australia* [2]*Graduate School of Business Queensland University of Technology, Brisbane Qld, Australia*

1. CONTEXT

Much has been written concerning the value of learning and education in delivering competitive advantage, particularly in knowledge based service industries (Karpin, 1995; Senge, 1990). There has also been much written about the necessity for real individual behavioral change to underpin effective organizational and cultural change (Quinn, 1996). The Queensland Audit Office (QAO) is a service knowledge-based organization, which despite having a legislative monopoly recognizes the competitive nature of its business. Over the last six years, QAO has undergone significant structural and organizational reform and has focussed on changing the people and the culture to align individual behavior with organizational values and direction. QAO has focussed on developing competitive advantage through development of its people, and particularly its middle managers.

QAO has been running its own in-house leadership programs since 1994. While these programs have relied on a range of external and internal speakers, the facilitation role had been managed generally by an executive with support from QAO's Professional Development Officer, and this was becoming increasingly time consuming as the programs gained organizational acceptance and consequently more participants.

In 1991, the Australian Government commissioned an Industry Task Force on Leadership and Management Skills. The Task Force's charter was to advise on measures to strengthen management development and business leadership within Australian enterprises. It was asked to identify effective management practices in a range of areas, to raise awareness of the need for improved leadership and management skills and to foster enterprise commitment to management development. In the report, Karpin (1995) identified a number of limitations to current Australian leadership and management practices.

"The Task Force's Research Program provides ample evidence that Australian enterprises and managers are failing in six critical areas: namely:
- low levels of education and training undertaken;
- over-reliance on short courses;
- over-emphasis on current rather than future skills;
- failure to handle the transitions from specialist to manager;
- failure to link management development to strategic direction; and
- failure to evaluate the effectiveness of management development activities."

QAO's internal program was designed to address some of these issues, but there was still a lack of rigor about the program, and participants put in a lot of effort with no academic recognition. Early in 1998 the QAO began negotiations with the Graduate School of Business to have the programs accredited by them so that:
- there would be acceptance and recognition of the high standard of the programs, both internally and externally;
- the design and facilitation role could be shared more widely and become less dependent on the good intentions of a few people;
- QAO would gain access to academic staff to present and run sessions;
- there would be greater academic rigor in the program;
- QAO would be able to market its programs within the government sector; and
- QAO participants would gain credit towards a recognized post graduate management award.

This accreditation process was finalized in June 1998, and the Graduate School of Business (GSB) has effectively taken over the supervision of these programs. This paper discusses the background of both organizations, the process used to attain accreditation, what has been learnt, and concludes with the expected outcomes for each organization.

2. BACKGROUND – A QUEENSLAND AUDIT OFFICE PERSPECTIVE

The Department of the Auditor-General was established in Queensland in 1860. Being an organization comprised primarily of auditors, it is not surprising that the culture of the office has been strongly conservative, concerned with detail, and fairly risk averse with a strong focus on centralized control and decision making. The legislation establishing the position of Auditor-General and the Queensland Audit Office places personal responsibility on the Auditor-General to give audit opinions and report on matters as required, and in the past this has led to a centralized decision-making style of management.

The QAO has a monopoly on all audits of public sector entities (some 620 in total including departments, local authorities, statutory bodies, and controlled entities of these organizations). The large majority of effort is devoted to financial and compliance regularity audits, and in the last two years, QAO has also been auditing performance management systems.

Management as a concept has been well understood in the QAO, with its focus on problem solving, has not always been the focus. As such, training for managers had given little attention to leadership development, and focussed on the planning, controlling, and monitoring aspects of management. "Soft skills" were perceived as being less useful for auditors, who were predominantly interested in doing audits and saw other corporate activities and training on matters other than technical accounting and auditing issues as of much lower priority.

2.1 Outline of 1997 Leadership Development Program (LPD)

QAO's LDP was based around developing Qld Public Service Senior Executive Service (SES) Officer competencies:
- Corporate Leadership
- Policy Development & Advice
- Managing for Outcomes
- Developing & Managing Resources
- Representation & Communication
- Self Management & Self Development.

Potential applicants were asked to complete an expression of interest setting out why they should be selected for the program and providing examples of either demonstrated or potential leadership ability. Participants were chosen by QAO senior management having regard to their application and referee reports, and also from personal observation of the staff involved. The program components were workshops, a workplace project, learning sets, and mentoring and possibly work placements. At the start of the program, participants completed a range of skills assessment tools including the Kouzes and Posner Leadership Practices Inventory; a Management Skills Self-Assessment (based on SES Competencies and reviewed by their managers); a Learning Styles Assessment; and a Team View 360-feedback process. The detailed program design was based on the results of the above assessments, although the overall corporate need was to develop leadership, self-management, and self-development, and change management skills.

Participants were required to read a range of texts from a prescribed list, and were provided with 4 – 6 articles every 4 – 6 weeks to read and discuss within the learning sets. Each person completed a work-based project involving organizational development issues. The participants also worked through case studies.

The program was a success, and led to a major focus across the organization on leadership development. In terms of individual outcomes, all five initial participants were promoted to senior management positions while in the program. Those people have taken on a significant role in facilitating other management development programs and have undertaken other corporate change projects. However, the program was resource intensive; lacked a thorough conceptual focus; and was largely dependent on continuing time consuming personal involvement of the facilitator. For these reasons, the Graduate School of Business at QUT was approached to advise on improvements to the program and to discuss accreditation. QAO and QUT have had a long association, and many QAO staff are graduates of QUT.

3. BACKGROUND – THE BRISBANE GRADUATE SCHOOL OF BUSINESS PERSPECTIVE

The Brisbane Graduate School of Business (BGSB) is a newly established (1995) post-graduate School within the Queensland University of Technology's (QUT) Faculty of Business. The BGSB offers a range of postgraduate, multi-disciplinary, applied programs leading to the award of MBA, Graduate Diploma in Business Administration or Graduate Certificate of Management.

QUT promotes itself as "The University for the Real World." As the "real world" changes, the BGSB is faced with the challenge of providing current, relevant applied learning opportunities to business and the community. Because of this "real world" focus, the BGSB has moved towards a range of initiatives in delivery and teaching that reflect contemporary business concerns. These include, the use of case studies, engaging business managers and leaders to conduct classes and the increasing use of real time projects in companies as part of course work.

While individual enrollment and company-sponsored enrollment in the MBA program is growing, it was felt that there was a significant number of opportunities for the BGSB to work with corporations to provide specially tailored programs. These programs would be designed to meet organizational needs, but also incorporate the conceptual rigor more normally associated with academic programs. The assumption behind such a partnership is that the worth of any program would be enhanced for the organization and the individual participants would receive external recognition for their learning achievement.

Fulmer (1997) discussing the relationship between practitioners and universities states:

"University should provide an individual with exposure to cutting edge thinking in a variety of disciplines. It should develop a commitment for honest inquiry and an attempt to seek new answers to old questions. Corporate experience adds the dimension of relevance. In a business setting, ideas have little currency unless they can be meaningfully applied in a specific situation."

Increasingly large organizations are establishing their own training and educational facilities and are running their own programs for middle and senior managers. In 1993 Jeanne C. Meister (Fulmer, 1997) identified 30 companies with corporate universities. By 1996 she reported that almost 1000 firms had begun or were actively investigating the feasibility of a corporate university.

The reasons for these developments range from a commitment by the organization to lifelong learning for employees, to disenchantment with the inflexibility of academic institutions in meeting their needs.

For smaller organizations, setting up their own educational facilities may not make economic sense. Even for large companies, setting up their own universities as has happened in the United States, may be duplicating resources that exist within local academic institutions. The ideal solution would appear to be for business organizations to work with academic organizations to design and deliver leadership development programs that meet the immediate and future needs of managers and potential leaders and that build on the expertise and resources of both organizations. If a common understanding can be achieved, all parties, and particularly the participants in the learning process, have much to gain.

4. THE PROGRAM APPROACH

The Assistant Auditor General at the QAO and the Director of the MBA Program at the BGSB looked at how they could design and deliver a Leadership Development Program that met the academic requirements of a post graduate business qualification, while meeting the development needs of the learners and the expectations and organizational demands of the QAO. This meant considering issues of content, learning process, timing, assessment strategies, mutual expertise and resources, administration and control, and relating learning to organizational as well as individual needs. The reasons that this conversation took place were concerns within the QAO about the continuation of the leadership program at the QAO and the relationship that already existed between the Assistant Auditor General and the Director of the MBA program. Before joining the BGSB, The Director had a career as a senior manager in the public sector and had been a consultant to the QAO, assisting with their strategic planning and change management processes. The relationship that was already established and the specific knowledge of the QAO enabled a partnership to be developed more easily than would otherwise have been the case.

There are traditionally a number of different ways in which leadership training is delivered. Jay Conger (1992) identified 4 categories of leadership training: Personal growth, skill building, conceptual development, and feedback. Csoka (1996) provides a simple overview of these strategies, which is used as a framework to understand the development and structure of the QAO program.

4.1 Personal Growth

Leadership training programs featuring personal growth emphasize the need for managers to become more aware of their inner talents, abilities, and limitations. QAO is very supportive of this approach and has included it as a critical element of their leadership program. The GSB, in reviewing its programs and their effectiveness in training competent managers is moving more to a recognition of personal development as an integral part of being successful in MBA programs, and as a manager. This is reflected in the marketplace where leading executive placement organizations have identified to BGSB personnel that the key attributes providing competitive advantage to individuals in the current employment market are self awareness, communication skills, and a capacity to work with others.

Because the employing organization recognizes the importance of personal growth as a critical element of leadership training, some of the difficulties identified (Csoka, 1996) when applying this new awareness in the work place are overcome. The support of the Auditor-General, as the CEO of the organization, has been particularly important in ensuring that participants in the program are able to use their new found self awareness.

QAO provides support and recognition for the personal growth element of the program through:
- The design of the program includes the requirements of each participant's own learning plans;
- Learning sets that provide mutual support for participants, coaching in leadership behaviors as well as a forum for resolving current business problems;
- Participants have either been promoted to more senior positions, or have been given special high profile corporate projects to complete.

4.2 Conceptual Development

This has traditionally been the strength of university leadership programs and works on the premise that if you know the concept you can act on it. Although this approach has fallen into disfavor in some quarters as being "out of touch" with the real world it does focus on the expertise required by leaders in contemporary society and provides the conceptual tools to deal with a rapidly changing environment. The structured program offered to QAO incorporated the thorough conceptual focus that was considered a welcome addition to the in-house leadership program.

QAO participants have benefited from the expansion of the conceptual framework part of the curriculum through being able to see the range of possible approaches, and being able to debate within the learning sets the applicability or practicality of any particular approach within their own organization. This approach to learning has also increased their confidence in their current roles, as the identification of the academic frameworks that support particular leadership responses diminishes the occasional feeling of isolation when dealing with particular business issues. Because most of the participants have worked only within the one organization throughout their working life, they have not had the exposure to many different organizational cultures and leadership styles, and the conceptual framework has proven to be illuminating by reducing the limits on experiential diversity.

4.3 Feedback

Feedback was a critical element in the Leadership Development Program as delivered at QAO. Individuals had to compete for places on the program and were tested against a wide variety of leadership, management, and personal style assessment tools. This element of the program will remain an important element of the program and assessment tools are used as part of assessment early in the program, and at the end of the program.

Participants gain feedback from the facilitators, lecturers, and from each other in the learning sets. The depth of discussion in the learning sets and the approach taken to how these particular articles/theories might apply within QAO also allows the participants an opportunity to learn from each other. The facilitators/tutors play a strong mentoring role within the program, and this is also an important part of the leadership development process.

4.4 Skill Building

This is perhaps the most commonly used method for leadership training because it has an intuitive appeal because of the practical approach which organizations need. This element of skill building is integral to the program through the incorporation of real projects as part of the course learning activities and assessment.

One example is one of the units already conducted, entitled Organizational Analysis and Consulting. The primary assessment in this unit is a report on a "real time" consultancy for a client organization. The learning groups within QAO contracted with the Assistant Auditor General to develop issues papers that would inform the QAO's strategic planning process. These issues papers had to identify the significance of the issue to the organization, make recommendations to the senior executive on how the issue could best be addressed and clearly articulate the implications for the organization of implementation of their recommendations. The report produced was incorporated into the strategic planning process within the QAO and had implications for the participants, senior management and the organization as a whole.

The conceptual frameworks taught during the course provided tools for the learners to use in collecting and analyzing their data, understanding how their organization worked and would respond to the changes they were recommending and the relationship that exists between the consultants and their client. Their presentation to the senior executive and the report prepared constitute a significant element of the assessment for the unit.

5. PROGRAM DETAILS

Built on the foundation laid by the Leadership Program, the Graduate Certificate of Management is an award-bearing program developed jointly by the BGSB at QUT and the QAO.

The program includes existing units from within the MBA program but the possibility exists in the future to include newly created units if required. These units include:
- Personal Development and Ethics;
- Human Resource Management;
- Organizational Analysis and Consulting;
- Leadership I and II

The units were chosen because they reflected the areas that the QAO wished to develop, and included the possibility of practical in-house projects as part of the learning experience. With the introduction of a 2nd cohort, it is possible to change the subjects offered to meet the needs of the organization and the individuals. The Personal Development and Ethics unit and the two Leadership units are considered essential, while the other two subjects may be altered in response to changing needs.

The delivery is in-house at QAO and uses a variety of methods based around learning sets. Information is provided to the learning sets through input sessions and workshops conducted by QUT and other providers and through independent learning and research supported by suggested reading. The learning sets are led by QAO staff members who are recognized as tutors of the Brisbane Graduate School. Participants have the opportunity of testing and applying their knowledge through discussion, practical projects, presentations, and assignments.

The program commences with significant self-assessment and the use of the Enneagram, 360 feedback tools and the development of a personal learning plan. This leads to an individualized learning plan that may require individuals to undertake different activities to ensure meeting the learning outcomes of the program as a whole. The learning sets are the focus of discussion and debate about what is learned. The program will conclude with a second self-assessment and 360-feedback process and the completion of a further ongoing leadership development plan. QAO staff acting as QUT tutors, supported by a member of the Brisbane Graduate School Academic Staff, facilitate the learning sets.

The Personal Development and Ethics Unit, as the title suggests, looks at models and frameworks for personal development and success. It explores personality models, interpersonal interaction, and the impact of a changing work environment on the individual. The focus of this unit is clearly in the personal growth area, though conceptual frameworks are used to facilitate the process of increasing self awareness. The unit raised a number of issues for participants whose previous experience of study had not included self examination.

The organizational analysis and consulting unit was run at the request of QAO in response to a particular organizational need. This unit clearly developed skills within an organizational development framework. Students undertook, in groups, a work related project, which had to be completed in a way that met the needs of the organization and the academic requirements of the unit. The outcome demonstrated enhanced skills of participants and improved quality of the project for the organization.

The 1st cohort is currently undertaking a Human Resource Management Unit which will again include a work based project of relevance to the organization and focus on skills development within a conceptual framework. The final unit, Leadership, to be completed in July 1999, will provide a conceptual understanding of leadership but also involve feedback and personal growth activities.

Because of the commitment to ensure that academic standards and that all four aspects of management education are integrated into the program, teaching staff have had to focus clearly on ensuring diversity in the learning and assessment strategies used.

The assessment for the program is consistent with the assessment for the same units run on campus. All assessment is the responsibility of the program coordinator at the Brisbane Graduate School. Although the assessment component is optional for participants in QAO's Leadership Program, the Graduate Certificate in Management will only be awarded to those participants who successfully complete all forms of assessment in accordance with QUT requirements. To date all students completing the units have been assessed.

Assessment strategies include: development of a personal profile, a personal journal, group presentations, case study examinations, project reports, short questions examinations, the development of an individual profile of a leader and a personal leadership development plan.

In developing the partnership considerable attention was given to the respective roles of QAO, the Brisbane Graduate School of Business and the participants. QAO responsibilities include:
- recruitment of participants,
- accommodation for the meetings of the learning sets and the input/workshop sessions,
- preparation for and facilitation of the learning sets,
- mentoring and support of participants, and
- the payment of the agreed student fees.
- QUT's responsibilities include:
- overall program coordination,
- support for the learning set facilitators,
- all assessment activities,
- providing readings and reading lists,

Leadership Education 27

- the award of the Graduate Certificate in Management to participants who successfully complete the program,
- access by participants to on-campus seminars,
- input and workshop sessions,
- providing access to the university library and other support services for the QAO facilitators; and
- off-campus access to student services for participants, such as access to student services, electronic database access etc.
- Program participants are expected to:
- participate in the learning sets,
- complete all program activities,
- undertake reading and home study, and
- complete assessment components in accordance with their agreement with QAO.

The program now has two cohorts. The first cohort has completed two units and will complete the final two units by July 1999. The 2nd cohort commenced in January 1999 and will do two units in 1999 and two units in 2000.

6. ORGANIZATIONAL OUTCOMES

For QAO, there have been ranges of positive outcomes that impact on both the current organizational performance and will also have a long range impact:

- Empowered leaders who are changing QAO's culture to that of an empowered leaning organization (Field 1998:74);
- Changed behavior of participants that has led to improvements in the way they lead their teams and the way they contribute to the leadership of QAO;
- Institutionalization of the Leadership Development Program, thus ensuring its longevity;
- Graduate Certificate in Management qualifications for many high potential managers;
- Demonstrated commitment by QAO to the concepts of being a learning organization and to truly valuing its people and investing in their development;
- Team building for management teams who now see their collective influence as agents of change;
- Many organizational improvement projects are now listed as "assignments." Being part of real life, they are of great learning value to the participants, and QAO gains great benefit from having its own staff

carry out these projects within a rigorous framework and for less cost (Haynes, 1998);
- Corporate recognition of the necessity of broadening QAO's past technical base (a key strength) to encompass other skills, and the strong links to competitive advantage;
- There has been a tremendous boost to QAO's strategic focus and overall morale of staff through the activities, behavior, and influence of a highly persuasive management team; and
- QAO's image and the perceptions of its clients has improved enormously through the high profile of the course, its marketing to other organizations, and the changed behavior of many senior staff who are dealing with clients on a day to day basis.

The relevance of the program depends on the integration of academic input and work experience and this in turn yields organizational and individual benefits. QAO is now producing highly qualified and experienced leaders who may take up senior management roles in both QAO and the Queensland Public Sector. This supports QAO's organizational aim of improving accountability within the Queensland Public Sector. As a long term research project, both authors will continue to monitor the effectiveness of the program, and its impact on organizational environment, culture, and strategic direction.

From a Brisbane Graduate School of Business perspective this program has provided an ideal opportunity to develop and trial a model of leadership development that incorporates a wide range of teaching strategies within a supportive organizational context which encourages the use of the newly acquired knowledge and skills. It also provides an opportunity to observe and assess the impact of such a program on individuals and the organization in which they manage. There is much to learn about improving the effectiveness of learning programs in their capacity to develop knowledge and skills that are transferred into the work place. The learning from this program can only improve the Graduate School's capacity to deliver effective, relevant and applied management and leadership programs.

7. KEY SUCCESS FACTORS

While the program is still in its early days, it is possible to identify a number of factors that have contributed to the success to date, and which will contribute to its long term success. There has been willingness on the part of QAO to accept the conceptual components and academic requirements (such as assessment) of the university. The Brisbane Graduate School has been willing to incorporate real life, real time projects in the program at times to suit QAO operational requirements rather than the university. There has been extraordinary support from the Auditor General and the Head of the Brisbane Graduate School which has enabled openness and flexibility at all stages of the development and delivery. The mutual knowledge and understanding of the organization and its culture has been critical in determining the focus of the program, its content, and its delivery. There is a degree of trust between the two organizations because of the previous experiences of two of the key players. Another success factor has been the clear understanding and acceptance of each organization's respective responsibilities. Perhaps most importantly there has been willingness on the part of each of the organizations to share ownership and to value the contributions made by the other partner.

The model will no doubt evolve and be improved in the light of experience. However, even at this early stage, there is considerable interest from other organizations in this as a model for the development and delivery of executive development programs, so this may be the first of many.

REFERENCES

Bourner, T. (1996). Effective management and the development of self-awareness: A plain manager's guide. *Career Development International, (1/4)*.

Conger, J. (1992). *Learning to lead: The art of transforming managers in leaders*. San Francisco: Jossey Bass.

Csoka, L.S. (1996). The rush to leadership training. *Across the Board, Vol33, No8*, 28-32.

Field, L. (1998). The challenge of "Empowered Learning." *Asia Pacific Journal of Human Resources, 36(1)*.

Fulmer, R.M. (1997). The evolving paradigm of leadership development. *Organizational Dynamics, Vol25 No4*, 59-72.

Haynes, P., & Setton, D. (1998). Move over Mckinsey, student projects are taking over. *Australian Business Review Weekly*, June 15.

Kaye, B. (1993). Career development – anytime, anyplace. *Training and Development, Vol. 47 No 12*.

Lester, R.K., Piore, M.J., & Malek, K.M. (1998). Interpretative management. *Harvard Business Review*, March-April.

Karpin, D.S. (1995). *Enterprising nation: Renewing Australia's managers to meet the challenges of the Asia-Pacific century. Report of the Industry Task Force on Leadership and Management Skills*. Commonwealth of Australia.

Meister, J.C. (1994). *Corporate quality universities*. Richard D Irwin Inc.

OECD (1995). *Continuing professional education of highly qualified personnel*. OECD.

Parry, K. (1996). Transformational leadership: A self-development challenge. *HR Monthly*, June.

Pedlar, M.I. (1997). *Action learning in practice* (3rd ed.). Gower Publishing Ltd.

Quinn, R.E. (1996). *Deep change – discovering the leader within*. San Francisco: Jossey-Bass.

Ruggles III, R.L. (1997). *Knowledge management tools*. Butterworth-Heinemann.

Scholtes, P.R. (1998). *The leader's handbook – making things happen getting things done.* McGraw Hill.

Senge, P.M. (1990). *The fifth discipline – the art and practice of the learning organization.* Random House Australia.

Teal, T. (1996). The human side of management. *Harvard Business Review, Vol. 74* (6).

Vicere A.A. (1996). Executive education: The leading edge. *Organizational Dynamics, Vol25 No2,* 67-81.

New Training Methods: A Giant Leap of Faith?

Des Monk
Department of International Business, University of Central Lancashire, Preston, UK.

1. INTRODUCTION

It is quite clear that there has been a dramatic interest in the use of flexible training methods in the past 10-15 years, in the UK. In particular, we might consider the following developments:
- the use of competencies;
- accreditation systems;
- an increased emphasis on "in-house" expertise, such as mentoring;
- the development of open/distance learning programs;
- a general desire that programs be delivered more flexibly. This has often meant that employers want "tailored" rather than "off-the-shelf" courses.

Sloman (1993) suggests that training is increasingly likely to play a strategic role in the future of many organizations. However, he goes on to say that such training is unlikely to be provided by the headquarters of such organizations. Rather, it will be provided via flexible means that will include the increasingly extensive use of open learning packages. Sloman and others (e.g. Littlefield, 1994) would stress the fact that during the 1990s, computer-based packages are going to become an increasingly important means of providing training. Employers want flexibility in terms of both provision and assessment. This means that a lot of training now has a more open-ended timeframe than it used to have; employees no longer have to attend a particular courses on a particular day of the week or attend a particular location in a specific month.

Two central questions are raise by this paper. Firstly, the issue of why employers have sought to introduce new training methods is considered; secondly, an attempt at evaluation is made. To examine the first question, a distinction is made between push and pull factors. Although much of the policy-led literature has emphasized positive (or pull) reasons for the adoption of new training methods, the argument put forward in section six of the paper is that there are several powerful push factors at work; certainly that would appear to be the case in this case study. In other words, employers are often under pressure to consider changes in training because they are encountering more difficult circumstances in their product markets; changes in labor market conditions have followed changes in product market conditions.

Attempts at evaluation are fraught with difficulties and some of these are discussed in sections 8 and 12 of the paper. However, it is the major contention of this paper that there has been something of a leap of faith, with respect to the adoption of new training methods. We do not really know if they are genuinely more efficient than traditional modes, even if senior management claim that they are, as they did in this particular case (Whitley & Martin, 1995).

2. A FALSE DICHOTOMY?

Obviously, it is possible to draw an overly stark distinction between "old" and "new" training methods. A distinction is made here for analytical purposes. One has to recognize that in practice, organizations have had, and will continue to have, a number of methods in use at any one time. Littlefield (1994) for example, rightly argues that it is difficult to be precise about the origins of open learning packages in the UK; one could suggest that they were the predecessors of correspondence courses that have been in existence for about a hundred years. However, it was the developments in computer technology in the 1980s and 1990s that really made open learning packages what they are today. Similarly, it is quite conceivable that a number of organizations had paternalistic figures who were in effect, unofficial mentors, in previous decades.

Whilst one recognizes such a danger, of drawing distinctions that are overly stark, it does seem as though there is a consensus in the UK that there has been a (desirable) shift away from lecture-based, traditional, standardized, taught courses towards a new mentality that has emphasized flexibility and the responsibility that an autonomous learner has for his/her own development (Mumford, 1985; Saggers, 1994; Torrrington & Hall, 1995).

3. HYPOTHESIS

There has been a shift towards new training methods in the past decade in the past decade (or so). These methods have emphasized the need for flexibility and autonomy. Whilst such methods may have some intrinsic merit, they have frequently been adopted because employers have been faced with increasingly hostile product market conditions. As yet, we do not know whether they genuinely represent a more efficient use of those resources which have been committed to training. So far in the UK, there has been a great deal of optimism about these methods, and at least some of that optimism seems to be misplaced.

4. TWO CAVEATS

Firstly, UK employers' training budgets were generally not cut in the 1990s, despite difficult economic conditions (CBI, 1993; Saggers, 1994). Instead, there was a shift in emphasis such that a bigger proportion of costs were shouldered by the employee (DFE, 1992).

Secondly, it is very difficult to gauge the effectiveness of training generally (Pickard, 1994) but that is especially so, given the open ended nature of the assessment procedures associated with new training methods. Many of the modularized programs on offer, and many distance learning packs, are considered attractive partly because there is a certain latitude allowed regarding the issue of student assessment. Students often can choose when they will sit an examination, or be tested for their competence in a particular area. The open ended time frames associated with modern training are, therefore, simultaneously an advantage to the trainee but an added source of methodological difficulties. It may be that a trainee has not undertaken any learning or assessment, for a long time in the context of a research project, but chooses to say that they will return to the program at a later date. However, traditional courses were often examined at a particular time and one could then see how many of a given cohort had passed or failed that test.

5. WHY THE SHIFT: SOME "PULL" REASONS

As with many socio-economic phenomena, we might categorize the reasons for the shift towards the new training methods under two headings, i.e. positive (or "pull") reasons and negative (or "push") reasons. One important positive factor to explain the advent of new training methods is concerned with the widespread adoption of competence-based training. As Torrington and Hall (1995) point out, the development of competencies has forced employers to think very clearly about exactly what knowledge or core skills are needed to do a job. Similarly, Armstrong (1995) and Fowler (1996) have suggested that job evaluation schemes are now increasingly likely to be amended by including competencies as a set of desirable characteristics that a person might bring to a job. In the past, it was thought that such evaluation schemes were simply designed to assess the worth of one job, compared to another; as such, they were not designed to assess the worth of one candidate with respect to another. Now the UK has a framework of competence-based learning (the NVQ scheme) that can be used to assist in a variety of management functions, such recruitment and job evaluation, that can also be used to identify existing skills and help to think about staff development. Baron (1995) has also suggested that management should identify competencies as a means of thinking about interview questions. Certainly in the organization studied here (British Gas), senior management were quite clear that internal promotion interviews in the mid-1990s would be competence-based. In other words, the development of competence-based training has helped to bring training and general business objectives together.

To explain the timing of the changes in training in the UK one could also point to the development of a national framework of accreditation (the NVQ system), that has only been in existence for about ten years (NCVQ, 1988). Prior to that, employees may well have been doing training that, potentially, might have been accredited but had to accept that such training was effectively firm specific, since it had not been graded according to the NVQ system. Clearly, such a lack of accreditation would effect an employees' motivation to do training especially in their own time. Government departments such as the DFE (Department For Employment) were quick to point out that accreditation schemes also make it more likely that employees will take responsibility for their own development, since they are now more likely to be able to take such training to other employers and have it recognized (DFE, 1992). Whilst there may be some truth in this suggestion, one has to add the caveat that such an assertion has yet to be tested empirically; like much of the discussion on new training methods, it has yet to be demonstrated in any rigorous way.

This theme, of taking responsibility for one's own development, is further taken up by two authors concerned with the training of nurses (Thorne, 1991; Howard, 1993). In particular, Howard suggests that new training methods emphasize the role of andragogy, rather than pedagogy. Andragogy suggests that the learner is an autonomous adult who is able to take charge of their own development; part of this process means that the learner is able to "take stock" of their existing knowledge and then see where they want to enhance their portfolio of skills, or competencies. This auditing process is a useful exercise in itself, as the learner has to gather together evidence of their skills, regardless of whether they were gained in a formal setting (such as a classroom) or an informal setting (for example, in having to learn about the demands of being a parent). Such a process, of emphasizing the learner's role in their development, has been hastened because universities (especially the so-called "new universities in the UK) have had to develop ways and means of assessing such portfolios of evidence. Whilst a lot of work-based training can be accredited via the NVQ system, other competencies can be assessed by admissions tutors, in the light of their course requirements.

Another characteristic of the new training methods is that they permit the learner to learn at their own speed. Just as one of the attractions of the Open University is that undergraduate courses are modularized and can be done over a period of time, so it said that open learning programs are similarly organized; people can learn at their own pace. Indeed, it is not only employers' organizations who advocate such usage (such as the CBI, 1993), but also the employees' representatives (such as the white-collar union UNISON, 1993). As UNISON rightly say, people have different commitments at different times and they also are able to absorb different skills at different rates, so once again, having open learning programs is deemed to be desirable but without any without any substantive evidence to back up this assertion.

The final pull factor concerns the development of computer technology. Littlefield (1994) suggests that it was only in the 1980s and 1990s that PCs became substantially cheaper and much more widely available than computer technology had been until these decades. Such a development in technology explains, he argues, the rapid development of the Open College in the UK, who run courses in a fashion similar to the Open University, but at a lower academic level. Their estimate is that open learning has expanded at a rate of 20% per annum, since 1987. Such orders of magnitude are consistent with the increased take-up of open learning that Whitley and Martin (1995) envisaged within British Gas, during the 1990s.

6. WHY THE SHIFT: SOME PUSH REASONS

However, one could also point to a number of push factors, to help to explain the development of these new training methods that put the matter in a different light. One critical factor to consider is the timing of such changes; surely one might expect that the sort of desirable (or pull) factors listed above would have been sought in previous decades. We therefore have to examine those factors which have been particularly relevant to the 1980s and 1990s. In other words, another way of looking at the adoption of new training methods is that UK employers were compelled to reappraise their training strategies, with a view to getting a more efficient use of the resources concerned.

If we consider the timing of these changes, it is striking that they are set against a backdrop of rapid globalization, with its attendant implications for increased competition in the product market place. Dunning (1996) points out that for the UK, stocks of outward foreign investment amounted to only 14.5% of GDP in 1967, but by 1993 this had escalated to 26.9%. He also suggests that this growth in globalization has been especially rapid since the mid 1980s; whereas world-wide FDI outflows only grew by 0.8% per annum between 1981-1985, they grew by 28.3 % per annum from 1986-1990 and by 5.6% per annum, from 1991-1993. Similarly, Storey (1992) suggests that many organizations began a serious and concerted move towards more flexible management strategies from the 1980s onwards because, inter alia, they faced an increased threat from global competitors . Prior to that date, world trade may well have been growing but in the 1960s and 1970s, it was not thought to be sufficiently important to instigate a swing towards HRM strategies. Storey argues that the development of HRM in Britain is uneven but that nevertheless, many employers are having to consider such a policy shift because they face more threatening conditions in their product market place. This has meant that employees now have to contend with more flexible job descriptions, more flexible (and increasingly individualized) contracts and it has meant that training strategies have had to change. More and more employers in the UK are having to accept that they become learning companies, in Storey's analysis; in his short article he does not explore this development in any depth but elsewhere (for example, Pedler et al, 1989), the supposition is that learning companies have to adapt themselves so that they are able to constantly learn new skills in order to compete. Such learning is often done on a flexible basis, because product market conditions demand such flexibility. A similar point was made by Charles Munn at the EDINEB conference held in Edinburgh last year (1997). The UK banking industry has had to adopt flexible (open) learning programs because the industry is now much more competitive than it was in the 1970s and earlier decades.

From the employees' perspective, it makes sense to accept these changes because they are, in effect, "buying" an insurance policy. As employees they might well want to have training done in the employers' time at a set time each week, but they accept the decision to undertake flexible training even in their own time, because they face the threat of losing their jobs if they refuse an implicit contract whereby they do more than is spelt out in their formal job contract (Manning, 1990). Clearly, there may well be both push and pull factors at work at the same time, but it is striking that both the UK government's publications (for example, the DFE 1992) and the management/practitioner literature (such as the CBI, 1993) has been noticeably enthusiastic about the alleged benefits of flexible training without much supporting evidence. One could equally well explain such developments by looking at push factors, in which case one might conclude that management were compelled to change their training methods.

At least one reference in a management journal has accepted that product market conditions prompted a change in training policy (Whitley & Martin, 1995). These authors were both senior training officers with British Gas and they accepted that exogenous changes had prompted a revision of training methods. In particular, they suggested that there was a need for more devolution when it came to training provision, because senior management had to accept that changed product market conditions warranted a less centralized training policy. The following quotations give one a "feel" for the sort of warm reception that was accorded to open learning:

> "Open learning is not cheap but it is certainly a cost-effective and flexible medium."

> "Currently around 16 per cent of our training is delivered through open learning ... In three years time we expect that 80 per cent of our training will be done through some form of open or flexible learning." (Whitley & Martin, 1995).

Whitley and Martin suggested that a changed culture had necessitated a new training policy that was much more devolved than had previously been the case. This devolution had partly been bought about because the company had undergone a far reaching business process reengineering program (see section 7 below). The company had been reorganized along functional (rather than regional) lines and there were to be four major sections of the company's actives in the UK; the most important of these was concerned with the transmission of natural gas along a high pressure pipeline, Transco.

An internal communication within Transco had this to say about new training methods:

> "New technology has made it possible for self-study material to be sent through Transco's computer network ... The benefits to shippers and Transco staff are the provision of immediate, up-to-date training- no having to wait for classes large enough to justify running a course."
> (British Gas, Transco, 1995)

What Whitley and Martin did not make explicit was the extent to which the company had its profits severely curtailed in the 1990s. Of course, there are a number of ways to measure profit, but in this case the different measures correlate reasonably well. The most common way to measure profit that was used within the company was after tax, and using a current estimate of the value of the gas used (rather than a historical) one. This procedure was slightly amended in 1997, when the accounts were drawn up on a historic-cost basis i.e. taking the value of the gas used at the time of purchase rather than the end of the financial year. It is also worth noting that 1997 was the first year that completely separate accounts had been drawn up for the two major wings of what was British Gas; from 1997 (see section 7 below) the transmission wing became a company called BG, whilst the trading arm became another organization called Centrica. In table 1, the estimate of profits for 1997 represents the amalgam of both of these new companies.

Table 1. British Gas's profits at nominal prices (in millions £)

Year	1987	1988	1989	1990	1991	1992	1993	1994	1995	1996	1997
Profit	1067	1018	1065	1063	1469	846	-613	918	607	-237	1251

Source: Annual Report (British Gas, various years)

The way that British Gas calculated its profits was itself a source of controversy; the company had a vested interest in showing its monopoly rent to be as low as possible. Critics pointed out that relations between the organization and its regulator (OFGAS) were frequently strained (Weston, 1996) and the level of profits was an obvious source of tension. It was to the company's advantage to show profits to be relatively low, as part of the battle over recommended pricing levels set by the regulator. The fact that a loss was recorded for 1993 was directly as a result of the company putting aside some £1.6 billion for the purposes of reorganization. It intended to spend that money over a three-year period (1994-1997) and if those costs were to be shown in the years concerned, then a surplus would have been recorded for 1993. Broadly speaking, however, one can accept that the profit levels indicated reflect the extent to which the company enjoyed a producer's surplus. Given that this is the case, it is quite clear that immediately after privatization (in 1986) the company still enjoyed a degree of monopoly rent; profits were consistently above the £1000 level until 1991. Indeed, within the company there was a certain degree of complacency regarding the commercial implications of privatization. The CEO (Cedric Brown) referred in 1994, to " the privatization that never was", meaning that the way that the company was run was very similar to the way that it had been run prior to privatization, a point also made by Ferner and Colling (1991). The important point here is that whilst they were a nationalized industry (and shortly afterwards), British Gas enjoyed a degree of producer's surplus and this extended to its provision of training, i.e. the company could afford to offer general training to its employees in office hours. As product market conditions tightened, the company sought to use more cost effective training (i.e. adopt new training methods), as Whitley and Martin indicated. In adopting this policy though, management within the company seemed to have underestimated the pitfalls involved.

7. THE INSTITUTIONAL BACKGROUND

In order to understand events in this study, it is necessary to outline the connection between the product and labor markets and this in turn makes it necessary to briefly outline the institutional history of the organization. Broadly speaking the 1980s were characterized by a limited degree of change, whereas the 1990s were characterized by a need for a more radical response to rapid exogenous change.

The UK Labor government established a number of nationalized industries in the late 1940s; the Gas Board (the predecessor to British Gas) was established in 1948. For the next four decades it enjoyed a considerable degree of market power; not only did British Gas enjoy pure monopoly power in the UK domestic market, but it also enjoyed monopsony power in the factor market for natural gas, from the mid-1970s. Although the organization was privatized in 1986, this did little to alter their market power as the legislative provision for third party carriage was not realized in that decade.

In the early 1990s the concern felt at the ex-nationalized industries' market power resulted in the adoption of Professor Littlechild's RPI-x formula in a number of cases. The formula was imposed on British Gas from 1991 onwards and is largely felt to have accounted for the fact that profit figures in the 1990s have not matched those of the 1980s (see section 6 above). Currently the trading wing of what was British Gas have to accept a pricing policy that is geared to an x figure of 4%. In real terms, of course, the cost of gas to the British householder has been falling for most of the 1990s. The equivalent figure for the transmission wing is 2%.

In 1993, the company was the subject of the biggest single reference to the MMC, (the Monopolies and Mergers Commission, the UK's anti-trust body). The Commission expressed renewed concern that British Gas was, simultaneously, an organization responsible for the transmission of gas around the UK, and one of a number of actual (and intended) shippers, responsible for selling gas direct to industrial and domestic consumers. By the early 1990s, the company's monopoly position had been breached in the industrial market but not in the domestic market for Britain's 18 million households. The company was to make arrangements to ensure that there would be competition in its core market, by publishing the prices that it would charge to consumers in advance and by splitting up the organization in order to prevent cross subsidy, in particular to prevent a situation whereby the transmission wing subsidized the trading wing. The company announced plans whereby it would shed a third of its workforce, some 25,000 employees, over a five year period.

In 1994, the company started the business process reengineering that was necessary as a prelude to the increased competition that it was likely to feel in its core (UK) market, the market for natural gas, sold to the nation's 18 million households. The organization abandoned its 12 regional centers, in favor of four functional units; of those, the most important were the transmission wing (Transco) and the trading wing. The monopoly power of Transco was confirmed by the Gas Act of 1995; only Transco was able to legitimately transmit gas along pipelines in the UK to customers. By the following year (1996), it was quite clear that a number of competitors were interested in entering the domestic trading market, as several independent shippers began to supply households in the south-west of the country in a pilot scheme that has since been extended to the whole of the UK.

Two major events occurred in 1997. Firstly, in February the transmission wing (now called BG) became a completely separate company with its own stock market listing, distinct from the trading wing (now called Centrica). Secondly, the hostility between the industry and its regulators continued with yet another reference to the MMC; this time, the problem centered on the pricing strategy that the transmission wing was to be allowed. The MMC confirmed OFGAS's (the industry watchdog's) suggestion that the prices charged by BG to the shippers should be pegged at RPI-2% for five years with a one-off fall of 21% that was imposed from October of that year.

The important point to be made in this section is that the exogenous changes faced by British Gas especially in the 1990s, brought about changes to their HRM policy. Arrangements for the provision of training within the company's internal labor market were critically affected by the government's (increasingly intrusive) regulatory policy. The argument in this paper is that senior management may well have thought that their strategy represented a rational response to such exogenous change, but they seemed to have underestimated the difficulties of using modern training methods.

8. METHODOLOGY: BRITISH GAS AS A CASE STUDY

To test the hypothesis outlined in section 3 it was felt that a case study methodology would be appropriate. Of course, there are obvious problems with such an approach; one is never sure whether the results are genuinely applicable, or not. At the very least, one can be sure that as a single entity, British Gas was one of the UK's key industries and therefore an important institution in its own right. It has been the biggest of the UK's (well-publicized) privatization ventures. It also had some 90,000 employees in 1986 (at the time of privatization), which made it one of the top ten employers. Moreover, like a number of other companies in the UK, it felt that the UK market was becoming increasingly saturated by the late 1980s and thus sought to extend its activities abroad. Again, like many other companies it sought to delayer its management structure in the 1990s; from having 14 different white collar grades in 1986, its successors (BG and Centrica) now have 10 such grades. Finally, like a number of companies (Saggers, 1994; King, 1993) British Gas did not reduce its training budgets in the 1990s; instead, it sought to alter the distribution of costs and put more emphasis on employees bearing the (indirect) costs of training, in terms of using their own time. In short, there are a number of reasons to suppose that British Gas represented an important case study that was illustrative of a number of trends in British industry in the 1990s.

British Gas was also chosen because it was so clearly in favor of the use of those modern training methods which have been outlined in the first section. Whitley and Martin, as two of the senior training officers within the organization had attested (in 1995) to the fact that the company were committed to the use of open learning centers. Moreover, the company were also committed to the concept of competence-based training and as such, made sure that they were able to independently assess the full range of NVQ competencies up to and including level four; the fifth (highest) level was the only one that required them to use external assessors. In common with the sort of developments described by Mumford (1985), British Gas had gone to some lengths to make sure that their graduate trainees were aware of the need to be responsible for their own development. The organization were also keen to move away from a culture that equated training with courses and as such, they were in favor of using mentors and in-house appraisals (British Gas, 1994).

To test the sort of assertion outlined in section 3 it was felt necessary to track a cohort of graduates over a number of years. In this case, that meant interviewing 30 graduates who had started on the company's GDP (graduate development program) in 1993. Actually, the company had recruited 70 graduates in 1993, but by the time access was gained to the group (in 1994), there were 60 graduates who were still with the company; of those, 53 agreed to complete a questionnaire and 38 (of these 53) agreed to be tracked. Of the 38 people who agreed to be tracked, 8 replies were discarded for logistical reasons (for example, because they were working in very distant locations).

9. METHODOLOGY: THE NATURE OF THE COHORT

In view of the sort of hypothesis being tested, it is worth saying something about the employees concerned. After all, if training policies are not as effective as management might wish for, then presumably one might say that this could be attributed to the sort of recruit into the organization. In this case, the company had grounds for believing that the employees concerned had already demonstrated a successful capacity for absorbing new information. They all had an honours degree from a British university. Moreover, they were working for an organization that had gone on record to confirm their commitment to the strategy of having its graduates professionally qualified (British Gas, 1994). This meant for example, that the organization was prepared to pay the fees required to sit examinations and give time off, for study purposes. The graduates had an incentive to train successfully, in that they were to be appraised (by their line manger) every six months and if that appraisal was adjudged to be successful, then the graduates were to receive an increment of £1,000, plus, of course, the possibility of extra career advancement. The majority were resigned to the idea of using their own time for training purposes; in the questionnaire replies 37/53 agreed with the statement that the company expected them to use their time for training. In short, we might expect on a priori grounds, that this case study would provide both an employer and a set of employees who would make the most of the new training methods available to them.

10. RESULTS

In terms of attrition, the 30 graduates interviewed in the autumn 1994 were reduced to 28 by the following year and they were further reduced down to 21 by the autumn of 1996. Of these quits, only three took voluntary redundancy, despite the fact that it (voluntary redundancy) was the major means by which the company shed the third of its employees referred to in section 7. Predictably, most (7/9) of the graduates that left did so in order to take up another job offer; one graduate was able to take up another job offer and also collect his £9000 lump sum for voluntary redundancy (worth approximately half of his salary).

Despite the fact that the company actively encouraged the graduates to become professionally qualified, a surprising number did not do so; after all, by refusing to become so qualified they were considerably reducing their chance of gaining extra salary and promotion either within, or outside of, British Gas. Of the group of 30 graduates described earlier, who were tracked, only 18 became "active joiners." Six graduates said that they had no intention of being professionally qualified and a further six were "other joiners", i.e. people who were able to claim professional status by virtue of a previous qualification (in 4/6 such cases this was by virtue of a Ph.D. and in the other two because of an MSc.). This clearly calls into question the extent to which graduates felt compelled to take responsibility to ensure that they met a target set for them by the company. Those who already had professional status could have indicated their ability (and willingness) to learn new skills in their own time by studying for another relevant qualification, such as the Open University's Certificate in Management Studies; being seen as an "active joiner" would have considerably increased their chance of gaining early promotion.

In 1996 the graduates were asked to evaluate the GDP; they all said that it was too long and the consensus was that a year would have been long enough. Of those interviewed at the end of their training period in 1995, 10 graduates had been promoted and all these came from the active joiner group. However, the promotion interviews that were held in 1995 and 1996 were competence-based. Several graduates said that it was therefore even more imperative that the objectives of their GDP should have been spelt out in competence terms, which they were not.

From a policy perspective, these results were interesting in that none of the graduates concerned were aiming for the NVQ scheme outlined earlier. Of the 30 graduates who were tracked, 18 were aiming for membership of a professional body such as the I.Mech.Eng. (the Institute for Mechanical Engineering) or CIMA (the Chartered Institute for Management Accountants; such membership applications usually meant having do demonstrate certain abilities by means of examination or by a range of practical tasks that were assessed Such professional status was felt to be a more useful means of signaling aspiration or ambition, than the NVQ system.

A third of all of the appraisal interviews that should have been done were not done. Bearing in mind that these interviews should have been the basis on which increments of a £1,000 were given (or withheld), then this was a surprising result. In fact, none of the graduates had their increment withheld; the money was simply paid, regardless of performance.

11. WHY WERE THE NEW TRAINING METHODS UNSUCCESSFUL?

One obvious question to emerge from this research concerns the reasons for the lack of success associated with new training methods. Open and distance learning programs were only used by 17/30 of the graduates who were initially tracked and were only considered useful by 6/28 of those graduates who were still in the survey a year later; see appendix two. Despite assurances by senior management that over 80% of training would be carried out via open learning (Whitley & Martin, 1995), those who were charged with the task of running open learning centers estimated that usage rates were low and running at no more than 20% (of the available time) and this is almost certainly an optimistic estimate. Similarly, appraisal interviews were the mechanism by which competencies should have been assessed and yet over a third (11/30) of the interviews that should have been done at the end of the first year of the training program had not been carried out; see appendix three. The company's own guide to the graduate training program stated quite clearly that graduates were expected to use at least some of their own time to become professionally qualified (see British Gas, 1994; 1995). However a significant minority (12/30) made it clear that their had no intention of pursuing this strategy. In six cases graduates argued that they had already achieved such status by virtue of a previous qualification (usually a Ph.D.), and in six cases employees simply stated that they had no wish to join a professional body. By the end of the three-year tracking period, all of the graduates had abandoned attempts to keep in touch with their mentors.

Three plausible reasons to explain these developments come out of the literature on the economics of education/training. The first useful starting point would be the distinction between the consumption and investment benefits associated with education/training. A number of textbook authors (such as Atkinson, 1983), have distinguished between the immediate short term gains to education (consumption benefit) and a longer term stream of benefits that would accrue to the person undertaking various courses (the investment benefit). Most of the graduates surveyed here were quite clear that they regarded training as a means of furthering their career; they were interested in the investment returns to training. Of the 53 questionnaire replies received, the vast majority (38) agreed that the major motivation for doing training was the extra earnings that could result in the future; see appendix four. Indeed, in many of the interviews, it emerged that these employees did not enjoy doing the courses that they were expected to do; there was little evidence of consumption benefit. The evidence suggests that these core employees were prepared to spend at least some of their own time in training; see appendix four, where it emerges that only two (out of 53) thought that they were expected to use an unreasonable amount of their own time in training. However, from the employees' perspective the rationale for using such time was as a means to an end, i.e. getting extra earnings in the long run. The perceived benefits of training were in investment, rather than consumption terms. Indeed, all five of the Ph.D. graduates claimed that they were very interested in the scientific nature of the work that they were employed to do. They claimed that they did not want to get promoted if such promotion would take them away from the specialist work that they were interested in. If graduates were not especially interested in promotion, then it may have been quite a rational policy not to use their own time to study for professional status.

Of the 30 graduates who were tracked in this study, twelve had no interest in using their own time to become professionally qualified. It is true that this meant that they were significantly less likely to get promoted (see appendix 5), but this trade-off may have been considered as a price worth paying, given that the training methods outlined above provided little or no consumption benefit and were predicated on the basis that they were sufficiently flexible that they could be used in the graduates' own time.

A second contribution from the economics of education literature comes in the form of the debate surrounding the screening (or credentialism) hypothesis. Arrow (1974) and others (Adnett, 1989), have suggested that employers and employees may well wish to use education/training qualifications as a means of sending (or receiving) signals. These signals may be used as proxy measures for what Blaug (1993) describes as desirable employment characteristics such as future "trainability", the ability to organize ones' efforts, or even more general traits such as politeness. The starting point for the hypothesis is that to accurately measure productivity or to gather reliable information about candidates is expensive and fraught with difficulties. Employers therefore wish to save on transactions costs and use qualifications as a readily available sifting device to weed out those applications that they do wish to consider any further. The more relevant signals that employees have, the more likely it is that employers are prepared to offer them a desirable job. This signaling process applies both to applicants for an initial port of entry job, as well as internal applicants who wish for a promotion post. There has been little by way of empirical evidence to support (or refute), this signaling hypothesis. Shah (1985) provides some "tentative" evidence to support the hypothesis, using British data. However, Shah's work was concerned with pre-entry screening; the evidence here suggests that post-entry credentialism has occurred. Graduates regarded the pursuit of professional status as the best means of sending out signals in the internal labor market. They were less concerned with the government's NVQ scheme, or maintaining links with their mentors, because these strategies were not seen as efficient means of sending out relevant signals. Ironically, many graduates regarded their progress whilst doing these examinations with some apprehension. Of the 18 graduates aiming for professional membership in the second round of the study, 8 of them said that they thought that this application was going badly. However, 5/8 of these employees still managed to gain promotion that year. The process of getting professional status seemed to be used as a means of sending out signals that implied that these graduates were ambitious and well organized, and as such, were prime candidates for promotion within the internal labor market. In pursuing this strategy, graduates were not overly concerned with the use of the new training methods alluded to earlier. The important that they wished to establish, within the company, was that they had the sort of desirable characteristics mentioned earlier, that would be sought after by managers who were about to decide who should be given promotion. The ambitious graduates' determination to become active joiners (of professional bodies) was the key element of their strategy; how they achieved this end was of less significance to them. As a consequence, some of these graduates signed up for evening classes, which one might regard as a traditional mode of learning; others simply took out books from local libraries to help them to pass their examinations. Very few of the graduates in this study fond that open learning programs were useful; in fact only 6/28 did so, in the second round of the study.

Thirdly, in economics the principal-agent has been recognized as having an important bearing on many different types of transaction, including the provision of education or training (Elliott, 1991). In this context, British Gas HQ may be thought of as the principal (the policy maker). It was this central body that considered the use of the new training methods as constituting an important part of future policy (See Martin & Whitley, 1995). The agents left to carry out the policy were the local managers, who had a number of other responsibilities apart from the development of those graduate trainees that happened to be working for them. These local managers had different agendas from the principals. Many managers felt that they, as individuals, were gaining little benefit from giving staff appraisals that were designed to assess the competencies gained by their graduate trainees. This distinction (between local management and British Gas HQ), is echoed in other organizations and the principal-agent goes some way towards explaining why competencies were not adequately monitored. Moreover, this finding fits into a more general context that is described in appendix four; the majority (27/53) of the graduates surveyed agreed that British Gas was insufficiently willing to assess the benefits of the training that were given. Indeed, 80% of the senior managers of one region of the company agreed that although the company was willing to devote resources to training, it was insufficiently willing to evaluate the effectiveness of such policies (British Gas West Midlands, 1993). The graduates surveyed here may well have gained extra competencies but in many cases there was little enthusiasm on the part of local managers to accurately monitor such developments. Of those appraisal interviews that did take place, nearly a quarter were dealt with in a summary fashion. The decision to award, or potentially withhold, a £1000 increment was made in a period of under 30 minutes, in 7/30 cases.

Two further explanations seem plausible, which are not from the economics of education literature. Firstly, the organizational flux suffered by the company has been described in section 7. The key point here is that such flux meant that mentors were often difficult to track down; as a consequence, graduates became disillusioned with the mentoring system. Moreover, many of the mentors were senior mangers who were quick to take advantage of the enhanced pension schemes, or voluntary redundancy being offered by the company, when it had to shed a third of its workforce in a five year period. Although, potentially, such mentors had skills and knowledge that could be passed on to their charges, in practice, the system fell into disuse quite quickly.

Finally, the relevant timeframe within which assessment could be carried out is an important consideration. Shackleton (1995) rightly argues that one of the very advantages of new training methods (i.e. open timeframes) is, simultaneously, a source of difficulty. With traditional off the job courses, a formal examination is frequently held (at a set time), to determine how well students have mastered the material. In the case of many new training schemes, such assessment does not occur in this fashion. Thus, those four graduates who took out open learning programs for modern languages (at the start of the training in 1993/4), all agreed (in 1996), that they were unlikely to finish them. Of course, the problem here is that it becomes very difficult to say exactly when the attrition occurred. The graduates concerned said that they thought that they might go back to their studies, at some (unspecified)

12. CONCLUSION

One has to be especially circumspect when suggesting any conclusions at the end of a study such as this. It is, after all, only one case study that featured one organization in the UK, and involved using a relatively small sample of questionnaire replies (53) and meant tracking an even smaller set of (30) graduates over a three year period. Clearly, one would have had more confidence in the results if they had measured the replies of thousands of people, over a longer period of time. It is also true that questionnaire replies suffer from the obvious defect that respondents are not responsible for their replies and they might well not be replying in a truthful manner. More research needs to be done. However, it is striking that a number of claims have been made about the benefits of modern training methods, in the practitioner/policy literature alluded to earlier, without supporting evidence. If these (alleged) benefits are to be assessed, then some sort of longitudinal study, done within one (or more) institutions would seem to offer a suitable means of evaluation.

It seems clear that there may well be a number of advantages to modern training methods (as described in section 5). However, to account for their adoption in the UK we also have to examine the sort of "push" factors outlined in section 6; certainly in this case as Whitley and Martin admit, the link between the product and labor markets is an important one. Economic necessity drove employers to consider fresh ways of gaining what they perceived to be a more efficient use of training budgets. In adopting a strategy that seemed rational, they seemed to have underestimated the sorts of difficulties that were involved and that were described in the last section (10).

We need to treat allegations of the merit associated with modern training methods very circumspectly. In the study here British Gas chose their graduates with great care; each one cost some £9,0000 transactions costs at the point of entry (British Gas, 1995). The point was made in section 9 that one might have imagined that the graduate employees in this study would succeed, given their previous track record and the fact that they had a number of (a priori) reasons for wanting to do well in their GDP. In fact the results of this study are distinctly mixed, from a management perspective. Given that British Gas was still spending some £35 million on the direct costs of training alone and given the attrition rates outlined earlier, then the case for swapping over to modern training methods is far from convincing.

Finally, one has to say that in this case the organization, whilst being committed to training, was even by its own admission, not sufficiently willing to evaluate the huge outlays involved. In a 1993 internal study, 80% of senior management thought that a former region (West Midlands Gas) did not sufficiently evaluate the money spent on training and that is certainly consistent with the evidence gleaned in this study. In that sense, it does seem as though the considerable sums that have been devoted to modern training methods represent a leap of faith.

APPENDIX 1 TRAINING WAS A KEY CONCERN OF THE GRADUATES AND WAS READILY AVAILABLE

Table 1a. My reason for staying with British Gas was

Reason for staying with B.G.	Frequency	Percentage	Cumulativ
2	8	26.7%	26.7%
3	1	3.3%	30.0%
4	14	46.7%	76.7%
5	2	6.7%	83.3%
6	4	13.3%	96.7
7	1	3.3%	100.0%
Total	30	100.0%	

Key:
Code	Reason
1	Seniority Rights
2	Nature of the work
3	Pay
4	Training
5	State of the Labor Market
6	Other
7	Pay back relocation expenses

NB This data was from the first round of the longitudinal study, i.e. collected in the autumn of 1994.

Table 1b. How easy/difficult, in the past year, has it been to make sure that you get the training that you want?

	VERY EASY	EASY	NEUTRAL	DIFFICULT	VERY DIFFICULT
	10	11	1	5	1

NB This data was from the second round of the longitudinal study, i.e. collected in the autumn of 1995.

Table 1c. How easy/difficult has it been to get any training you may have wanted, this past year?

	VERY EASY	EASY	NEUTRAL	DIFFICULT	VERY DIFFICULT
	5	9	1	2	4

NB This data was from the third round of the longitudinal study, i.e. collected in the autumn of 1996.

APPENDIX 2: OPEN/DISTANCE LEARNING PACKAGES WERE USED BUT WERE NOT CONSIDERED VERY USEFUL

Table 2a. Have you used any open learning packages

OPEN LEARNING PACKAGES	Frequency	Percentage	Cumulativ
+	17	56.7%	56.7%
-	13	43.3%	100.0%
Total	30	100.0%	

Key:
Code   **Open learning packages**
+   Yes
-           No

NB This data was from the first round of the longitudinal study, i.e. collected in the autumn of 1994.

Table 2b. How useful did you find any open/distance learning materials?

	VERY USEFULL	USEFULL	NEUTRAL	VERY LITTLE USE	COMPLETELY USELESS
	2	4	2	2	18

NB This data was from the second round of the longitudinal study, i.e. collected in the autumn of 1995.

Table 2c. How useful have you found open/distance learning materials ?

	VERY USEFULL	USEFULL	NEUTRAL	NOT USEFULL	NOT AT ALL USEFULL	N/A
	0	5	1	1	3	11

NB This data was from the third round of the longitudinal study, i.e. collected in the autumn of 1996.

APPENDIX 3: STAFF APPRAISALS

Table 3a. Have you had two staff appraisals?

STAFF APPRAISALS	Frequency	Percentage	Cumulativ
+	19	63.3%	63.3%
-	11	36.7%	100.0%
Total	30	100.0%	

Key:
Code	Staff Appraisals
+	Yes
-	No

Table 3b. How long did your staff appraisals last on average?

STAFF APPRAISAL LENGTH	Frequency	Percentage	Cumulativ
1	6	20.0%	20.0%
2	1	3.3%	23.3%
3	0	0%	0%
4	22	73.3%	96.7%
5	1	3.3%	100.0%
Total	30	100.0%	

Key:
Code	Staff Appraisal length
1	0 Minutes
2	Under 30 Minutes
3	Between 30 Minutes to 1 Hour
4	Between 1 to 2 Hours
5	Over 2 Hours

NB This data was from the first round of the longitudinal study, i.e. collected in the autumn of 1994

APPENDIX 4: RESPONSES TO ATTITUDINAL SURVEY

Table 4.

	STRONGLY AGREE	AGREE	NEUTRAL	DISAGREE	STRONGLY DISAGREE
C1	1	1	5	31	15
C2	12	33	3	5	0
C3	3	24	16	9	1
C4	3	28	15	6	1
C5	0	10	6	24	13
C6	6	32	6	7	2
C7	31	21	1	0	0
C8	10	35	5	2	1
C9	1	14	10	20	8
C10	3	14	10	20	8
C11	3	4	10	31	5
C12	1	7	6	33	6
C13	0	7	32	13	1
C14	5	18	14	15	1
C15	5	27	9	9	3

Section C Questions

1) The amount of my own time that I have to invest in training is unreasonable.
2) The training that I receive is sufficiently general as to be applicable in a range of organizations.
3) British Gas is sufficiently willing to assess the benefits of my training.
4) British Gas is sufficiently willing to assess the costs of my training.
5) The major motivation for training is the extra salary it is likely to generate in the short run (i.e. within the next two years).
6) The major motivation for training is the extra salary it is likely to generate in the longer run.
7) The major motivation for training is to enhance my long term career prospects.
8) British Gas is committed to training.
9) Far too much of my time at work is spent doing menial tasks that are not commensurate with my position in the company.
10) My long term career aim is to stay with British Gas and get a senior managerial post.
11) In order to achieve a full range of competences I am obliged to change locations more often than I would wish.
12) In order to achieve a full range of competences I am obliged to change jobs more often than I would wish.
13) The main company rationale for on-the-job training is the chance that it gives British Gas to disseminate company values.
14) The company expects me to use my own time to gain extra competences as part of my development.
15) I feel that I have been fairly treated by the staff appraisal system in the way that my training needs have been assessed.

NB This data was collected from the 53 questionnaire replies received in the autumn of 1994.

APPENDIX 5: CROSS TABULATION OF MEMBERSHIP OF A PROFESSIONAL BODY AND PROMOTION (CHI-SQUARED TEST)

	Promotion		Total
	Yes	No	
Membership of a Professional body			
1	0	1	1
2	5	2	7
4	2	3	5
5	3	2	5
n	0	10	10
Total	10	18	28

NB The data above is from the second round of the longitudinal study, i.e. collected in the autumn of 1995.

Key:
Code	Application Status
1	Getting on very badly with application to join professional body.
2	Getting on badly with application to join professional body.
4	Getting on well with application to join professional body.
5	Getting on very well with application to join professional body.
n	Not currently applying to join professional body.

The expected value in a number of cells is less than 5. Chi-squared test is not valid.
Chi-square =11.32, Degrees of freedom=4, p value = 0.02314980

In the absence of the problem discussed above, one would be inclined to hold the H1 hypothesis (i.e. accept that there was some relationship between the variables) and reject H0 (the null hypothesis). If one collapses some of the cells together so that rows 1/2/4/5 are combined and compared to row n, then the cell values do, of course, become higher. However, in this situation, there is one degree of freedom and there is still one cell with an expected value of less than 5; the problem is not resolved.

REFERENCES

Adnett, N. (1989). *Labor market policy.* Harlow: Longman.

Armstrong, M. (1995). Measuring work: The vital statistics. *Personnel Management,* September, 34-36.

Arrow, K. (1974). Higher education as a filter. In K. Lumsden (Ed.), *Efficiency in Universities.* New York: Elsevier.

Atkinson, G.B.J. (1983). *The economics of education.* London: Hodder & Stoughton.
Baron, H. (1995). Highlights from a fair question. *Saville and Holdsworth Newsline*, 21, September, 2.
Blaug, M. (1993). Education and the employment contract. *Education Economic*, (1), 21-33.
Boyatzis, R. (1982). *The competent manager.* New York :Wiley.
British Gas (1986 onwards). *Annual report.* London: British Gas.
British Gas (1993; 1994*). The graduate development program.* London: British Gas.
British Gas West Midlands (1993). *Investor in people survey.* Solihull: British Gas.
British Gas (1995). *Graduate development and recruitment strategy.* London: British Gas.
British Gas Transco (1995). More training is planned. *The Link Letter*, 4, September, 1.
Brown, C. (1994). *CEO's Address to Conference.* Presented to British Gas Graduate Development Conference, Solihull, September.
CBI (1989). *Towards a skills revolution.* London: CBI.
CBI (1993). *Routes for success.* London: CBI.
DFE (1992). *Pickup in progress.* 28, Autumn.
DfEE (1995). *Labor market and skill trends.* Nottingham: DfEE.
Dunning, J.H. (1996). Globalization, foreign direct investment and economic development. *Economics and Business Education*, 4 (2), 46-51.
Elliott, R. (1991). *Labor economics: A comparative text.* London: McGraw-Hill.
Ferner, A., & Colling, T. (1991). Privatization, regulation and industrial relations. *British Journal of Industrial Relations*, 29 (3), 391-409.
Fowler, A. (1996). How to pick a job evaluation system. *Personnel Management*, February, 41-43.
Howard, S. (1993). Accreditation of prior learning-andragogy in action or a cut-price approach to learning? *Journal of Advanced Learning*, 18 (11), 1817-1824.
King, S. (1993). Business benefits of management development. *Management Development Review*, 6 (4), 38-40.
Linbeck, A., & Snower, D. (1988*). The insider/outsider theory of employment and unemployment.* London: MIT.
Littlefield, D. (1994). Open learning by PC or paper. *Personnel Management*, September, 55-58.
Manning, A. (1990). Implicit contract theory. In D. Sapsford, & Z. Tzannatos (Eds.), *Current issues in labor economics.* London: Macmillan.
McNabb, R., & Ryan, P. (1990). Segmented labor markets. In D. Sapsford, & Z. Tzannatos (Eds.), *Current issues in labor market economics,* London: Macmillan.
MMC (1993). *Gas.* Cmnd 2314. London: HMSO.
MMC (1993). *British Gas plc.* Cmnd 2315. London: HMSO.
Mumford, A. (1985). What's new in management development? *Personnel Management*, May, 30-32.
Munn, C. (1997). *The changing education and training needs of the financial services Sector.* Paper presented to the fourth EDINEB conference. Edinburgh, September.
NCVQ (1988). *Assessing competence.* London: NCVQ.
OFGAS (1993; 1995; 1996). *Annual report.* London: OFGAS.
Pedler, M., Boydell, T., & Burgoyne, J. (1989). Towards the learning company. *Management Education and Development*, 20 (1), 1-8.
Pickard, J. (1991). What does the investors in people award really mean? *Personnel Management*, March, 9-10.
Saggers, R. (1994). Training climbs the corporate agenda. *Personnel Management*, July, 40-45.

Shackleton, J.R. (1992). *Training too much?* London: IEA.
Shah, A. (1985). Does education act as a screening device for certain British occupations? *Oxford Economic Papers*, 37, 118-124.
Shackleton, J.R. & Walsh, S. (1995). *National vocational qualifications: The story so far.* Paper presented to ERSC conference. London, February.
Sloman, M. (1993). Training to play a lead role. *Personnel Management*, July, 40-45
Storey, J. (1992). HRM in action: The truth is out at last. *Personnel Management*, April, 28-31.
Taylor, M. (1996). *Higher education and management NVQs.* Paper presented to NVQ seminar. Preston, March.
Thorne, P. (1991). Assessment of prior experiential learning. *Nursing Standard*, 6 (10), 32-34.
Torrington, D., & Hall, L. (1995). *Personnel management.* Hemel Hempstead: Prentice Hall.
Unison (1993). *Distance and open learning: A guide to courses.* London: Unison.
Weston, C. (1996). Regulator takes a tough line. *Guardian* 4/10/1996, 20.
Whitley, T., & Martin, L. (1995). Devolving the power of training. *Practical Training*, April, 26-28.
Whiteway Research (1993). *Graduate training and development survey.* London: Whiteway Research.

The Economics of the Learning Organization and the Role of Economics in the Organization of Learning

Joseph G. Nellis & Stephen Regan
Cranfield School of Management, Cranfield University, UK

1. INTRODUCTION

The aim of this paper is to present a model of an organization as a learning system drawn from organization theory and to enhance this with models of learning which are becoming increasingly prominent in economics. We find that the two paradigms have the potential to enrich each other's understanding of the same topic. We then consider two implications of this for the organization of learning within the business school world: first, for the role of the business school in partnership with corporate clients which are assumed to be "learning organizations," and second, we consider the impact upon the nature of the economics curriculum within MBA programs.

Our analysis develops further the thinking behind Nellis (1998) and reflects how the pedagogic and research concerns outlined in that paper have progressed. Nellis suggests that a crisis grips academic economists in the UK and emphasizes that: " ... there is now a growing question concerning not only the role of economics but about the future of economics education." (Nellis, 1998). Further evidence to support this view is not hard to find. In particular, enrolments to study single honours economics degrees in British universities have been falling steadily for many years. Along with this, there is a growing realization amongst British academics that the average 'quality' of undergraduate and graduate students is declining. Furthermore, the role of economics within the growing market of vocationally relevant business degrees is being questioned quite sharply – as evidenced by the fact that economics is taught as a discrete subject on only a very small minority of MBA programs within the UK.

In addressing this 'crisis' facing the academic economists we examine whether the gap between economic theory and business practice has been overstated, and whether economists have been serving their subject as well as they might by failing to realize the potential value and excitement to be had in teaching more directly a curriculum which reflects current research in the subject. As an example of this we track two apparently unconnected phenomena: first, the development of learning as an important theoretical concern for organizational theorists (see Grant & Spender, 1996; Adler & Cole, 1993; Adler, 1992; and Tsoukas, 1994); and secondly, the recent development of interest in learning within economics (see Marimon, 1997; Borgers, 1996). We assert that economic theories of learning are rarely presented to managers and that this failing overemphasizes the perceived irrelevance of economics which many managers and students feel as they approach the subject.[1]

The argument of this paper proceeds as follows. In Section 2 we present a brief overview of organizational learning which reflects the character of recent work in organization theory. The principle feature of such models is that they are non–economic: they describe *how* learning takes place, and relate it to causal factors using systems theoretic frameworks, or to metaphors drawn from psychology. These models of learning are incomplete in that they fail to address learning in an economic context, and thus in Section 3 we present a summary of the economics of learning. Sections 2 and 3, taken together, amount to a more general theory of learning, describing both *how* (Section 2) and *why* (Section 3) learning comes about. Section 4 then draws some implications from this theory of organizational learning to develop some conceptual frameworks for how Business Schools might view relationships with their 'clients'. Our key ideas for educational innovation are presented in this section: namely the concept of a *learning*

---

[1] Consider for instance the role of game theory in the New Industrial Organisation which has hardly touched the way economic principles courses are taught. In addition, models of public choice have greatly enriched what we understand about regulation of business. The economics of development has a great deal to say about normative and ethical matters of great relevance to business. The new theories of growth are very rich in matters which could only be described as sociological and new trade theories are steeped in realities of political behaviour.

partnership and the notion of a *learning organization*. Section 5 gives an illustrative example of how these innovations affect one aspect of the work of a Business School, specifically the economics curriculum.

2. THE ORGANISATION AS A LEARNING SYSTEM

Learning is becoming more important: organizations need to learn (adapt) in order to survive and the rate of change of market and non–market (e.g. regulatory) environments is now so fast that the importance of learning is rising up the hierarchy of key competencies of most (but unfortunately not all) organizations. An extreme view of this strategic imperative towards the learning organization is presented by Quinn et al (1990) who assert that the firm is best viewed as an 'intellectual entity' and that products are simply the results of the firm's knowledge resources. This is consistent with a well-established vein of economic reasoning within Industrial Organization Theory and associated with Schumpeter (1954) and Penrose (1959). Schumpeter sees the essence of competition to be related to innovation, a struggling for intellectual leadership between ever more knowledge-intensive businesses. Penrose, who has become fashionable with strategy scholars as providing an early view of the importance of management as an intellectual resource, insists that the firm is a bundle of resources which only have value in that they are able to provide a flow of benefits, and that this flow of benefits is very dependent on the intellectual resources of the firm's management. Given the ubiquitous nature of the proposition that organizational learning is valuable, the obvious question which presents itself is *how* do organizations actually learn?

2.1 How Organizations Learn

Although all organizations learn, they do not all learn in the same way. Each organization has a preferred learning style, just as human beings and other organisms do. We now define three dimensions to this learning style or orientation, the *focus*, the *process* and the *scope* of organization learning.

The *focus* aspect of learning concerns *what* the organization learns. In particular, whether the organization learns (i.e. adapts) by changing its products and/or services; or whether the organization prefers to learn by adapting its processes (e.g. substituting technology for labor, or one type of labor for another; or changing its business model, for example, by outsourcing). Thus organizations learn either by doing different things in the same way, or the same things in different ways. Most organizations will do both, but organizations may have a bias towards one or the other.

The process dimension concerns *how* the organization learns (adapts) rather than what it learns. Thus an organization may learn by adapting either what it makes, or how it makes them, but there are alternative learning *processes* by which this adaptation can be achieved. We scale the organization's preferences in this dimension according to whether the learning process is open or closed. An open learning organization is flexible in the means it uses to effect adaptation. A closed learning organization is one where there are fixed rules and procedures about how learning takes place.

The *scope* dimension of organization learning concerns *who* learns. This is either narrowly defined, in which case there is a very targeted approach to learning, and little attempt to create 'cascades' or spillovers. Different product groups or functional specialists or layers of management learn different things. If the focus is broad, then there is an active attempt to treat learning as a single pool, a common resource shared throughout the organization.

The essential point is that organizational learning is at least as complex as individual learning. This complexity requires a great deal of thought on behalf of educationalists who seek to develop relationships with organizations as entities which learn. Furthermore, the key role of learning as part of sustainable competitive advantage will place at a premium the skills needed to manage this relationship.

3. THE ECONOMICS OF LEARNING

Recent work in applied industrial economics has traversed the same territory as the models of organization learning referred to above. In particular, within evolutionary theory (see Nelson, 1995) as well as within the related Resource Based Theory of the firm (see Teece et al. 1990), the notion of learning is central to a dynamic theory of the firm. Equally, theoretical economics has been full of research into how expectations and beliefs are formed within the context of a 'learning process'.

The economics of learning has four main strands. First, there is the research program concerned with bounded rationality, which posits learning as an alternative to rationality as a basis for the theory of choice (for instance, Neural Networks and artificial intelligence models – see Holland, 1995). Secondly, there is a strand of learning theory which is concerned with justifying the existence and stability of the equilibria in economic models which are sensitive to the assumptions made about the nature of rationality which agents possess (Kreps, 1990). Thirdly, there is a need for learning theories in order to show not only how an equilibrium is stabilized but how it is selected from a potentially very large set of multiple equilibria (Grandmont, 1994). Fourthly, and finally, there is a need to explain observed behavior which is out of equilibrium, highlighting that there is something fundamentally wrong in the models themselves, but which is often then corrected when learning is explicitly incorporated into them (Marimon, 1997).

In order to make a link between the economic theories of learning and the Organization Theoretic (OT) models of learning, it is useful to compare these different 'learning' paradigms, i.e. that of management and that of economics. There is one striking similarity which is that both approaches define learning as *adaptive* behavior by agents. Moreover, both the organizational theory and the economic theory approaches are happy with the notion of the *organization* as an agent – for instance, economic models of learning are happy to conceive of learning as taking place at the level of the firm.

However, the model of learning that economists have in place has a slightly different purpose to that of the organization theorists. Principally, economics is not concerned to explain learning as an end in itself. To put it very starkly – just because learning is the way firms actually behave is not a good enough reason for an economist to study it, though it may be for an organization theorist.[2]

The reason for this is that if we discover that learning simply explains *how* our models achieve equilibrium, they have added nothing very much to our tool kit – except they may add some complexity to the story we tell. On grounds of parsimony, at least, we would thus exclude the theory of learning from future research, since we can achieve the answers we want by simpler means.

However, if learning allows us to change the predictive content of models, then it is of significant interest to economic theorists. If, for instance, we need learning to explain how the equilibrium is selected over another, and if both these equilibria are indistinguishable within our more axiomatically rational choice models, then a theory of how organizations learn is a necessary part of the economic theory of the firm. If this is so, there is also an important policy prescription from learning theory. If we show that learning is important for equilibrium selection and justification, then we have the possibility that a particular equilibrium may be achieved more easily when it is learned more easily. Thus, learning can become an

---

[2]Many observers would argue that realism is not perceived by economists as being an important concern in economic models, implying that only predictive efficacy is essential.

important part of policy development at all levels. In this area, the concerns of the economist and the organization theorist converge. The organization theorist is concerned with learning in organizations and wants to understand how organizations reach their equilibria, (i.e. their strategies) regardless of whether there is a less realistic, more elegant model which explains which strategies they reach. The economist only wants to understand learning if there is no alternative, reduced-form model.

However, in the context of policy formation and the response by an organization to it, these interests converge. The organization theorist is interested in how organizations learn, and the applied policy work these theorists do is identified to assist in the management of this learning. Equally, an economist would want to improve the ability of the organization to make the correct response to policy changes, and would be concerned with how organizations actually do learn. An understanding of how organizations learn will improve the efficacy of policy decisions. Thus there is a case for economic models being enhanced by Organization Theory models in ways which add something to economic theory and policy.

Equally, the process of incorporating the Organization Theory perspective on the effectiveness of learning into economic models of learning may throw up some very precise definitions about what exactly constitutes a 'learning algorithm.' The mathematical formalism which characterizes economic theory may add something to the field when coupled with the more contextual, cognitive process model in Organization Theory (see above), since the formal model is often much more general. Thus economics may (and we believe will) add greatly to the understanding of learning in organizations.

4. THE LEARNING PARTNERSHIP AND LEARNING ORGANISATION

One outcome of this interest in the role of learning for both organization theorists and economists is the possibility that relationships between Business Schools and the organizations that use their services may have to alter. What do economists have to offer MBA students in addressing organizational change, for instance, when they understand organizations to be evolving in a behavioristic way rather than as neoclassical production function optimizers as argued by economists? How does a Business School alter the executive courses it offers to its clients when it sees those clients to be continuously engaged in a process of learning already? For example, if organizations such as Motorola or British Aerospace or Microsoft decide to

Learning & Organization 63

manage learning as a key strategic competence, what does this mean for the relationships they form with external providers of education and training?

One possible framework for the role of a Business School in such interactions is represented in figure 1 below, which seeks to capture the essence of the *'learning partnership'* approach. The cyclical nature of the diagram captures the self sustaining nature of the partnership: this is a dynamic relationship between the partners.

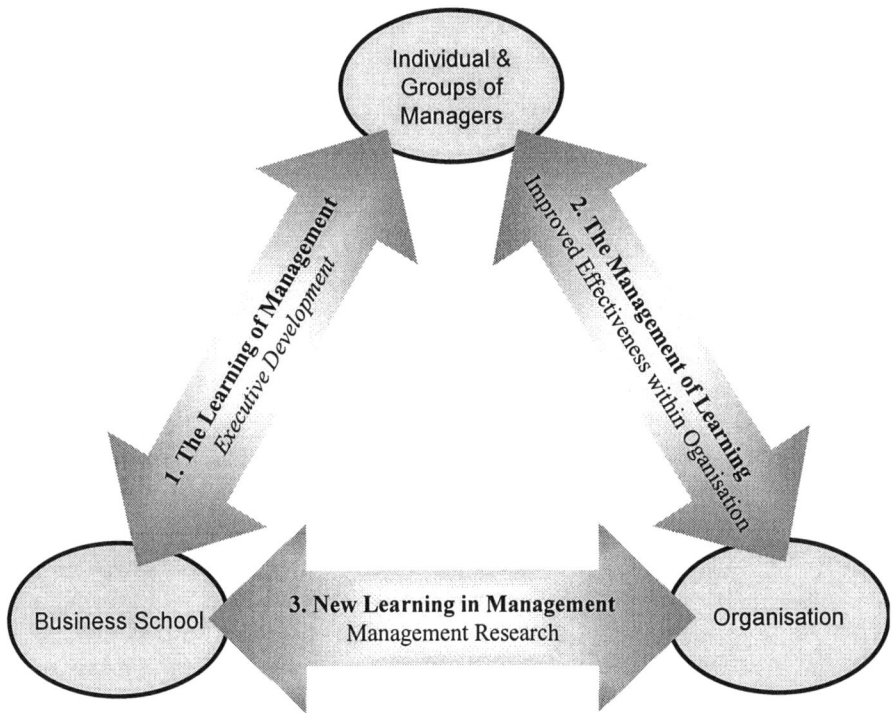

Figure 1. The Learning Partnership Model.

There are three elements to this learning partnership model: (a) the relationship between the manager and the Business School; (b) the relationship between the manager and the organization; and (c) the relationship between the Business School and the organization. We describe each in turn.

First, the relationship between the manager and the business school is defined by the extent to which the manager is able to realize the human capital which the learning in the business school develops. This realization of the value can only take place in an organizational context, and thus the role of the business school is to develop in the manager not only a skill but an ability to transfer his or her skills into the organization. This generally means that the manager will learn not only technical skills, such as finance or strategy, but softer, behavioral or affective skills. Thus, the manager learns skills as an individual, and these skills may be transferable skills which have wide applicability for the mangers future career. But the manager also learns *the skill of transfer*, since without this he/she is unable to fully realize the value of the cognitive skills. We define this element of the three-way learning partnership between the managers and the business school, as the '*learning of management*'.

The second element in the three–way partnership is that between the manager and the organization. The concept of a learning contract is useful in this context: both partners will usually have agreed objectives for the learning which is to take place, which will often be defined as measurable outcomes and may even form part of the formal appraisal process. The individual manager expects a commitment from the organization, say, in terms of career progression as a consequence of the commitment to develop new skills. Moreover, the organization needs to be aware of how to capture the value of the training in which it makes a joint investment with the manager. Specific mentors and /or sponsors within the organization who hold a stake in the learning process and its outcomes will often be appointed. Thus the organization and the manager are engaged in a process which could be described as *The Management of Learning*, which is an essential adjunct to the *Learning of Management* between the manager and the Business School. An effective learning partnership requires that both of these processes are present, that both contracts exist and support each other.

Third, there is the relationship between the Business School and the organization. Clearly, there is often a financial contract between the business school and the organization, but there is also an implicit learning contract between these two in the learning process which is our primary concern in this paper. Acting as providers of management learning, at whatever level, is just one aspect of the work of a Business School. If set within a University context, the Business School is (or should be) dedicated to learning, and this means the creation of organizationally relevant knowledge (whether pure or applied) as well as the dissemination of this knowledge. Thus the third learning contract in the three–way learning partnership is a research agenda, which supports the other two elements in the partnership. It is difficult to imagine a learning partnership lasting over time without this ongoing development of new knowledge and it is equally difficult to imagine how such knowledge could come about without some form of engagement with business organizations.

Thus, the *Learning Organization* in the title of this paper is a three-way partnership between managers, organizations and Business Schools. It is not the company, nor the managers, nor the Business School in isolation which are defined as 'the learning organization' in themselves, but this new organization they create between them. Creating this partnership is what we mean by '*The Organization of Learning*'.

There are various implications of such a concept of learning organization for the process of educational innovation, a few of which we now consider. First, there are striking potential linkages between the idea of the learning partnership and the new models of a university, which are being developed by the leading–businesses. For instance, the corporate universities of McKinsey or Motorola seem to fit well with this concept. Equally, the term 'virtual university' has started to be used with particular reference to a 'University for Business'. At the level of the partnership the concept outlined in this paper is just such an entity in the sense that the learning goes on within an abstract, intangible entity, which is made up of nevertheless very real constituents: real managers, real businesses and real universities.

5. IMPLICATIONS FOR THE CURRICULUM: EXAMPLES FROM ECONOMICS

Notions of knowledge management and learning are not only changing the relationship between Business Schools and the organizations they serve, but they are also changing the nature of the curriculum within the Business School. In this final section of the paper we review the ways in which the curriculum has altered in line with these new organizational and academic imperatives. Our aim is to illustrate such changes rather than to develop generalized rules, and thus we confine ourselves to the economic curriculum, the area we know best.

The growing concern of economics with knowledge formation, which explores the boundaries between learning and rationality, has been reflected in the way the content of core economics courses has been changed within some (especially British) Business School MBA programs. In this final section we refer to examples of how this has occurred.

Today, much more time is typically given over to a careful analysis of the nature of the firm as a behavioral entity, covering such topics as agency theory, information economics, incentive compatibility and tournament theory. Typically, in both the US, the UK and Europe, innovative economics courses are concerned with strategic interaction between the firm and the market, often using game theory, stressing the role of conduct (strategy) in determining industrial structure. Such courses are now almost entirely concerned with imperfect competition and particularly oligopoly theory, and hence deal head–on with competitive rivalry, analyzing strategic management within an economic paradigm. Typical issues on such a course, like strategic pricing, marketing activity in different environments, innovation and R+D and investment decisions are treated as being both highly relevant as well as rigorously based in theory.

The consequences of these recent innovations in changing the nature of economics presented to a business audience are encouraging for a number of reasons.

- First, students become aware of economics as a discipline which links theories of organization with theories of strategy. This has important implications for the future role of economics in Business School curricula: the value of studying economics is that it is a particular "way of thinking" rather than a set of problems of concern to only economists. The case for integrating economics into a single, core program, say by a series of linked cases and common assessment is strongly supported by this experience. This is particularly important in a Business School where every issue which an economist addresses has to fight for attention from other perspectives. Thus, labor market economics contends with HR models which are at least in part non-economic and, similarly, with models of competitive processes, where economics is in debate with strategy, or consumer theory where economics must fight for attention with some very seductive models based on sociological and psychological paradigms.
- Secondly, the models of organizations and markets presented in economics are immunized from the standard criticism that economics is too abstract to be included on, say, MBA programs. This critique usually asserts that economic theory requires an assumption of too much rationality for the models to be of any use to practicing managers. Our concern with adaptive behavior and bounded rationality and the economics of learning greatly weakens this challenge. Economics gains in credibility by starting from the same sort of grounded assumptions that marketing, finance and strategy make.
- Thirdly, the pedagogy needed to deliver this kind of teaching is different to traditional economics teaching methods. In order to teach and to assess such material there is a need to develop a number of case studies and some of these have been useful research exercises both from an academic and from a pedagogic perspective.
- Finally, the results of our experience in applying these principles have been very encouraging in terms of building the status of economics within one economics curriculum. There has been a significant increase in the rigor of the economics we teach in our attempt to incorporate more realistic assumptions about the real workings of the economy. This is because many of these new theories are at the forefront of the

academic profession's research agenda which makes this material challenging and new even for those of our students who have had previous training in economics.

We would conclude, therefore, that as Business School economists we have some confidence in the future since our discipline is developing theoretical tools which are directly relevant to the business world and models of learning are but one example of this. Moreover as Business School academics we are also hopeful that the rise in status of knowledge and its management within firms is likely to lead to an increased rather than a diminished role for the business schools as *partners* with organizations. Finally, as educationalists interested in innovation, we offer the concept of 'The Learning Organization' developed in this paper, and reiterate its key features. First, it is (at least potentially) virtual; second, it is a jointly owned and jointly managed entity and hence inherently co–operative.

REFERENCES

Adler, P.S. (Ed.) (1992). *Technology and the future of work.* New York: Oxford University Press.

Adler, P.S., & Cole, R.E. (1993). Designed for learning: A tale of two auto plants. *Sloan Management Review,* Spring, 85-95.

Borgers, T., & Sarin, R. (1995). *Naïve reinforcement learning with endogenous aspirations.* Mimeo: University College London and Texas A + M University.

Grandmont, J.M. (1994). Expectations formation and stability of large socioeconomic systems. *Working Paper No. 9424.* Paris: CEPREMAP.

Grant, R.M., & Spender, J.C. (1996). Knowledge and the firm: Overview. *Strategic Management Journal, Winter Special Issue,* 5-11.

Holland, J. (1995). *Hidden order: How adaptation builds complexity.* Menlo Park, CA: Addison–Wesley.

Krepps, D. (1990). *Game theory and economic modelling.* Oxford: Clarendon Press.

Marimon, R. (1997). Learning from learning in economics. In D. Kreps & W. Kenneth (Eds.), *Advances in Economics and Econometrics.* Econometric Society Monographs, No26. Cambridge: Cambridge University Press.

Meyer, M.H., & Utterback, J.M. (1993). The product family and the dynamics of core capability. *Sloan Management Review,* Spring, 29-49.

Muth, J.F. (1960). Optimal properties of exponentially weighted forecasts. *Journal of the American Statistical Association, 55,* 299-306

Nash, J. (1950). Equilibrium points in n-person games. *Proc. Nat. Acad. Sci. USA, 36,* 48-49

Nellis, J.G. (1998). The Future of Economics. In R.G. Milter, J.E. Stinson, & W.H. Gijselaers (Eds.), *Educational Innovation in Economics and Business III.* Boston, London, Dordrecht, the Netherlands: Kluwer Academic Publishers.

Nelson, R. (1995). Recent evolutionary theorizing about economic change. *Journal of Economic Literature, XXXIII,* 48-90.

Nelson, R., & Winter S. *An evolutionary theory of economic change.* Cambridge Mass.: Belknap/Harvard University Press.

Nonaka, I., & Takeuchi, H. (1995). *The knowledge creating company.* New York: Oxford University Press.
Penrose, E. (1959). *The theory of the growth of the firm.* New York: Wiley.
Quinn, J.B., Jordan J., Baruch, J.J., & Zien, K.A. (1996). Software Based Innovation. *Sloan Management Review, Summer,* 11-25.
Schumpeter, J.A. (1954). *History of economic analysis.* New York: Oxford University Press.
Simon, H.A. (1947). *Administrative behavior.* New York: Macmillan.
Teece, D., Pisano, G., & Shuen, A. (1990). Firm capabilities, resources and the concept of Strategy. *Working Paper EAP 38.* University of California at Berkeley, 9-11.
Tsoukas, H. (1994). Refining common sense: Types of knowledge in organizational studies. *Journal of Management Studies, 31,* 761-780.
Weibull, J. (1995). *Evolutionary game theory.* Cambridge Mass: MIT Press.

PART II

TECHNOLOGY AND INNOVATION

The IS Department Defines the Future of the College of Business

James Perotti
MIS Department, College of Business, Ohio University, Athens Ohio, USA

1. INTRODUCTION

There is a compelling logic justifying, even lauding, the beliefs and practices of traditional business programs. After decades of acceptance of, even commitment to, that logic, it is very difficult for faculty to question it, much less overcome it. The typical Information Systems (IS) department rejects that logic, and suggests an alternative way to think about business programs. The traditional logic encompasses the purpose of the department, the pedagogy, the priority of research; it defines the roles of the faculty and of the students. It can be called the discipline-based model. The mission of the department, it asserts, is to discover, develop, protect, and explain the discipline. The profession's body of knowledge is valuable in its own right, not because practitioners find employment in the field. The faculty is the preeminent experts and developers of the knowledge base. They develop the discipline both by research and publication; they train new students to become experts in the field. Teaching is then understood as an initiation into the profession, the way in which to convey knowledge and understanding of the discipline. A few of the best and the brightest students succeed in the ultimate testimony to the faculty by completing the Ph.D. and becoming new faculty.

The alternative logic, again one which defines the purpose of the department, the pedagogy, the roles of students and faculty, is the "student customer" model. IS departments typify and exemplify this model. It is a service model, giving priority to discovering and satisfying the customers needs. It assumes that business students elect their majors with the clear objective of using the degree to start a career in that professional field. The mission of customer-oriented business departments is to prepare students for careers in the field. Continuous placement of students with companies requires keeping employers satisfied; hence both students and employers are customers. Employers are better and better at articulating the skills and competencies which they want in new hires; they want students who can perform the professional work on the first day; they want to avoid the costs and uncertainties of training new employees. Both employers and faculty are coming to the realization that "performance" criteria, the skills and competencies to perform the professional tasks, are best learned by practicing them. The traditional pedagogy, based upon textbook "cover-the-materials" approach, is not nearly enough; applied skills cannot be learned by reading about them, they must be performed over and over again.

There are widening conflicts between professional practitioners in the workplace and the faculty in academic departments. The often-stated belief about the value of research-model is that research advances the discipline, while keeping the faculty and curricula up-to-date. Employers and students alike dispute that claim, both express concern that students lack the skills to practice their profession. The widespread usage of calculators in the business curriculum indicates a disconnect between business training and business practice. Financial functions and tasks are performed with computers in the workplace, but not in the curricula. This paper will take a stereotypical look at two departments: Accounting and Information Systems. Accounting is the best example of a discipline-based model, Information Systems of a student-centered model. Accounting is the most out-of-date, and its majors are disappearing; Information Systems is the most in touch with real-world careers, and its majors are rapidly growing.

2. INEVITABILITY

In business contexts with short product life cycles, survival depends on innovating, creating products or services which meet the needs of fickle customers. The survival of the business college depends on its having customers, both students majoring in its programs as well as business employers. Customer retention, in turn, depends on staying focused on the ever-changing career requirements of business fields. Only then will the internal rate of change begin to accelerate, as it attempts to close the gap between its content and business practices.

Herman Hesse's Magister Ludi is a critique of the superior German intellectuals who seclude themselves from the chaos of the real world. This book seems an apt description of many of our research universities. The discipline-based model justifies the emphasis on the discipline and the disdain for business practices, since they often don't measure up to the ideal. A symptom of the problem is that innovations in business practice, which prove themselves in the marketplace, reports take years to be accepted into the scholarly literature and into the classroom; by that time, more recent innovations have become "best practice" in the workplace. Students starting business careers experience a time warp, a feeling of not being prepared frustration with their faculty. When employers hire, they often see little difference in relevant skills between business majors and political science or communication majors. That is really damning.

Many business colleges are experiencing declining enrollments. But business Colleges with good records of placing students into professional careers cannot meet the demand for their services. The brighter students want business careers, and they will seek out colleges where the reputation of the college all but assures placement into a career. Nowhere is this phenomenon clearer than in IS departments; programs with good reputations are literally overwhelmed by the number of students. At the same time and in the same college, the numbers of majors in accounting, operations, human resource management, management, etc. are dropping. Student customers are rational; good academic programs grow and succeed, poor service drives away students.

3. IS AS PROTOTYPICAL

A prototype is a realistic model, predictive and descriptive of how the real thing will turn out. Other business departments can view their own futures by considering the essential characteristics of the current IS departments. Accounting, Finance, Marketing, Management, HRM will be forced to become more like IS – that future is inevitable. That is the claim.

Here are the characteristics of IS that are prototypical:
1. Faculty and curriculum are focused upon careers for the student customers; this is the defining characteristic for successful professional business programs.

2. Employers' technology requirements shape the curriculum, shape the students' preparation for IS careers.
3. These technology requirements are continuously changing as business operations are redesigned, hence IS skills must be continuously upgraded to reflect best business practices.
4. Employers want IS graduates to bring skills and competencies to the workplace, not just "knowledge" about IS, hence the pedagogy must include hands-on "action learning."
5. IS learning is embedded in real-world business contexts, the pedagogy must be project-based solving business problems.
6. The IS pedagogy casts faculty in the roles of mentor and coach, and faculty interaction with students builds student satisfaction with that humane and caring environment.
7. Since business computing is ubiquitous, faculty computing expertise should surpass student expertise and be continuously upgraded and expanded.

Many IS departments, my own included, are experiencing unprecedented growth in the major, unprecedented demand to get into courses, accolades from graduates whose average salary last year exceeded $40,000, and accolades from prominent employers. Employers, students and IS faculty hold up the IS department as a model for other departments, exhorting them to be more focused on preparing graduates for business careers in their fields. An excellent way to validate the prototype is to invite prominent business people to be guests of the IS program and invite the President and Provost for lunch. Partners from the Big 6 Consulting firms, whose continuing growth depends upon good IS programs for new employees, speak convincingly about the value of the IS programs. Steve Alexander, interprets ComputerWorld's 1999 mid-year salary survey, which lists salaries by specific title and by location; he summarizes his concern about the unmet demand for IS positions and how it is driving up salaries:

> "If 1998 was a great year to be in IT, 1999 looks to be more of the same: rising salaries, personnel shortages that spell tremendous opportunity and signing bonuses for those who are most in demand. Salaries have risen so sharply in the past year and a half that information technology managers are struggling to keep up with market rates — or to even know what they are." (Alexander, 1999).

Faculty from traditional business departments find it easy to reject IS' leadership. Discipline-based departments dismiss as irrelevant the growing number of IS majors, the career successes of the graduates, the gratitude of parents and students. And this is where their credulity breaks down. Their response echoes from the distant past, the glory days of yesteryear. Faculty from discipline-based departments respond by pointing out that IS is not a real discipline, IS teaches only techniques and skills, IS lacks any substantial content and a substantial knowledge base. Academic administrators, bewildered by the demand for IS and unwilling to provide needed faculty, argue that computing is a fad, like the internet; the author noted his concern that electricity and phones were also fads. But it is clear that the non-traditional IS department cannot find acceptance as a prototype for other departments, when one starts from the assumptions of the discipline-based model. The discontinuity must be understood and addressed if there is to be progress in moving other departments to a student-centered approach.

4. AN EPISTEMOLOGICAL ASIDE

Aristotle's influence on psychology and education still holds sway after all these years. The Greek term "episteme," translated as knowledge, is divided into scientific (theoretical) knowledge (judgements about the universal and necessary) and practical knowledge (deliberations about politics or ethics). Business knowledge would be an oxymoron for Aristotle. Business expertise is really art, "techne," technique or the ability to create things; art is learned from experience, from practicing. Generalizations or concepts are inferred from the successful practice of the art and are passed on to the apprentices. Few IS faculty have pretensions of conveying scientific knowledge or great wisdom, as will be noted below, IS is not a discipline.

Can we learn how to swim by reading a book? Learn how to ride a bike that way? Learn how to do business that way? Knowledge is an ambiguous term; constructivist views are now popular, but Aristotle and Kant's views might be more instructive. All knowledge is empirical knowledge, all knowledge derives from sensation: "Nihil in intellectu, nisi prius in sensu." We organize and interpret the perceived objects of sensation and make judgements about them, employing the concepts already in our minds. Randomly grabbing a textbook from my shelf and randomly opening it yields this concept: "Horizontal differentiation focuses on the division or grouping of organizational tasks to meet the objectives of the business." There is no context for learning, no experience to situate these conceptual terms. The author (and faculty teaching from this book) make a tacit assumption that "a priori" knowledge. the direct grasp of concepts without experiencing the objects, is possible. The philosophers dispute the possibility of direct a priori knowledge, Aristotle's Christian followers attribute such knowledge to angels: "Angelus scit a priori sed homines scit a posteriori."

Book learning also fails to build skills and competencies because the concepts are too simplistic, the tasks large and more complex. Again, experience would have inform us of the size and complexity of the task, the amount of expertise needed to perform it. Trying to become a financial manager by reading an Accounting textbook is a good example. The typical textbook approach of teaching concepts to students who lack an experiential context in which to place them, results in filling their heads with free-floating abstractions—mere data, mere words, not even information.

In the terminology of Constructivism, in which knowledge (mental models) are built from relevant information, textbooks offer pre-packaged "knowledge," saving students the effort of "constructing" it. Textbooks often provide tables of principles, categories, or procedures with little information about the inferences which created them. Even more serious is Peter Senge's claim that mental models are often wrong, and because we do not reflect on them, much less modify them, mental models can readily impede learning.

> "Contemporary research shows that most of our mental models are systematically flawed. They miss critical feedback relationships, misjudge time delays, and often focus upon variables that are visible or salient, not necessarily high leverage." Senge (p. 203).

Learning is much more difficult than constructing mental models. Mental models are inherently simplifications, perspectival, often too vague and too static to deal with dynamic and complex tasks, e.g., business processes. As the philosophers Hegel and Nietzsche noted, learning occurs after reflection on the inadequacies of our mental models forces us to construct more sophisticated models; Nietzsche would say that learning occurs when we overcome our truths. The 1956 Taxonomy of Educational Objectives still stands as the defining standard for levels of learning; Bloom's (the editor) taxonomy lists these six "educational behaviors from simple to complex:" knowledge, comprehension, application, analysis, synthesis, evaluation. (Bloom, 1956). Bloom equates "knowledge" with the acquisition of information, the "processes of remembering," the lowest level kind of learning. Textbook learning cannot meet the demands of a professional school. It falls short of the task of preparing business students who can apply concepts and models, who can analyze and synthesize, who can evaluate and reconstruct.

Like the music, theater, and TV Production departments, the IS department is acutely aware of the role of skills in performing the requisite tasks. Skills such as analysis, synthesis, evaluation of processes are part of the day-to-day tasks of an IS consultant or a financial manager. Students need to learn a suite of "competencies" in order to be effective performers. Hamel and Prahalad use the term "competency" which they define as the "package of skills and technologies giving mastery of a key process" (Hamel & Prahalad, 1994). Richard Boyatzis defines competencies as "the characteristics of a person which results in superior job performance; the characteristics include knowledge, skill, motivation, etc," (Boyatzis, 1982) Competencies include skills, concepts, and technologies; effective performance requires that all three function together.

The IS departments' pedagogy evolved and developed in such a way that, now after the fact, the competency-based approach represents a good description of the approach used. Much like Constructivism, learning takes place by practice building mental models of how the task is to be performed. The models are learned from experiencing the processes. The IS vocabulary is familiar before the skills are developed; the models and concepts are learned after the fact from the experiences of completing the tasks. What is different is the emphasis given to the computer tools and skills, which are regarded as essential to the learning, to the performance of the task.

Employers want graduates who can add value to the company on the first day of work, i.e., graduates with the typical competencies required in the functional area. An Accounting or Finance major who have never used accounting software must spend weeks in training before they are ready to really do the job; but an English or Philosophy major—we have all heard how wonderful they are as employees—must spend months in training learning about business in general, the functional area, and the computer tools.

5. THE SAD STORY OF ACCOUNTING

A feature story in the New York Times tells the story of how and why the accounting departments, indeed the accounting profession, shot itself in the foot. Some of the ways to look at the wound:

- The article reports that the number of college students graduating in accounting has declined by 50%.

- The number of public companies requiring audits is growing.

- Only 12.5% of applicants taking the C.P.A. exam pass it on the first try, the lowest percentage since 1985 when the exam was inititated.

- The SEC has expressed its concerned about the quality of audits.

During the decade from 1970 to 1980, the accounting profession was perceived as an attractive profession, with continuing growth all but guaranteed, with high starting pay and lots of opportunity for promotions into very high paying jobs. During this period, the accounting profession erected a number of barriers to entry, both to restrict the number of accountants, and to ensure the quality of profession: 1). The C.P.A. exam was made more difficult, 2) the C.P.A. required two years of experience, 3) and the educational requirement to sit for the C.P.A. exam was raised from a 4 year bachelor of business program to a 5 year degree. The barriers worked. College students are deciding that it is not worth 5 years of college and 2 further years of apprenticeship to sit for a C.P.A. exam designed to flunk 87% of them. Enrollment is falling across the country.

Accounting is a good example of a business program in which faculty see their primary allegiance to the profession, not the students. The profession, arrogantly confident of its allure, chose to impose very high standards for the accounting majors, and now the accounting departments must live with rapidly declining enrollments and the profession must struggle to ways to audit a growing number of companies with fewer licensed auditors. The profession is now fully aware of the problem which it created and will probably lower the barriers to entry, but that will have little effect on the decline in enrollments until it is a reality. But the accounting faculty, still committed to the profession rather than the students, reject the notion that they have an obligation to facilitate the career aspirations of the business students. So the student customers, with a wide range of career opportunities, are going elsewhere.

Accounting is more like mathematics or business law than other business fields, in the sense that its concepts and rules are human artifacts, rather than abstractions from business practice. Management, Marketing, and IS curricula are based upon business practice. Faculty in Accounting can truly master their content, because it is a man-made, internally consistent system of principles and concepts. Unlike other business disciplines, accounting has answers which are true or false; because accounting has an artificial internal consistency, its answers are tautologically true.

Applying these principles and rules to the ambiguous and changing realities of business operations suggests a distinction between the practice of accountancy, e.g., preparing tax forms, and the discipline of accountancy, e.g., mastering tax laws. Understandably, most accounting faculty are not interested in preparing students with the skills to practice accountancy; the accounting curriculum emphasizes mastery of the principles. Unfortunately, the C.P.A. exam focuses upon applying the principles. The 12.5% average rate of passing the exam illustrates the validity of the distinction. The pedagogical emphasis is now seen as a major concern.

Not every faculty member puts the emphasis on the established content of the field. A professor of Accountancy at Miami University (of Ohio) thinks that his tax course should prepare students to help businesses minimize their tax obligations to the federal government. The course is not about tax regulations, he makes all the tax regulations accessible on a CD-ROM drive—there is no point of memorizing the regulations when tax people just look them up. He assigns the students a typical real-world tax problem: "show me how IBM (look up their financials on Edgar) can save $1 million by smart usage of the latest tax revisions." He gives away the information in order to move to application, analysis, and creativity. The irony here is that students really learn the relevant tax regulations! The students love this emphasis, readily understanding that someone who knows how to save big money on taxes is highly employable.

There is an irony to adding a 5th year to the accounting program, having the C.P.A. rate decline to its lowest level since its inception, at the same time the profession demands more experience. The New York Times article expressed concern about the efficacy of the Accounting programs' pedagogy: "The classroom is a great primer, but it sure doesn't get you there." While it is a simple matter to design an exam so difficult that no one can pass it, the embarrassingly low pass rate is a strong indictment of the accounting programs' pedagogy. The emphasis on "concepts" and the trivial calculator problems has failed to produce competent practitioners. So two years of experience are required before certification because the textbook learning fails to develop the requisite skills. The chairman of Kansas' licensing board had this comment about textbook learning: "It's only by live experience in public accounting…that you can gain the skills and objectivity that we believe are key." At this point very little has changed in the accounting departments. Acutely aware that the 5th year requirement was a serious mistake, faculty fear next year's consequences, since the requirement does not take effect until the June 2000 graduates.

6. IS IS NOT A DISCIPLINE

"IS is not a discipline," is an oft heard criticism. It is hard to know what that means. Clearly it is a way of finding fault with student-oriented programs based upon assumptions and beliefs of the discipline-based faculty. To some it means that IS lacks sufficient content to be taken seriously as a discipline or department. But it might well be a sign of the gulf between knowledge-based disciplines and performance-based "art" programs. Colleges of Arts and Sciences have difficulty accepting "Art" departments, because of their lack of content, and have pushed them out into Colleges of Fine Arts. It even seems as if Arts and Sciences would like to rid itself of the physical science departments by pushing them into Engineering. Arts and Sciences has perverted "science" such that pseudo-sciences, such as sociology and psychology, are more prestigious than physics and chemistry.

Indeed, the Ohio University Provost holds the Psychology Ph.D. program up as the model for other programs to emulate, even though very few of the graduates can find employment in that field. The conflict, writ large, is that the discipline-based perspective holds up the master-the-content "scientific" knowledge disciplines as examples, while performance-based "Art" departments, such as IS and engineering, point to the successes of their students in real-world businesses and ridicule the traditional disciplines as irrelevant, out-of-touch pseudo-sciences.

IS is not a discipline because it does not have well established foundational theories or principles which would define its scope and purpose. The theoretic foundations for disciplines come after-the-fact, after the practice is well established. The theory is abstracted from the practice. While Law and Medicine are well established disciplines (the first doctorates were granted in 1240 and 1270), engineering never made it at Oxford because it did not date back to the 13th century. IS practices are rapidly changing, radically changing, making it impossible to define what it is and where it is going. There are concepts and mental models aplenty. There is a flood of published material about IS. IS, in that sense, has more content than other business disciplines. IS concepts are invented daily, e.g., a virtual office consists of a portable device incorporating a cellular or satellite modem and software enabling on-line interaction with other business partners. And IS truly experiences paradigm shifts, e.g., the cover of Business Week suggests that PCs are obsolete, radically new mental models of the field; these obsolete the old theories and concepts and redefine the possible. The sheer amount of information about IS products and events is daunting. Every day there are hundreds of announcements on the internet about new computer devices, new software. There are daily editions of popular computer magazines published on the internet; there are weekly paper copies of these magazines freely distributed to MIS professionals. The content is both huge and fast changing. No single person or textbook can claim mastery of the field. So what do IS faculty elect to teach? The curriculum is shaped by what the employers use!

7. HOW OTHER DEPARTMENTS WILL FOLLOW THE IS LEADER

What does it take for a group to redefine itself? Probably a "burning platform," to make the current situation untenable, e.g., declining enrollments and faculty reductions, and a vision of the future that appears to improve upon the current situation. Many business departments are experiencing declining enrollments; but the fire is ignited when faculty are terminated because of fewer students. Accounting departments across the country are losing faculty and feeling the heat, but they do not seem capable of rethinking their basic logic. These accounting faculty need the dean to redefine their mission for them. The discipline-based approach justifies ignoring students' needs; the student-centered approach would react to student concerns and find ways to better serve their needs. When business students' expectations for a high-paying job are unmet and ignored by the faculty, the rationality for majoring in business is removed. Students "walk." Were the business college redefined by a vision of business students being successfully placed into business careers, faculty goals and students' goals would be the same. Students buy in, find satisfaction as they make progress toward a career, they direct other students to the program, enrollment grows.

The transition from the discipline-based role, where faculty are the self-defined experts, to a service role, where faculty serve students, is a humbling one. Often the underlying impediment to change is that faculty are unaware that they are acting upon and committed to a mental model—the discipline-based logic—which they have not articulated. Faculty need to be part of a facilitated discussion where they are asked to make their tacit assumptions about their relationships with students explicit. Only then can these assumptions be critiqued and rethought. Peter Senge, influenced by Hanover, Argyris, Beckett and others, suggests four steps to help people rethink and critique their mental models so that they can then be open to change:

- Recognizing "leaps of abstraction" (noticing our jumps from observation to generalization)

- Exposing the "left-hand column" (articulating what we normally do not say)

- Balancing inquiry and advocacy (skills for honest investigation)

- Facing up to distinctions between espoused theories (what we say) and theories-in-use (the implied theory in what we do) (Senge, 1990).

Once faculty recognize their service role, their dependence upon students, the redesign of the curricula can begin. This second step is a defining one; faculty must develop curricula that provides the skills and competencies which employers need. Employers define the needed modules, not the specialties of the faculty. Faculty must abandon the paternalistic "we know what's good for these students." Once business realities shape the curricula, changing business practices should drive continuous upgrading of the curricula. "Changing business practices" does not mean that the IS curriculum should jump from programming language to programming language, for example. It does mean that major long-term changes in business practice like Business – to – Business / E-Commerce practices or Microsoft's domination of the network server market need to be made part of the curriculum.

The third step, that of redesigning the pedagogy, is also driven by the requirements of the workplace. Students have skills and competencies even more than concepts and principles. The "cover-the-material-in-the-textbook" pedagogy has to yield to pedagogy which develops performance, skills, competencies. It seems self evident that talking about IS, engineering, mathematics, accounting, etc does not prepare students to write programs, build bridges, graph a dynamic event, or do an audit. Yet most faculty reared in the traditional pedagogy find it impossible to rethink what they are doing. What is proposed here is dismissed as heretical and wrong-headed. The inability to rethink the pedagogy is the biggest obstacle to the effective preparation of students for specific careers. Interactions with students are time consuming, humbling, and often frustrating. IS faculty have lots of experience with coaching, mentoring, and facilitation—that's what we do.

> "This new faculty role represents a paradigm shift calling for new skills. The paradigm shift has been expressed as moving from being the "sage on the stage" to serving as the "guide on the side." The basic skills required to be the "guide on the side" (active listening, coaching, mentoring, and facilitation) are not characteristic of a significant number of faculty members, and thus they must be learned" (Stinson & Milter, 1996).

Getting faculty to give up their "sage on the stage" role is very difficult, they just don't understand how students can learn without the lecture method. The "sage on the stage" controls the classroom interactions and is very empowering; the coach watches her or his team perform with few opportunities for input. The point is that student learning only results from their individual struggles; when faculty cover-the-material and students sit passively, little learning occurs.

8. CONCLUSION

This paper suggests that there is too much distance between the practice of auditing, investing, programming, marketing, and managing and the preparation for these careers in the typical business college. Employers are unhappy that business graduates cannot perform the required tasks without training. Students are unhappy that they are poorly prepared and offered little help in finding jobs. So students are electing other majors and enrollment is declining, although the jobs are there, e.g., "Shortage of Accounting Students." is the title of the New York Times article.

Even a cursory study of academic business departments reveals why this problem exists. Faculty have an agenda and a reward system in which serving students' career needs is but a very small part. The discipline-based model and the priority of the research agenda justifies giving low priority to employers and students' career needs. The accounting story exemplifies how the academic department can continue to ignore the realities of the workplace. Since the accounting principles and concepts are a man-made construct, and not derived from the evolving practices in the workplace, there is a clear rationality for the faculty to pay little attention to the workplace. That justification works for accounting, but it cannot excuse management, marketing, IS, investment finance, etc.; these disciplines abstract their concepts from rapidly evolving accepted practices in the workplace. They would like to see themselves as social sciences, but the rapid pace of change in the workplace and the slow pace of publishing research forces faculty to accept their role as after-the-fact chroniclers of business practice. Teaching concepts and ignoring practice only works in an imaginary world where change does not occur.

Consistent with the research agenda is a pedagogy which emphasizes mastering content, rather than developing workplace skills. Somehow the notion has become accepted that textbook memorization is adequate preparation for the workplace, i.e., that talking about how people work is much the same as practicing the tasks, that business tasks are accomplished when a good grade on a multiple choice test about the task is awarded. It will be very difficult to move faculty from their comfort with textbook teaching to the recommended "learn by doing," "learn by experience" pedagogy which the IS department has adopted.

IS faculty struggle with the criticism of business college colleagues, but the success of their graduates and the praise of employers dulls the criticism. In most business colleges IS enrollments grow and grow, while Accounting enrollments go down and down. But the success can turn to failure and the failure to success. Academic Administrators punish the IS department by failing to add faculty commensurate with student growth, thereby driving away students who cannot get into required classes. Accounting is rewarded with lighter teaching loads, fewer students and the same number of faculty, giving them more time to publish and reap the rewards of the research agenda. But the reality of the marketplace eventually reaches into business colleges. When the college's enrollment drops, the Provost reduces the college budget or removes faculty lines. Gee, why have enrollments dropped when there is such a strong demand for business careers? It's much easier to make changes now. But there is a strong accepted logic underpinning current departmental practices that has to be overcome before the college can redefine faculty goals, rewards and roles in terms of serving students' career aspirations.

REFERENCES

Alexander, S. (1999) No cure in sight. Computerworld Midyear Salary Survey, *ComputerWorld, March 29.*

Aristotle. (1947). *Nichomachean Ethics.* In R. McKeon, *Introduction to Aristotle*, Chicago: University of Chicago Press.

Bloom, B. (Ed.) (1956) *Taxonomy of educational objectives.* New York: David McKay Company, INC.

Boyatzis, R. (1982). *The competent manager.* New York: John Wiley & Sons.

Hamel, G., & Prahalad, C.K. (1994). Competing for the future. Boston, MA.: Harvard Business School Press.

Johnson-Laird, P.N. (1983). *Mental models.* Cambridge, MA: Harvard University Press.

Kant, I. (1964). *Groundwork of a metaphysic of morals*, translated by H.J. Patton. New York: Harper Torchbooks.

Petersen, M. (1999). Shortage of accounting students raises concern on audit quality. *The New York Times, A-1 and C-3, (February 19).*

Rouse, W.B., & Morris, N.M. (1986). On looking into the black box: Prospects and limits in the search for mental models. *Psychological Bulletin, 100*, 349-363.

Senge, P. (1990). *The fifth discipline.* New York: Doubleday Currency.

Stinson, J., & Milter, R. (1996). Problem-based Learning in Business and Education, *New Directions for Teaching and Learning, no. 68*, Winter 1996, 33-42.

Treacy, M., & Wiersema, F. (1995). *The discipline of market leaders.* New York: Addison-Wesley.

Zuboff, S. (1984). *In the age of the smart machine.* New York: Basic Books.

Informatics Engineering and Business Informatics in the Ict Society: Substitutes Or Complements?

Hans Heijke & Ger Ramaekers
Research Centre for Education and the Labour Market (ROA), Maastricht University, the Netherlands

1. INTRODUCTION

In the sixties and seventies, automated information systems in the form of large computers were primarily used for processing mass data to back up administrative and industrial processes. In order to provide the necessary computer programs, various methods and techniques were developed. In the eighties, personal computers and local area networks emerged and information and communication technology (ICT) penetrated all levels and almost all work places within organizations. In the early nineties, when organizations were confronted with poor company results and ever increasing costs for ICT, organizations began to question the contribution of ICT to the amelioration of company results. As a consequence, in developing, implementing and applying new ICT, the management of organizations started to not only take technical aspects into consideration but also economical and organizational consequences (Looijen, 1995, pp. 13-16).

In view of the developments outlined above, the sixties and seventies saw the emergence of technical studies aimed at the development of embedded software (studies in *basic informatics*) and techniques for industrial automation and industrial process operation (studies in the *technical application of informatics*). In the eighties, studies were set up in economics that focussed on the development of automated systems for the management, administration and running of organizations (studies in the field of *information systems*). Technical education also offered studies in information systems to complement the already existing studies in *basic informatics* and the *technical application of informatics*.

On the basis of the above, one would expect that, as far as ICT is concerned, informatics studies in economics focus mainly on the development of automated systems for the management, administration and running of organizations (*information systems*), whereas informatics studies in engineering also focus on the development of embedded software (*basic informatics*) and techniques for industrial automation and industrial process operation (*technical application of informatics*). As a consequence of this difference in focus, the occupational domains of informatics studies in engineering and informatics studies in economics may only partly overlap (indicating the degree in which these two kinds of studies are substitutes and hence compete with each other). The more these types of studies play complementary roles in the labor market and the overlapping occupational domain is smaller, the more we should consider these two studies as useful though distinct preparations for later occupational careers. Insofar as the two domains overlap and studies can be regarded as substitutes, there is a reason to wonder whether it is useful to maintain the two studies side by side without any modifications. To be able to compare the two types of ICT studies, we should, however, consider more aspects than merely the overlap of occupational domains. It is important, for example, to know whether the graduates from these two types of studies are expected to meet different requirements in terms of knowledge and skills in order to be able to successfully do their jobs, whether they experience any deficiencies in their studies in these respects, and which study requires additional training in order to lift graduates to the required level. In this paper, we shall try to obtain greater insight in the building blocks for a framework to determine the positions of these two ICT studies in relation to each other.

In the analysis, we shall use as a reference an analysis that we carried out before and in which we examined the importance of informatics-skills for economics graduates (Heijke & Ramaekers, 1997). This previous paper included not only economics graduates from informatics studies but graduates from all economics disciplines. We found that economics graduates are more likely to participate in training in the field of ICT if much knowledge of ICT is required in the job and if they feel that they have acquired insufficient knowledge of ICT during their economics study.

Furthermore, we found that employers transfer to the workers the costs involved in the necessary ICT training (both costs resulting from low productivity and direct training costs) in the form of lower wages. Apparently, these skill deficiencies are regarded as a lack of general skills and the required training effort therefore offers no exclusive benefits for the employer involved. The paper ends with the conclusion that there could be a task here for university studies to provide better general ICT skills.

The structure of the present paper is as follows. Section 2 describes the curricula developed within technical and economic university education that focus on ICT. The data on the graduates who will be used are described in Section 3. The similarities and differences on the labor market between informatics studies in economics and informatics studies in engineering will be examined empirically on the basis of three research questions. In Section 4 we want to characterize the labor market of these two kinds of studies by occupation, sector of industry, firm size, economic sector and required knowledge and skills. Furthermore, we examine whether graduates choose those jobs in which the required knowledge and skills best meet their field of expertise. The second part of the research examines the deficiencies in knowledge and skills experienced by the graduates (Section 5), and estimates the probability that these graduates will participate in training in the fields of ICT and business administration (Section 6). In the third part of the research (Section 7) we want to estimate the factors that determine the economic value of these graduates for their companies (as indicated by their wages). Lastly, Section 8 brings together the conclusions of the paper.

2. EDUCATION IN INFORMATICS

In order to provide society with the necessary knowledge of ICT, curricula have been developed within both engineering sciences and economic sciences, which are directed at this kind of knowledge. For the analyses in this paper, we were able to use labor market data on graduates from the study of informatics engineering at Delft Technical University and the informatics studies within the economics faculties of Tilburg University and Erasmus University Rotterdam.

The four-year study of informatics engineering at Delft Technical University is aimed at training engineers, using scientific knowledge and methods, to directionally contribute to the analysis of problems of a technological, managerial and societal nature with the aim of developing automated solutions. They must also be able to develop, realize, implement and maintain such solutions. In the last year of their studies, students specialize in one of the following three topics. The first topic, called *basic informatics*, is directed at the development of embedded software with the theoretical foundation of algorithm development and programming. The second topic, *information systems*, is directed at developing information systems for determining the policy and the management of companies and institutions. *Technical application of informatics* is the third topic and is directed at techniques for industrial automation and industrial process operation (Diependaal, 1997, pp. 1-2).

For the second topic of informatics engineering (*information systems*), there are counterpart studies within economics, namely the four-year study of business informatics at Tilburg University (including the university's 'own' first-year study in business informatics) and the three-year study of business informatics of Erasmus University Rotterdam (which comes after the first-year study of economics). Both studies focus on information systems for managing, administrating and running organizations. The emphasis in these studies is on organizational issues, although technological devices such as computers also play an important role. Business informatics studies focus on determining information needs; the analysis, design, building, testing, implementation and running of information systems; the management and security of information systems; the collection, recording, processing and filing of data; computer-aided cost-benefit analyses; the use of computers in decision support systems; business management information; communication issues (data flow); and the modeling of organizations and their functioning with the aid of computers (Studiegids 1995-1996, Economische Wetenschappen, Erasmus Universiteit Rotterdam, p. 423).

In the last year of their four-year studies, business informatics students at Tilburg University may specialize in one of the following three topics. The first topic, called *information knowledge*, both broadens and deepens the knowledge of information systems and is recommended for students who want to take the postgraduate accountancy study. *Business organization*, the second topic, deepens the organizational knowledge by focusing on the relation between the way in which firms or institutions are organized and the goals of such firms or institutions. The third topic broadens the knowledge of *informatics* with respect to expert systems, AI techniques, computer networks and mathematical aspects of the use of computers (Studiegids 1995-1996, Faculteit der Economische Wetenschappen, Katholieke Universiteit Brabant, pp. 65, 69).

The three-year study of business informatics at Erasmus University Rotterdam consists of about 25% mathematics and mathematical operations research, 50% informatics and 25% economics. In the last year of their studies, students may choose one of the following topics: *information knowledge, informatics* and *decision support systems*. The first two topics resemble those at Tilburg University. The third topic deepens the knowledge of the use of computers in decision support systems.

In summary, we distinguish two kinds of informatics studies in this paper, namely business informatics (BI) and informatics engineering (IE). BI includes both the four-year study of business informatics at Tilburg University and the three-year study of business informatics at Erasmus University Rotterdam. IE consists of the four-year study for informatics engineer at Delft Technical University. As far as ICT is concerned, BI is directed mainly at the development of automated systems for managing, administrating and running organizations, whereas IE also focuses on the development of embedded software and techniques for industrial automation and industrial process operation.

3. THE DATA

ROA annually carries out labor market research among graduates from five economics faculties in the Netherlands. Since 1996, ROA has also carried out labor market research among graduates from Delft Technical University, including informatics engineers. This research project, known as the University Education Monitor, examines both the characteristics and the qualifications of graduates and their current labor market position.

The research data for this paper were obtained from the two latest postal surveys, carried out late 1996 among graduates from the academic year 1994/□95, and late 1997 among graduates from the academic year-1995/'96. Because the surveys are held between 12 to 18 months after graduation, the study observes graduates at the beginning of their professional careers. In total, 133 graduates of BI and 99 graduates of IE responded to these surveys.

Table 1 shows the distribution of these 232 respondents over a number of characteristics relevant for this paper. As can be seen, BI graduates significantly more often completed a tertiary-level education prior to their studies and more often have committee experience than IE graduates. Furthermore, BI graduates are employed significantly more often in large organizations than IE graduates. With respect to personal characteristics, it can be observed that IE has a significantly greater share of male graduates than BI.

Table 1. Characteristics of respondents

	IE	IB	Total	
Personal characteristics:				
- sex: male*	91%	80%	85%	
- average age in years	26.5	26.4	26.5	(2.9)[a]
Additional qualifications before graduation:				
- previous tertiary education*	0%	13%	7%	
- earlier relevant work experience	49%	51%	50%	
- internship experience	83%	84%	84%	
- committee experience*	35%	54%	46%	
Additional qualifications after graduation:				
- participation in training	66%	74%	71%	
- average number of months in current job	13.6	14.8	14.3	(15.3)[a]
Work characteristics:				
- job at university level	30%	40%	36%	
- supervisory position	22%	23%	23%	
- average gross hourly wage (Dfl)	24.5	24.4	24.5	(6.2)[a]
- private sector	95%	93%	94%	
- large organization (>= 100 workers)*	70%	83%	78%	

* Difference between tracks is significant at 5% level
[a] Standard deviation

4. CHARACTERIZATION OF THE LABOUR MARKET

This section characterizes the labor market of BI studies and IE studies by occupation, industrial group, firm size, economic sector and required knowledge and skills, respectively.

4.1 Occupation and Industrial Group

The next two tables characterize the labor market by occupation (Table 2) and industrial group (Table 3). The occupations and industrial groups are mentioned only if at least 5% of all paid working BI graduates or IE graduates work in them.

Table 2 shows a great degree of overlap in occupations between the two groups of graduates. Only the ranking of their occupations differs. As can be seen, BI graduates work relatively slightly more often as advisors in the fields of automation/information, whereas IE graduates work slightly more often as systems analysts/designers.

Table 2. Characterization of the labor market by occupation

Occupations* of BI graduates:	
- administrative automation advisors/information analysts	18%
- administrative automation and information project advisors	9%
- technical automation advisors/information analysts	7%
- assistant accountants	6%
- programmers (scientific applications, technical)	5%
- administrative system analysts/designers	5%
- organizational experts	5%
Occupations* of IE graduates:	
- administrative system analysts/designers	11%
- technical system analysts/designers	10%
- technical automation advisors/information analysts	8%
- administrative automation advisors/information analysts	8%
- systems programmers (scientific applications, administrative)	6%
- systems/network managers	6%
- programmers (scientific applications, technical)	5%
- administrative automation and information project advisor	5%

* Share at least 5%

Not only with respect to occupations, but also with respect to industrial groups, there is a high degree of overlap between the two groups of graduates (Table 3). Nevertheless, BI graduates work slightly more often in accountant firms (7% versus 1%), while IE graduates work in systems design/systems analysis/programming services (8% versus 3%).

Table 3. Characterization of the labor market by industrial group

Industrial groups* of BI graduates:	
- automation companies	34%
- computer service/IT firms	9%
- management consultancies	8%
- accountants	7%
- banking	6%
Industrial groups* of IE graduates:	
- automation companies	30%
- computer service/IT firms	13%
- systems design/systems analysis/program services	8%
- management consultancies	6%
- banking	6%

* Share at least 5%

4.2 Firm Size and Economic Sector

The labor market of BI graduates and IE graduates is characterized in Table 4 by firm size and economic sector. The results show that while most BI and IE graduates work in large organizations, informatics engineers more often than BI graduates find employment in small and medium-sized organizations. We can also see that almost all BI and IE graduates work in private organizations.

Table 4. Characterization of the labor market by firm size and economic sector

	BI	IE
Firm size:		
1-9 workers	3%	7%
10-99 workers	14%	22%
∃ 100 workers	83%	70%
Economic sector:		
private sector	93%	95%
public sector	7%	5%

4.3 Required Knowledge and Skills

Although the occupational domains appear to overlap a great deal, there may be a difference between the qualifications expected from graduates from one type of study and from the other. We shall look at this in greater detail. On the basis of literature on job analysis (Algera, 1991) we compiled a list of 25 'qualification items' that may be used to indicate demands for knowledge, general skills and personal skills. These three clusters of knowledge and skills, and the qualification items which compose them, are shown in Table 5. The qualification items are formulated in such a way that they can apply to people working in a variety of different fields. The graduates could indicate under each item how important they thought that particular qualification item was for them to perform well in their current paid activities. The response categories ranged from 1 to 5, corresponding to the responses 'very unimportant', 'unimportant', 'neither important nor unimportant', 'important', and 'very important', respectively. Table 5 shows the importance of the different kinds of knowledge and skills for both BI and IE graduates. The table contains for each qualification item the percentage share of graduates who stated that the knowledge or skill involved is (very) important for them to perform well in their current paid activities.

Table 5. The importance of knowledge and skills for BI and IE graduates

	BI	IE
Knowledge:		
- specialized professional knowledge	78%	81%
- subject-specific methods and techniques	72%	72%
- keeping up with recent developments in the field	85%	80%
- understanding of information & communication technology (incl. computer use): ICT	91%	83%
- understanding of legal regulations relevant to the profession*	**26%**	**12%**
- understanding of operational management (organizational, financial, administrative): BA **	**76%**	**49%**
General skills:		
- application of (theoretical) knowledge and techniques in practice *	**79%**	**66%**
- analytical and diagnostic (research) skills	71%	71%
- quantitative (research) skills	39%	36%
- gathering and documenting information, data management	60%	59%
- linguistic skills (command of foreign languages)	51%	53%
- verbal presentation, fluency **	**91%**	**72%**
- written presentation, writing skills*	**84%**	**73%**
- negotiating and commercial skills	68%	60%
- planning, co-ordination and organization of activities*	**88%**	**75%**
- leadership skills	48%	37%
- teaching and training skills (incl. giving directions, knowledge transfer)	51%	43%
- making and maintaining contacts with other people	88%	78%
Personal skills:		
- capacity for independent work*	**95%**	**86%**
- initiative, creativity	91%	92%
- ability to cope with stress**	**94%**	**81%**
- accuracy, precision	83%	82%
- adaptability*	**88%**	**77%**
- loyalty, integrity, dealing with conflicts of interests**	**87%**	**70%**
- systematic evaluation of results, establishing and using feedback	77%	71%

* Difference is significant at 5% level.
** Difference is significant at 1% level.
Significant differences are shown bold

The most important occupational requirements of BI graduates and IE graduates are specialized professional knowledge, keeping up with recent developments in the field, knowledge of ICT, planning skills, social skills, capacity for independent work, initiative/creativity, ability to cope with stress, accuracy/precision and adaptability (Table 5). At least 75% of both BI graduates and IE graduates mentioned that these knowledge and skills are (very) important for their daily work. Least important for the work of BI graduates and IE graduates are an understanding of legal regulations relevant to the profession, quantitative (research) skills and leadership skills. Less than 50% of both BI graduates and IE graduates mentioned that these knowledge and skills are (very) important for good performance of their current paid work.

When looking at the job requirements we find that certain knowledge (understanding managerial matters and relevant legal regulations), certain general skills (practical application of knowledge, planning skills and verbal & writing skills) and certain personal skills (capacity for independent work, ability to cope with stress, adaptability and ability to deal with conflicts of interests) are significantly more important in jobs of BI graduates than in jobs of IE graduates. It is striking that none of the 25 knowledge items and skills proves to be more important in jobs of IE graduates than in jobs of BI graduates. This indicates that BI graduates, in spite of the fact that the occupational domain overlaps a great deal with that of IE graduates, have to meet higher job requirements. In this respect, the study of BI appears to play a complementary role to the study of IE in the labor market.

4.4 The Graduates' Field of Study and the Required Knowledge of ICT and Business Administration

Both IE graduates and BI graduates are specialists in the field of ICT. BI graduates, however, have the additional advantage that they are also specialists in the field of business administration (BA). IE graduates will probably have more knowledge of ICT. It may be expected that graduates choose those jobs that best meet their field of expertise. By means of linear regression analysis, we have tried to estimate whether graduates choose those jobs that best match their field of study. This is to say that BI graduates more often choose jobs in which a great deal of knowledge of BA is required, while IE graduates more often choose jobs in which a great deal of knowledge of ICT is required. In the questionnaire, knowledge of BA is defined as an 'understanding of operational management (organizational, financial, administrative), and knowledge of ICT as an 'understanding of information & communication technology (including use of computers)'. The dependent variables in the estimates are the importance of knowledge of ICT and BA in the job. As mentioned above, these variables were coded on a 5-point scale, ranging from 'very unimportant' to 'very important'.

In these estimates, the probability of getting a job in which a great deal of knowledge of ICT or of BA is required, is explained by personal characteristics, the graduates' knowledge of ICT and BA as indicated by their field of study, and by their additional qualifications acquired before graduating. The personal characteristics incorporated in the equation are 'sex: male' and 'age'. These act as control variables, whose expected sign is not clear.

As mentioned above, the most important factor that may determine the probability of getting work requiring a great deal of knowledge of ICT or BA, is the graduates' field of study. Since IE is chosen as the reference category in the equations, a positive sign may be expected with respect to choosing jobs in which much knowledge of BA is required and a negative sign with respect to jobs which require much knowledge of ICT. Apart from their field of study, graduates may have obtained additional knowledge of ICT and BA from previous education (especially if they had already completed a matching tertiary-level education), from experience on a management committee (for instance a student association), from work experience relevant to their field of study or from gaining internship experience. These factors were included in the analysis as the variables 'previous tertiary education', 'committee experience', 'relevant work experience' and 'internship experience'. Committee experience and relevant work experience could be acquired either before or during their studies; internship experience only during their studies. Appendix 1 provides an overview of all variables. All variables used in this equation are recorded as dummy variables, except for the age in years.

The results of the regression analyses in Table 6 show that the graduates from the field of study that generates most knowledge of BA, namely BI, indeed most often get jobs in which much knowledge of BA is required. This indicates that the BI study is complementary to the IE study when it comes to required knowledge of BA.

Furthermore, no significant effect is found with respect to the field of study when it comes to getting jobs in which knowledge of ICT is important. This confirms our basic assumption that both fields of study educate specialists in the field of ICT, and hence are potential substitutes with respect to this kind of knowledge.

The finding that committee experience significantly increases the chance of getting ITC-intensive jobs but does not increase the chance of an BA-intensive job is surprising, since committee experience does not generate special skills in the field of ICT. It is also surprising to find that relevant work experience significantly reduces the chance of finding ITC-intensive work, since this work experience is expected to increase the knowledge of ITC of both groups of graduates.

Table 6. Linear regression analysis of the importance of knowledge of ICT respectively BA in the job

	Importance of ICT		Importance of BA	
	Coefficient	t-value	Coefficient	t-value
Personal characteristics				
- sex: male	0.12	0.78	-0.02	-0.09
- age	-0.04	-1.82	-0.01	-0.30
Additional qualifications				
- previous tertiary education	-0.40	-1.75	0.00	0.01
- committee experience	0.30*	2.53	0.13	0.92
- relevant work experience	-0.23*	-2.03	0.17	1.24
- internship experience	-0.03	-0.20	0.05	0.27
Qualifications				
- BI study	0.19	1.60	0.65**	4.51
Constant	5.22*	8.65	3.40**	4.79
R-squared	0.08		0.12	
S.E.	0.83		0.97	
F	2.73**		4.18**	
N cases	218		215	

* Significant at the 5% level
** Significant at the 5% level

5. DEFICIENCIES IN REQUIRED KNOWLEDGE AND SKILLS

This section examines the deficiencies in knowledge and skills experienced by BI and IE graduates. Table 7 shows for each qualification item the percentage share of paid working graduates who indicated that their studies should have paid more attention to this qualification item. As can be seen, both BI graduates and IE graduates often experienced deficiencies in the fields of keeping up with recent developments, verbal & writing skills, and negotiating & commercial skills. More than 50% of both BI graduates and IE graduates stated that their studies should have paid more attention to these skills. Both groups seldom experienced deficiencies with respect to their specialized professional knowledge, understanding of relevant legal regulations, quantitative (research) skills, capacity for independent work, accuracy/precision, and adaptability. Less than 25% of both BI graduates and IE graduates stated that the study they had completed should have paid more attention to these knowledge items and skills.

Table 7. Attention needed for knowledge and skills (% more attention needed).

	BI	IE
Knowledge:		
- specialized professional knowledge	23%	16%
- subject-specific methods and techniques	29%	30%
- keeping up with recent developments in the field	62%	63%
- understanding of information & communication technology (incl. computer use): ICT**	**38%**	**19%**
- understanding of legal regulations relevant to the profession*	**12%**	**23%**
- understanding of operational management (organizational, financial, administrative): BA **	**25%**	**53%**
General skills:		
- application of (theoretical) knowledge and techniques in practice **	**52%**	**34%**
- analytical and diagnostic (research) skills	32%	23%
- quantitative (research) skills	9%	5%
- gathering and documenting information, data management*	**18%**	**31%**
- linguistic skills (command of foreign languages)	34%	35%
- verbal presentation, fluency	73%	68%
- written presentation, writing skills	56%	60%
- negotiating and commercial skills	58%	62%
- planning, co-ordination and organization of activities	48%	57%
- leadership skills	34%	41%
- teaching and training skills (incl. giving directions, knowledge transfer)	36%	38%
- making and maintaining contacts with other people	48%	53%
Personal skills:		
- capacity for independent work	16%	19%
- initiative, creativity	32%	33%
- ability to cope with stress*	**26%**	**14%**
- accuracy, precision	20%	16%
- adaptability	19%	21%
- loyalty, integrity, dealing with conflicts of interests**	**44%**	**26%**
- systematic evaluation of results, establishing and using feedback	32%	31%

* Difference is significant at 5% level.
** Difference is significant at 1% level.
Significant differences are shown bold

Table 7 also shows that Business Information graduates more often experienced shortcomings than informatics engineers in their knowledge of ICT and their ability to apply knowledge in practice, and in their ability to deal with conflicts of interest and to handle stress. Informatics engineers more often experienced deficiencies than business information scientists in their institutional and organizational knowledge (knowledge of legal regulations and understanding of organizational, financial & administrative matters) and their skills in dealing with data.

Diagram 1 confronts the experienced deficiencies in knowledge and skills with their importance for occupational practice. If at least 50% of the graduates states that a certain knowledge or skill item received too little attention, then we consider their studies as having failed with respect to that particular knowledge or skill. This is more serious when that knowledge or skill item is (very) important for the occupational practice of at least 75% of the graduates. If, on the other hand, less than 50% of the graduates states that a certain knowledge or skill item received too little attention, then we consider their studies as having paid sufficient attention to that particular knowledge or skill. This is even better when that knowledge or skill item is (very) important for the occupational practice of at least 75% of the graduates.

The results in Diagram 1 demonstrate that both studies show serious shortcomings regarding the topic of keeping up with recent developments in the field. The BI study also shows also serious shortcomings with respect to the practical application of knowledge and verbal & writing skills. The IE study also fails when it comes to verbal & writing skills. This is, however, less serious because these skills are less important for IE graduates. More serious is the fact that the IE study fails in stimulating planning skills and social skills.

Diagram 1 also shows that both studies score well with respect to certain important knowledge and skills, such as specialized professional knowledge, knowledge of ICT, capacity for independent work, initiative/creativity, the ability to cope with stress, accuracy/precision, and adaptability. The BI study also performs well in the fields of understanding managerial matters, planning skills, social skills, dealing with conflicts of interests, and systematic evaluation.

If graduates think that a knowledge or skill item that is (very) important for good performance in current paid activities should be given more attention, they believe that their level of the required knowledge or skill item is insufficient. In this case, it is to be expected that they are more likely to participate in further training. In the next section, we will estimate the probability of graduates participating in training.

Diagram 1. Comparison of acquired and required knowledge and skills

	BI graduates	IE graduates
Serious deficiencies 1):		
• keeping up with recent developments in the field	X	X
• application of (theoretical) knowledge and techniques in practice	X	
• verbal skills	X	
• writing skills	X	
• planning skills		X
• social skills		X
Less serious deficiencies 2):		
• negotiating and commercial skills	X	X
• understanding of operational management		X
• verbal skills		X
• writing skills		X
Sufficient, but less relevant knowledge and skills 3):		
• subject-specific methods and techniques	X	X
• understanding of legal regulations relevant to the profession	X	X
• application of (theoretical) knowledge and techniques in practice		X
• analytical and diagnostic (research) skills	X	X
• quantitative (research) skills	X	X
• gathering and documenting information, data management	X	X
• linguistic skills (command of foreign languages)	X	X
• leadership skills	X	X
• teaching and training skills	X	X
• loyalty, integrity, dealing with conflicts of interests		X
• systematic evaluation of results, establishing and using feedback		X
Sufficient, relevant knowledge and skills 4):		
• specialized professional knowledge	X	X
• understanding of ICT	X	X
• understanding of operational management	X	
• planning skills	X	
• social skills	X	
• capacity for independent work	X	X
• initiative, creativity	X	X
• ability to cope with stress	X	X
• accuracy, precision	X	X
• adaptability	X	X
• loyalty, integrity, dealing with conflicts of interests	X	
• systematic evaluation of results, establishing and using feedback	X	

1) % (very) important >=75 and % more attention needed =>50
2) % (very) important <75 and % more attention needed =>50
3) % (very) important <75 and % more attention needed <50
4) % (very) important >=75 and % more attention needed <50

6. PARTICIPATION IN TRAINING

Deficiencies with respect to the required knowledge and skills can be dealt with in two ways. One way is to prevent them from occurring by giving the knowledge and skills concerned more attention in initial education. Another way is to reduce these deficiencies in knowledge and skills by means of participation in training after graduation. In the questionnaire, the graduates were asked if they had taken any training course or company training after leaving university and, if so, to list the most important subjects of this training course or company training (if they had taken more than one training course or company training after leaving university, they were asked to list the most important subjects of the most recent training course or company training). Most BI graduates (74%) and IE graduates (66%) had participated in training (courses and company training) after leaving university. Table 8 shows that most training was in the field of ICT, followed by business administration and communicative skills. On balance, 47% of IE graduates and 29% of BI graduates participated in training in the field of ICT, 1% of IE graduates and 10% of BI graduates in the field of business administration, and 4% of IE graduates and 6% of BI graduates in the field of communication skills.

Table 8. Fields of Training

	BI	IE	Total
ICT	43%	72%	55%
Business Administration	14%	2%	9%
Communicative Skills	9%	6%	8%
Banking	8%	2%	5%
Other fields of training	26%	18%	23%

* Share < 5%

This section estimates the graduates' chances of having participated in training in the field of ICT and the field of BA after graduation. In these logistic regression equations, the probability of participating in training is explained by personal characteristics, the graduates' formal qualifications (as indicated by their previous education and their current field of education) and their informal, additional qualifications acquired before graduating. In our analysis this chance also depends on the knowledge of ICT or BA that the individual graduates acquired during their studies, the required knowledge of ICT/BA in the job, the length of time that the graduates have worked in their current jobs, and the organization in which they worked. It may be expected that graduates are more likely to participate in training in the field of ICT/BA if they have acquired insufficient knowledge of ICT/BA during their studies, if a great deal of such knowledge is required in the job, and if their firm offers ample training facilities.

The knowledge of ICT or BA that the individual graduates had acquired during their studies is first indicated by the field of study in which they graduated. It may be expected that IE probably generates more knowledge of ICT than BI, while BI probably generates more knowledge of BA. Since IE acts as the reference category in the equation, a positive sign may be expected with respect to participation in ICT training and a negative sign with respect to participation in training in the field of business administration.

Before or during their studies, graduates may have obtained extra knowledge of ICT and BA from previous education, from experience on a management committee, from work experience relevant to their studies, or from internship experience. It may be clear that if a certain knowledge or skill item should be given less or the same amount of attention, the graduates thought that they had acquired the required knowledge or skill item at a sufficient level. On the other hand, if a certain knowledge or skill item (in this case knowledge of ICT or BA) should be given more attention according to the graduates (the variables 'ICT needs more attention' and 'BA needs more attention'), they thought that their knowledge of ICT or BA was insufficient and hence they were more likely to participate in ICT or BA training. The chance of having participated in training will also increase the longer the graduate has worked in the present job.

It may be assumed that graduates who work in large organizations are more likely to participate in training because large organizations can offer more training facilities than small organizations. Due to competition, private organizations have a greater urge to implement new ICT and to give BA much thought than public organizations and hence a greater urge to implement training activities in these fields.

The graduates' chance to participate in ICT or BA training is explained by two personal characteristics ('age ' and 'sex: male'). It may be expected that the incentive to participate in training decreases with age. This is due to the fact that the time span in which returns to the investment in training can be earned back decreases with age (see for instance Mincer, 1974). Considering the expected possible loss of human capital when interrupting or even ending working life for raising children, 'sex: male' is expected to have a positive effect on the participation in training (see for instance Green, 1993; Shackleton, 1995). Appendix 1 provides an overview of all variables. All variables used in this equation are recorded as dummy variables, except for the age in years and the number of months in the current job. The results of the regression analysis are shown in Table 9.

Table 9. Logistic regression analysis of the graduates (chance of participating in training)

	ICT training		BA training	
	Coefficient	S.E.	Coefficient	S.E.
Personal Characteristics				
Sex: male	.98*	.48	!.86	.69
Age	.05	.06	!.00	.11
Additional qualifications before graduation				
Previous tertiary education	!.40	.64	!.30	1.20
Committee experience	!.46	.32	.28	.65
Relevant work experience	!.09	.31	!.09	.64
Internship experience	.06	.43	!.62	.83
Acquired and required qualifications				
BI study	!.30	.33	2.24*	1.13
ICT needs more attention	!.22	.35		
ICT is important	.03	.46		
BA needs more attention	.19	.72		
BA is important	.13	.77		
Number of months in job	.01	.01	!.01	.03
Work organization				
Private sector	1.54	.86	!0.80	1.09
Large organization	.82*	.39	.85	1.09
Constant	!5.30*	2.08	!4.17	4.08
2 Log Likelihood	281.0		97.3	
Likelihood Ratio	19.0		14.8	
N cases	210		208	

* Significant at the 5% level

6.1 Participation in ICT Training

The results in Table 9 show that the chance of participating in training in the field of ICT depends on the graduate's sex and the size of the organization in which he/she works. As was expected, men are more likely to participate in training (but only in the field of ICT) than women. As was also expected, graduates are more likely to participate in training (but again only in the field of ICT) if they work in large organizations. Surprisingly, participation in ICT training does not depend on the importance of ICT in the job, nor on the knowledge of ICT which the individual graduates have acquired during their studies. It seems that BI and IE graduates do not take ICT training because they feel that they have acquired insufficient knowledge of ICT during their studies and hence because they want to reduce deficiencies in their knowledge of ICT. It may be that BI and IE graduates, who are specialists in the field of ICT, participate in ICT training because they want to professionalize further in their field of expertise or because when they entered the firm, they were confronted with firm-specific requirements with respect to ICT that were not reflected in the more general questions regarding the importance of ICT knowledge and skills in the current jobs.

6.2 Participation in BA Training

The results of the regression analysis displayed in Table 9 show that the only variable that has a significant effect on the chance of participating in training in the field of BA, is the graduate's field of study. As can be seen, BI graduates participate more often in BA training than IE graduates. In this respect, it should be borne in mind that knowledge of BA is to a larger extent required in the jobs of BI graduates than in the jobs of IE graduates (see Table 5). The fact that the graduates do not feel that they have acquired insufficient knowledge of BA during their studies (no significant effect of the variable 'BA needs more attention'), indicates that BI graduates do not participate in BA training in order to reduce deficiencies in their knowledge of BA. BI graduates, who are specialists in the field of BA, may participate in BA training because they want to professionalize further in their field of expertise or because when they entered the firm, they were confronted with firm-specific requirements with respect to BA that were not reflected in the more general questions regarding the importance of BA knowledge and skills in the current jobs.

7. WAGES

This section examines whether deficiencies in the required knowledge of ICT and BA had a negative effect on the graduates' economic value for their company as indicated by their wage level. For this purpose, we estimated a wage function, with the knowledge of ICT and BA required in the job and acquired in the study being incorporated as explanatory variables.

In the wage function, the natural logarithm of the gross hourly wages is explained in a linear equation on the basis of personal characteristics, additional qualifications acquired before or after graduation, the graduates' shortcomings with respect to knowledge of ICT and BA, the job requirements regarding knowledge of ICT and BA, and the level and supervisory nature of their job. By incorporating in the wage function not only the graduates' level of acquired knowledge of ICT and BA but also the degree in which this knowledge is required in his job, we follow the economic theory that takes explicit account of whether the applicability of a person's knowledge and skills is context-specific, namely the job matching theory (for an overview, see Sattinger, 1993). In this theory, it is assumed that the knowledge and skills that individuals possess, do not give them any absolute advantages in employment, but rather that their productivity is partly determined by the characteristics of the specific function that they perform. By utilizing their knowledge and skills where these will generate the highest productive output, they can achieve comparative advantages. The job matching theory differs in this respect from the human capital theory, which supposes that people's knowledge and skills generate the same output wherever they are applied, so that it makes no difference how the labor supply is allocated between the available jobs (for a broad outline of the human capital theory, see Schultz, 1961).

The personal characteristics that have been incorporated in the wage function are: 'sex: male', 'age' and 'age squared'. 'Sex: male' is expected to have a positive effect on wages, due to the possibility that employers expect a loss of human capital for women when they interrupt working life to raise children. 'Age' is also expected to have a positive effect, because one's work experience increases with age. 'Age squared' is expected to have a negative effect because productivity increase declines with age (see for instance Mincer, 1974). The expected effects of an individual's knowledge and skills are also positive.

The additional qualifications before graduation, which have been incorporated in the wage function, are expected to increase a graduate's amount of human capital and hence productivity as indicated by the wages. The incorporated additional qualifications after graduation are: 'participation in ICT training', 'participation in BA training' and 'number of months in job'. The last variable is expected to have a positive sign because the length of experience in the current job enhances the productivity of the graduate in this job. The variables 'participation in ICT training' and 'participation in BA training' may affect wages in two opposite ways. The effect of training on wages may be positive through the mechanism of increased productivity (see for instance Becker, 1975). On the other hand, the mere fact of participating in training implies direct costs, which the employer may shift on to the worker in the form of lower wages.

The variables 'ICT needs more attention' and 'BA needs more attention' indicate a deficiency of knowledge in these fields and hence are expected to have a negative effect on productivity and therefore on wages.

The job characteristics, incorporated in the wage equation, refer to a job for which the employer requires a university-level education ('job at university level'), having supervision over other workers ('supervisory position') and the degree in which knowledge of ICT and BA is required in the job (the variables 'ICT is important' and 'BA is important'). The variable 'job at university level' is expected to have a positive effect on wages because the level of the job matches the graduate's educational level. The job requirements with respect to knowledge of ICT and BA act as control variables whose expected signs are not *a priori* clear.

All explanatory variables are recorded as dummy variables, except for the age in years and the number of months in the current job. Appendix 1 provides an overview of all variables.

Table 10. Linear regression analysis of the gross hourly wage (ln)

	BI graduates Coefficient	t-value	IE graduates Coefficient	t-value
Personal characteristics				
Sex: male	!.020	!.52	!.097	!1.04
Age	!.037	!.58	.062	.61
Age squared	.000	.93	!.000	!.37
Additional qualifications before graduation				
Committee experience	!.010	!.31	.065	1.11
Relevant work experience	.052	1.68	!.079	!1.39
Internship experience	!.076	!1.64	.167*	2.40
Additional qualifications after graduation				
Participation in ICT training	.017	.50	.115	1.87
Participation in BA training	.010	.19	!.251	!.96
Number of months in job	.000	.56	.007	1.84
Acquired knowledge				
ICT needs more attention	!.043	!1.34	.006	.08
BA needs more attention	.023	.61	!0.020	!.34
Job characteristics				
ICT is important	!.090	!1.70	.199**	2.96
BA is important	!.015	!0.40	.013	.23
Job at university level	.059	1.73	.167*	2.46
supervisory position	.009	.22	.047	.68
Constant	3.57**	3.82	1.577	1.05
R-squared	.38		.38	
S.E.	.15		.23	
F	3.79**		2.92**	
N cases	108		88	

* Significant at the 5% level
** Significant at the 1% level

The wage equations for BI graduates and IE graduates, respectively, were estimated using linear regression analysis. The results in Table 10 show that IE graduates who completed an internship during their studies earn higher wages, indicating that this particular form of experience enhances their human capital and hence productive value. The wages of IE graduates also increase as the required educational level for the job matches the university-level education of the graduates, indicating that the university-level knowledge and skills which they possess can be put into use most productively in jobs in which university-level knowledge and skills are required. Lastly, IE graduates earn higher wages in jobs that require much knowledge of ICT, indicating that their ICT knowledge can be used most productively in jobs in which this particular kind of knowledge is required.

For both BI graduates and IE graduates, the wage level does not depend on the experienced deficiencies in knowledge of ICT or BA that individual graduates have acquired during their studies, nor on participation in training in these fields. The mere fact that employers do not shift on to the graduates the training costs in the form of lower wages, indicates that there are no deficiencies in generally applicable knowledge of ICT or BA. On the contrary, it seems that employers invest in ICT or BA training for these specialists because they want to invest in the further professionalization of their specialist workers with a view to their future role in the firm or because the ICT or BA training of these young specialists is aimed at removing any firm-specific deficiencies in these areas, meaning that their training is aimed at qualifications that only have productive value within the firm itself (Becker, 1975; Hashimoto, 1981).

8. CONCLUSIONS

In this paper we compared the labor market position of graduates from two fields of study that specialize in ICT, namely the technical study of informatics engineering and the economics study of business informatics. As far as knowledge of ICT is concerned, BI is directed mainly at the development of automated systems for managing, administrating and running organizations, whereas IE also focuses on the development of embedded software and techniques for industrial automation and industrial process operation. Both fields of study educate specialists in the field of ICT. However, BI graduates probably acquire more knowledge of BA than IE graduates. IE graduates probably acquire more knowledge of ICT.

We found that the occupational domains of the two groups of graduates show a great degree of overlap, indicating substitution on the labor market. However, certain knowledge and skills (e.g. understanding managerial matters, planning skills, verbal & writing skills, ability to cope with stress and to deal with conflicts of interests), are more important in jobs of BI graduates than in jobs of IE graduates. None of the 25 knowledge items and skills proves to be more important in jobs of IE graduates than in jobs of BI graduates. This indicates that BI graduates have to meet higher job requirements and that the BI study is, at least in these aspects, complementary to the IE study.

By means of linear regression analysis, we estimated whether graduates choose those jobs which best match their field of study. We found that the graduates from BI, the field of study which generates most knowledge of BA, indeed most often have jobs that require much knowledge of BA. This indicates that the BI study is complementary to the IE study when it comes to required knowledge of BA. When it comes to finding a job in which knowledge of ICT is important, no significant effect of the field of study was found, indicating that both fields of study educate specialists in the field of ICT, and hence are substitutes with respect to this kind of knowledge.

With respect to knowledge of ICT and BA, business information scientists state more often than informatics engineers that their studies should have paid more attention to knowledge of ICT. Informatics engineers indicate more often than business information scientists that their studies should have paid more attention to knowledge of BA.

The majority of both BI and IE graduates take part in training courses or company training after leaving university. Most training is in the field of ICT, followed by BA and communicative skills. We found that participation in ICT training does not depend on the importance of knowledge of ICT in the job nor on the knowledge of ICT that individual graduates have acquired during their studies. It seems that BI and IE graduates, all of whom are specialists in the field of ICT, do not take ICT training to reduce deficiencies in their knowledge of ICT. With respect to BA training, we found that BI graduates more often take training in this field than IE graduates. It seems that BI graduates (who are specialists in the field of BA) do not participate in BA training to reduce deficiencies in their knowledge of BA.

We also found that the wages of these graduates are not significantly affected by their experienced deficiencies with respect to the available knowledge of ICT or BA nor by their later participation in training in these fields. It is possible that these specialists do not take ICT or BA training in order to reduce deficiencies in required knowledge, but because their employers want to invest in their further professionalization with a view to their future functioning within the firm. Another explanation could be that the ICT or BA training of these specialists is aimed at removing certain firm-specific deficiencies in these areas, which manifest themselves when graduates enter the firm concerned. In both cases, there is no incentive for the employer to shift the training costs on to the workers in the form of lower wages. In this respect, the training of these specialists differs from the ICT training of economists in general. In an earlier study (Heijke & Ramaekers, 1997), which included graduates from all economics disciplines, we found that employers shift on to economics graduates the costs involved with ICT training in the form of lower wages. This points at training as a way of reducing deficiencies in basic, general applicable knowledge of ICT. Another indication for this was our finding in this study that economics graduates who stated that economics studies should pay more attention to ICT more often took ICT training than economics graduates who indicated that their studies had paid sufficient attention to ICT.

With respect to the subject contents of the economic studies, the previous study therefore argued that more attention should be paid to generating ICT knowledge and skills in the programs themselves. The present study shows that this does not apply to the economic study programs that specialize in ICT. In the field of ICT knowledge and skills, they experience slightly more deficiencies than the technical studies that specialize in ICT, but employers do not regard this as such a shortcoming of the study that this requires more training in this area, the costs of which would then be shifted on to the graduates. Although the occupational domains of the technical and economic ICT studies overlap to a great extent, it seems that graduates of the economic ICT studies must meet higher demands with regard to knowledge and skills. This concerns in particular knowledge and skills in the field of business administration. They therefore have a greater chance of ending up in jobs that require such skills, but without having a smaller chance of a job in which it is the ICT skills that are important. Although the graduates themselves indicate that more attention should have been paid to ICT knowledge and skills in their programs, they have no greater chance of receiving training in this area and, in spite of the experienced deficiencies in their studies, their employers do not pay them less, not even if this knowledge and these skills are important for their proper functioning in their jobs. They do, however, have a greater chance of taking part in further training in the field of business administration, but presumably more as an investment in the future or to obtain firm-specific knowledge than as a means of removing any deficiencies resulting from their studies. With regard to the technical ICT studies, we may carefully draw the conclusion that, in order to widen their scope in the labor market, they could pay more attention to knowledge and skills in the field of business administration during their studies.

9. REFERENCES

Algera, J.A. (Ed.), 1991. *Analyse van arbeid vanuit verschillende perspectieven.* Amsterdam/Lisse: Swets & Zeitlinger.

Becker, G.S. (1975). *Human capital, a theoretical and empirical analysis with special reference to education.* New York: Columbia University Press, second edition.

Diependaal, R.J., et al. (Ed.) 1997. *Technische Informatica studeren aan de TU Delft*. Faculteit der Technische Wiskunde en Informatica. Technische Universiteit Delft.

Green, F. (1993). The determinants of training of male and female employees in britain. *Oxford Bulletin of Economics and Statistics, 55*, 1.

Hashimoto, M. (1981). Firm-specific capital as a shared investment. *American Economic Review, 71*, 475-482.

Heijke, J.A.M., & G.W.M. Ramaekers (1997). Importance of informatics-skills for economics graduates. Paper presented at the Conference on *Educational Innovation in Economics and Business*, 1-3 September 1997, Edinburgh.

Looijen, M. (1995). *Beheer van informatiesystemen*. Deventer: Kluwer Bedrijfsinformatie b.v.

Mincer, J. (1974). *Schooling, experience and earnings*. New York: NBER.

Sattinger, M. (1993). Assignment models of the distribution of earnings. *Journal of Economic Literature, 31*, June, 831-880.

Schultz, T.W. (1961). Investment in human capital. *The American Economic Review, 11*, 1-17.

Shackleton, J.R. (1995). *Training for employment in Western Europe and the United States*. Aldershot/Vermont: Edward Elgar Publishing Limited.

Studiegids 1995-1996. Economische Wetenschappen. Erasmus Universiteit Rotterdam.

Studiegids 1995-1996. Faculteit der Economische Wetenschappen. Katholieke Universiteit Brabant.

An Innovative Approach to Teaching Investments Using Information Technology

Richard J. Curcio
Kent State University, USA

1. INTRODUCTION

The purpose of this paper is to explain and demonstrate an innovative, action-learning, online approach for teaching investments.

Appropriate investment analysis, portfolio selection and management depend upon an understanding of basic financial concepts, information and good judgment. Until recently, one of the greatest constraints to effective investment management, at least for the average investor, was accessibility to information. The Internet, or online computing, of the 1990's has dramatically alleviated that limitation. The shared computing of the 1970's with expensive terminals, slow communications and user-**un**friendly software made it difficult to share information between systems. In the 1980's the inexpensive micro-processor-based PC brought computing power and local area networks to the people. While these networks helped users reach beyond their workstations, that reach extended only to other users and researchers within their organizations. Today, the ever-expanding electronic phenomenon known as the Internet (NET), which connects millions of computers around the world, is eliminating the technical and geographical

obstacles that have been restraining the Information Revolution. The Net provides easy, almost instant access to:
1. up-to-the-minute financial news,
2. mountains of information on the U.S. and other economies, financial and real asset markets of the world,
3. detailed information on individual industries, companies, securities, mutual funds and real assets,
4. financial forecasts,
5. technical analysis,
6. financial education,
7. financial discussion groups,
8. financial software and online calculators,
9. online brokerage and other financial services,
10. a market for some initial public offerings (IPO's) and
11. a virtual finance library including financial newspapers, periodicals, journals and research working papers.

This information is accessible at lightning speeds and with desktop convenience. With the impending development of still higher speed telephone and cable modems, accessing web sites is expected to become as easy as changing channels on your television.

The Internet has leveled the investment playing field between the individual and institutional investor. Coupled with the explosive expansion of the Net has been the development of today's extremely powerful desktop computers and ever more sophisticated, but increasingly user-friendly, software.

During this same period, we have experienced rapid growth in mutual fund investing and an expanding securitization of real assets. Further, the decline of communism and the world-wide spread of capitalism has given way to enormous growth of global investment opportunities and an ever-increasing number of world investors and investment capital. The Net will not only alter the relationship between professional and individual investors, but will facilitate this global investment revolution and will, likely, impact the entire investment process itself.

The financial and economic information richness and convenience of the NET opens significant possibilities for innovative approaches to teaching investments. This paper details one such approach in which a number of hands-on projects, which directly involve the use of the NET, are the principal learning vehicles.

The suggested experiential learning projects include:
1. a security portfolio selection and tracking exercise;

2. a top-down investment analysis assignment involving an investment valuation and recommendation of the common stocks of from three to five publicly-traded corporations in a given industry;
3. a comparative evaluation of the historical portfolio performance and future investment prospects of several mutual funds within a given mutual fund category, and
4. a common stock screening project for selecting companies, from a vast universe of corporations, that meet specified investment criteria for possible inclusion in a portfolio.

Suggested internet websites for obtaining the economic, financial market, sector and industry information, as well as company financial data, ratios, historical price graphs, technical charts, earnings and earnings growth forecasts, all necessary for implementing the above projects, are provided. Additionally, there is a generalized explanation of how to effectively integrate information and communication technology in this approach to teaching investments.

Learning theory demonstrates that an individual's understanding, recall and retention of new information is significantly enhanced when that information is presented in a comprehensive and meaningful manner. Recall from basic psychology, the experiment in which subjects are read 10 words and then, subsequently, asked to take one minute to write down all the words that they can recall from memory. The experiment is conducted in three sets. On the first pass, the subjects are read 10 nonsense syllables and asked to write down as many as they can recall. Because the words are unfamiliar, the recall rate is typically low. In the second set, the subjects are read 10 familiar words. The recall rate is much improved. On the third pass, the subjects are read 10 words in a complete sentence. Since the words are linked in a comprehensive, meaningful way, the recall rate is significantly greater than in the first two sets.

It is conjectured that greater comprehension and retention of investment definitions, concepts, theories and strategies occurs when teaching involves integrative, real-time, internet-based, experiential-learning projects. Traditional teaching of investment's courses usually involves lectures on the various investment topics. Students are generally assigned readings and, additionally, exercises involving questions and problems at the end of the chapters. Subsequently, they are tested on their ability to identify definitions and concepts in a multiple choice exam, solve problems and/or write short essay answers to related questions. Typically, the topics are covered one at a time and, for the most part, in isolation. While teaching does progress from descriptive materials to higher level concepts and theories, simultaneous integration of all pertinent knowledge, skills, strategies and perspectives for making effective investment decisions is minimal or non-existent. Hence, it is argued that the effectiveness of traditional teaching of investments can be significantly enhanced through the use of integrative, real-time, internet-based, experiential projects. It is hypothesized that the integrative, information technology approach described in this research stimulates, for students, greater interest, more intensive preparation efforts, greater comprehension of complex concepts and longer retention than occurs with traditional teaching.

Based on my experience testing this approach on at least six undergraduate and MBA level investments classes in the past two years, it appears that these real world, internet-based, action-learning projects stimulate intense student interest and motivation because of the realism. Additionally, students comment that this approach to learning basic investment definitions, concepts and strategies is much more meaningful than traditional teaching methods, thus resulting in greater retention of the newly learned knowledge. Finally, the projects are quite simple to implement, requiring no special arrangements, case books, simulations, databases, diskettes or similar materials. However, this approach does require that students have access to a computer with internet capabilities, either through the educational institution or their personal equipment, and that they have basic knowledge for internet usage, or can receive introductory instruction on internet usage.

Section II describes how to implement project (1) using the NET. Similarly, sections III, IV and V explain, in detail, the use of the internet in correspondingly carrying out projects (2), (3) and (4). Section V provides the summary and overview of this approach to teaching investments.

2. PORTFOLIO SELECTION AND TRACKING PROJECT

The first project involves choosing and tracking one or more hypothetical portfolios. The choices may constitute exclusively, common stock, mutual funds, options (puts and calls) or bonds or a combination of some or all of these investments.

At the instructor's option, the students may simply buy and hold or be allowed to trade throughout the semester (or term) with gains (losses), holding period returns (HPR's) holding period yield's (HPY's) and annualized holding period yields being calculated and reported at the end of the investment period. The project should be assigned early in the course after some introductory instruction regarding the characteristics of the different types of investments and an explanation of how to read price quotes on the financial pages and on the internet. At this stage, the selection of the investments may be based on intuition or involve only a minimal amount of research. Numerous internet websites provide price quotes and permit portfolio tracking. Some of these websites are:

Information Provider	Internet Address or URL
First Call Estimates on Demand	http://www.wsbi.com/firstcall/
Wall Street City	http://www.wallstreetcity.com
Data Broadcasting Corp.	http://www.dbc.com
Stock Point	http://www.stockpoint.com
America Online (AOL)	AOL, (channel) Personal Finance, (selection) Portfolios (if AOL is your internet service provider)
STOCK-TRAK ®	http://www.stocktrak.com

Note: As of this writing, the first five listed websites provide portfolio selection and tracking as a free service. STOCK-TRAK ® does charge a fee per student(s) account but permits, and accounts for, frequent trading. A sample of the portfolio tracking web pages from First Call Estimates on Demand are provided in Tables 1, 2 and 3.

3. TOP-DOWN INVESTMENT VALUATION PROJECT

Consider an investment valuation project in which the student gets to choose an industry (e.g., computer software, pharmaceuticals, beverage etc..) and from three to five companies within the industry to be comparatively evaluated for investment purposes. A comprehensive top-down investment evaluation entails: first, a global macro-economic and financial market analysis, second, a major sector and industry analysis and third, an analysis and evaluation of the investment prospects of the object companies.

An analysis of the U.S. and global political macro-economic and financial market environment may entail, for example, (for the U.S) forecasting: real GDP growth, inflation, Consumer Price Index (CPI), interest rates (long-term – 30 year T-Bond rate and short-term – 30 day T-Bill rate), corporate profit growth rate, stock market price levels (DJIA or S&P 500), unemployment rate, currency exchange rates (yen/$, D.M./$) and other pertinent measures. For other countries or regions of the world the analysis may entail forecasting at least, real GDP growth, inflation (CPI) and other pertinent economic variables.

Table 1. Portfolio Manager Gain/Loss.

Symbol	Trade Date	Trade Price	# of Shares	5:03 p.m. (ET) Price	Gain/Loss $	%
AOL	10/20/96	12.50	200	111.50	19,800	792.00
BUD	9/15/92	36.00	300	50.63	4,388	40.60
CSCO	6/15/97	37.50	300	100.19	18,806	167.20
DELL	12/28/93	6.00	400	109.56	41,425	1726.00
DIS	8/22/95	12.00	500	33.50	10,750	179.20
GE	6/09/95	50.00	50	90.75	2,038	81.50
GER	2/10/93	2.50	500	17.06	7,281	582.50
GM	2/10/93	28.00	200	68.75	8,150	145.50
MCD	11/18/91	12.50	400	65.75	21,300	426.00
PZZA	10/25/95	12.00	225	30.00	4,050	150.00
				Total	**137,988**	**276.00**

Reprinted from First Call Estimates on Demand Portfolio Page

Table 2. Portfolio manager market value.

Symbol	Issue Name	Amount Invested	% of Total Invested	Market Value ($)	% of Total Value
AOL	America Online Inc.	2,500	5.00	22,300	11.9
BUD	Anheuser-Busch Companies	10,800	21.60	15,188	8.1
CSCO	Cisco Systems Inc.	11,250	22.50	30,056	16.0
DELL	Dell Computer Corporation	2,400	4.80	43,825	23.3
DIS	Walt Disney Company	6,000	12.00	16,750	8.9
GE	General Electric Company	2,500	5.00	4,538	2.4
GER	Germany Fund	1,250	2.50	8,531	4.5
GM	General Motors Corporation	5,600	11.20	13,750	7.3
MCD	McDonald's Corporation	5,000	10.00	26,300	14.0
PZZA	Papa John's Int'l, Inc.	2,700	5.40	6,750	3.6
	Total	**$ 50,000**	**100.00**	**187,988**	**100**

Reprinted from First Call Estimates on Demand Portfolio Page

Table 3. Portfolio Manager Quotes.

Symbol		Open	High	Low	Last Price	Net	Volume	Last Time
AOL	+	106.000	111.500	105.563	111.500	7.063	6,593,900	5:03pm
BUD	+	50.250	50.625	49.938	50.625	0.375	1,273,900	4:00pm
CSCO	−	98.750	101.125	98.500	100.188	2.063	12,268,500	4:01pm
DELL	+	112.250	114.125	109.000	109.563	−1.000	23,962,400	4:01pm
DIS	−	32.688	33.625	32.125	33.500	1.313	5,796,500	4:20pm
GE	−	89.375	91.313	89.375	90.750	1.438	4,291,300	4:18pm
GER	−	17.063	17.063	17.063	17.063	0.250	30,100	3:43pm
GM	+	67.875	68.750	67.063	68.750	0.750	1,927,200	4:09pm
MCD	−	65.000	66.125	64.938	65.750	0.813	1,535,000	4:01pm
PZZA	+	29.500	30.375	29.063	30.000	0.625	323,800	4:00pm

These 20-minute delayed quotes were generated 8/18/98 5:59:49 p.m. ET.
Click the 'GO' button above to refresh the quotes.

Reprinted from First Call Estimates on Demand Portfolio Page

4. TOP-DOWN INVESTMENT VALUATION PROJECT

Consider an investment valuation project in which the student gets to choose an industry (e.g., computer software, pharmaceuticals, beverage etc..) and from three to five companies within the industry to be comparatively evaluated for investment purposes. A comprehensive top-down investment evaluation entails: <u>first</u>, a global macro-economic and financial market analysis, <u>second</u>, a major sector and industry analysis and <u>third</u>, an analysis and evaluation of the investment prospects of the object companies.

An analysis of the U.S. and global political macro-economic and financial market environment may entail, for example, (for the U.S) forecasting: real GDP growth, inflation, Consumer Price Index (CPI), interest rates (long-term – 30 year T-Bond rate and short-term – 30 day T-Bill rate), corporate profit growth rate, stock market price levels (DJIA or S&P 500), unemployment rate, currency exchange rates (yen/$, D.M./$) and other pertinent measures. For other countries or regions of the world the analysis may entail forecasting at least, real GDP growth, inflation (CPI) and other pertinent economic variables.

While there are numerous websites which provide information to assist this U.S. and global macro-economic analysis, following are two sites which are particularly useful:

Information Provider	Internet Address or URL
Dr. Ed Yardeni's Economics Network	http://www.yardeni.com
The Economist Intelligence Unit on AOL	AOL, Keyword: EIU

Table 4, figure 1 and table 5 provide samples of the type of information available through these websites.

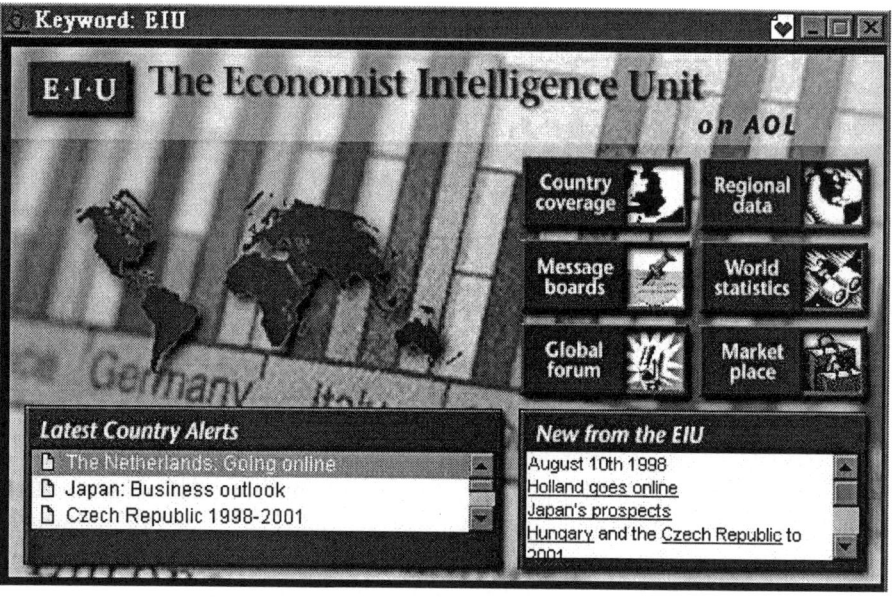

Figure 1. Reprinted from: The Economist Intelligence Unit on AOL.

Table 5. Asia, regional forecasts

	1997	1998	1999
GDP (real % change)			
Australasia	2.8	2.3	2.7
ASEAN	4.6	-5.0	0.7
Greater China	8.0	5.8	6.6
South Asia	4.2	4.6	5.4
Japan and the NICs	1.9	-0.0	1.6
Asia & Australasia, incl Japan	3.1	1.0	2.7
Asia & Australasia, excl Japan	5.8	2.8	4.6
Consumer price inflation (%)			
Australasia	0.5	1.6	1.6
ASEAN	5.2	25.6	9.0
Greater China	2.8	3.8	5.0
South Asia	7.3	9.4	8.5
Japan and the NICs	2.0	1.3	1.5
Asia & Australasia, incl Japan	2.6	4.0	3.2
Asia & Australasia, excl Japan	3.8	8.1	5.8
Current account balance (US$ bn)			
Australasia	-26.4	-27.9	-31.0
ASEAN	-6.1	11.9	11.1
Greater China	26.4	28.4	21.2
South Asia	-10.3	-8.1	-11.1
Japan and the NICs	101.7	154.7	167.0
Asia & Australasia, incl Japan	69.4	147.9	149.0
Asia & Australasia, excl Japan	-25.1	25.7	9.0
Merchandise trade balances (US$ bn)			
Australasia	-3.7	-3.8	-4.9
ASEAN	2.0	20.6	16.6
Greater China	42.4	45.3	39.3
South Asia	-13.7	-11.1	-13.4
Japan and the NICs	91.8	140.3	148.4
Asia & Australasia, incl Japan	124.8	196.8	195.0
Asia & Australasia, excl Japan	23.2	78.2	67.0

(a) Excluding Japan

Reprinted from: The Economist Intelligence Unit on AOL. ASEAN: Association of Southeast Asian Nations; Indonesia, Malaysia, Philippines, Singapore. NICs: Newly industrializing countries; Hong Kong, Singapore, South Korea, Taiwan Greater China: China, Hong Kong, Taiwan.

Table 4. Deutsche Banc Alex. Brown Economic Forecasts (reprinted from www.yardenic.com)

Item (1)	1999				2000				99/ 98A	00/ 99
	Q1A	Q2A	Q3A	Q4A	Q1E	Q2E	Q3E	Q4E		
Real GDP	3.7	1.9	5.7	5.8	4.1	3.2	4.0	4.5	3.9	4.3
Final Sales	4.6	3.4	4.5	4.6	4.9	3.8	4.0	4.1	4.3	4.3
Personal Consumption Exp.	6.5	5.1	4.9	5.3	5.0	3.7	4.0	4	5.3	4.6
Durable Goods	12.4	9.1	7.7	11.8	8.3	2.8	4.7	4.2	11.4	7.1
Nondurable Goods	8.9	3.3	3.6	6.1	3.4	2.2	2.6	2.4	5.3	3.5
Services	4.2	5.2	5.0	3.5	5.0	4.6	4.6	4.8	4.0	4.6
Nonresidential Fixed Investment	7.8	7.0	10.9	2.5	13.0	13.4	14.5	12.9	8.3	10.6
Structures	-5.8	-5.3	-3.8	-5.3	5.9	1.6	0.8	0	-2.7	0.0
Producer's Durable Equipment	12.5	11.2	15.7	4.9	14.6	16.2	17.7	15.7	12.0	13.5
Residential Fixed Investment	12.0	5.5	-3.8	-1.2	3.2	1.1	0.0	1.1	7.2	0.7
Inventory Invest. (Billion 92$)	50.1	14.0	38.0	65.4	47.4	33.4	33.4	41.4	41.9	38.9
Net Exports (Billion 92$)	-284	-319	-338	-256	-381	-401	-426	-441	-324	-412
Total Government Purchases	5.1	1.3	4.5	8.4	4.4	1.9	2.0	0.9	3.7	4.0
Federal Government Purchases	-0.5	2.1	4.1	16.0	3.6	3.2	2.8	1.4	2.9	5.5
State & Local Gov't Purchases	8.3	0.9	4.8	4.4	4.9	1.2	1.6	0.7	4.1	3.1
Real GDP (2)	3.7	3.6	4.0	4.0	4.2	4.7	4.3	3.9	4.0	3.9
Industrial Production (2)	2.8	3.2	3.7	4.5	3.8	3.5	3.8	3.7	4.5	3.7
Car&Light Truck Sls Mill. Units	15.5	16.0	16.4	16.0	16.4	15.9	15.7	16.1	16.0	16.0
Cars	8.4	8.8	8.8	8.8	9.0	8.7	8.5	8.8	8.7	8.8
Domestic Models	6.9	7.1	7.1	6.8	7.2	7.0	6.8	7.1	7.0	7.0
Imported Models	1.5	1.7	1.7	2.0	1.8	1.7	1.7	1.7	1.7	1.7
Light Trucks	7.1	7.2	7.6	7.3	7.4	7.2	7.2	7.3	7.3	7.3
Housing Starts (Million Units)	1.8	1.6	1.7	1.7	1.7	1.6	1.7	1.6	1.7	1.7
Unemployment Rate (Percent)	4.3	4.3	4.2	4.1	4.0	4.0	3.9	3.9	4.2	4.0
Consumer Price Index (3)	1.5	2.9	4.2	2.2	1.5	1.2	1.0	1	2.7	1.2
Implicit Price Index, GDP	1.9	1.4	1.0	2.0	1.2	0.1	0.8	0.8	1.4	1.0
Unit Labor Costs, Nonfarm Bus.	1.5	4.4	-0.4	1.2	1.0	2.0	1.5	1.1	1.9	1.3
Hourly Comp., Nonfarm Bus.	4.3	4.6	4.9	4.4	4.4	4.5	4.7	4.7	4.8	4.6
Productivity, Nonfarm Bus.	2.5	0.7	5.1	3.2	3.4	2.5	3.2	3.6	2.8	3.2
Book Profits After Taxes (2)	3.9	5.5	10.9	14.7	8.5	10.6	12.3	11.9	8.7	10.8
Real Disposable Personal Income	0.3	2.9	3.1	4.4	6.8	3.7	3.6	4	3.0	4.5
Personal Savings Rate (Percent)	3.0	2.5	2.1	1.9	2.3	2.3	2.2	2.2	2.4	2.3
Prime Rate (Percent)	7.8	7.8	8.1	8.4	8.7	9.0	9.0	9.0	8.0	8.9
3-Month Treasury Bills (Percent)	4.4	4.4	4.6	5.0	5.7	6.0	6.0	6.0	4.6	5.9
30-Year Governments (Percent)	5.4	5.8	6.0	6.3	7.0	6.7	6.5	6.2	5.9	6.6
Trade-Weighted Dollar	100.0	102.0	100.0	101.0	103.0	105.0	107.0	107.0	100.8	105.5

A = Actual. E = Estimate. (1) Quarterly and annual average percent change. Forecasts are rough estimates based on very limited information & are subject to frequent and large revisions as new information becomes available. (2) Four-quarter percent change. (3) Percent change based on last month of quarter or year.

The industry analysis might entail gauging the impact of the projected global, economic and market events on the chosen industry. Of interest is, identifying the major factors that may affect future demand, prices, costs, profitability and growth rates in the industry. Useful websites for obtaining information for completing this portion of the project include:

Information Provider	Internet Address or URL
Wall Street City	http://www.wallstreetcity.com
Dr. Ed Yardeni's Economics Network	http://www.yardeni.com

Students might supplement the information provided through the internet with library references such as Value Line Investment Survey's industry rankings and individual industry analyses. Figures 2, 3, 4, 5, and 6 provide illustrative examples. The analysis of the individual companies in the industry entails gauging the relative competitive strengths and weaknesses of these object companies. Typically, this involves a financial evaluation including a ratio analysis (comparative and trend) encompassing the categories: (a) liquidity, (b) asset management, (c) debt management, (d) profitability and (e) market value. The analysis also entails assessing company risks and forecasting company sales, earnings per share (EPS), dividends per share (DPS), price/earnings (P/E) multiples, growth rates and share prices under most likely, optimistic and pessimistic scenarios.

In addition to the above fundamental analysis, technical analyses of the general markets as well as the individual companies may be required as part of this project[3]. Such analyses might, among others, involve consideration of (1) stock price and volume techniques, (2) support and resistance levels, (3) moving average lines, (4) relative strength indicators and (5) breadth of the market indicators such as the advance – decline line.

Finally, the investment evaluation requires the preparation of an investment recommendation regarding the industry and each of the object companies.

---

[3] While academicians are split on the usefulness of technical analysis, numerous investment practitioners believe in and use technical analysis. Also, large investment houses devote extensive resources to technical analysis and many media reporting on developments in the securities markets is from a technical perspective. Hence, whether one believes that investment decisions should be based on fundamental analysis, technical analysis or the acceptance that markets are efficient, students should, at least, be aware of the principles and practice of technical analysis.

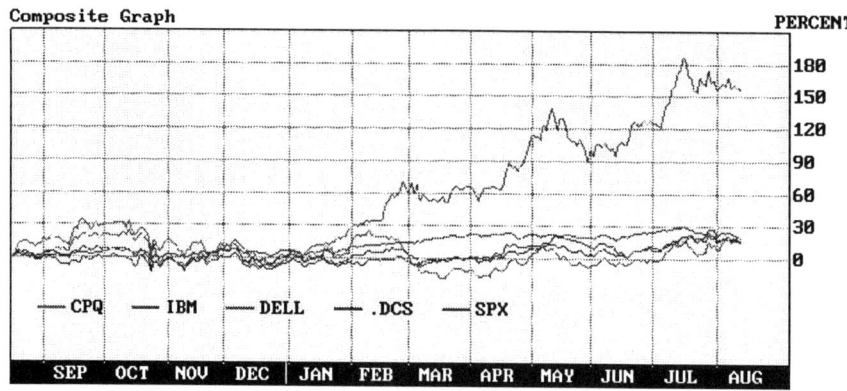

Figure 2. Comparison Graph – One Year. Reprinted from: www.wallstreetcity.com

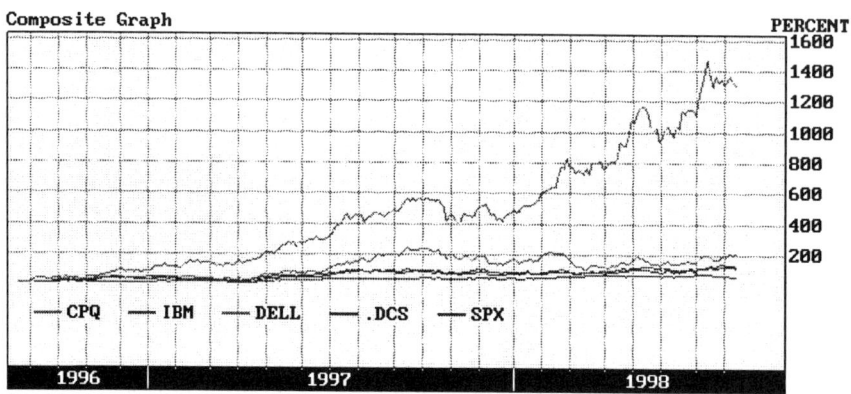

Figure 3. Comparison Graph – Two Year. Reprinted from: www.wallstreetcity.com

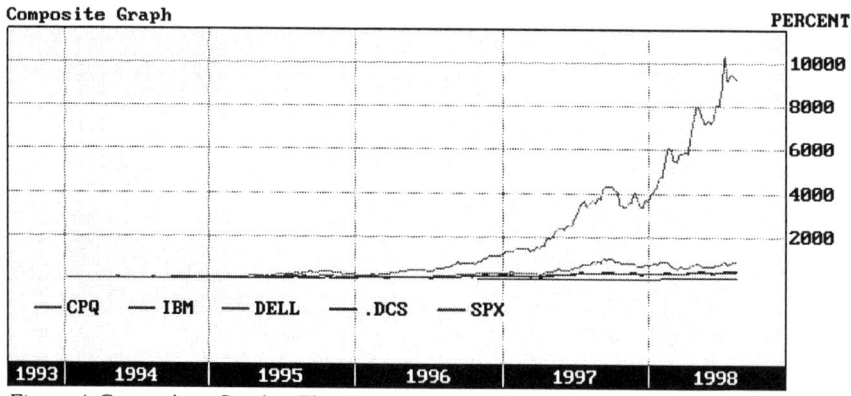

Figure 4. Comparison Graph – Five Year. Reprinted from: www.wallstreetcity.com

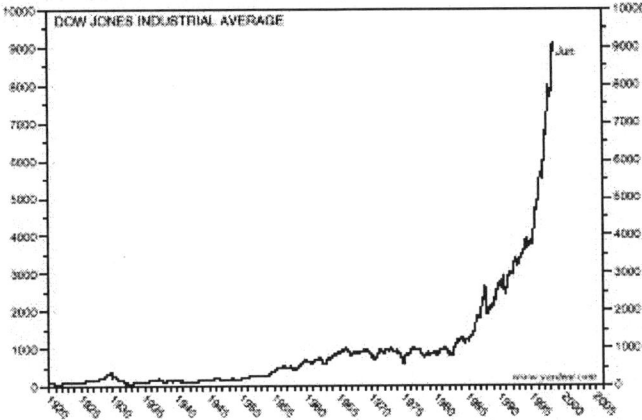

Figure 5. Dow Jones Industrial Average 1920 – Present. Reprinted from: www.yardeni.com

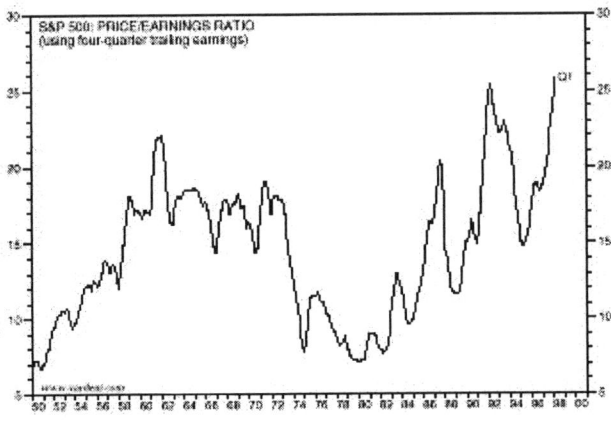

Figure 6. S&P 500: Price / Earnings Ratio. Reprinted from: www.yardeni.com

Considerable assistance in preparing these fundamental and technical analyses, forecasts and recommendations can be obtained from the following web sites:

Information Provider	Internet Address or URL
Wall Street Research Net	http://www.wsrn.com
Market Guide	http://www.marketguide.com
Wall Street City	http://www.wallstreetcity.com
Data Broadcasting Corp.	http://www.dbc.com
Investorama	http://www.investorama.com
Stock Point	http://www.stockpoint.com
Decision Point Timing & Charts on AOL	AOL, (channel) Personal Finance, (selection) Investing Forums

As an example of how this project can be implemented, a detailed outline for undergraduate students to follow in preparing their Top-Down Investment Valuation Project is included here.

Outline for Top-Down Investment Valuation Project
Industry Analysis of Three Companies

Table of Contents

Executive Summary – A two page summary of the analysis, forecasts and recommendations.

I. **Introduction** – State the purpose of your report, identify and describe your chosen industry and the three companies to be analyzed. Explain the organization of your report.

II. **Macroeconomic Analysis & Forecasts** – provide your two-year economic & financial market forecasts of the U.S. and major regions of the world. Refer to www.yardeni.com, The economist Intelligent Unit on AOL at AOL, Keyword: EIU.

III. **Industry Analysis & Forecasts** – Provide your assessment of the timeliness and future prospects for your industry. Focus on major factors which will impact the expected revenues, costs and profits for this industry. See Valueline's industry timeliness rankings and industry analysis data sheets and/or Standard & Poor's investment advice on www.personalwealth.com.

IV. **Company Analysis**

    A. Conduct an historical, comparative ratio analysis of your three companies. The ratio categories should include (1) liquidity, (2) asset management, (3) debt, and (4) profitability and (5) market value as described in handouts and references entitled - Investment Valuation. The analysis should cover the past five years. Many of the ratios can be found on the Valueline company analysis pages. Also, refer to www.wsrn.com and www.marketguide.com for ratios, graphs of ratios and comparisons with industry and general market levels.

    B. Conduct a technical analysis of your three companies focusing on current prices in relation to the 50-day and 200-day moving averages, relative strength indicators, volume, support & resistance levels and trends. Refer to the handouts and references entitled – Technical Analysis. Also, refer to www.marketguide.com, www.dbc.com, www.wsrn.com, www.investorama.com, www.stockpoint.com and Decision Point Timing and Charts on AOL through AOL, (channel) Personal Finance, (selection) Investing Forums.

C. Plot a graph of the comparative stock price performance of your three companies, the S&P 500 (symbol is SPX) and your industry (you need to look up the symbol) for one, two and five years! Take note of the 52-week high and low and the current price.
D. Based on your two-year economic and financial market forecasts, fundamental ratio analysis and technical analysis, provide a two-year forecast of each of your companies': sales, earnings per share, dividends per share, P/E multiples and share price (end of 1999 and end of 2000). Refer to Valueline's projections and also professional analysts' forecasts on www.wsrn.com and www.marketguide.com.

V. **Investment Recommendation** – Indicate whether you would recommend a strong buy, buy, hold, sell or strong sell for your companies. Support your recommendations. Refer to www.wsrn.com and www.marketguide.com and Valueline for professional evaluations of these companies and timeliness and safety ratings.

5. MUTUAL FUND PORTFOLIO EVALUATION PROJECT

This project entails a comparative analysis and evaluation of several mutual funds within a selected mutual fund category (e.g. aggressive growth, growth, growth and income, balanced, sectors, global and others). While this project can be assigned to an individual, it lends itself well to a student group or team investigation in which each member of the team is responsible for researching and analyzing one mutual fund of their choosing within the group's chosen or assigned mutual fund category. The whole group is then responsible for the comparative analysis and evaluation of all the mutual funds examined by the members. The evaluation should include a comparison of returns, risks, the size and nature of the sales load (if any), 12b-1 fees, expense ratio, turnover ratio, relative performance during bear markets and any other important characteristic. The comparative evaluation should especially emphasize the relative return/risk performance. Definitely, students should plot all of their group's mutual funds on a capital market line and also on a security market line with, say, the S&P 500 portfolio coordinates proxying for the market portfolio in each case and the 90-day Treasury Bill as the risk-free rate. Other return/risk measures include the Sharpe ratio, alpha and Morningstar's star rating. The analysis should also identify the sector weightings as well as the top 5 – 10 stock holdings of each mutual fund. Finally, based on their analysis and future projections on the economy, individual sectors, industries and companies, each group should rank-order the mutual funds which they have evaluated and make an investment recommendation with regard to those mutual funds and the mutual fund category. The following internet websites provide very useful information for enabling the above project.

Information Provider	Internet Address or URL
Morningstar	http://www.morningstar.net
AOL	AOL, (channel) Personal Finance, (selection) Mutual Funds

Students might supplement the information provided through the internet with library references such as <u>Morningstar Mutual Funds 500</u>.

6. COMMON STOCK SCREENING PROJECT

This assignment involves screening large populations of securities on the basis of specific attributes in order to narrow the choices to a list which meets the investor's criteria. While there is much debate about the effectiveness of attribute screens, a number of academic research studies as well as several reported in the popular financial press have found evidence that choosing investments through attribute screening can lead to superior investment performance.

Regardless of one's disposition on this issue, stock screening does allow investors to restrict their search to those securities meeting their desired characteristics.

The stock screening attributes might include such items as: size (as measured by sales and/or market capitalization), price/earnings (P/E), price/sales (P/S), price/book (P/B), earnings growth rates, dividend payout ratio, return on equity, debt/equity, beta, stock price range and others.

A very useful internet website for this project is:

Information Provider	Internet Address or URL
Wall Street Research Net	http://www.wsrn.com

7. SUMMARY

The purpose of this paper was to explain and demonstrate an innovative, action-learning, internet-based approach for teaching investments. Vast amounts of information pertaining to the U.S. and global economies, financial and real asset markets, individual sectors, industries, companies, securities, mutual funds, real assets, financial forecasts, technical analysis and up-to-the-minute financial news is now accessible at lightning speeds and with desktop convenience. The internet, that ever-expanding electronic phenomenon which connects millions of computers around the world has made this possible.

The financial and economic information richness and convenience of the NET has opened significant possibilities for innovative approaches to teaching investments. This paper detailed one such approach in which a number of hands-on projects, which directly involve the use of the NET, are the principal learning vehicles. The experiential learning projects included (1) a security portfolio selection and tracking exercise, (2) a top-down industry investment analysis, (3) a mutual fund portfolio evaluation and (4) a common stock screening assignment. Suggested internet websites necessary for implementing these projects, along with sample printouts, were provided.

Based on my experience of testing this approach, at both the undergraduate and MBA levels during the past two years, I have found that this method stimulates intense student interest and motivation because of the realism. Also, students comment that this approach to learning basic investment definitions, concepts and strategies is much more meaningful than traditional teaching methods, and results in greater retention of newly learned knowledge. Finally, the projects are quite simple to implement, requiring no special arrangements, case books, simulations, databases, diskettes or similar materials. However, the approach does require that students have access to a computer with internet capability and that they have basic knowledge for internet usage, or can receive introductory instruction on internet usage.

The extent to which a traditional investments textbook and traditional investments teaching are used in conjunction with this internet-based, action-learning approach may depend upon the prior educational preparedness of the students and the experience of the instructor.

8. REFERENCES

Pettijohn, J.B. (1996). A guide to locating financial information on the Internet. *Financial Practice and Education*, 102-110 (Fall/Winter).

Ray, R. (1996). An introduction to finance on the Internet. *Financial Practice and Education*, 95-101 (Fall/Winter).

Reilly, F.K., & Brown, K.C. (1997). *Investment analysis and portfolio management*, Fifth Edition. Orlando, FL: The Dryden Press.

People, Knowledge, and the Internet: Redefining Categories, Concepts, and Models

Tatyana Dumova
School of Communication Studies, Bowling Green State University, Ohio, USA

1. INTRODUCTION

The 20th century revolution in information and communication technologies has dramatically altered the way people live, work, think, and learn. Its impact has been compared with the impact of the scientific revolution in the 16th century and the industrial revolution in the 17th-19th centuries (Bossert, 1997; Castells, 1997; Denning & Metcalfe, 1997; Tapscott, 1996). Milestones of the progress of technology such as the invention of the steam engine, printing press, radio, television, or the microcomputer are all responsible for profound socio-economic transformations. This is especially true with regard to the roles played by knowledge in contemporary society. The "age of information," "knowledge age," "information society," "knowledge-based society," "information economy," "knowledge economy," and "knowledge era"-- are all labels scholars currently use to define technological and societal changes of the present time (Chaffee & Rogers, 1997; Dutton, 1996; Marien, 1996; Tapscott, 1996). I propose that these labels reflect the changing nature of the relationship between people and knowledge. Instead of a single linear association among people (P) and knowledge (K), we now deal with a three dimensional relationship involving at least three, rather than two, variable factors: people (P), knowledge (K), and technology (T) including the Internet.

In an attempt to explore this hypothesis, the present historiography presents a heuristic overview of recent scholarly writings on how the advent of new electronic technologies affects knowledge creation. The need for a research on knowledge and the Internet is crucial. Scholarly research may provide answers as well as alternatives to many practical questions, may help make knowledge production more effective, and may stimulate further growth of knowledge including scientific knowledge. For example, according to Schank (1997), effective integration of knowledge of virtual learning opportunities into corporate training systems by Andersen Consulting, Diamond Technology, and Anixter, Inc. is an advantage that provides these companies a secure place in the future (p. 174). Furthermore, integrating insights from a wide literature base on knowledge is a task that needs to be done if scientists are truly responsible for the production of knowledge in contemporary society.

The purpose of this study is to identify, explore, and contextualize the changing nature of knowledge formation in contemporary society, specifically as it applies to the integration of the Internet and the World Wide Web into the analysis. The study is not intended to describe or explain the nature of knowledge itself, but rather suggest possible directions for analyzing as well as redefining existing explanations. I must say, that in this study, I am not getting into philosophical discussion of what the nature of knowledge is in terms of "knowing", or how we "get to know" or how we do know that "we know", neither am I considering knowledge from a physiological viewpoint as a state of mind or awareness. The way knowledge is perceived here is rather generally in an objective sense as understanding, gained from observation, experience, or learning. Before proceeding, I also need to specify that the terms knowledge "production", "formation", and "generation" are treated here as synonymous. With all of these terms, I refer to the development of new knowledge, improvement of existing knowledge, and knowledge growth.

In the first section, I define relevant models grounded in objective-empiricist theoretical tradition. These models originated in traditional disciplines such as psychology, education, and economics. In addition, I identify the principal variable factors and categories of analysis as well as suggest probable relations among variables and concepts. In the second section, I reexamine some interrelated nontraditional concepts from education, information science, and communication studies that may help to explain the evolving nature of knowledge generation in contemporary society. These are embedded in hermeneutic empiricist theoretical approach and include: learning paradigm, computer-mediated communication, Internet education, and "abstraction in chaos." Some tentative conclusions and recommendations for further analyses are suggested in the discussion section.

2. DEFINING CATEGORIES OF ANALYSIS

In order to create a solid foundation for redefining knowledge creation concepts through the introduction of technology, it may be useful to examine several traditional empirical knowledge models. People have long sought to explain the nature, the source, the process of formation, the limitations, and the validity of knowledge. Plato looked upon knowledge as a discovery that takes place during the orderly process of rational thought. Empiricists, on the other hand, insisted that human knowledge is obtained from experiences provided by the five senses. The English philosopher John Locke, for example, considered the human mind as a receptacle that receives, stores, and combines sensations.

Scientific epistemology of knowledge has become a combination, although complex and controversial, of both rational and empirical perspectives. The scientific perspective is based upon a rigorous sequence of procedures by which a body of knowledge is built. According to this perspective, the successive steps of creating knowledge include systematic observation, collection of facts, organization, and classification of collected data, as well as formulation, testing, and verification of hypotheses.

It is important to acknowledge the value of traditional objective-empiricist theoretical perspective. According to this perspective, there is an objective reality out there and knowledge is independent and autonomous from the observer: "knowledge without a knower" and "knowledge without a knowing subject."[4] Consequently, in many cases knowledge is viewed as being directly transferred from a producer of knowledge to a learner. In this section, three distinctive objective-empiricist approaches to knowledge in the information age will be outlined: the knowledge pyramid, knowledge as a result of learning, and knowledge as an economic resource.

2.1 Knowledge Pyramid

One example of a scholarly delineation of knowledge is the so-called knowledge pyramid (Vogt, 1994, p. 100). This concept originated among scholars in psychology and education and is grounded in traditional

---

[4] Popper, K. (1972). *Objective knowledge.* Oxford: Clarendon Press, 108-109, 111, 116, 118.

empirical research. It provides a scientific model of stores of human knowledge as well as a visual perspective on the nature of knowledge formation. As Karl Popper pointed out, knowledge in an objective sense encompasses problems, theories, and arguments. At the same time, Popper distinguishes between the world of facts, or physical world, and the autonomous "III world", consisting of products of human activity, or "pure" science.[5]

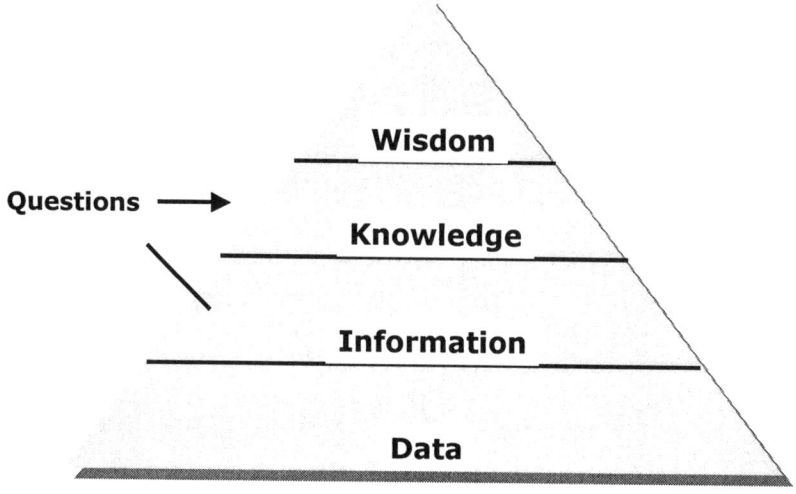

Figure 1. Knowledge Pyramid.

Source. Vogt, E.E. (1994). The Nature of Work in 2010: Convergence and the Workplace. In *Crossroads on the information highway: Convergence and diversity in communication technologies* (p. 100). United States of America: Institute for Information Studies.

Similarly to Popper's objective-empiricist perspective although not precisely along the same lines, the knowledge pyramid model places knowledge above the masses of available facts and data. considering it an intermediate step between information and wisdom (see figure 1). The role of knowledge here is to enable a shift from recording observations and facts to answering questions, creating models, and generating new perspectives including theoretical. Wisdom is regarded as synthesized knowledge. That includes worldviews, paradigms, theories, concepts, and models. (Compare with Popper's "objective theories", "objective problems," "objective arguments", scientific hypotheses, and discussions.[6])

---

[5]Ibid., p. 112-116.
[6]Ibid., p. 108-109. 111, 154.

The nature of knowledge growth, according to Popper, lies in interaction between people and the III world. It is this interaction that allows scientists to promote the growth of knowledge about the world of facts. For Popper, criticism or critical discussions are major instruments in producing knowledge. Thus consumption of theories, for example, means criticizing them, changing them, and replacing false theories by better ones while the growth of knowledge is viewed as a process of error elimination.[7]

An expanded version of the knowledge pyramid model presented in figure 2 also emphasizes the hierarchical nature of knowledge but distinguishes more levels of abstraction. Intelligence is viewed here as an inference applied to information, and wisdom as synthesized knowledge at the top of the "Facts to Wisdom Hierarchy" (Haeckel & Nolan, 1993, p. 6):

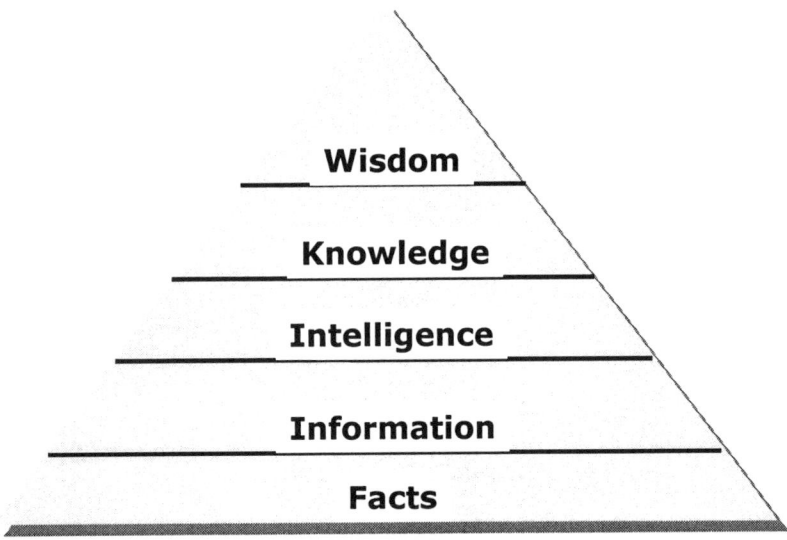

Figure 2. Facts to Wisdom Hierarchy.

Source. Haeckel, S.H., & Nolan, R.L. (1993). The role of technology in an information age: Transforming symbols into action. In P.J. Myer (Ed.), *The Knowledge Economy: The nature of information in the 21st century*. Annual review of the Institute for Information Studies (p. 6). United States of America: Institute for Information Studies

It is significant to speculate how the emerging electronic technologies fit with the hierarchical structure of the knowledge-formation process. Technology may be regarded as an application of scientific knowledge to the

[7] Ibid., p. 112, 286-287.

production process, including both the production of goods and ideas. Technology undoubtedly fits all the stages preceding the synthesizing stage. Stephen Haeckel and Richard Nolan (1993) assert that technology can be used and is used "to capture, digitize, codify, store, process, deliver, and present information" (p. 6). Although technology can be used to process information, only human beings can generate knowledge and wisdom (Haeckel & Nolan, 1993, p. 6).

Because the proliferation of technology into our lives evolves so rapidly, scientists may no longer view creation of knowledge as a linear process involving only two elements, namely, people (P) and knowledge (K):

Figure 3. Knowledge Formation: Linear Model.

Source. By the author.

The relationship between people and knowledge in this model is simple: it is a bivariate linear association. People produce knowledge. Knowledge affects people.

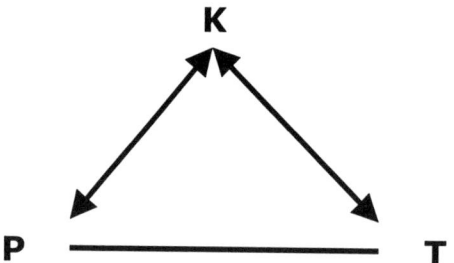

Figure 4. Knowledge Formation: Non-Linear Model.
Source. By the author.

My claim is that technologies are creating a significant transformation in this relationship. In the era of information technologies, the model becomes more complex and involves at least three, rather than two, variable factors: people (P), knowledge (K), and technology (T). Instead of a single linear association, we now deal with a three dimensional relationship (figure 4).

This triangulation consists of three pairs of relationships that can be interpreted in at least three ways. (1) People create technologies. Technologies induce knowledge. Knowledge changes people; (2) People produce knowledge. Knowledge creates technologies. Technologies affect people; or: (3) Technologies change people. People generate new knowledge. Obviously, there are many other interpretations, for example, people produce knowledge, knowledge is consumed by people, knowledge creates technologies, and, finally, technologies affect knowledge and change people. Given the complexity of discussed associations, scholars must be aware of the variety of possible relations among variables that can subtly shift the emphasis of knowledge dynamics.

The people category of this analysis is composite and would require a lengthy discussion on its own. Depending on the context of the research, scientists use different subjects in their analyses: students, learners, users, receivers, audience, producers, and consumers. However, it is because of the proliferation of technologies, including the Internet and the World Wide Web, in our lives that people can no longer be viewed as either producers or consumers of knowledge. Technology allows learners to perform both as consumers of information and producers of knowledge.

2.2 Knowledge as a Result of Learning

A second instructive way of viewing knowledge from traditional empiricist perspective is looking at it from an educational perspective--as a product of a learning process. Barbara Kurshan and Cecila Lenk (1995) have studied the changing nature of the relationship between knowledge and learning, on the one hand, and technology, on the other. They hypothesize an *evolutionary* rather than *revolutionary* impact of technology caused by an increasing access to information. Ideally, they believe, technology can contribute to bringing about revolutionary changes in accessibility of education to students of any age and place and, consequently, on the production of knowledge. However, in real life this may not happen without radically reforming the educational setting on a broader scale involving not only students and teachers, but also families, practitioners, businesses, and policy makers (Kurshan & Lenk, pp. 130-131).

Not just scholars and educators demonstrate the changing nature of information and knowledge. Eric Vogt, president of Micro Mentor, Inc. portrays an interrelationship between the knowledge hierarchy and the learning process (see figure 5):

> ... As one progresses higher in the triangle [knowledge hierarchy], one can be said to have "learned more." ... Facts can be sensed; information and intelligence are essential in interpreting the context/meaning of facts; the certitude that begets knowledge enhances the quality of any decision-making process; and action guided by wisdom is certainly superior--especially if there is wisdom enough to link the elements of a learning loop into a self-reinforcing cycle (Quoted in Haeckel & Nolan, 1993, p. 7).

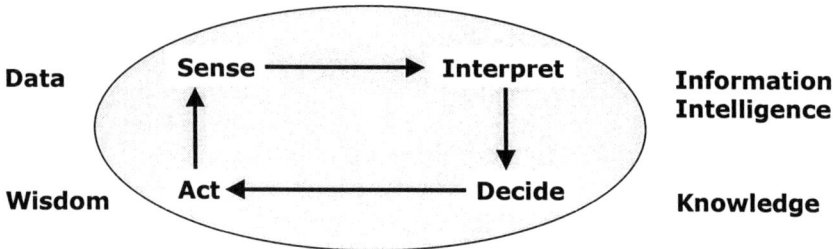

Figure 5. Learning loop.

Source. Haeckel, S.H., & Nolan, R.L. (1993). The role of technology in an information age: Transforming symbols into action. In P.J. Myer (Ed.), *The Knowledge Economy: The nature of information in the 21st century*. Annual review of the Institute for Information Studies (p. 8). United States of America: Institute for Information Studies.

Accordingly, Haeckel and Nolan (1993, p. 12) identify four specific levels of learning, namely: observation, orientation, decision, and action (figure 6). Observation is sensing environmental signals; orientation is interpreting the meaning of captured signals; decision means selecting from a range of available responses; while action is executing the selected response. This schema presents a passive way of learning. Nevertheless, researchers believe that by enhancing the connecting, sharing, and structuring of information, technology can force information to change its nature from passive and descriptive to active and transforming (Haeckel & Nolan, 1993, p. 10).

2.3 Knowledge as an Economic Resource

A third productive way of approaching knowledge within empirical paradigm is considering it as an economic resource. Many believe that in the knowledge-based society, intellectual capital has become an important means of production (Castells, 1996, p. 66; Melody, 1996, p. 316; Romer, 1993, on-line; Tapscott, 1996, p. 68). Research has shown that in the United States, between the 1940s and 1980s, nearly 40 percent of improvement in labor productivity accounted for the maintenance and improvement of educational resources and about 33 percent for the diffusion of new knowledge (Denison, 1985, p. 98). According to Tapscott (1996, pp. 64, 68), with the emergence of the newest electronic technologies, knowledge becomes a basis for the transition of humankind toward a new economy--a knowledge-based global economy (figure 7).

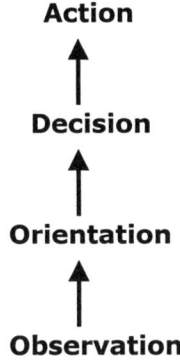

Figure 6. Levels of Learning.

Source. By the author.

Economist Paul Romer, the "Adam Smith of Silicon Valley," seeks to challenge conventional economic theory by tying knowledge and technology within the concepts of economic growth and development (Samuels, 1996, on-line). He talks about the "idea-driven economy," the "economy of ideas," and the "knowledge economy." Contrary to classical economists, Romer states that ideas and technologies, not labor and capital, are the real engines of growth and wealth (figure 8). According to Romer (1993, on-line), among the most important ideas are "meta-ideas," or ideas that indicate how to produce and transfer other ideas (see figure 8). However, the "economics of knowledge" has not yet been established in mainstream economics.

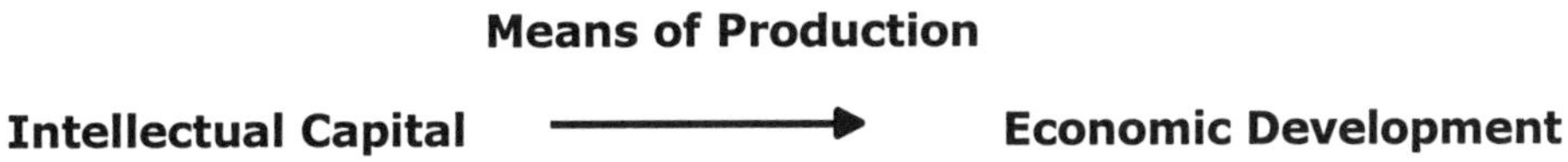

Means of Production

Intellectual Capital ⟶ **Economic Development**

Figure 7. A Knowledge-Based Economy.

Source. By the author.

This view of knowledge as an economic resource is also grounded in objective empiricist theoretical framework. To me, the idea of a knowledge-based economy, or economy of ideas that enable economic growth and development, is similar to Popper's thesis of interaction between people and the world of objective theories that provides the growth of knowledge.

Ideas ──────▶ Economic Growth

Figure 8. Knowledge Economy is the Economy of Ideas.

Source. By the author.

In an attempt to apply traditional empirical analysis to new technological phenomena, however, the models discussed above largely fail to consider the qualities and specific features of technology itself. Therefore, although these models serve well in considering two of the three variables, namely, people and knowledge, they do not help in understanding the implications of technology and fail to explain why this last variable may or may not have an effect on creating knowledge. Since this study focuses on emerging electronic technologies, namely, the Internet and the World Wide Web, an interdisciplinary approach to technology is used along with the following discussion of four innovative concepts that more extensively depict the impact of new media on knowledge.

3. REDEFINING RELEVANT CONCEPTS

In order to integrate the technology variable into the analysis of the people-knowledge relationship, it is essential to depart from the traditional empirical approach with which scholars from many academic disciplines have been viewing issues related to the effects of the Internet on knowledge production and consumption. This section attempts to identify the following hermeneutic empiricist concepts: learning paradigm, computer-mediated communication (CMC), Internet education, and "abstraction in chaos." These concepts are variations of a hermeneutic empiricist approach that encompasses both postmodernist and constructivist theoretical traditions.

A major point of departure in hermeneutic empiricism is that there is no external reality independent of individual's mind. Therefore, rather than transmitted from a producer to a consumer (as is the case with objectivist models), knowledge, according to Jurgen Habermas, is created or constructed by each learner. Moreover, each individual is responsible for his or her own knowledge construction.[8]

Not only is each individual performing as an observer and interpreter, he also becomes a partner in a dialog. Knowledge is viewed by postmodern

---

[8]Habermas, J. (1971). *Knowledge and human interests.* Boston: Beacon Press, p. 172, 176, 179-181.

tradition as understanding, understanding as communicative experience, and experience as mediated by the interaction among the participants.[9] The relationship between an observing subject and an observed object is replaced here by that of a participant subject and a partner. A new shared knowledge may be also generated through interaction among active learners.[10] As to constructivist hermeneutic perspective, knowledge is the domain constituted from different elements that are related to each other as parts to whole. Knowledge is also viewed as a field of coordination and subordination of statements in which concepts are developed, applied, and transmitted.[11]

3.1   Learning Paradigm

Assuming that both teaching and learning are scholarly acts equally contributing to the construction of knowledge, Michael Brooks (1997) and Beverly Hunter (1997) describe a discrepancy reflecting the coexistence of two opposite epistemological approaches. The traditionally dominant *teaching paradigm* places an emphasis on the teacher as a primary source of knowledge. As in the case with other traditional empiricist models, constituent elements of a learning process are primarily viewed here as different actors playing different roles and specified either as learners and consumers of knowledge (students) or knowledge producers (scholars). Also, there is a category of intermediaries such as librarians, teachers, and publishers. Because teaching is considered an art rather than a science, it cannot be evaluated or measured. Learning is viewed as a private act, taking place between the teacher, that produces knowledge and the student, that consumes it. Consequently, learning is teacher-centered and teacher-controlled and students are viewed as passive respondents of knowledge (Brooks, 1997; Hunter, 1997).

On the contrary, according to the alternative *learning paradigm* rooted in constructivist theoretical approach, knowledge is built through active and collaborative learning (Brooks, 1997; Deden, 1998; Hunter, 1997). The emphasis is now being made not on recipients of information and knowledge but rather on participants of the knowledge-formation process (Watters, Conley & Alexander, 1998). Because of the technological and social transformations of contemporary society, learning is currently viewed as a two-way relationship allowing learners to perform both as consumers of

---

[9] Ibid., p. 179-182.
[10] Ibid., p. 179-180.
[11] Foucault, M. (1972). *The archaeology of knowledge*. New York: Pantheon Books, p. 182-183.

information and producers of knowledge (Brooks, 1997; Hunter, 1997; Smyth, 1996).

Not only scientists and practitioners detect a paradigm shift in education from a teaching paradigm to a learning paradigm. The thesis developed by many observers is that new technologies are pushing education and learning in the direction of becoming "virtual education" (Brooks, 1997), "virtual learning" (Mather, 1997), and "hyperlearning" (Denning, 1997). "Virtual learning" is often defined as a traditional mode of learning enhanced by the use of advanced electronic technologies (Brooks, 1997, p. 7). A "hyperlearning" environment is an emerging type of learning: non-traditional, nonlinear, and multidimensional (Denning, 1997, pp. 275-276). While the domain of education "is losing its monopoly on knowledge creation," "virtualization" of education enables new models of learning and working and is revolutionizing education (Gell & Cochrane, 1996, pp. 253-256). Virtual reality, computer simulations, and role-playing can make learning and training truly effective and can make knowledge a valid economic resource (Schank, 1997). Closely linked to the virtual learning is the concept of computer-mediated communication.

3.2 Computer-Mediated Communication

Computer-mediated communication (CMC), a constructivist deviation from traditional empiricism, has become a focus of a long-standing controversy between scholarly "computerphiles" and "computerphobes" (Hiltz & Wellman, 1997, p. 44). While "computerphiles," or computer advocates, argue that computer-mediated communication is a technological breakthrough, "computerphobes," or opponents of computers, accuse technology of making face-to-face communication obsolete and turning real life into a code. In view of these debates, Starr Hiltz and Barry Wellman (1997) emphasize the socializing nature of computer-mediated communication, in which computer networks increase socialization by connecting not only computers but also people. Hiltz and Wellman examine essential characteristics of different types of computer-mediated communication and seek to investigate what kinds of virtual communities best fit into learning.

Discussions of the effects of computer-mediated communication on learning have distinguished two basic types of social computer networks: computer-supported cooperative networks and virtual communities. Computer-supported cooperative networks unite people on the basis of common tasks and accomplishments. They tend to be more homogeneous but are limited in terms of people's specializations and spatial relationships. A virtual community is a community which no longer requires a physical location, but rather focuses on values and beliefs as well as the means of communication that provides the interrelationship between members of the learning community (Hiltz & Wellman, 1997, p. 45; Nguyen & Alexander, 1996, p. 105). Virtual communities have neither spatial limits nor group constraints and may be broadly based (Foster, 1997, pp. 24-25; Rheingold, 1993, p. 5).

Virtual communities, in turn, vary. Electronic mail, bulletin board systems, newsgroups, computer conference systems, multiple-user domains (MUDs), and virtual classrooms are different methods of online communication made possible by the progressive development of technology (Bromber, 1996; Healy, 1997; Lockard, 1997; Tepper, 1997). Many researchers believe virtual classrooms benefit the learning process (Denning, 1997, p. 278; McCormack & Jones, 1997; Phillips, 1998, p. 41; Schank, 1997). The virtual classroom environment, defined as both an instrumental group and a community in which students and teachers seek to accomplish their goals, is enabled by an asynchronous learning network, which is a part of a computer-mediated communication system (Hiltz & Wellman, 1997, p. 46).

Virtual classrooms present another unit of analysis for those who seek to explore the issue of virtual learning (McCormack & Jones, 1997; L. Porter, 1997). The methodology of research includes matched comparisons, pre/post-course questionnaires, direct observation, and interviews. The results of research of at least one study by Hiltz and Wellman (1997) confirm the hypothesis that command of the material and outcomes of learning in a virtual classroom were equal or superior to a traditional classroom. Students reported higher motivation and gratification of learning in virtual classes as compared to a traditional setting (p. 47).

However, it is important to acknowledge not only the advantages of the virtual learning, such as varieties of pedagogy and teaching methods, collaborative learning, active participation, increasing flexibility, interactivity, and decreasing the sense of isolation (Hiltz & Wellman, 1997, pp. 46-47; McCormack & Jones, 1997, p. 198) but also the disadvantages. The latter include limited opportunities for new friendships, lack of face-to-face communication and physical cues, non-regular meetings, synchronicity (necessity for the participants to be on-line at the same time), information overload, timing, ineffective use of unreliable computer systems (Hiltz & Wellman, 1997, p. 48; McCormack & Jones, 1997, pp. 198-200; Weinreich, 1997, on-line), and sometimes rule-breaking behavior. For example, free-riding (asking questions rather than answering, gathering information rather than distributing), lurking (reading discussions without participating), grandstanding (posting many unrelated messages), and flaming (provocative or hostile posting) all have a negative impact on learning (Kollock & Smith,

1994, on-line). Furthermore, although computer-mediated communication can provide elements of real human communication, such as sociability, emotional support, and sense of belonging, the nature of the virtual classroom still poses many organizational, conceptual, and methodological problems.

3.3 Internet Education

Some explorers seek to find solutions to the above problems in the World Wide Web's enormous potential as an educational tool (Carvin, 1996; Deden, 1998; McCormack & Jones, 1997). Andy Carvin (1996) considers the hypertext architecture of the Web, as well as its interactive character, to be critical for the roles it takes in society (p. 78). Among these roles, Carvin delineates four: The Web as Tutor; The Web as Publishing House; The Web as Forum; and The Web as Navigator. Indeed, the WWW does provide students with guides to on-line resources and enables in-depth involvement in on-line publishing. It presents a forum for discussion and a marketplace of ideas. Carvin suggests that the Web creates a new learning environment and all of its four functions contribute to creation of knowledge.

Others believe that accessibility of information on the Web by itself does not create knowledge (Contradictions, 1996, pp. 124-125; Humming, 1997, p. 73; Sunal, et. al., 1998, p. 13). Simply using the WWW to access information cannot guarantee production of knowledge. Information is not a substitute for knowledge (Nguyen & Alexander, 1996, p. 118). It is true that linking the Internet and the WWW with the learning process "gives power to students and teachers, enabling them to construct meaning from current information and integrate it into an ever-increasing body of knowledge" (Sunal, et.al., 1998, p. 14). This power, however, may be misleading as well as useless without knowledge-producing work on the part of learners. What qualities of the World Wide Web, then, are better contributing to active learning and creating knowledge as opposed to mere consuming or gathering of information widely spread over the Internet? As some observers point out, "the idea that the Internet is full of knowledge as opposed to information is false" (Contradictions, 1996, p. 126).

3.4 "Abstraction in Chaos"

Anthony Rutkowski (1997) attempts to fill the gap in scholarly understanding of the Internet as a technological phenomenon. He offers a rich mixture of insight and observation on the qualities of the Internet, viewed as a newly emerging paradigm, as well as on its technical and institutional dimensions. What Rutkowski has suggested is a new model of investigating the qualities of the Internet based on the application of the chaos theory well known to mathematicians.* Rutkowski (1997) defines the Internet as an abstraction built on top of the underlying physical components such as personal computers, access devices, and operating systems (p. 2). Furthermore, he demonstrates that multiple applications such as the World Wide Web, electronic mail, and file transfer protocol (FTP) are built on the Internet platform (p. 2). Even more so, these elements of the Internet architecture relate to each other as parts to whole.

Moreover, all these "layers of abstraction" that constitute the Internet environment have two patterns in common. First, contrary to old "top-down" information models, rooted in objective empiricist tradition, these evolve as "bottom-up" infrastructures capable of self-organization. From a constructivist perspective, the Internet structures provide a domain where ideas and concepts are created, stimulated, developed, and transmitted. Secondly, at any level ranging from global, national or regional to campus network or an individual home, the autonomous components of the Internet follow a self-replicable pattern. Finally, features such as adaptiveness, robustness, diversity, pluralism, interactivity, and self-organization make the Internet a truly unique communication medium as compared to traditional media including print, radio, and television (Hindle, 1997, pp. x-xii). Rutkowski (1997) further delineates the implications of this model by arguing that not only physical components of the Internet architecture develop in a chaos-like pattern, Internet users also do (p. 3).

As it appears from Rutkowski's (1997) model, the chaos-like and asynchronous pattern of Internet development, self-organization, and self-replicability are truly critical to the explanation of the changing nature of the relationship between people and knowledge in modern society. Also important are the Web's "superconnectivity," or non-restricted interconnections by means of computer networks (Turoff & Hiltz, 1998), continuous operation and backward compatibility (i.e., later browser versions can read earlier versions) (Connolly, 1998), decentralized decision making ("all experts are equal"), and interoperability ("all computers are equal") (Brenda, 1998). Knowledge may infinitely grow from "bottom" to "top" at any autonomous level. The Internet technology has the potential to stimulate active and continuous learning practices as well as to facilitate constant development and innovation.

---

*Compare with Nietzsche's "... one must have chaos in one, to give birth to a dancing star..." (Quoted in Nguyen & Alexander, 1996, p. 123).

4. DISCUSSION

Scholars in a variety of academic disciplines have explored how the emerging technologies including the Internet and the World Wide Web are shaping the relationship between people and knowledge in contemporary society. I suggest that these technologies are creating a significant transformation in the relationship between people and knowledge. Knowledge creation has been evaluated as a collaborative, interdisciplinary, and inquiry-based process in which people perform not only as consumers but also as producers of knowledge. Some argue that there is an evident paradigm shift toward learning and knowledge production, rather than teaching and knowledge consumption; others believe that the Internet itself is a newly emerging paradigm.

This historiography has demonstrated that there are numerous ways of how leading scientists employ traditional empiricist concepts of knowledge. The principal categories of variable factors such as knowledge, technology, and people have been defined through analyzing epistemological models grounded in empiricist theoretical framework: the knowledge pyramid, knowledge as a result of learning, and knowledge as an economic resource. These models, however, seem not to work well in investigating the ways new technologies, the Internet and the World Wide Web, affect knowledge production and need reconsidering. Although conceptual approaches that originated within traditional paradigm of research are useful in explaining the hierarchical nature of knowledge, they largely fail to integrate the unique attributes of the emerging media into analysis.

In contrast, new concepts that originated within hermeneutic empiricist theoretical framework provide an effective basis for reconsidering the ways the Internet and the World Wide Web affect knowledge dynamics. In particular, learning paradigm, computer-mediated communication, Internet education, and "abstraction in chaos" may serve as more useful conceptual frameworks for guiding future research. They integrate the unique properties of the Internet such as self-organization, self-replicability, and a chaos-like asynchronous pattern of growth, into the analysis and may be successfully applied to studying knowledge formation in contemporary society.

One interesting direction for further analysis may be the concept of knowledge work, which was left outside this discussion. Another is computer-assisted organizational learning that may become central not only to the issue of virtual learning but also to knowledge. Finally, distance learning is becoming an increasingly important educational model and a significant aspect of scholarly investigation. About two-thirds of American institutions of higher learning involving more than five million students are reported to implement some form of distance learning today (Chepesiuk, 1998, p. 52).

Yet, whatever the case, as it appears from the historiographical analysis of writings by scholars from a variety of academic disciplines, the complexity of the Internet phenomenon requires a comprehensive foundation for understanding, scrutinizing, and regulating its impact on knowledge production and consumption in contemporary society. Thus, while there has been much research on the Internet and the World Wide Web and the ways they affect the formation of knowledge, many related questions still remain unanswered. How does the concept of knowledge change in modern society? How should people reconsider the relationship between knowledge and technology? How does computer technology alter the dynamic of information-processing and knowledge generation? What further steps should be taken to utilize the Web's great educational potential? A lot of vital questions are still waiting for their researchers. This discussion suggests that a comprehensive interdisciplinary theory of knowledge is needed to provide a theoretical and methodological foundation for both present and future research on people, knowledge, and the Internet in the era of revolution in information and communication technologies.

5. REFERENCES

Bossert, P.J. (1997). Horseless classrooms and virtual learning: Reshaping our environments. *NASSP Bulletin, 81* (592), 3-15.

Brenda, M. (1998). Shaping the Internet: The dynamics. *IEEE Internet Computing, 2* (1), 87-90.

Bromber, H. (1996). Are MUDs communities? Identity, belonging, and Consciousness in Virtual Worlds. In R. Shields (Ed.), *Cultures of Internet: Virtual spaces, real histories, living bodies* (pp. 143-152). London: Sage.

Brooks, J.M. (1997). Beyond teaching and learning paradigms: Trekking into the virtual university. *Teaching Sociology, 27* (1), 1-14.

Carvin, A. (1996). More than just hype: The World Wide Web as a tool for education. *The High School Journal, 79* (2), 76-86.

Castells, M. (1996). *The rise of the network society: Vol. I. The information age: Economy, society and culture*. Malden, Mass.: Blackwell Publishers.

Chaffee, S.H., & Rogers, E.M. (Eds.). (1997). *The beginnings of communication study in America: A personal memoir by Wilbur Schramm*. Thousand Oaks: Sage Publications.

Chepesiuk, R. (1998). Internet college: The virtual classroom challenge. *American Library, 29* (3), 52-55.

Connolly, D. (1998). Dan Connolly on the architecture of the Web: Let a thousand flowers bloom. *IEEE Internet Computing, 2* (2), 22-31.

Contradictions in cyberspace: Collective response. (1996). In R. Shields (Ed.), *Cultures of Internet: Virtual spaces, real histories, living bodies* (pp. 125-132). London: Sage.

Craig, I. (Ed.). (1994). *Crossroads on the information highway. Convergence and diversity in communications technologies. Annual review of the Institute for Information Studies* (pp. 109-134). United States of America: Institute for Information Studies.

Deden, A. (1998). Computers and systemic change in higher education. *Communications of the ACM*, 41 (1), 58-63.

Denison, E. (1985). *Trends in American economic growth, 1882-1982*. Washington, D.C.: Department of Labor.

Denning, P.J. (1997). How we will learn. In P.J. Denning & R.M. Metcalfe (Ed.), *Beyond calculation: The next fifty years of computing* (pp. 267-286). New York: Copernicus, Springer-Verlag New York.

Denning, P.J., & Metcalfe, R.M. (1997). *Beyond calculation: The next fifty years of computing*. New York: Copernicus, Springer-Verlag New York.

Dutton, W.H. (Ed.). (1996). *Information and communication technologies: Visions and realities*. Oxford: Oxford University Press.

Firestone, C.M. (Ed.). (1997). *The Internet as paradigm. Annual review of the Institute for Information Studies*. United States of America: Institute for Information Studies.

Foster, D. (1997). Community and identity in the electronic village. In D. Porter (Ed.), *Internet culture* (pp. 23-38). New York, London: Routledge.

Foucault, M. (1972). *The archaeology of knowledge*. New York: Pantheon Books.

Gell, M., & Cochrane, P. (1996). Learning and education in an information society. In W.H. Dutton (Ed.), *Information and communication technologies: Visions and realities* (pp. 249-264). Oxford: Oxford University Press.

Habermas, J. (1971). *Knowledge and human interests*. Boston: Beacon Press.

Haeckel, S.H., & Nolan, R.L. (1993). The role of technology in an information age: Transforming symbols into action. In P.J. Myer (Ed.), *The Knowledge Economy: The nature of information in the 21st century. Annual review of the Institute for Information Studies* (pp. 1-24). United States of America: Institute for Information Studies.

Hamming, R.W. (1997). How to think about trends. In P.J. Denning, & R.M. Metcalfe (Eds.), *Beyond calculation: The next fifty years of computing* (pp. 65-74). New York: Copernicus, Springer-Verlag New York.

Healy, D. (1997). Cyberspace and place: The Internet as middle landscape on the electronic frontier. In D. Porter (Ed.), *Internet culture* (pp. 55-68). New York, London: Routledge.

Hiltz, S.R., & Wellman, B. (1997). Asynchronous learning networks as a virtual classroom. *Communications of the ACM, 40* (9), 44-49.

Hindle, J. (1997). The Internet as Paradigm: Phenomenon and paradox. In C.M. Firestone (Ed.), *The Internet as paradigm. Annual review of the Institute for Information Studies* (pp. v-xxi). United States of America: Institute for Information Studies.

Hunter, B. (1997). Learning in an Internetworked world. In C.M. Firestone (Ed.), *The Internet as paradigm. Annual review of the Institute for Information Studies* (pp. 103-21). United States of America: Institute for Information Studies.

Kollock, P., & Smith, M. (1994). Managing the virtual commons: Cooperation and conflict in computer communities [WWW Document]. [On-line].(8/18/98)URL: http://www.sscnet.ucla.edu/soc/csoc/papers/virtcomm/Virtcomm.htm

Kurshan, B., & Lenk, C. (1994). The technology of learning. In I. Craig, (Ed.), *Crossroads on the information highway. Convergence and diversity in communications technologies. Annual review of the Institute for Information Studies* (pp. 109-34). United States of America: Institute for Information Studies.

Leidner, D.E., & Jarvenpaa, S.L. (1995). The use of information technology to enhance management school education: A theoretical view. *MIS Quarterly*, September, 265-291.

Lockard, J. (1997). Progressive politics, electronic individualism, and the myth of virtual community. In D. Porter (Ed.), *Internet culture* (pp. 219-232). New York, London: Routledge.

Locke, J. (1974). *An essay concerning human understanding*. New York: Doubleday.

Marien, M. (1996). New communication technology: A survey of impacts and issues. *Telecommunications Policy*, 25 (5), 375-387.

Mather, M.A. (1997). Virtual learning gets real. *Technology and Learning*, 17 (5), 51.

McCormack, C., & Jones, D. (1998). *Building a Internet education system*. New York: Wiley Computer Publishing.

Melody, W.H. (1996). The strategic value of policy research in the information economy. In W.H. Dutton (Ed.), *Information and communication technologies: Visions and realities* (pp. 303-318). Oxford: Oxford University Press.

Myer, P.J. (Ed.). (1993). *The Knowledge Economy: The nature of information in the 21st century. Annual review of the Institute for Information Studies*. United States of America: Institute for Information Studies.

Nguyen, D.T., & Alexander, J. (1996). The coming of cyberspacetime and the end of polity. In R. Shields (Ed.), *Cultures of Internet: Virtual spaces, real histories, living bodies* (pp. 99-124). London: Sage.

Nietzsche, F. (1972). *Thus spoke Zarathustra*. (R.J. Hollingdale, Trans.) Harmondsworth: Penguin Books.

Phillips, V. (1998). Virtual classrooms, real education. *Nation's Business, 86* (5), 41-45.

Popper, K. (1972). *Objective knowledge*. Oxford: Clarendon Press.

Porter, D. (Ed.). (1997). *Internet culture*. New York, London: Routledge.

Porter, L.R. (1997). *Creating the virtual classroom: Distance learning with the Internet*. New York: Wiley Computer Publishing.

Rheingold, H. (1993). *The virtual community: Homesteading on the electronic frontier*. New York: Harper Collins.

Roget's II the new media thesaurus. (1980). By the editors of the American Heritage Dictionary. Boston, Mass.: Houghton Mifflin Company.

Romer, P. (1993). Economic growth. In D.R. Henderson (Ed.), *The Fortune Encyclopedia of Economics*. New York: Time Warner Books [On-line]. (8/24/98) URL: http://www.stanford.edu/~promer/Econgro.htm

Rutkowski, A.M. (1997). The Internet: An abstraction in chaos. In C.M. Firestone (Ed.). *The Internet as paradigm. Annual review of the Institute for Information Studies* (pp. 1-22). United States of America: Institute for Information Studies.

Samuels, D. (1996). The Adam Smith of the Silicon Valley. *Worth Online*,9 [On-line].(8/24/98)URL: http://www.worth.com/articles/Z9609F01.html

Schank, R. (1997). *Virtual learning: A revolutionary approach to building a highly skilled workforce*. New York, McGraw-Hill.

Shields, R. (1996). *Cultures of Internet: Virtual spaces, real histories, living bodies*. London: Sage.

Smyth, R. (1996). Students as producers: Using the World Wide Web as publishing house. *The High School Journal*, 79 (2), 87-92.

Sunal, C.S., Smith, C., Sunal, D.W., & Britt, J. (1998). Using the Internet to create meaningful instruction. *The Social Studies, 89* (1), 13-17.

Tapscott, D. (1996). *The digital economy: Promise and peril in the age of networked intelligence*. New York: McGraw-Hill.

Tepper, M. (1997). Usenet communities and the cultural politics of information. In D. Porter (Ed.), *Internet culture* (pp. 39-54). New York, London: Routledge.

Today's news. (1998). American Internet User Survey [WWW Document]. [On-line]. (2/9/98) URL: http://www.prnewswire.com:80/cgi-bin/stories.pl?ACCT=104&STORY=/www/story/1-27-98

Turoff, M., & Hiltz, S.R. (1998). Superconnectivity. *Communications of the ACM, 41* (7), 116.

Vogt, E.E. (1994). The nature of work in 2010: Convergence and the Workplace. In I. Craig (Ed.), *Crossroads on the information highway: Convergence and diversity in communication technologies* (pp. 89-108). United States of America: Institute for Information Studies.

Watters, C., Conley, M., & Alexander, C. (1998). The Digital Agora: Using technology for learning in the social sciences. *Communications of the ACM*, 41 (1), 50-57.

Webster's new encyclopedic dictionary. (1993). New York: Black Dog & Leventhal Publishers.

Weinreich, F. (1997). Establishing a point of view toward virtual communities. *CMC Magazine*, (February) [On-line]. (8/24/98) URL: http://www.december.com/cmc/mag/1997/feb/wein.html

Integration of Groupware Into a MIS Curriculum

Gail Corbitt, Ben Martz & Lauren Wright
California State University, Chico, California, USA

1. INTRODUCTION

Recently, organizations have discovered that their employees are not adept at handling the demands of an increasingly fast-paced, diverse global environment. The ability to work in groups, the capacity to integrate knowledge across several functional areas and "the ability to maintain productive user/client relationships" (Trauth, Farwell & Lee, 1993) are skills that students must have in order to meet the needs of prospective employers. Since all of these skills relate to the ability to work effectively in teams, software tools and environments that support groups and teams are playing an increasingly important role in business school curricula.

In addition to this external pressure, business schools must respond to the internal demand to include creativity (Couger, 1996) and to change their education delivery paradigm (Barr & Tagg, 1995). Couger's summary of the report, "*IS '95: Model Curriculum and Guidelines for Undergraduate Programs in Information Systems,*" notes the explicit recommendation to include the topic of creativity and innovation in a business school curriculum. Barr and Tagg discuss the gap between academia's "espoused theory" and academia's "theory in use." Methods must be found to place students in "real world - like," learning, work group environments.

One such solution is a Collaborative Student Environment (CSE). We define a CSE as a computer-augmented, group-oriented, student-based, learning environment. As a learning environment, a CSE contains structured interactions between students in addition to the traditional student and teacher interactions. For our purposes, the conceptual basis for the learning environment portion of a CSE may be found in Chickering and Gamson's *"Principles for Good Practice in Undergraduate Education"* and the AAHE's *"What Research Says About Improving Undergraduate Education."* Specifically, these position papers point to a list of characteristics for quality instruction including: active learning; assessment and prompt feedback; collaboration and integrating education with experience.

The salient component of the CSE reviewed in this paper is the use of GroupWare – a type of software geared toward enhancing the productivity of groups – within a curriculum. We believe students who have the opportunity to use this state-of-the-art technology to complete group assignments and to enhance the project team approach to learning leave the university better prepared to meet the needs of their future employers. The objective of this paper is to describe the use of GroupWare in a business school curriculum.

2. CRITICISMS OF BUSINESS SCHOOL CURRICULA

In an American Assembly of Collegiate Schools of Business (AACSB) study (Porter & McKibben, 1988), the AACSB surveyed both educators and employers and reported their findings regarding business schools and their graduates. The results indicated that there was too little emphasis in the following areas: people skills; communication skills; creative problem-solving; the importance of the external environment; the global aspects of business; and business ethics. Business schools were also criticized for focusing too heavily on quantitative analytical techniques. Another study, entitled *Five Years Out*, described the criticisms graduate students had of their MBA programs 5-10 years after graduation (Louis, 1990). The results paralleled those of the AACSB study. Five years after graduation, more than half the MBAs felt that they lacked the necessary people skills for their current jobs. Two-thirds of the graduates believed that their business school backgrounds had not prepared them for the realities of working within an organization.

An additional indication that traditional business school curricula may be inadequate to prepare the employees of the future comes from a general report issued by the US Labor Secretary's Commission (1991). This report

states that American citizens must have the following competencies to be prepared for the workplace of the future:
1. the ability to organize resources;
2. the ability to work with others;
3. the ability to acquire, evaluate and use information;
4. the ability to understand complex systems; and
5. the ability to work with a variety of technologies (including computers).

Even in disciplines where people skills may seem de-emphasized (e.g., Information Systems), prospective employers rank the need to maintain good user/client relationships first (Trauth, Farwell & Lee, 1993).

As final support of this dilemma, over the past five years the CSU Chico MINS program has conducted focus group surveys of recruiters and managers in its industry council. The council includes companies varying in size, technology-emphasis, recruiting emphasis, etc. For example, Andersen Consulting, Chevron, Cisco, Fireman's Fund Insurance Company, Foundation Health Systems, Hewlett-Packard, IBM, Intel and Visa International have all participated in these focus groups. Consistently, these recruiters and managers have rated teamwork in the top three important characteristics for a business school graduate (Table 1).

Focus group participants insisted that the definition of teamwork be based on the fundamental characteristic that individual members must work with and rely on other members of the team. This was accomplished by defining teamwork as a student's ability to function in a team where dependence on other group members to successfully complete the project is required. As can be seen in Table 1, this characteristic was ranked consistently in the top three desired exit skills – number two in 1993, number three in 1994, number one in 1996, number 2 in 1997.

Table 1. Focus Group Survey Responses
(Ranking of Desired Exit Skills in Graduates)

Desired Exit Skills	Oct 93	Nov 94	Apr 96	Apr 97
Logical Approach to Problem Solving	1	2	7	N/A
Ability to Function in a Team Where Dependence is Required	2	3	1	2
Ability to Work with a Group	3		2	
Interpersonal & Communication Skills	4/5*	1	3 tie	1
Understanding System Development Life Cycle	6	4	3 tie	N/A
Self Motivation			5	N/A
Ability to Own a Problem and Solve it			6	N/A
Leadership Skills		5		3

* identified as two different items in 93; only appeared once in 94, 96, 97.

Many business schools have responded to the complaints and concerns by changing their programs to provide more active, experiential learning opportunities for their students (Greising, 1989). This trend in business schools toward participatory, collaborative methods of instruction parallels a pervasive trend in higher education. By 1989, over 450 colleges and universities were using collaborative learning techniques (compared to approximately 100 schools in 1980). The changes may be in part a reaction to recent reports indicating that students must be actively involved and engaged to facilitate the learning process (Goodsell, Maher & Tinto, 1992; Graham, 1992; Johnson, Johnson & Smith, 1991; Light, 1992; Nicastro & Jones, 1994). Instructors are now being encouraged to adopt new teaching methods. These techniques attempt to transform students from passive receptacles to be filled with knowledge by an expert instructor into involved participants who are helping to construct their own knowledge. Some of the active learning methods used most often in business schools include: case study discussions; cooperative learning projects; simulations; group exercises plus in-class discussion; and structured controversy (conflict resolution).

The active learning techniques are not without problems. In general, the concerns center around the efficiency and effectiveness of collaborative group efforts within the class curriculum. While there is an obvious need to increase the number of group activities and to offer more opportunities for students to be actively engaged, the same barriers that plague team efforts in the workplace exist in the classroom as well. A number of authors have documented drawbacks to typical work group environments (Fox 1987; Nunamaker, et al. 1991; Shockley-Zalabak, 1991). Drawbacks that relate most directly to the classroom situation include:
1. air fragmentation - or who gets to talk first and/or next (Nunamaker, et.al., 1991);
2. interpersonal barriers like dominance, hidden agendas, conflicting goals among participants, socializing, free riding, etc. (Nunamaker, et.al., 1991; Shockley-Zalabak, 1991);
3. time-consuming activities related to getting all ideas out, offering all students the opportunity to talk, etc., all within a 50-75 minute timeframe (Fox 1987);
4. fear of negative evaluation (by classmates or the teacher), which may inhibit some students (Nunamaker, et.al., 1991).

Given the increasing emphasis on teamwork and the issues that can arise regarding group activities that are traditionally used in classrooms, the CSE provides an effective way for students to increase both their group-related learning and their in-class productivity.

3. GROUPWARE AND THE COLLABORATIVE STUDENT ENVIRONMENT

For our purposes, a Collaborative Student Environment (CSE) is defined as a computer-augmented, group-oriented, student-based, learning environment. This definition narrows the broad environment for our discussion. First, the environment is computer-augmented, meaning that computers are available for use but are not required in all situations. Second, a CSE is geared specifically toward supporting group work by incorporating the use of GroupWare. Third, the individuals are students, not experienced group members or politicos. Finally, and most importantly, the CSE is a fairly "safe" learning environment where it is not necessarily to make a mistake.

Specifically, the CSE described here is found within the College of Business at California State University, Chico. It includes a 16-person electronic meeting room, a breakout conference room, GroupSystems software, University-wide email system, listserve capability, five electronic classrooms and a student-team oriented curriculum. This means that the application of the GroupWare system stretches beyond a particular functional area (i.e., management, marketing or accounting) in this setting. For example, Money (1996) has used GroupWare in his exploration of students learning formal Structured Analysis (SA) techniques while Shepherd et. al. (1996) and others explore the interaction of GroupWare and creativity.

We have applied GroupWare to many general, group-oriented applications within the functional areas and disciplines. These applications include: electronic discussions; real-time testing, developing evaluation criteria; peer evaluation, team project definition, group writing activities; and conflict resolution. A final application is the development and delivery of an elective MIS course based on GroupWare fundamentals and group problem solving concepts.

3.1 Electronic Discussions

Class discussion is a teaching technique that is utilized in nearly all business school courses. Students discuss films, articles, books, lecture content and other discipline-specific topics. Typically the instructor has a list of questions that he or she poses to the class, to which various students respond. Usually, only the most prepared and/or the most outspoken students participate actively in the discussion. Unless the instructor is particularly skilled at drawing out the less vocal students, most class discussions are dominated by the same few students each time.

Electronic discussions help equalize the input (Benbasat & Lim, 1993; Gallupe et. al.), since every student has the same opportunity to offer ideas, opinions or criticisms. Questions can be "tossed out" for the class to discuss via Electronic Brainstorming (EBS) or Topic Commenter (TC) – two modules of the software used. EBS was designed around manual brainwriting methodologies from Osborn and Whiting (Osborn, 1953; Whiting, 1958). The fundamental concepts proposed by Osborn for group productivity have been automated. This software supports a free-flowing series of comments based around a pre-determined topic. On the other hand, Topic Commenter was patterned after a less divergent process such as 5-M method (IBM, 1989). In this problem-solving methodology, participants focus on pre-defined areas such as Money, Material, Manpower, Mechanisms, and Management. In this way, the software exposes students to many divergent and convergent group productivity methodologies such as Nominal Group Technique, Stakeholder Analysis, Delphi, etc.

The CSE adds strategically different characteristics both benefits and drawbacks to the student's learning environment. First, after starting the session, the instructor has the opportunity to become an anonymous participant and may act as an unobtrusive catalyst in the discussion. Second, because all comments are anonymous, students cannot distinguish which comments come from the teacher and which are from fellow students. This attribute of electronic discussions has two supporting advantages: it equalizes input for all involved; and it discourages students from "talking" to impress the teacher when they may not actually have much to add to the discussion. Finally, one confounding drawback is that the teacher is not aware of who participates most and has little way to assess individual students' preparation for the discussion.

3.2 Real-Time Testing

One of the more interesting GroupWare applications in the CSE is that of team-based final exams. In a team-based final exam, each student in a team of five or six is asked to complete an open ended discussion question. The questions are encoded into, and recorded by, the GroupSystems software. Each student then opens the assigned question and responds. A second pass is initiated where each student opens a second question, reads the original student response and comments. Under the guidelines of the test, the second student may agree or disagree with the original answer but must explain his or her new response. The final phase of the team-based exam asks the whole team to look at each set of original and secondary responses, and to discuss them verbally with the instructor.

Initial reactions to the team-based exams have been positive. Students get immediate feedback; not necessarily grades, but a reaction to their answers from instructors and peers. Students are provided multiple methods to communicate and relate their knowledge on a subject. The instructor now has three levels of student response by which to establish a grade: the classic historical response; a secondary critical response; and verbal interaction in the final phase. In this scenario, anonymity may be disabled if individual grades need to be assessed.

3.3   Developing Evaluation Criteria

Another use of the CSE with broad applications is student participation in determining course or project grading criteria. The list of criteria can be generated in the software tools. A comment section under each criterion is used to specify how each item can be measured and who is responsible for measurement. Once everyone understands what the criteria are and how they are assessed, students can vote on the number of points to be allocated to each item. Points can be allocated for an entire course or for a single project. For example, 100 points can be used if the evaluation criteria apply to the whole course. If points are to be allocated for a single project that is worth 25% of the course, then 25 points may be the maximum number allocated for the project. More than one vote is usually required to reduce the criteria to a manageable set since students come up with more criteria than can be accomplished within the scope of the project or course. An initial yes/no vote can be taken on the criteria to determine which items on the list can be eliminated (or two votes via allocation can be used to achieve similar results - Table 2). One interesting observation of the outcomes of this process is that students are often more harsh in their grading criteria than the teacher.

3.4   Peer Evaluation Criteria Development

Criteria for peer evaluation can also be developed in the CSE. For example, if 20 percent of the total course points are allocated to the group's performance as a whole, an additional 10 percent can be used to adjust the project grade for individual students based on peer evaluation. This adjustment is a way of recognizing that all students in a group may not participate equally and that some students in a group may have contributed substantially more than others. In this situation, students are asked to develop a list of peer evaluation criteria. Some examples of student-generated items include: willingness to participate; knowledge of the subject; actual time spent on group-related activities; ability to participate in group - related activities; and in-class presentation skills. Since students typically rate each other on these criteria, they also need to specify how performance on the criteria are measured and what percent of the total peer evaluation points each of the items is worth. This method of peer evaluation helps students be more accountable to each other and discourages students from trying to "witness" their way through a group project. For these reasons, peer evaluation should always be included in the grading criteria when group projects account for a percentage of the overall course grade. Students often push for including peer evaluation as part of a group project grade. They feel that this makes group members behave more responsibly and that the overall group grade is more fair because there is an adjustment for individual performance.

Table 2. Course Evaluation Criteria Based on Two Rounds of Voting by Allocation of 100 Points

Item	Mean	Sum of Points
First Vote:		
Exams	20.00	180
Class Discussion	15.00	135
Group Project	13.89	125
Individual Project	12.22	110
Project Presentation	10.56	95
Group Case Study	10.56	95
Report of Class Tours	9.44	85
Current Topic Presentation	5.56	50
Individual Case Study	2.78	25
Second Vote (after eliminating last 3 items and specifying exams):		
Final Exam	16.67	150
Midterm Exam	16.67	150
Individual Project	16.67	150
Group Project	16.11	145
Group Case Study	14.44	130
Class Discussion	12.22	110
Individual Presentation	7.22	65

3.5 Peer Review Process

One of the toughest aspects of any team environment, whether it is student or real-world based, is group member performance evaluations. Free-riders exist both in the real world and in the class environment. The CSE has been used to evaluate student teams. At the semester midpoint and again at the end of the semester, teams of students responded to a 17-item performance evaluation (Appendix A) encoded in the Survey tool of

GroupSystems. During the semester, team members were asked to evaluate each other and their team leader; one time using paper and pencil, and one time in an electronic environment. When compared, there was little difference in the aggregate and relative ratings given team members. No method significantly produced higher team member ratings than the other. The main difference between the methods lies in the satisfaction recorded by the team members. Seventy-two percent of the students indicate that, given the choice between manual and electronic reviews, they prefer electronic. This level of satisfaction seems to be based upon the anonymity characteristic of the software and speed of completing the review.

3.6 Student Team Project Definition

A common response to the request for additional communication skills is to include group presentations on salient topics related to the course content. The compelling question, in a Collaborative Student Environment, is "salient to whom?" Old- fashioned teaching says let the instructor decide; new learning centered education says help the students decide. To this end, the CSE has been used to help students develop a set of topics salient to the members of their class. The software facilitates the creation of a list of pertinent topics that students want to have answered or addressed by the team presenting that topic. In the example from the capstone MIS class below, one team decided on the topic "Making Money on the Internet" and the class responded by entering related questions and suggestions for the presentation. One of the main criteria for grading the presentation was how well the presenting team covered the questions.

Example "Making Money on the Internet"
- How much money can actually be made?
- Need good examples.
- Is it possible with the current state of the internet?
- Who is making this money?
- Is this for all businesses or a specific target audience?
- Do consumers trust electronic commerce enough?
- Has anyone seen INTERCASINO, internet gambling, it is run out of Canada. Talk about making big bucks.
- Shouldn't the Internet remain free?
- Aren't there commerce channels already in existence?
- What problems are there now with unethical ways of making money?
- Big Government will choke power users, it will never happen!
- How would transactions be done on the Internet? Is encryption safe?

This interchange creates a better learning environment on several levels. First, the students have participated in identifying and choosing the topics of interest for the class. This helps the teams commit to their topic as they are now aware of the stated interest by fellow students. Second, specific topical areas for teams to address are pinpointed. This helps the teams research and target their final presentations. Finally, the coverage (or lack) of the defined topic areas provides a measure for the instructor to evaluate the presentation based upon the class criteria.

3.7 Group Writing

Students in business courses are often required to turn in group papers or reports. The typical method of completing these written documents involves several steps. First, each group member is assigned responsibility for completing a different part of the paper. Each person then completes his or her part separately. Finally, someone synthesizes all the separate pieces of writing into a single document. While this process can produce a satisfactory end product, it is not truly a collaborative effort. Group members do not have the benefit of seeing what others are writing and responding to it as they work on their own parts, since each person is working in isolation. However, GroupSystems offers an electronic alternative that allows groups to truly collaborate in completing written assignments. By setting the appropriate options in the software, group members can work simultaneously on the same document. Although only one participant can work on a particular section of a document at a time, the section becomes available for others to view or edit as soon as that person is finished with the section. In this environment, group members can create a document together that reflects true collaborative work.

3.8 Team Journal

Another type of group writing used in many disciplines is the team journal. For this activity, the instructor typically enters questions related to course content in a notebook that is kept in an accessible location (e.g., a specially designated place in the library). Throughout the semester, groups are responsible for reacting to the instructor's questions and to the comments of other groups. They can also pose questions or raise issues of their own. When this technique is used, students become actively involved in exploring the course material. They also "teach" others the course material through their responses to other groups' journal entries. The team journal activity can be greatly enhanced by using Group Outliner, the hierarchical outlining function in GroupSystems that helps organize ideas into different categories. The instructor (or team members) can designate categories that correspond to separate questions or issues. New categories can be added at any time, and group members can easily access or respond to the comments in each category throughout the semester.

3.9 Groupware Course and Practice

The availability of the CSE provides the capability to introduce the conceptual foundations of GroupWare and decision support systems into the curriculum. The conceptual foundations of individual and group problem solving can be demonstrated instead of simply discussed. The course the authors have implemented is taught in two phases. The first phase introduces the students to the concepts and demonstrates those concepts with the software. The second phase requires the students (usually in two person teams) to identify, organize and facilitate at least two real meetings for a real group. The groups are usually obtained from on campus but have also included off-campus groups such as county and charitable organizations.

4. STUDENT RESPONSE

In all cases where GroupWare has been used in the CSE, feedback from students has been positive. Talkative students do not agonize over whether they are speaking too much or dominating the conversation. Less outgoing students appreciate the chance to express their opinions more easily. In experiential observations along with self-reported feedback from two case studies (Corbitt & Wright, 1997), international students report that they: are more comfortable expressing disagreement; feel they have more opportunity to participate; and can participate at their own pace. This medium ("written communication") may be more comfortable than verbal conversation, since most international students have a better command of English in written form than in conversations (especially when their American counterparts speak with an accent or faster than normal).

Students also respond positively when they are able to establish their own grading standards and course content (as described above). With respect to formal grading standards, Table 3 provides data for two separate terms of project grading criteria. Students in each of the two classes created their grading standards without any knowledge of previous grading criteria, yet the results were very similar. Nearly identical criteria and weights are developed by independent groups of students in the same class from one term to another. Thus, grading criteria remain fairly consistent from one term to the next. And since the students are usually harder on themselves than an instructor is, the grading criteria are usually comprehensive and complete.

Table 3. Two Terms of Project Grading Criteria Developed By Undergraduates

Criterion	Percent-1st Term	Percent-2nd Term
Percent Complete	15	12
Actual Costs/Benefits	4	N/A
Quality of Report	14	16
Creativity of Solution	9	N/A
Logic of Solution	N/A	11
Completeness of Report	14	13
Class Presentation	14	9
User Satisfaction	15	14
User Documentation	9	9
Difficulty of Project	N/A	5
Individual Performance	6	11

Team-based exams have created a method for instructors to triangulate a grade for a student using the historical testing methodology of question and response, plus two additional methods of critical review and verbal discussion. The CSE produces a positive impact on the sensitive area of peer performance evaluations for teams. Students are more satisfied (72% preferred) with the speed and anonymity of electronic-based evaluations than with manual evaluations.

5. LIMITATIONS OF THE CSE

The implementation of a CSE does present some challenges for the classroom environment. Briggs, Nunamaker and Sprague (1998) provide a good starting point in their "unanswered questions." For example, without removing the anonymity inherent in GroupWare product usage, it is more difficult to attribute and to assess the input of individual students in discussions and writing activities. However, this issue can be minimized if anonymous, electronic activities are not used for all class discussions or writing activities and are not the only basis for a student's final grade.

Another problem arises occasionally when students take advantage of the fact that all input is anonymous and use the medium to make lewd, sexist, or otherwise unprofessional comments. Reinig, Briggs and Nunamaker (1998) describe an electronic classroom and attempt to develop a model on the impact of "flaming." In practice, these comments are always openly discouraged by the facilitator and are eliminated from the final document that is distributed to classmates. We have found this problem is more typical in brainstorming activities with younger, student participants and has rarely been an issue with upper-division undergraduates or graduate student groups, especially if guidelines for appropriate behavior are established at the start of a session.

Finally, there is a set of limitations around the socialization issues of members in a group. In a lot of work groups, there is a need for groups to work together and "bond," not just to remain task oriented. For example, some international students reported that the electronic meetings felt too "impersonal." Technology and anonymity again may reduce the perceived ownership of the actions or plans, which in turn may lower commitment to the decisions.

6. CONCLUSION

Measuring the real effectiveness of the CSE described here is problematic. Clearly, from a research methodology perspective, McGrath's (1984) "horns of the [research] dilemma" are exposed here at their sharpest. There are few controls and multiple confounds. Any conclusions are suspect, so the researchers are left with field study observations from which to derive conjectures and hypotheses for future exploration.

Based upon our experiences, our conjectures include: 1) One of the major benefits of the CSE, in the business school environment, may be its ability to modify the traditional curriculum to better meet student and employer needs. 2) The capability of the GroupWare software to allow simultaneous and anonymous input helps create a dynamic environment where a greater amount of high-quality work can be completed than in a typical class period. 3) Students are more involved in actively constructing knowledge and creating/evaluating their own learning experiences; thus, they have the opportunity to learn in a more interesting, engaging atmosphere. 4) Since the emphasis is on team work, communication skills and creative problem solving, students who have used GroupWare in classes should be significantly better prepared to meet the demands and expectations of their future employers than those who have been exposed only to the traditional classroom environment.

In addition to the authors' observations listed here, there are surrogate "observations" demonstrated by external environments such as student demand and employer recruiting. For example, external employer recruiting measures, such as recruitment (16% increase in companies recruiting; 39% increase in job offers) and student starting salaries (MIS is 22% above non-MIS) seem to indicate more employable students. Student demand (student enrollment has increased 300% in options where the CSE is used) indicates significant interest and response. All of these observations hint at some underlying factors that may be determined further through researching these conjectures.

In summary, we believe that implementing the concepts underlying the student learning environment, and more specifically a Collaborative Student learning Environment, have helped address one of the major issues concerning business schools today – providing skilled students who can work in a team environment. Our support for this proposal is generated both with internal data and observations centered around student reported satisfaction with the peer review process and with external data and observations centered around aggregate positive input and output measures defined as program growth and employer perceived value, respectively. The exploration of the major factors contributing to this improvement is left to more formal examination of the conjectures established from these observations.

APPENDIX A: PERFORMANCE EVALUATION

Students in a Human Resource Management course as part of their performance evaluation project developed the questionnaire items below. Seventeen criteria were divided into three categories. The evaluation criteria were on a five-point scale: Clearly Outstanding, Exceeds Expectations, Meets Expectations, Below Expectations, Unacceptable.

CATEGORY / CRITERIA	DEFINITION
Job Knowledge Category	
Knowledge Of Job Related Principles And Practices:	Has sufficient knowledge, acquired through experience or training, to perform duties of the job.
Application Of Knowledge To Practical Situations:	Applies sound judgment, makes recommendations or decisions that are timely and reflect consideration of alternatives.
Understanding Of Work Relationships:	Understands the general relationship of own work activities to the activities of the primary work group, team or other teams.
Productivity Category	
Quality Of Work:	Produces work that is accurate and completed according to instructions.
Quantity Of Work:	Produces an acceptable volume of work.
Timeliness Of Work:	Completes assignments within established time limits.
Punctuality:	Includes days absent or late as basis for assessment. Note significant improvement or consistently high performance.
Organizational Skills Category	
Organization Of Work:	Schedules and plans work assignments to effectively meet job responsibilities
Adaptability:	Adjusts to changes in priorities and procedures, and normal day-to-day job demands.
Innovation:	Recommends changes to existing systems, policies and/or equipment that result in improvements.
Decision Making:	Makes a decision to meet job responsibilities by considering the pertinent facts, issues, and alternatives.
Improvement Of Job Performance:	Accepts and follows through on recommendations for improved job performance.
Communication Of Necessary Information:	Provides information regarding work progress and problems to team leader, co-workers, and other employees and teams.
Ability To Work With Others:	Cooperates with and obtains the cooperation of others to meet job responsibilities.
Oral Communication Skills:	Communicates information orally in a clear and understandable manner.
Written Communication Skills:	Communicates information in writing in a clear and understandable manner.

REFERENCES

AAHE (1996). What research says about improving undergraduate education. *AAHE Bulletin*, April 1996.

Barr, R.B., & Tagg (1995). From teaching to learning - a new paradigm for undergraduate education. *Change, November/December*, 13-25.

Benbasat, I., & Lim (1993). The effects of group, task, context and technology variables on the usefulness of group support systems: A meta analysis of experimental studies. *Small Group Research, vol. 24, 4*, 340-462.

Briggs, R.O., Nunamaker, & Sprague (1998). 1001 Unanswered research questions in GSS. *Journal of Management Information Systems, Vol. 14, No. 3*.

Chickering, A.W., & Gamson (1987). Principles for good practice in undergraduate education. *The Wingspread Journal, June.* Johnson Foundation, Inc.

Corbitt, G., & Wright, L. (1995). Lessons learned in multi-cultural settings. Paper presented at INFORMS, San Diego, May 1997.

Corbitt, G., Martz, B., & Wright, L., (1999). Addressing the challenges of the future: Implementing a collaborative student environment. *Proceedings 32nd Hawaii International Conference on Social Sciences, January.*

Couger, J.D. (1996). Creativity: Important addition to national joint undergraduate i.s. curriculum. *Journal of Computer Information Systems*, 39-41.

Fox, W.A. (1987). *Effective group problem solving.* San Francisco, CA: Jossey-Bass Publishers.

Gallupe, R.B., Bastianutti, & Cooper. Unblocking brainstorms. *Journal of Applied Psychology.*

Goodsell, A., Maher, & Tinto (1992). *Collaborative learning: A sourcebook for higher education.* University Park, PA: National Center on Postsecondary Teaching, Learning and Assessment.

Graham, E. (1992). Dewey disciple. *Wall Street Journal, September 11*, B1, B4.

Greising, D. (1989). Chicago's B-School goes touchy-feely. *Business Week, November 27*, 140.

IBM (1989). QIT effectiveness training handbook. FSD Owego, New York.

Johnson, D.W., Johnson, & Smith (1991). *Active Learning: Cooperation in the College Classroom.* Edina, MN: Interaction Book Company.

Light, R. (1992). *The Harvard Assessment Seminars: Second Report.* Cambridge, MA: Harvard University Press.

Louis, M.R. (1990). The gap in management education. *Selections: The Magazine of the Graduate Management Admissions Council, Winter*: 1-12.

McGrath, J.E., Martin, & Kulka (1984). Judgment calls in research. Sage.

Money, W.H. (1996). Applying group support systems to classroom settings: A Social Cognitive Learning Theory Exploration. *Journal of Management Information Systems, Vol. 12., No. 3.*

Nicastro, M.L., & Jones (1994). *Cooperative learning guide for marketing teaching tips for marketing instructors.* Englewood Cliffs, NJ: Prentice-Hall.

Nunamaker, J.F., Dennis, Valacich, Vogel, & George (1991). Electronic meeting systems to support group work. *Communications of the ACM, 34, (7)*, 40-61.

Osborn, A.F. (1953). *Applied imagination.* New York: Charles Scribner's and Sons.

Porter, L.W., & McKibbin (1988). *Management education and development: Drift or thrust into the 21st century?* New York, NY: McGraw-Hill.

Reinig, B.A., Briggs, & Nunamaker (1998). Flaming in the electronic classroom. *Journal of Management Information Systems, Vol. 14*, (3).

Shepherd, M.M., Briggs, R.O., Reinig, B.A., Yen, J., & Nunamaker Jr., J.F. (1996). Invoking social comparison to improve electronic brainstorming: Beyond anonymity. *Journal of Management Information Systems, 12*, 3.

Shockley-Zalabak, P. (1991). *Fundamentals of Organizational Communication*, New York, NY: Longman Publishing.

Trauth, E., Farwell, & Lee (1993). The IS expectation gap: Industry expectations versus academic preparation. *MIS Quarterly, Sept.*, 293--307.

U.S. Labor Secretary's Commission (1991). Report from the *Secretary's Commission on Receiving Necessary Skills*. Washington. D.C.

Whiting, C.S. (1958). Creative thinking. Reinhold Publishing Co., New York.

(1) GroupSystems and Electronic Brainstorming are registered trademarks of Ventana Corporation. Topic Commenter and Survey are trademark names of Ventana Corporation.

PART III

INNOVATIVE LEARNING METHODS

Innovative Business Education: 'Problem-oriented Learning' – Some Results

Nienke Bastiaans & Louk Paul
Faculty of Management and Organization, University of Groningen, Groningen, The Netherlands

1. INTRODUCTION

This article describes some of the University of Groningen Faculty of Management and Organization's experiences and results with the development and implementation of a fundamentally new Business curriculum. Firstly, we briefly describe the problems with the 'old' curriculum and the central goals for the new curriculum. Secondly, we explain the problem-oriented learning concept and describe the design of the new curriculum: what does the program actually look like? Thirdly, we report our method of designing the curriculum. After that, we describe our first experiences and results with our new program. What do students learn with regard to the educational goals? What are students' and teachers' opinions on this issue? We also pay special attention to the Faculty staff's acceptance of the new curriculum.

A central feature will be the way in which staff gradually seem to accept the new coaching role in the new curriculum. Finally, we shall pay attention to the improvements we plan to make and already are making in our innovative Business program.

At the end of 1994, the Faculty began the challenging task of developing the innovative curriculum that was finally implemented in September 1996. A number of weak points perceived in the 'old' curriculum triggered the development of a new curriculum. These weaknesses included:
- Reproduction of knowledge dominated, at the cost of application of knowledge.
- The program confronted students with design and change issues and problems too early in their study, and paid too little attention to creating a solid foundation in how to describe and diagnose organizations. Also in 1994, the Faculty did research on her Business graduates at the labor market (Van der Weele, 1994), to find out what their position was. What kind of functions do the graduates have? What requirements do they have to fulfil? From this research, more weaknesses in the curriculum appeared:

The graduates were ill-prepared for the labor market. Their teamwork skills were underdeveloped, and often, where students could choose from a vast array of electives, the Faculty was unable to help them focus sharply on their decisions. In the research, the graduates proposed to the Faculty to decrease the number of electives, towards circumscribed specialisms in functional areas.
- The study program confronted students with tactical and strategic issues too early in their study, without them having a sufficient basic knowledge of primary processes in organizations, knowledge of the shop floor and knowledge of operational activities.
- Lack of coherence and integration between disciplines and gaps and overlaps were perceived to exist between the contents of various courses and between core disciplines.

Related to this lack of integration, is the following result from this labor market research. The respondents were asked to specify the amount of disciplines which they needed in their first and in their second function.

Table 1. From Van der Weele, 1994, in % (267 questionnaires were returned for a return rate of 55%). The amount of important disciplines in 1st and 2nd function.

# important disciplines	1-2	3	4	5	6	7	8-10
1st function	9	19	23	23	13	6	5
2nd function	7	9	17	21	17	17	8

Regarding to their first function, most respondents seem to have a job in which 3-6 disciplines are important. This amount seems to increase in their second function. Above this, 84% of the respondents say the relations between disciplines is an important part of their function.

In order to address these five weaknesses mentioned before, the Faculty formulated central goals for a new curriculum. The overarching goal was to establish a closer link between business education - which is by definition regarded as multi-disciplinary (Gijselaers, 1995) - on the one hand and the needs of professional training and practice on the other hand, which is reflected in a multidisciplinary orientation of curricula (Nijhuis & Van Witteloostuijn, 1998) and thereby supplying the labor market with graduates possessing adequate professional knowledge and practical skills, including social and communicative competencies. From this goal, a number of design principles for the new curriculum were derived:

- Coherence and integration between courses and between core disciplines. According to the table derived from the labor market research mentioned before, graduates working as managers often use the combination of different disciplines (Van der Weele, 1994).

A sequential structuring of the program, in which the focus gradually shifts from a) primary processes to tactical and strategic issues, and b) from diagnosing organizations to design and change issues.

Circumscribed specialisms for students to follow.

A didactic approach which activates students and which fosters an attitude among students of owning their own learning processes, and which helps students to develop the necessary insights and skills to apply Business knowledge in a variety of situations. The last principle was made more concrete when the Faculty adopted and developed a new learning concept which was called '*problem-oriented learning*'.

2. PROBLEM-ORIENTED LEARNING

Distinctive characteristics of the new learning concept are the following.

Students work together in small teams on cases and projects, learning different skills like working together, presenting and interviewing. This is, under the condition that different skills are an integral part of the education process (Milter & Stinson, 1995).

Cases and projects stimulate students to learn how to integrate the core disciplines, with reference to Milter and Stinson (1995), saying: "learning is approached holistically rather than within the boundaries of artificial discipline-based compartments."

By means of cases and projects, students learn to apply the business knowledge provided in the literature and in supporting lectures. Cases and projects are strongly related to Management themes, so that students learn in a rich context. Like Milter and Stinson stated (1995, p. 36):

"If these are the desired learning outcomes (or, in this case, the described distinctive characteristics of the new learning concept), how do we change the educational processes to accomplish the outcomes? There is no simple solution. Certainly, we are going to have to experiment broadly and share the result of that experimentation."

Well, this article is an attempt to share some results from our Faculty experimentation. First, we will show you how our innovative program looks like. Then we will examine if Faculty really lives up to the expectations with the new learning concept. What do students learn? What is their opinion and their teachers' opinion about it? But first we will explain to you our vision on the differences between problem-oriented and problem-based learning concepts.

2.1 Differences Between Problem-Oriented and Problem-Based Learning Concepts

The 'problem-oriented' learning concept is not a completely new one. Some of the elements in this concept are comparable to elements in problem-based learning curricula. The similarities mentioned below are derived from Van Woerden (1997), who describes similarities between problem-based learning and project learning. Characteristics of project learning are the use of real life problems and the application of knowledge. The *similarities* are:
- students work independently in small teams on assignments;
- the coach guides the learning process of the team;
- during the cooperative work, the coach guides the interaction processes in the team;
- the team is in a learning environment, in which there are enough sources and materials available - or to acquire- to fulfil the task;
- the coaches themselves are part of the learning environment, in their role of 'resource person';
- the assignment needs to meet some criteria to guarantee the intended independent approach. The most important criterion is, that proper information is available -or to acquire- to fulfil the assignment. The second criteria is that the assignment is relevant for the profession.

So, there are some similarities between problem-based learning and problem-oriented learning. To get a clear picture of the concept of problem-oriented learning, we want to make a second comparison between problem-based and problem-oriented learning, to try to find some *differences*. Although there are different features of problem-based learning in different settings (Gijselaers, 1995), you can compare problem-based learning to problem-oriented learning. Some important differences between them must be mentioned.

- The first difference between many problem-based learning curricula and the new problem-oriented Business curriculum in Groningen is the amount of freedom that students have. Our problem-oriented learning concept is characterized by more pre-programming of students' activities. First and foremost, the problem-based learning curriculum requires students to choose their own literature and other learning materials (Moust, 1997); in our curriculum, the literature is completely specified. Remarkable is the fact, that according to Van Woerden (p. 197, 1997) problem-based learning gives students less freedom than project learning. He states that students in project learning can decide themselves, which knowledge and skills to use.
- Secondly, according to the 'Seven-Jump' (Moust, 1997), students in a problem-based learning curriculum, formulate their own learning objectives so that they can link these to the knowledge and insights they already possess. As Tempelaar (1998) states, since prior knowledge between students diverges, different groups will define different learning objectives. In our curriculum, the Faculty has already formulated these learning objectives; so, in contrast with a problem-based learning curriculum, the learning objectives are the same for all the students (although they can often choose the organization they want to go to or the kind of project they want to do).
- The third difference between many problem-based learning curricula and the new Business curriculum in Groningen, consists of the kind of goals that are targeted. In the most problem-based learning curricula, the major concern and starting point for students in the learning process is the *acquisition of knowledge by students* (Delhoofen, 1996). Whereas the *use of knowledge by students in the newly formulated projects* is more important and the starting point on which students are taken into account for, for the problem-oriented Business curriculum. This is related to the former described difference, that students in a problem-based learning curriculum formulate their own learning objectives, while in the problem-oriented curriculum learning objectives are already formulated by the Faculty. In this curriculum, students are expected to already studied the literature before coming together; in a problem-based program step 5 'Formulate learning objectives' from the 'Seven-Jump' (see table 2) forms the starting point for study-activities (Moust, 1997).

Table 2. The "Seven-Jump" (Gijselaers, 1995)

The "Seven Jump"	
Step 1	Clarify terms and concepts not readily comprehensible
Step 2	Define the problem
Step 3	Analyze the problem
Step 4	Draw up an inventory of the explanations discussed in step 3
Step 5	Formulate learning objectives
Step 6	Collect additional information outside the group
Step 7	Synthesize and test the newly acquired information

- A fourth difference between problem-based and problem-oriented learning is the kind of problems that are used. The problems in the PBL-concept are most of the time formulated in a short way; often they do not contain very rich, diverse information. The problems in the problem-oriented concept are real life problems. They often contain cases with all kind of data. This difference is related to the difference is goals that are targeted. The 'problem-based problem' is meant to conduct students to acquire new knowledge; while the 'problem-oriented problem' is meant to conduct students to apply already learned knowledge.

One reason for choosing for a somewhat more pre-programmed curriculum is that one of the central goals, integration between courses and between core disciplines, can be realized more easily and with more depth. A conceivable disadvantage can be, that not only literature and learning objectives are pre-programmed but also, in a manner that can be perhaps too narrow, that the outcome of analyses and the design tasks that students have to fulfil can be also too restrictive; the 'find-the-one-and-only-one-answer' syndrome. This is something the Faculty wants to prevent. Later on in this article, we will examine if this disadvantage of restrictiveness is realistic and if students do realize the aimed integration. We think, our task is to develop students to be critical and creative human beings instead of people who are searching for one specific correct answer which, in an organizational world, often does not exist.

3. WHAT DOES THE PROGRAMME LOOK LIKE?

The new curriculum lasts 4 years. Each year is divided into 3 trimesters, each of 14 weeks. The problem-oriented learning concept is introduced in the first two years of the program and in the first trimester of the third year. In practice, students work together in teams of 12 on cases and projects. They receive support from their tutor, who is their coach and examiner, and (from the second year onwards) also an expert in one of the core disciplines in the program. Like in problem-based learning curricula, in comparison to more traditional programs, the role of the teacher is different in this learning concept (Gijselaers, 1995). Instead of the omniscient expert, the teacher has to fulfil the role of a 'coach' who coaches the learning process of the students while they are working on their projects.

About 40% of the curriculum is developed according to the problem-oriented concept, consisting of assignments and projects. The other 60% is offered in the more traditional way, with only lectures and self study activities. However, a strong coherence has been created between this more traditional part and the problem-oriented part; to be able to fulfil their projects, students have to apply knowledge from traditionally organized courses. Regarding the way students approach their study, we aim to have students gradually develop their skills in organizing their study independently. This is reflected in a shift in the design of projects across the various trimesters; they change from short-term assignments to long-term projects. In the first year, an assignment may take only a few days. At this stage, the emphasis is on helping students to learn how to be responsible for and how to 'manage' their own learning process. From the second year onwards, projects last longer, sometimes even one complete trimester.

Table 3. Example of a first year assignment

First trimester, assignment in week 2, 1998-1999
Goal
The most important goal of this week is to learn how to describe organizations using concepts which are widespread in Organizational Theory. We would like you to use this weeks literature.
Literature and other materials
• Paul, J.C.L. et al. Organisatie en Gedrag [Organization and Behavior], Chapter 2.
• Other prescribed material
• Case of Firm Teeninga
• Fragments of Kasta (CD-ROM). You can see them via the Website: http://www.bdk.rug.nl/bio/bio1/
Assignment
Describe the formal organization structure of the Kasta organization and the Firm Teeninga. Compare the organic structures of the Kasta organization and the Firm Teeninga and try to give an explanation for the differences and similarities you found. Use relevant concepts form the literature you had to study for today.
Compare the organic structures of the different parts of the organization from Firm Teeninga with each other and try to explain the differences and similarities.
Describe the factual structure from the Firm Teeninga. Which differences do you see between the factual and organic structure?
What does it mean for an organization advisor to know the organization structures of a certain organization?
From: Studiehandleiding (like a blockbook) first trimester 1998-1999, Faculty of Management & Organization, University of Groningen.

Table 4. Example of a second year project

First trimester second year, long term project 1997-1998
The integrating issue in this trimester is the 'Market report'. In this report, research is done on the possibilities of introducing a new product into the market. The new product is deodorant. To write the Market report, you have to make 5 intermediary products which will be assessed. You work together in this trimester in groups of three students. The intermediary products are: • Operationalisation of the terms • Environment analyses • Questionnaire • Data-analyses • Productdesign We expect to get these intermediary products on specified dates. *From: Studiehandleiding (like a blockbook) fourth trimester 1997-1998, Faculty of Management & Organization, University of Groningen.*

For students, it is essential to have co-operation in order to fulfil the projects. In this way, supported by training, students develop social and communicative skills. In their 'offices', students have their own meetings, led by a student chairman and a student secretary whose functions rotate. During meetings, students discuss issues like their project assignment, literature, their project planning and their division of tasks. They also have to present their results verbally to their coach.

First-year projects are primarily aimed at gaining a thorough business knowledge at the level of operating processes. Students often have to visit an organization and subsequently describe its primary processes. The knowledge that students need to apply in order to carry out the projects is introduced in lectures and literature. From the second year onwards, functional Business areas are central. In second-year projects, students need to apply this knowledge in an integrated way.

In the third and fourth year, students are confronted with strategic and tactical problems. In order to realize depth in the curriculum, students are stimulated to use the knowledge they have learned in the first two years. This is especially the case in the 'Management Game', in which students have to simulate an organization.

A new organization structure

The Faculty not only changed the content and learning concept, but also the organization structure (see also section 5, about the staff's acceptance). This new structure was implemented to realize coherence and integration between the courses provided and between the core disciplines.

A typical feature of the new structure is the implementation of 'trimester managers'. This type of manager co-ordinates the teachers and the operational processes within one trimester; he or she is also the chairperson at the meetings of the trimester development team (see also section 4). This team consists of teachers who are responsible for the courses. The trimester manager is responsible for the integration between the courses in the trimester. Each trimester manager is a member of the 'Education committee', which is chaired by a director who is responsible for the quality of the program. This committee monitors the lines of the curriculum in the program and the coherence between the trimesters.

4. DESIGNING THE PROGRAM

The design and implementation of the new business program can be characterized as a 'snowball method'. The development started with a small group of key persons, which was regularly extended when new groups of staff got involved at different stages. In this way, we realized a growing support among staff for the new program. This is not to say that acceptance among staff could be taken for granted. In a later section we shall dwell upon various factors which affected the process of growing acceptance.

In more concrete terms, the 'snowball method' we adopted in designing the new program started with the establishment of a small committee consisting of a selected group of full professors. They developed a prototype of the new program (Faculty of Management and Organization, 1995). Components of this prototype report included the goals to be achieved by means of the new curriculum, the problem-oriented learning concept, the courses and the new specialisms for students to follow. After the report had been finalized, the committee handed over the practical development of every trimester to a trimester development team. Each team was commissioned to develop a complete trimester with student projects, lectures, blockbooks and literature. Each team consisted of teachers from different disciplines, in order to stimulate the development of integrated education. In this way, every time a trimester had to be developed, other members of the Faculty were involved in the curriculum development. Each time the operational design of a trimester was completed, all other members of the Faculty received a short report stating the most important issues.

Three months before the start of each trimester, the Faculty organized workshops in which the 'coaches' became involved in the new program. These coaches were invited to give their opinion about the new program first of all. Discussions in workshops sometimes led to modifications in the program. Secondly, the coaches received more detailed information about the content of the new program, and thirdly, the coaches were trained in their new role.

5. EXPERIENCES AND RESULTS WITH THE NEW PROGRAMME

The design and implementation of a 'problem-oriented' Business program is challenging. Faculty members from different disciplines have to work together to develop an integrated program. For most of these developers, working together in an interdisciplinary team is a very positive experience in which they learn a lot from each other. In addition, as we will see in section 5.2, many of the coaches are positive about their new role as a coach of a team of students, although there are also coaches who prefer to cling on to their old role of lecturer, presenting their own expertise (see also section 6, on the staff's acceptance).

The Faculty has just started doing research on students' and teachers' opinions on the new program. As promised earlier, we will examine in this section if Faculty really lives up to the expectations with the new problem-oriented learning concept (see section 2). To find out, we developed one questionnaire for teachers, acting as coaches and one for the students, who take part in the new program. All the teachers and students from the first trimester of the first year in 1998-1999 received a questionnaire. Both of them were filled out anonymously; 30 were returned by the teachers for a return rate of 81%; 393 were returned by the students for a return rate of 87%. The students' questionnaire had 5 answer categories: entirely disagree, disagree, agree, entirely agree, not applicable. The teachers questionnaire consisted of the five-point Likert scale, ranging from entirely agree to entirely disagree. Both questionnaires consisted of questions about the realization of the educational objectives with the new program in general and questions about student teamwork more specific. What is the opinion of students and teachers about the new program? Do we reach the objectives? What is their opinion about the teamwork?

5.1 Students' Opinions

What opinion do students in the first trimester have concerning the teamwork in the new Business program?

Table 5. Students' opinions concerning teamwork (first trimester)

Question	% agree	% disagree	% not applicable
Team Meetings Productive?	78	16	4
Team Meetings Useful?	75	19	5
Team Meetings useful for written exam?	42	52	7

Innovative business education

What opinion do these students have concerning to what extent the educational objectives are reached?

Table 6. Students' opinions concerning to what degree educational objectives are reached (first trimester)

Question	% agree	% disagree	% not applicable
Assignments challenging	53	41	6
Learn to Apply Knowledge	80	16	4
Learn Interrelationships courses	67	28	5
Better Picture of being a Manager	76	19	4
Enthusiasm increased for Business	67	29	4
Overall Opinion for Business Program	68 (good/enough)	30 (bad)	2

5.1.1 Interpretation

The students indicate that concerning the aspect of learning to work together, the team meetings were useful (75%) and productive (78%). Besides, they learned how to apply knowledge (80%) and to see interrelationships between courses (67%). They also got a better picture of what it really means, being a manager (76%). The overall opinion about the new program is positive for 68% of the respondents. The enthusiasm for studying Business did not increase for 29% of the respondents. This probably occurred because part of the group is going to attend another program, namely the technical variant of the general Business program. The group meetings were not useful for 52% of the students for their preparation of their written exams. This is probably caused by the fact, that in the written exam students are asked questions about their insight in the courses, not the extend to which they can apply Business knowledge. Students filled in the questionnaire before the oral exams, so there was no question considering the usefulness of the team meetings for preparing the oral exams, in which students are assessed on applying knowledge.

Astonishing is the percentage of students in the first trimester saying the assignments were *not challenging (41%)*. This is probably related to the amount of freedom students have and, coherent with this, to two of the differences between problem-based curricula and this problem-oriented curriculum. Namely, the way the assignments and projects are designed in this problem-oriented curriculum is characterized by the learning objectives already formulated for the students and by the literature already prescribed for the students (see section 2).

The third difference mentioned before, consists of the kind of goals that are targeted with problem-oriented learning. The 'use of knowledge by students' seems to be more important and the starting point for the students within this concept. According to the students, 80% say they learned to apply knowledge. So, there seem to be no negative sounds according to this third difference.

5.2 Teachers' Opinions

What opinion do the teachers from the first trimester have concerning the teamwork from students in the new Business program?

Table 7. Teachers' opinions concerning students' teamwork (first trimester)

Question	% agree	% neutral	% disagree
Students Discussed Literature in Useful way	25	32	43
Students Structured Meetings well	64	18	18
Discussion regarding Assignments was Useful	75	18	7
Students made a Motivated Impression	72	24	3
Students sticked to Agreements	83	17	0
Students learned well to Work together	82	18	0
Students studied Literature Enough before a Meeting	54	25	21

What opinion do these teachers from the first trimester have concerning to what extent the educational objectives are reached?

Table 8. Teachers' opinions concerning the degree in which educational objectives are reached (first trimester)

Question	% agree	% neutral	% disagree
In assignment results the Integration was realized Well	65	15	20
Assignment results are a good Indicator for Understanding courses	70	11	19
Students could Apply literature well	31	45	24
Assignments were of good Quality	57	32	11
Assessment Discriminates enough between students	82	11	7
Assessment is good Predictor for rest study	35	35	31
All students Contributed enough to assignments	78	11	11

5.2.1 Interpretation

The teachers, working as a coach, indicate that concerning the aspect of learning to work together, the students in the first trimester learned to work together well (82% of the teachers). Students structure meetings well (64%), they discuss in a useful way about the assignments (75%), they sticked to agreements (83%) and made a motivated impression (72%). Remarkable is the fact, that 43% of the teachers indicate that students do not discuss literature in a useful way. 54% of them indicate, that students do study literature before the meetings, while almost half of them (45%) is neutral about students applying literature (24% in negative and 31 % is positive). Maybe the way students study the literature is less thorough.

So, teachers seem to be less satisfied about the extent to which students meet one of the central goals, namely application of knowledge. The teachers are more satisfied about the other central goal, namely the way students integrate between the different courses in the first trimester.

5.2.2 Student performances

With the start of the new program in September 1996, student performances improved considerably (table 9). In the old program, only about 10% of the students finished their first year in one year. In the first (1996) and second year (1997) in which the new program was implemented, the student performances were three times better. However, we need to be careful with these data; they mean nothing with regard to educational goals concerning content.

Table 9. Student performances in new program, compared to old program

Cohort	% of students who finish 1st year in 1 year
1993	8
1994	11
1995	10
1996	30 (new program)
1997	30 (new program)

6. STAFF'S ACCEPTANCE

As mentioned, this section will briefly address the question of the Faculty Staff's acceptance of the new curriculum. A central issue is the way in which the staff gradually seem to accept their new coaching role in the newly formulated projects. Two things should be made clear in advance. First, although the 'snowball-method' succeeded in fostering commitment among those who had been involved in any of the development and design phases, the majority of staff had still been onlookers when the actual implementation was at hand. Second, regarding all these staff members, at some point in time a Faculty policy had been formulated which stated that virtually all

Staff members were supposed to participate in any one of the first seven trimesters of the new program, in a new coaching role. This new teaching obligation, which, for many, was surrounded by insecurities, was the watermark of the new curriculum. Acceptance or rejection of the new curriculum hinged upon favorable acceptance of the projects.

In order to describe our experiences in this respect, a number of issues that heavily influenced the process of acceptance should be elucidated. The first concerns the time factor. Due to external pressures, the organization was forced to quicken its pace of renewal considerably. The implementation of the new plans was accelerated by one year. This put an enormous strain on the organization, especially on the first-trimester's development team, since its development time was reduced from nearly one-and-a-half years to nearly six months. This left little time - next to the pure and simple development of course material and so on - for getting the future coaches on board. In the meantime, the allocation of members of staff across the various trimesters was only decided upon when the development was well underway. All in all, it turned out that getting people aboard in this context could be little more than 'tell and sell'. The occasions to do that were, firstly, during a voluntary plenary meeting of all staff (not well addressed), and secondly, during the training of the elected coaches 'in trimester batches' for their new roles. During this training, the staff were familiarized with, on the one hand, the content of the new program which, due to the tight time-frame had only partially been finished, and, on the other, the novel coaching role and its accompanying style which was intended to replace the traditional teacher's role.

A second factor that is worth mentioning concerns the Faculty's varied organizational-cultural make-up which in recent years had been showing a gradual widening of inter-unit differentiation. This development was triggered a few years ago. At that time, an adjoining higher organizational layer, made up by sections each of which consisted of several units, was abandoned. Since then, the organization consisted of a wide variety of units each harboring different disciplines, no longer held together at an intermediate level. Across these units, attitudes towards the new program and, of course, especially towards its most prominent, problem-oriented course elements, varied. This could eventually mean, for instance, that one of our trimester's staff population would be heavily dominated by members of one particular unit whose attitudes were rather negative. At the same time, the staff who were elected to act as coaches in another trimester comprised a cohesive and positively motivated group.

Notwithstanding these differences, a commonly felt issue was the question involving the extent to which the new demands on staff were at variance with professional development and status. Especially the first-year projects, in which the bulk of Faculty staff were supposed to act in their new roles, tended to stress a learning-process oriented role instead of a role in which staff could depend on disciplinary know-how. On top of that, as far as helping the students was relevant with respect to the course content, the staff were supposed to invest some of their time to acquaint themselves with the basics of different disciplines in order to provide this help.

A fourth ingredient in the change process to be mentioned concerns aspects of the general Faculty context, especially the fact that staff members are exposed to varied and sometimes conflicting organizational demands. The new assignment of coaching students was only one of these. Other demands were, for instance, to deliver a certain amount of research output, the involvement in one or more other courses (sometimes courses in a totally different curriculum provided by the same Faculty), or management tasks. As to the research output demands, during the introduction of the new curriculum, policies regarding staff assessment and advancement were sharpened.

Another element of the Faculty's context has already been mentioned - the broad range of disciplines that are present in the composition of the staff. Different scientific disciplines each nurture their own theories and their own flavor of scientific and teaching methods. This made one group of colleagues more susceptible to innovation than the other.

Now, taking the present situation at the Faculty and provisionally trying to draw up a balance of what has been reached, we can conclude that time heals many wounds. At the start of the implementation of the new curriculum in September 1996, trimester-development teams had to operate in a situation in which resistance to change varied across staff. Now it seems that with time, experience with the new teaching role has lessened the insecurities initially felt. However, some resistance remains and the renewal has not yet been institutionalized completely.

7. IMPROVEMENTS TO MAKE

There are some issues that can be improved. First and foremost, improvements can be made in the further design of the new program. One point is the nature the projects and assignments have. The projects and assignments need to be changed into more challenging projects, in which students have more freedom and are more responsible for their own learning process. In this respect, the Faculty should consider the option, in which students can formulate their own learning objectives and choose their own literature. This will lead to more freedom and more challenge; but the Faculty should take into account the possibility, that other learning goals will be reached than the Faculty has in mind. The short-term assignments need to change towards long-term projects, in which students also have more freedom to plan and divide tasks, etceteras.

Another point for improvement is related to the central curriculum goals 'integration of disciplines' and 'application of knowledge'. The demands, placed on the Business students, with regard to the projects need to be increased concerning content.

Furthermore, at this moment the systems for monitoring and evaluating our performance have not yet been fully developed and need to be fine-tuned to our new educational goals. For instance, monitoring the performance of our new coaches is vital for assessing our problem-oriented program. On the other hand, having trimester teams designing trimester content has led to a formalization of this program level in the organizational structure. Formally appointed trimester managers have recently come into function. They have turned out to be capable of playing a vital role in monitoring their trimester. At this moment, we aim to assign them an important task in the system of monitoring, evaluation and quality improvement of our education.

Improvements can be made in the staff's acceptance. From a management perspective, with hindsight and in a tentative manner, at least two demands on management can be formulated. The *first* one has to do with the management of context. Given the diversity of the Faculty's context, and the sometimes contradictory stimuli this context provides, careful policymaking and signaling of how different demands are to be met are important factors in fostering acceptance. Often this turns out to be a difficult balancing act.

The *second* demand on management, less general of character, has to do with the nature of the staff allocation across projects which was decided upon. Especially in the first-year trimesters, this was more or less a division of staff, across the board, across trimesters - more informed by pure capacity considerations than by consideration of matching a trimester's subject matter to the staff's relevant disciplinary skills. The selection of coaches in the second year was based far more on a careful selection of an appropriate set of skills and know-how. Now, we see that the level of acceptance, or even enthusiasm, differs greatly between the two years; second-year coaches have become involved and enthusiastic teachers.

8. CONCLUSIONS

The development and implementation of the innovative Business program at the University of Groningen was challenging. Faculty members from different disciplines have to work together to develop an integrated program. For most of these developers, working together in an interdisciplinary team is a very positive experience in which you *learn a lot from each other*. We 'are going to have to experiment broadly and share some results' (that is: learn from each other), is what Milter and Stinson wrote in 1995 (p. 36). Well, this article is an attempt to share and learn with others from some results from our Faculty experimentation.

There seem to be some differences between our problem-oriented curriculum and the better known problem-based curricula. The differences have to do with the amount of freedom students have in the program. In the problem-based programs, students formulate their own learning objectives and choose their own literature. In our program this is more restricted and therefore, prescribed. Also, the application of knowledge is more important and the starting point for students in their learning process in the problem-oriented approach, whereas the acquisition of knowledge is the major concern and starting point in the problem-based curricula.

The Faculty did research on students' and teachers' opinions about the new curriculum. What did students learn from the new curriculum, according to both of them? Both students and teachers say students learned specific skills in working together in a team, which is one of the central goals of the new program. The team meetings were useful, students discussed in a useful way, they sticked to agreements and made a motivated impression. Teachers seem to be less satisfied than students about the extent to which students meet one of the central goals, namely application of knowledge. The teachers, like the students, are more satisfied about the other central goal, namely the way students integrate between different disciplines.

Astonishing is the percentage of students saying the assignments were not challenging. The Faculty wants to improve this, by giving students more freedom and more responsibility for their own learning process. How this will take place, needs to be reconsidered: does more freedom mean, students formulate their own learning objectives? What happens to the learning objectives the Faculty wants to reach?

Because much of the pressure for educational change has recently come from stakeholders other than the Faculty, it is easy to forget that curriculum innovation is the primary responsibility of the faculty. The process of curriculum change must start with significant faculty involvement, or it will not get far (Boyatzis, Cowen & Kolb, 1995). Faculty involvement in our organization is realized by using the 'snowball method'. The development started with a small group of key persons, which was regularly extended when new groups of staff got involved at different stages (section 4). But still, improvements can be made in the staff's acceptance. From a management perspective, at least two demands on management can be formulated. Given the diversity of the Faculty's context, careful policymaking and signaling of how different demands are to be met are important factors in fostering acceptance. The second demand on management has to do with the nature of staff allocation. Especially in the first year, this was more or less a division of staff, informed by pure capacity considerations than by consideration of matching a trimester's subject matter to the staff's relevant disciplinary skills. The selection of coaches in the second year was based far more on a careful selection of an appropriate set of skills and know-how. Now, we see that the level of acceptance, or even enthusiasm, differs greatly between the two years; second-year coaches have become involved and enthusiastic teachers.

REFERENCES

Bastiaans, N. (1999). *Probleemgeoriënteerd onderwijs: De nieuwe rol van docenten.* [Problem-oriented learning: The new role of teachers]. Paper presented at national conference in Enschede.

Boyatzis, R.E., Cowen S.C., & Kolb, D.A. (Eds.). (1995). *Innovation in professional education. Steps on a journey from teaching to learning.* San Francisco: Jossey-Bass Publishers.

Faculty of Management and Organization (1995). *Prototyperapport.* Rijksuniversiteit Groningen.

Delhoofen, P. (1996). *De student centraal. Handboek zelfgestuurd onderwijs.* [The student central. Handbook on self directed learning]. Groningen: Wolters-Noordhoff.

Gijselaers, W.H. (1995). Perspectives on problem-based learning. In W.H. Gijselaers, D.T. Tempelaar, P.K. Keizer, J.M. Blommaert, E.M. Bernard, & H. Kasper (Eds.), *Educational innovation in economics and business administration: The case of problem-based learning* (pp. 39-52). Dordrecht: Kluwer Academic Publishers.

Milter, R.G., & J.E. Stinson (1995). Educating leaders for the new competitive environment. In W.H. Gijselaers, D.T. Tempelaar, P.K. Keizer, J.M. Blommaert, E.M. Bernard, & H. Kasper (Eds.), *Educational innovation in economics and business administration: The case of problem-based learning* (pp. 30-38). Dordrecht: Kluwer Academic Publishers.

Moust, J.H.C. (1997). *Probleemgestuurd leren.* [Problem-based learning]. Groningen: Wolters-Noordhoff.

Tempelaar, D.T. (1998). Congruence of assessment and instructional system: The case of problem-based learning. In D.T. Tempelaar, F. Wiedersheim-Paul, & E. Gunnarsson (Eds.), *Educational innovation in economics and business administration II: In search of quality* (pp. 197-211). Dordrecht: Kluwer Academic Publishers.

Weele, van der, A. (1994). *Bedrijfskundigen op de arbeidsmarkt* [Business graduates on the labor market]. Rijksuniversiteit Groningen, Centrum voor Onderzoek van het Wetenschappelijk Onderwijs.

Woerden, van, W. (1997). De ontwikkeling van activerend onderwijs: Probleemgestuurd leren en Projectonderwijs [The development of activating education: Problem-based learning and Project learning]. In G.T. ten Dam , J.F.M.J. van Hout, C. Terlouw, & J. Willems. *Onderwijskunde hoger onderwijs. Handboek voor docenten.* (pp. 186-213). Van Gorcum, Assen.

Competitions and Problem-Based Learning: The Effect of an Externally Set Competition on a Cross-Curricular Project in Marketing and Design

Frances Brassington[1] & Alan Smith[2]
[1]*The Business School, Buckinghamshire Chilterns University College, UK,* [2]*School of Business and Management, University of Teesside, Middlesbrough, UK*

1. INTRODUCTION

This paper discusses the further development of a problem-based learning (PBL) project undertaken at the University of Teesside in 1998. The project brings together undergraduate students from the faculties of business and design and requires them to work together in the roles of client and consultant respectively. Thus groups of business students, all majoring in marketing, develop a new product and then negotiate with and commission a group of design students to produce the design work to fulfil their requirements. The project has run for one semester every year since 1992 using briefs developed jointly by the design and marketing staff, ensuring that learning and assessment objectives are met for both design and marketing students. The student feedback has always been very positive, justifying the time and effort put into the project by the co-ordinating staff. The rationale behind developing such a project in the first place, the benefits derived from it for all parties concerned, and the evolution of the project over the years are all discussed in Brassington and Smith (1997).

In 1998, it was decided to develop the nature of the project further by adding an external element to it. The project brief was, therefore, based upon a competition set by the UK's Institute of Direct Marketing (IDM). The objective of this paper is to examine how involvement in an external competition had affected:

- project design and academic objectives,
- interaction between the marketing and design students, and
- student motivation within the project.

These issues will be examined within the context of PBL philosophy. The following section, therefore, presents a brief literature review establishing the importance of PBL as a means of preparing students for complex problems in the real world. Then, the operational detail of the design and implementation of the competition-centered PBL exercise are described. Section 4 presents and analyses feedback from students, staff and the IDM which provides a foundation for conclusions on the extent to which the inclusion of the external element in the project was successful. This experience will also provide further insights into comments drawn from the literature.

2. PBL CONTEXT

PBL is a well established technique (see, for example, Boud & Feletti, 1991) which is especially relevant to undergraduate business education. Chaharbaghi and Cox (1995) discuss work by Perry (1970) which defines the way in which undergraduates' thinking develops along a nine-point scale during degree studies. They concluded that as a result of 'traditional' teaching methods, many graduates do not even get half-way along the scale, that is to a point where knowledge is considered to be relativistic and contextual. This means that when graduates go into industry, they find it difficult to cope with real problems requiring more than just knowledge for their solution. Clearly, this is a problem for employers. Gilbert and Guerrier (1997), for example, investigated the perceptions of managers in the hospitality trade. The managers interviewed felt that graduates coming into the industry had had too theoretical an education and thus needed more exposure to practical problem-solving. Moves towards PBL approaches within hospitality courses were thus welcomed by the trade. As Chaharbaghi and Cox (1995) conclude, therefore:

"... it is crucial to incorporate active-learning processes directed towards solving life-like problems."

It is, however, not that easy for academic staff to design mechanisms for delivering these active-learning processes to inexperienced students. Nevertheless, as pressure increases upon educators to provide more 'vocationally-relevant' courses, producing graduates who can deal with complex problems, the importance of PBL becomes clearer in delivering two of Norman's (1994) learning strategies: *Skill development* and *Conceptual Development*. As Guzdial *et al* (1996) point out:

> "A hard problem, addressed with support for successfully solving the problem and for reflecting on the problem, will lead to deep, transferable knowledge and skills. ... Authentic problems, problems that are real, that might arise in a student's [professional] life ... have enormous potential for learning."

Although Guzdial *et al* are talking about engineering, regardless of the subject area these "deep, transferable knowledge and skills" are valued by potential employers. Employers also value an employee's ability to work in teams. There is thus an important role for group work within PBL situations. Guzdial *et al* (1996) feel that groups can tackle much more complex and interesting problems that individuals can alone.

Indeed, given the pressures of work on final year students in particular, academic staff see group work as being an essential tool if large-scale, integrative tasks are to be set. Group work has other, educationally challenging benefits too, of course. The authors of this paper have found that students have to:
- articulate their ideas
- persuade others to accept those ideas and/or ...
- ... learn to evaluate and accept the ideas of others objectively and to compromise when necessary
- plan and manage tasks as a group with respect to deadlines
- plan and manage tasks as a group with respect to the efficient use of everyone's time and skills, while ensuring that it is all done towards the final goal
- plan and manage tasks as a group with respect to a fair contribution from everyone, motivating the lazy, developing the weak, capitalizing on strengths
- co-ordinate all this work to create a seamless final report or whatever is required.

Chaharbaghi and Cox (1995) in describing a PBL course in manufacturing summarize the importance of group work thus:

"The introduction of peer groups lies at the heart of the learning process enabling the group members to share their knowledge and experiences as well as negotiating and making sense of new ideas."

Guzdial *et al* (1996) go further than this by talking about 'synchronous and asynchronous collaboration'. The former requires the group to work together, brainstorming, planning and allocating tasks, whereas the latter is more reflective, collaborating after the task is completed to complete the group's learning process. They see it as a simple equation:

Complex problem-solving + Reflection = Learning.

The idea of action-reflection (Schon, 1983; 1987) within post-experience management education (Lowenthal, 1986; Dixon, 1990; Marsick et al., 1992; Robinson and Wick, 1992; Small and Cullen, 1995) is accepted. Managers can take their own, real experience and analyze, or reflect upon it perhaps within the context of a theoretical framework or comparing it with other professionals' experiences or reactions. With undergraduate students, however, there is little or no significant professional experience and the kind of problems that PBL throws at them, even if they are taken from real situations, are bound to regarded as somewhat hypothetical[12]. This makes it somewhat likely, therefore, that the initial focus of any reflection will mainly be on the *process* that the students have been through (how the group worked together, how tasks were allocated, how time was managed, what sources were used etc.) rather than on the *content* or on *professional* issues. Nevertheless, with adequate support (as recommended by Savery & Duffy, 1994), an appreciation of both the practical professional and theoretical implications of what has been done does come (Brassington and Smith, 1997).

The following section discusses the design and implementation of the project taking into consideration these issues of preparation for the real world, the role of group work and the importance of encouraging reflection as well as activity.

---

[12] Assignments at both the University of Teesside and Buckinghamshire Chilterns University College requiring students to act as consultants in real small businesses prove that PBL can be made extremely 3-dimensional for undergraduates. Such exercises, however, are fairly difficult to set up and can only work well with small groups of students.

3. PROJECT IMPLEMENTATION

Staff were faced with a number of issues in designing, implementing and running the project, each of which will now be discussed.

3.1 The Competitive Brief

Staff have been running a cross-curricular project for several years using a PBL approach (see Brassington and Smith, 1997) using briefs designed by the staff. There was thus initial concern about whether the IDM competition brief was suitable. Could it be adapted to the project? Was the problem sufficiently 'messy'? Would the integrity of the project be enhanced or compromised by the brief? Could the competition's timescale be fitted within the time available for the project? After discussion, staff decided that the nature of the brief offered by the competition could fit the academic needs of both sets of students and would provide a challenging PBL project. In terms of the timing, it was decided that although the IDM's timescale was tight, there would be sufficient time for students to work on the problem, be assessed, and send their project reports to the IDM by the competition's closing date.

The essence of the IDM's brief was to launch a customer benefits card for BMW GB using direct marketing. The brief did not, however, specify the type of card (i.e. whether it would be a loyalty card, credit card or affinity card), nor did it define the kind of technology to be used, for example a smart card or a swipe card. A further constraint imposed by the IDM was that students should work in small groups of a maximum of four, but coaching and supervision from tutors was allowed. It was thus felt that the problem set by the brief was sufficiently open, or 'messy', to enable students to develop problem-solving and group working skills, and to acquire new knowledge to resolve the problem. The brief was felt to provide a useful context for new learning in such areas as direct marketing, customer loyalty, and card technology, areas within which students would need to acquire knowledge. Comparisons were made with PBL criteria (i.e. that PBL should provide a context for new learning, that it should require the acquisition of knowledge and the development of problem-solving skills, and that the problem should come first and dictate the kind of knowledge needed, Eitel & Gijselaers, 1997, p. 5), and the decision was taken to adopt the brief and enter the competition. The added dimension of being part of a national competition and being answerable to an external body was also felt to be useful and challenging for both staff and students.

In designing and implementing the project, staff found guidelines suggested by Savery and Duffy (1994) helpful. Of particular value were the

four guidelines relating to PBL design (as grouped by Kirch & Carvalho, 1998):
1. All learning should be anchored to a larger task or problem.
2. The learner should be encouraged to develop ownership of the overall task or problem.
3. The task must be authentic.
4. The task and the learning environment must be designed to reflect the complexity of the environment in which the learner will be expected to function at the end of the learning.

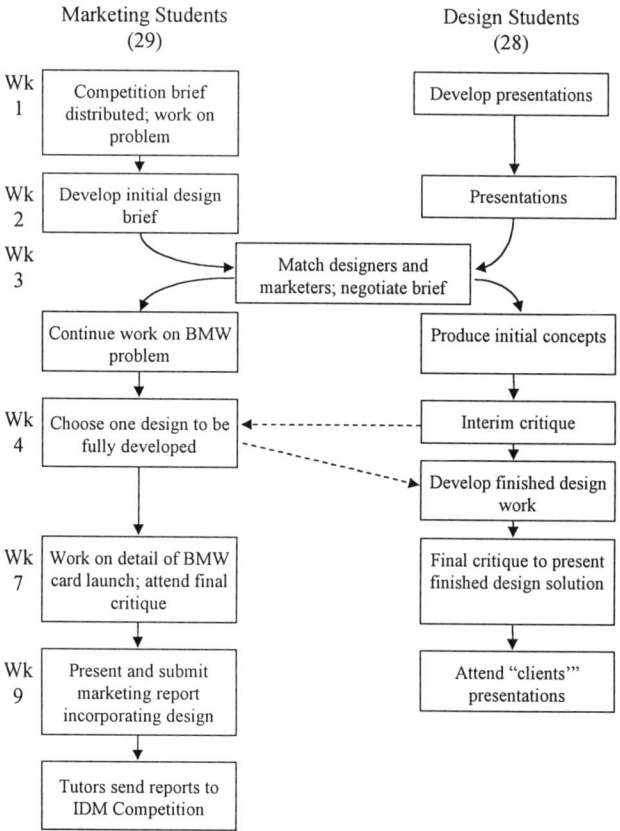

Figure 1. Project Summary.

The first guideline was fulfilled by putting the brief into the context of the larger task of experiencing the role of marketing practitioner. With the second guideline in mind, staff briefing the students emphasized the need for students to assume problem ownership because the IDM competition rules stipulated that staff could only supervise the project. The use of a 'real' problem and a 'real' client provided authenticity in accordance with the third guideline, not only in terms of the brief itself but also in terms of the role of the students as consultants in the position of having to pitch competitively against unknown rivals from other institutions. Finally, the learning environment was engineered to reflect realistically the day-to-day working relationship between the marketers and the designers, with deadlines, real budget constraints, frequent meetings, creative pitches and even the occasional working lunch!

The competition essentially dictated the pace and structure of the project. The key stages in the project, along with an indication of the timescale involved are summarized in fig.1.

In week 1, marketing students were provided with an in-depth briefing by staff on the competition brief and the implications of the PBL approach. At this stage, five students dropped out, leaving 24 marketing students to form small management teams. The marketing students immediately began to translate the BMW problem into a creative design brief for the design students, and to identify the knowledge inputs required to solve the problem. Meanwhile, the design students prepared to sell their creative talents to the marketers through multi-media presentations. This was the first time the design students, in the role of design consultants, had had to justify their work to non-design-literate clients. After the designers' presentations in week two, the marketing teams were matched with their design consultants and left to finalize the details of the design brief and to develop a protocol for meetings. Marketing students were given weekly meetings with marketing staff, but were permitted to consult with staff outside the prescribed times, which they frequently did.

From week three onwards, design and marketing students worked together on a variety of tasks. Working to the marketers' creative brief, the designers produced a number of initial concepts for BMW card designs, point-of-sale display material, dealer displays and mail shots, in rough artwork form. These were presented to their marketing client teams in an interim critique during week four, at the end of which the marketers chose one concept to be fully developed into finished design work. This work was presented to the design tutors for assessment in a final critique in week seven, to which the marketers were invited. Meanwhile, the marketing students had also been producing detailed launch strategies for their proposed BMW card, which they formally presented to marketing staff in week nine using the design work they had commissioned as a presentation aid.

At the end of the presentations, the marketing teams handed their reports to staff for submission to the IDM competition. Included in the reports were copies of the creative design work produced by their design teams. The deadline for reports to reach the IDM was the end of week nine, so staff had little opportunity for detailed checking of the reports before they were sent off. Staff had earlier provided students with the IDM competition rules, asking them to ensure that their reports conformed. Apart from this, as project supervisors, the staff could have no other input into the content of the report, which meant that there was considerable pressure on the students to 'own' the problem in every respect.

The IDM Competition rules, contained in a twenty-page document, were both comprehensive and stringent. Marketing students had to acquaint themselves in detail with the rules before submitting their reports to the competition's judging panel. The rules covered elements such as how to submit an entry and the report format, as well as specifying the type of binding to be used, team codes and double-spaced laser printing. Prizes on offer to national competition winners included a day at a motor racing school; cash prizes of over £2,000 and a trip to the DMA forum in San Francisco for the winning project supervisor. The project supervisors at Teesside University were therefore delighted when one of their project teams won a merit award, which effectively ranked them fifth out of the forty-five competing UK universities.

The judging panel was made up of prestigious leading industry players who provided detailed written feedback to the project teams, using evaluation criteria supplied by the IDM. Project reports were assessed against seven specific criteria on a scale of 1 to 10. Scores were described as "incomplete or unimaginative" for a 1, or "innovative, imaginative, breakthrough" for a score of 10. The criteria were specified as follows:

- Relationship marketing strategy
- Plan for BMW card
- Direct marketing strategy
- Media plan
- Creative plan
- Budget
- Presentation quality.

Although the IDM competition proved to be a valuable learning experience, the effect of competition *per se* was less clear cut. The weight of research evidence (see for example Adams, 1983; Kohn, 1986; Johnson et al., 1981, Ibbetson & Newell, 1997, 1999) suggests that competition can have a negative impact on student learning, whereas collaboration and cooperation between individuals and teams can have a more beneficial;

effect. The IDM criteria were adopted by the Teesside tutors and used to produce a grade for each of the project teams, ranked A through E. The grades were then used as part of the comprehensive feedback to the marketing teams (see section 3.4), with the breakdown of the final grade explained. Tutors awarded two A grades, 2 Bs and one C, which is higher than the usual grade profile for a module in marketing. This suggests that the external competition might have had a beneficial effect in this case.

3.2   Group Work

Once the project was underway, the issues and problems surrounding group work soon began to emerge.

Students required different group work skills at different stages of the project. Nunamaker et al (1996/97) identify three levels of collaboration or group work:

1. *Individual level*: uncoordinated individual effort towards a goal (analogous to a sprinter).
2. *Co-ordination level*: co-ordinated but independent effort towards the goal (analogous to a relay team).
3. *Group Dynamics level*: concerted effort towards a goal (analogous to a crew working together).

The first level occurred when the problem brief was issued and all students had their own ideas about how to resolve the problem. This was a particularly lively session, given the open nature of the BMW brief. The second level saw separate tasks allocated to each team member, for instance one undertaking secondary research into the car industry, one researching relevant theory, another contacting companies involved in card technology. The third level then saw the group pooling material and working purposefully towards the final report.

3.3   Managing the Constraints

The competitive brief, together with the IDM rules and regulations, imposed a number of constraints on the project implementation. The timescale was non-negotiable, as was the brief, and staff were unable to clarify or interpret the brief on behalf of the students. Marketing students had to structure and interpret the problem for themselves in order to provide the designers with a creative brief, and had to make fundamental strategic decisions about the type of customer card to launch, the card technology to use and the direct marketing campaign. At the end of the nine-week project period the students felt drained by the intensity of the experience, and no doubt the challenges and constraints of the competition played a key role in this. A later discussion with the IDM revealed that a number of teams from other institutions had found the competition too demanding and had dropped out.

3.4 Review and Reflection

Savery and Duffy (1994) suggest that PBL tutors (or learning managers) should provide time for supported reflection. This was implemented by building a whole day into the project for each of the marketing teams to work with tutors and reflect on their experience. Each student was encouraged to review his or her contribution as a team member and to reflect on the development of the group's problem solving skills and acquisition of knowledge. To aid this process, the completed evaluation questionnaires from the designers were used as feedback to the marketing students on their project management skills. Although this was slightly uncomfortable for some students, the opportunity to "see ourselves as others see us", as the poet Burns wrote, proved invaluable.

At this point in the project, it was important for staff to utilize the de-briefing skills they had gained over the years. Any negative peer feedback was therefore reflected back as a positive learning experience, and students counseled to this effect. For the learning managers, the provision of a period of reflection and the development of de-briefing skills were felt to be key elements of a PBL approach to this project.

3.5 Operational Problems

Kirch and Carvalho (1998) discuss a number of problems that they encountered with PBL projects, closely mirroring those experienced by staff during this project:

- *Grades*: PBL motivates students differently from other types of teaching and as Kirsch and Carvalho found, overall grades in this project were higher than average, as discussed above.
- *Time commitment from faculty*: although PBL is student centered, it is time consuming for staff as students want to discuss complex and fuzzy problems. Tutors involved in this project found that it is much more demanding than traditional teaching.
- *Student centered problems*: PBL does rely on students actually being self-directed and taking responsibility for their learning. Especially as group work was involved, staff had to be aware that there could be students who were not contributing fully. Learning might not take place also where a student just takes on those parts of the task that can easily be done rather than those which require learning new skills. The small

group size in this project, however, did make it difficult for any student to 'hide'.
- *Substitution*: as Kirch and Carvalho put it, "Is it learning that I'm seeing?" Students should not be allowed to substitute activity for learning and thinking, although in reality this is difficult for learning managers to control without direct intervention, and some students were observed in classic displacement-type activity. Spending hours in a library gathering data might make a student feel as if a valuable contribution is being made, but that student also needs to be stretched to ensure that those data are rigorously analyzed. Perhaps staff need to consider intervention strategies in order to pre-empt this substitution effect, although again, the small group size tended to mean that all members had to participate in every element of the project.

Other problems encountered by Kirch and Carvalho, namely those of heresy and differences among faculty members, were not experienced by staff. Heresy is explained as the propensity for staff who do not really understand PBL or its management to revert to non-PBL activities under the PBL banner. Fortunately, design staff and marketing staff have been involved in this project over a number of years and have developed a good working relationship and understanding of PBL. Any differences or elements of heresy have, therefore, long since been eliminated.

4. FEEDBACK AND EVALUATION OF THE PBL EXPERIENCE

In order to assess the effects of the BMW brief, students were asked to complete the same questionnaire used in previous years (Brassington and Smith, 1997). The questionnaire comprised a mixture of open ended questions and semantic scales in order to assess how the students felt about their experiences and how they would like to see such a project evolve. With the open ended questions, responses were categorized using a crude post-content analysis. It was also felt to be important to gather the reflections of both marketing and design staff involved in the project and this was done through one to one semi-structured interviews. The IDM was also contacted to find out their view of the competition.

Responses from marketing students and design students are presented in sections 4.1 and 4.2, with feedback from the marketing staff and design staff in sections 4.3 and 4.4 respectively, while the response of the IDM is discussed at the end in section 4.5.

4.1 Marketing Students

Table 1 summarizes the main points from the marketing students' questionnaire. In terms of developing their understanding of marketing communication, the external brief made little impact on previous scores. The scope of the brief was considered to be about right by 90% of the respondents, a significant improvement on the previous year. Further comments indicate that the open nature of the brief increased the students' flexibility. the time allowed for the whole project was generally thought to be about right. However, a significant number considered the time allowed for the involvement of the designers to be too short. Nevertheless, comments made by the students suggest that they thought the time pressure added a realistic element to the project.

Table 1. The Impact of the External Brief on Marketing Student Evaluations.
Marketing students who considered the scope of the brief, the time allowed to complete the brief, and the amount of designer involvement to be 'about right'

Evaluation factor	1998 (%)	1997 (%)
The scope of the brief	90	75
Time allowed to complete the project	57	65
Amount of designer involvement	33	57

The involvement of the designers produced some very positive feedback. Most of the comments centered around the insights gained from working with designers, as well as encouraging creativity, enthusiasm, professionalism and a "more responsible attitude." A number of ways in which working with the designers might offer valuable experience were suggested, and students were asked to rate them on a scale between excellent and poor. Excellent and very good responses were aggregated and termed 'strongly positive'. As with the previous project, strongly positive ratings were given to the area of visualizing brand concepts. In addition, the external brief seems to have had its most positive overall impact on the areas of managing consultants, broadening thinking, and setting deadlines, all of which improved their ratings compared with previous years. Two groups who had experienced difficulties with their designers, however, rated coping with and setting deadlines as poor, as well as inter-disciplinary liaison. When asked to comment on the experience of working with designers, the most frequent comments were on the value of working with others and gaining valuable insights into the design process. One comment was made to the effect that it:

"Highlighted differences in the interpretation of the brief."

Asked what they liked best about this project, students cited the 'real world' aspect most frequently, together with working with designers and seeing their results visualized. The open nature of the brief also gave rise to a number of comments with regard to 'freedom'. Tutors were also pleased to see a number of students commenting that this was the most interesting module they had studied. Under the 'least liked' heading, the time constraint elicited the most frequent comments, along with the late arrival of the competition rules and regulations, an issue for the IDM.

Very few changes to the running of the project were recommended by the students, although 43% did suggest a longer timescale. This was probably because the competition deadline closely coincided with the students' own dissertation deadlines. A number of very positive closing comments were made that the project had been "useful", "good experience", and "enjoyable." Several students suggested that this learning approach should be extended to other modules. A couple of closing comments are also worth noting:

"The competition gave the project an extra dimension."

"This has been the best project of my university career."

4.2 The Design Students

Overall, there was a very clear relationship between the designers' rating of the project and the tutors' grading of the marketing teams' performance. The higher the grade awarded to the marketers, the more positive the ratings given to the project experience by their partner design team. Clearly, the more the marketers worked at being professional, communicating openly with their designers and creating a genuine dialogue, the more the designers enjoyed the experience.

Whereas in previous years the design students saw the main value of the project in improving their understanding of design, in 1998, 71% of students rated the project as useful in developing their understanding of marketing. A few comments on the design constraints imposed by some marketing students were in evidence, as in previous years. Table 2 summarizes the students' responses which are very much in line with the responses from the marketing students in section 4.1 above.

Table 2. The Impact of the External Brief on Design Student Evaluations.
Design students who considered the scope of the brief, the time allowed to complete the initial concepts, and the time allowed to complete the final concept to be 'about right'

Evaluation factor	1998 (%)	1997 (%)
The scope of the brief	54	80
Time allowed to complete initial concepts	79	87
Time allowed to complete final concept	50	47

When asked "to what extent did the involvement of the marketers affect your attitude to the project?", 45% of students commented on the lack of feedback from marketers, or that they were "too laid back", clearly a major issue of concern to the designers. This would suggest that many design students reacted less positively to the ill-structured nature of a PBL approach and were looking to the marketers to define and structure the problem on their behalf. Other designers, however, commented that the marketers' involvement created a more positive and motivating attitude to the project.

The designers were then asked to consider ways in which working with the marketers might offer valuable experience and the results are shown in table 3. As with the marketers, each factor was rated on a scale between excellent and very poor. Overall, all nine factors were rated positively, with strongest support for 'producing commissioned work' and 'coping with deadlines' amongst 80% of students. One of the weakest ratings was given to the area of 'interpreting the brief', in total contrast to the previous evaluation where this received the most positive rating. Presumably students felt that the imposition of an external brief limited their interpretive design talents. Again, the area of 'broadening thinking' gained less enthusiastic support.

Table 3. The Value of Working with Marketers for Design Students.
Percentage of design students rating the factors in this table as 'excellent' or 'good' (aggregated scores). Remaining students rated factors as 'average', 'poor' or very poor'.

Evaluation factor	1998 (% of students rating as 'excellent' or 'good')	1997 (% of students rating as 'excellent' or 'good')
Producing commissioned work	80	93
Acting as a consultant	76	93
Broadening your thinking	62	80
Coping with deadlines	80	80
Interpreting a brief	62	100

It would seem, therefore, that some design students felt constrained in their thinking and creativity by the BMW brief. Later comments suggest, however, that this could be resolved if the marketers worked at involving designers earlier, at creating a genuine team dialogue, communicating openly with their designers, and providing feedback. Additional comments on the value of working with marketers reflect the 'real world' experience gained by the design students. As in previous years, many students commented on the value of working with others and indeed the word 'professional' was used by a number of students to describe the experience of working with the marketers.

The prestigious nature of the BMW brief seems to have had more impact on the designers than the marketers. On being asked what they liked best about the project, 25% of students specifically mentioned BMW or said that the BMW brief made it more interesting, whereas only one marketing student mentioned BMW. Some 33% used the words 'live' or 'realistic' to describe the most positive aspects of the project.

In contrast to previous years, a number of consistent themes emerged from the responses about the least liked aspects of the project. These can be characterized as a lack of feedback, involvement and enthusiasm from the marketers, and arose where a state of disharmony seemed to have developed between teams. It should be noted, however, that not all conflicts resulted in disharmony. As Souder (1988) observes:

"Professional disagreement appears to be a very healthy and enlightening climate for its members."

In terms of the interaction between design and marketing students, it would seem that healthy conflict can lead to creativity. Furthermore, disharmony might be avoided by designers and marketers understanding and appreciating their reciprocal roles (see Souder, 1988). Other comments on the least liked aspects centered on the pressure felt by the designers and the vague or ambiguous nature of the brief, which, according to Bruce and Cooper (1997), can be a source of major problems in a project.

Several suggestions were made for improvements (shown in table 4), should a similar project run next year. Some 42%, felt that the brief should be clearer or more specific. This ties in with earlier comments and suggests that designers are more comfortable if the marketers impose form and structure on the brief and specify the design outcomes. As one member of the marketing staff put it:

"The better the brief, the better the design work."

Most students considered the timescale to be acceptable, although 25% requested more time. The plea for more dedication was made by 17%, with 50% of designers wanting more feedback and greater enthusiasm from the marketers: clearly an issue if the project is to be run with an external brief next year. A number of comments on the need for an explicit system of contact and liaison with the marketers were made.

Table 4. Design Students' Suggested Areas For Improvement

Area for Improvement	Percentage of Design Students Citing Factor
More dedication from the marketing students	17
More enthusiasm from marketing students	17
More feedback from marketing students	33
A clearer, more specific, brief from marketing students	42

Finally, judging from the number of students who took the opportunity this time to comment on their own experience, the project seems to have had a profound impact. Students were in agreement that the experience, whether positive or negative, had been a useful one, 46% labeling the experience "useful" or "enjoyable." Many other comments were made to the effect that it had helped to improve design skills and teamworking, with one student observing that:

"Marketers should learn about design."

The need for more direction and communication from the marketers was specifically noted by several students, with one or two requesting more feedback from design tutors and the clarification of the marketers' role.

Overall, the external brief seems to have given the project a greater impetus and sense of reality, with designers gaining valuable insights into the interface with marketers, but needing a good clear brief, earlier involvement in the problem, open communication and lots of feedback.

4.3   The Marketing Staff

Overall, staff were pleased with the project and very positive about using an external brief. Having a 'live' client had been very motivating for both staff and students. The only problems encountered by the staff involved the logistics of facilitating and organizing the student learning experience, in particular ensuring that students met the IDM deadline for submission of reports. This was non-negotiable, and in fact worked to the staff's advantage to the extent that a slightly conspiratorial "us and them" relationship developed in meeting the very tight deadlines imposed by "them", i.e. the IDM.

Marketing staff had initial worries that the direct marketing brief might limit the scope of the design students. This proved not to be the case and the design staff were pleased that the nature of the brief and the client (BMW) facilitated a great deal of problem solving Behavior, with design students using their initiative to search the internet for BMW graphic images, which helped them to produce highly professional artwork.

Some conflict occurred, both inter- and intra-group, but this was largely creative conflict and was viewed positively by all parties as reflecting the 'real world' aspect of resolving management problems and achieving results through others. One slightly disappointing aspect was that the performance of the weaker students was not lifted by working with stronger, more motivated, students. Perhaps staff had been over ambitious in their hope that this might be a project outcome. Staff were, however, pleased to observe the development of problem-solving skills, with the problem itself providing a useful vehicle for new learning. Students had quickly identified the knowledge inputs required to bring about problem resolution, and had acquired knowledge of such areas as customer loyalty cards, relationship marketing, card technology, media costs, and of course the creative design process. Staff felt that this provided clear evidence for the value of a PBL approach to the project. Indeed, such was the degree of immersion in the problem, that many students commented afterwards that they did not wish to hear the words loyalty card or BMW mentioned ever again!

The staff enjoyed their role as facilitators, the involvement in students' problem solving, and responding to students who challenged the brief. The effect of the competition was motivating for staff and provided a useful added dimension. Staff themselves became quite absorbed in the brief and perhaps the desire to do well in a national competition fired corporate pride. They also found that PBL needs time and involvement if done properly, that it is more than just sending students off to the library to find something out for themselves. As Kirch and Carvalho (1998) found, the experience was more demanding for staff than traditional teaching. However, the staff found it to be more rewarding. and felt more stretched and challenged by the PBL approach.

In conclusion, staff felt that the impact of a 'live' external brief had been valuable in meeting the learning objectives of the project and that the PBL approach had been appropriate. The IDM brief and student competition would therefore be incorporated next time the project was run. It was felt that the competition had helped significantly in achieving the broader objectives of PBL, i.e. increased motivation, higher order thinking skills, providing authenticity, and seeing relevance and context (see Brassington and Smith, 1997).

4.4 The Design Staff

After some initial misgivings about the scope for design creativity provided by a direct marketing brief, the design staff became very enthusiastic about the project. An added sense of excitement in having a prestigious, high quality brief from BMW was observed and felt to be a positive motivator. Design students produced extra work for the project and showed a higher level of commitment, with no group conflict apparent which had been a negative feature of previous years. Thus design staff were happy that the learning objectives for the project had not only been met, but exceeded.

Because of the studio-based nature of the design course, staff could observe most of the interactions between the design students and their marketing 'clients' when meetings were held, which was particularly useful in seeing the working relationships developing. Staff were impressed by some of the marketing teams, especially in the way they set up an early dialogue with the design students, involving them in their strategic thinking and setting out clearly defined design outcomes. This was felt to be a good indicator of a strong working relationship, and staff noted the frequent meetings held by these teams with specific points of action agreed. It soon became evident to staff that design students wanted to be involved in the problem at a more strategic level and felt they had something to contribute.

Those designers who had been involved early in the life of the problem seemed to be more motivated; "they feel they have something to offer" was a frequent comment from staff. However, the designers still required the marketers to articulate a clear strategic vision rather than the vague brief some of the designers felt they had received. From this point of view, the designers seemed less comfortable in dealing with the messier, ill-defined aspects of a PBL approach, even though they were producing the desired responses in seeking new knowledge and developing new design skills.

The availability of BMW graphics, mainly via the Internet, was seen by the design staff as a very positive aspect of the brief, and it was felt that this gave added impetus to the project as well as the kudos of designing for a prestige client. In this respect, the comments of the staff reflected those of the design students in their evaluations and is worth noting for future projects.

4.5 The Institute of Direct Marketing

The IDM direct marketing competition is modeled on a competition run in the USA by the Direct Marketing Educational Foundation. The competition is one of several ways in which the IDM actively supports direct marketing teaching and research in UK universities and colleges. According to the IDM, the competition has been designed to give UK students "the opportunity to apply theory to practice by developing a 'live' direct marketing campaign. Students are challenged to combine their knowledge, skills and creativity to solve a real direct marketing problem." The IDM see direct marketing skills such as decision making, interpersonal communication and creativity as important in preparing students for entry into the business world.

The competition is open to both undergraduate and postgraduate students, and this year some forty-five universities and colleges entered teams. This year has seen a tough, close-run competition with several teams dropping out. The IDM feel that to become a finalist and to receive an award is a real achievement for a student's CV, and they are justifiably proud of the many finalists who go straight in to direct marketing jobs.

5. CONCLUSIONS

This paper discussed how an external competition was incorporated into a PBL project and how it affected:
- project design and academic objectives,
- interaction between the marketing and design students, and
- student motivation within the project.

5.1 Project Design and Academic Objectives

In terms of project design, the main impact of the competition was that:
- Staff had no flexibility to vary the brief nor, because of time constraints and the volume of work required by the competition brief, could additional elements be added to achieve any additional academic objectives.
- The external competition timescales had to be incorporated into the project and deadlines met. Staff again did not have the flexibility to alter deadlines, if, for instance, they had felt that extending the deadline for report submission would have led to a more thorough piece of work.
- The extent to which staff could become involved in the students' work was constrained by the competition rules, but this had the positive effect of reinforcing the students' ownership of the project.
- Students had a 'real' prestigious client, BMW, and an externally set brief, adding realism and perhaps moving students away from reliance on tutors.
- Overall, the competition was felt to offer suitable opportunities for the students to engage in the kind of problem definition, data gathering, analysis, project management and client - consultant liaison activities that staff have built into PBL projects in previous years. Certainly, the intangible benefits, such as developing professionalism, creativity, dealing with others, managing deadlines etc. have been just as evident in 1998 as in previous years.

5.2 Interaction Between Marketing and Design Students

The use of a competition brief does not seem to have made any major difference to the interaction between the two groups of students. As in previous years, some partnerships worked very well indeed while one or two foundered. The marketing students largely appreciated the designers' inputs and enjoyed:

- seeing their ideas turned into tangible designs and having quality artwork to include with their reports
- dealing with other professionals and experiencing the synergy of such interaction
- the project management involved in dealing with consultants
- gaining insights into the design process.

In general, the designers' experience was also largely positive, but some frustration is evident despite the benefits of the project. Although the competition helped to improve the extent to which the project developed the students' understanding of marketing, some designers felt that:

- some marketers imposed too many constraints on them ...
- ... and yet some marketers were not being prescriptive enough
- some marketers were not giving them enough feedback
- some marketers were not perhaps involving the designers enough or making the most of their professional talents.

Perhaps this all goes to show that the students are indeed being well prepared for the real world through this project!

5.3 Student Motivation

The competition was seen to have a strongly positive motivating effect on the students as it was not seen as a contrived assignment imposed by staff and actually encouraged partnership between staff and students. The designers in particular were excited at having a prestigious, high quality brief from BMW and were motivated to produce extra work for the project. Design staff generally felt that there was greater commitment and a more professional approach from their students as a result of the competition. The marketing students too seemed to feel that they had something to prove with all groups taking full responsibility for their own learning and working hard to fulfil the competition. The higher than average grades awarded for the project and winning a merit award for one of the submissions to some extent supports a claim that students were motivated to perform well.

The effect of competition on the students' learning and performance are illustrated in the following verbatim comments taken from their questionnaires: "at the start of the brief, inter-group competition became too intense" "work groups could be smaller", "challenging and enjoyable", "liked the freedom and competition best", "disliked nothing really - apart from the stress!", "competition gave it an extra dimension", "least liked group conflict. Group motivation low at times" (designer), "The pressure" (designer). Those above comments indicate a fairly mixed reaction to the effects of competition, but do seem to illustrate that competition in a marketing project is not necessarily a good thing.

5.4 Evaluation of the PBL Approach

As far as the experience reported in this paper goes, the PBL approach proved valuable because:
- it helped achieve the complex educational goals for the project
- the students enjoyed the freedom and flexibility of the PBL approach and asked for it to be applied to more modules
- it allowed the incorporation of a real problem and experience of the role of the practitioner, and the use of the competition highlighted this
- the students found the feedback and the time for reflection required of PBL valuable.

Reflecting on Savery and Duffy's (1994) guidelines for PBL design, three more guidelines can perhaps be added:
1. Debrief the PBL participants thoroughly, with positive comprehensive feedback.
2. Encourage the involvement of all the problem's stakeholders early in the life of the problem (adapted from Souder, 1988).
3. Be a PBL enthusiast! There was a clear relationship between the enthusiasm of the marketers and the positive ratings of the PBL experience given by their design teams.

Peters (1985) advocates the encouragement of enthusiasm in business school teaching. He argues that if anything, the active suppression of enthusiasm is taught. Through PBL, perhaps we can begin to redress the balance.

REFERENCES:

Adams, J. (1973). Effects of competition and open receptivity on creative productivity. *Catalogue of Selected Documents in Psychology, 3*, 16-7.

Boud, D., & Feletti, G. (Eds.). (1991). *The challenge of problem-based learning*. London: Kogan Page.

Brassington, F., & Smith, A. (1997). The design and implementation of a cross-curricular project in marketing and design. *Zeitschrift fur Hochschuldidaktik*, Special Issue, Problem-based Learning: Theory, Practice and Research, *21 (1)*, 81-96.

Bruce, M., & Cooper, R. (1997). *Marketing and design management.* London: Thomson.
Chaharbaghi, K., & Cox, R. (1995). Problem-based learning: Potential and implementation issues. *British Journal of Management, 6 (4),* 249-257.
Dixon, N. (1990). Action Learning, action science and learning new skill. *Industrial and Commercial Training, 22 (4),* 10-16.
Eitel, F., & Gijselaers, W.H. (Eds.). (1997). *Zeitschrift fur Hochschuldidaktik,* Special Issue, Problem-based Learning: Theory, Practice and Research, *21 (1),* 5.
Gilbert, D., & Guerrier, Y. (1997). UK Hospitality managers past and present. *The Service Industries Journal, 17 (1),* 115-132.
Guzdial, M. et al, (1996). Computer support for learning through complex problem solving. *Association for Computing Machinery, Communications of the ACM, 39 (4),* 43ff.
Ibbetson, A., & Newell, S. (1999). A comparison of a competitive and non-competitive outdoor management development program. *Personnel Review, 28 (1/2),* 58-76.
Ibbetson, A., & Newell, S. (1996). Winner takes all: An evaluation of adventure-based management training. *Journal of Management Learning, 27 (2),* 163-185.
Johnson, D. et al, (1981). Effects of cooperative, competitive and individualistic goal structures on achievement: A meta analysis. *Psychological Bulletin,* 89, 47-62.
Kirch D., & Carvalho, G. (1998). the delivery of accounting in the problem-based learning environment. In R.G. Milter, J. Stinson, & W.H. Gijselaers (Eds.), *Educational innovation in economics and business III: Innovative practices in business education* (pp. 131-143). Boston, London, Dordrecht: Kluwer Academic Publishers.
Kohn, A. (1986). *No contest: The case against competition.* Boston: Houghton-Mifflin Co.
Lowenthal, D. (1986). Developing community enterprise managers. *Journal of European Industrial Training, 10 (1),* 22-28.
Marsick, V. et al (1992). Action-reflection learning. *Training and Development, 46 (8),* 63-66.
Norman, D. (1994). *Things that make us smart: Defending human attributes in the age of the machine.* Reading: Addison Wesley.
Nunamaker, J.F. et al, (1996/97). Lessons from a dozen years of group support systems research: A discussion of lab and field findings. *Journal of Management Information Systems, 13 (3),* 163-207.
Perry, W. (1970). *Forms of intellectual and ethical development in the college years: A scheme.* New York: Holt, Rinehart and Winston.
Peters, T. (1985). *A passion for excellence.* New York: Harper and Row.
Robinson, G., & Wick, C. (1992). Executive development that makes a business difference. *Human Resource Planning, 15 (1),* 67-76.
Savery, J., & Duffy, T. (1994). Problem-based learning: An instructional model and its constructivist framework. *Educational Technology,* Sept-Oct, 31-38.
Schon, D.A. (1983). *The reflective practitioner: How professionals think in action.* London: Temple Smith.
Schon, D.A. (1987). *Educating the reflective practitioner,* San Francisco: Jossey-Bass.
Small, M., & Cullen, J. (1995). Socialization of business practitioners: Learning to reflect on current business practices. *Journal of Business Ethics, 14 (8),* 695ff.
Souder, W. (1988). Managing relations between R&D and marketing in new product development projects. *Journal of Product Innovation Management,* 5, 6-19.

A Problem-Based Learning Approach to Business Software Skills

Victor Perotti, Patricia Sorce & Ben Isselhardt
Rochester Institute of Technology, College of Business, Rochester NY, USA

1. INTRODUCTION

Today, computer software skills are a fundamental requirement for every businessperson. It is difficult to imagine how an individual could even survive in the current business atmosphere without the ability to use basic computer applications. Thus, the instruction of these skills has become an important facet of all Business education. Unfortunately, the traditional lecture and repetition approach to these skills seldom works well. It becomes very obvious that learning computer software requires practice with the software, rather than lengthy discourse on the subject. This paper presents an overview of our transition to an alternative teaching methodology, problem-based learning, for the instruction of computer skills.

1.1 The Course and its History

Business Computer Applications is the name of RIT's computer skills course required for all College of Business students. The intent of the course is to give the students a set of intellectual and computer skills to enable them to excel in their other courses and later in a business career. About one half of the students in the course are first year College of Business students, with the remainder being higher level undergraduates and adult students. In addition, there is a growing number of older students who are taking the course as part of a new Management Information Systems Certificate program. In addition to the wide span of ages taking this course is an even greater diversity of students' technological experience. The least experienced students often have no computer experience at all, while the most advanced do computer consulting.

Business Computer Applications has changed content in every year since its inception in 1993. Including version changes, a total of fifteen different computer applications have been covered in that time. These rapid changes are made necessary by several factors. First, to best prepare the students for the current marketplace, it is important to try and stay up with the rapid changes in business computer software. For example, since 1993, three new Microsoft Windows operating systems, and four new versions of Microsoft Office have been released (www.microsoft.com). Second, the course has changed to cover that software which emerges as the de facto standard. For example, during the late 1980's and early 1990's, Freelance Graphics enjoyed wide use, but was soon overtaken by Microsoft Office. Finally, and perhaps most importantly, the course has had to change in order to deal with a remarkable growth in the students' computer sophistication. In its earliest incarnation, the majority of students needed to learn simple topics including using a mouse, manipulating windows and dealing with directories and folders. In the most recent year, the average student had experience with Windows, Internet Browsers, Microsoft Word and Excel. Some exceptional students were computer consultants and Internet entrepreneurs.

1.2 Reasons for and Nature of the Change

The dramatic advances in technology put the Business Computer Applications faculty in a very difficult race to try and stay ahead of the student expertise and to keep abreast of the rapidly changing software. The continual learning and revisions to the course meant a lot of work for the instructors. In addition to the time requirements for keeping up with the software, there was considerable demand on the instructors' time due to the courses' traditional teaching methodology. A typical course meeting included a lecture on a particular software feature, followed by students working through a set of problems at the end of the textbook chapter. On one day, for example, students learned about the formatting of cells in Microsoft Excel. They were assigned three or four problems, and worked on them during the second half of class. Typically they would submit a single printed sheet with their solutions on them. Significant instructor time was then spent coordinating, grading and recording the results from these exercises.

By early 1997, instructor and student enthusiasm for the course was reasonably low. For instructors, the volatility and high time demand made this course less attractive than those where the same lectures and exams could be used year after year. In addition, the class was set up to use very dry "here is how to" lectures, with little opportunity for instructor or student creativity. Students, perhaps sensing a lack of instructor involvement, showed little interest in the assigned problems, and skipped class frequently. For the advanced students, the problems were too easy. The beginners, on the other hand, could walk through a problem's step by step instructions, but in the end did not feel as if they were learning anything. To quote one student, the class had become "a joke."

Given the obvious need for change, the MIS program team met to discuss new ideas for how the course could be delivered. The problem-based learning approach was accepted almost immediately, however there was minimal instructor experience with this methodology. As a first step towards defining our problem-based learning implementation, the instructors agreed that the computer applications should be covered as tools to be used *in concert* to achieve a desired end, rather than as an end in themselves. This insight led to an even greater one: that the students in the course should really be learning business skills and not simply computer skills. By revising our conception of the course, it became easy to articulate the student **outcomes**: business research, analysis, written communication and oral communication skills. In this high level framework, the individual computer applications are simply tools, and like any tools they can be added, eliminated, replaced or improved. For example, the desired research and oral communication outcomes required the addition of new skills in Internet searching and Microsoft Word formatting.

2. OUR IMPLEMENTATION AND METHODOLOGY

Our implementation of problem-based learning borrows heavily from that already in use at Ohio University (see for example, Stinson & Milter, 1996). Specifically, teams of five or six students participate in three problem cycles during a ten-week quarter. The goal of each team is to produce a set of deliverables, usually taking the form of a ten to fifteen page paper and/or an in-class presentation. At the beginning of each problem cycle, a brainstorming session is held to allow students to take inventory of their individual and group skills, and to compare them to what will be required to complete the problem. While brainstorming, the students are encouraged to consider not only the low-level application skills, but also the high-level problem solving and teamwork skills that will be needed.

2.1 The Co-Developed Problem Calendar

The next step in each problem cycle represents a new idea for delivering problem-based learning. In this phase, a problem calendar is jointly developed by the instructor and the class. The calendar specifies topics and activities to be covered for each class meeting. Early in the problem cycle, for example, the students frequently ask the instructor to talk about specific computer techniques, such as how to conduct Internet research. Alternately, the class may wish to spend the early part of the problem discussing information about the problem domain. Later in the problem cycle, the students might request information about advanced application techniques, or they may prefer to have an entire class session to meet with their teams and have one-on-one discussions with the instructor.

The process of creating the problem calendar allows students to learn several skills apart from the brainstorming itself. First, the class learns to *prioritize* the many skills that emerge from the brainstorming session. In our implementation, there are usually five or six class meetings between brainstorming and the delivery of the students' solutions. In essence, this means that time with the instructor is a scarce resource, which the class works to schedule and utilize. A second opportunity for learning from the problem calendar is an *analysis of how specific topics can be best learned*. Some skills really benefit from lecture-based instruction, while others can be better acquired when individuals follow a textbook example. Finally, the development of the problem calendar requires *group decision making*. Frequently, students in the class disagree about what should be covered, the extent of the coverage, or the order of coverage. The ensuing negotiation and eventual resolution of these disagreements is an important part of the learning.

After the calendar has been developed, the activities for the remainder of the problem cycle are completely specified. The course proceeds with the schedule from the calendar and the instructor alternately serves as a source of information and as a mentor. As an information source, the instructor gives demos, lectures or brings in experts to provide their viewpoints. In the mentor role, the instructor encourages the various teams to question their assumptions, consider more possibilities or to improve the quality of their deliverables. Some instructors also encourage the teams to submit outlines or drafts of their work so that they can give feedback before the end of the problem cycle.

At the conclusion of each problem cycle, the students submit any printed deliverables to the instructor and deliver their presentations to the entire class. The other students in the class ask questions during the presentations, and complete forms to evaluate both the content and the delivery of the information. The instructor prepares a one or two page summary of these evaluations with his or her own comments for the team. This summary is probably the most important form of feedback that the students receive, since it details not just how well they did, but also why they did well or poorly and how they can continue to improve.

The final class meeting for each problem session includes a debriefing session, which requires the students to review in their own minds, what they have learned. For our implementation of problem-based learning, the debriefing has proved to be very important, since without some consideration, it can be easy for certain students to say they have not learned anything. As the class discusses what they have learned, it is clear that they have advanced their knowledge on several levels. For example, the early stage in the debriefing typically includes a list of all of the computer application skills that were required to complete the problem. However, as the discussion progresses, higher level skills like time-management, teamwork, and problem solving are often mentioned.

2.2 The Use of Technology

Even though the course has always focused on learning computer skills, students before last year were seldom encouraged to use any technology beyond the specific applications covered in the classroom. In fact, instructors and students have almost always communicated through simple pieces of paper including syllabi, assignments, exams, course notes, evaluation forms, and feedback forms. With the move to problem-based learning has come a move towards delivering and receiving course information electronically. Beginning last year, the primary form of communication between the instructor and the student, as well as among the students themselves has become email. However, the most significant technological change has been the creation of a course web site as a central point of information about the course. Students can receive syllabi, tutorials, suggested links, grades, problem assignments and calendars from this page. They can also use the WebPages to send anonymous feedback about the course to the instructor.

The limitations of using paper for communication are even more serious when one considers that students' submission of assignments and exams has also been limited to simple printouts. It is very difficult, if not impossible to evaluate how well someone uses a computer given only some printed results of their work. To address this issue, assignments and exams are both delivered to the class and submitted to the instructor using file sharing on our local area network. When a student completes an exam, they can simply save their work directly to the hard drive of the instructor. This gives instructors much more information about the way students use the software, but also eliminates the need to deal with many individual floppy or zip disks.

In the coming year, another form of electronic communication will be available for Business Computer Application students through the collaboration program FirstClass. Using this software, individuals will be able to conduct team meetings, send email, or exchange applications through a single interface. This will be especially important since the diverse mix of students mean that it is often difficult to gather an entire group in one place at one time. FirstClass and other GroupWare applications allow users to work from anywhere and at any time.

3. THE RESULTS

The methodology described above constitutes a great change in the way the Business Computer Applications course is both delivered and received. In an effort to understand the impact of this change, we will discuss several factors: high level benefits of the approach, changes in student work, individual student evaluation, and overall student evaluation for all sections.

The adoption of a problem-based learning methodology has provided some subtle benefits for the instructors of the Business Computer Applications. For one, since the course is no longer centered on specific applications, it is much more robust to radical changes in information technology. In its new form, the faculty address only a small subset of the available features of a given application, instead spending time on how to integrate that application with others, or introducing other skills that are not centered around a particular application. Another benefit of this approach is that students with many different levels of computer knowledge can learn significantly in the class. Advanced students with extensive computer skills are challenged and valued, while beginning students have the opportunity to learn from the instructor and all of their classmates. More important than these high level advantages are the dramatic changes in the work submitted by the students.

Before the transition to problem-based learning, the students were asked to complete simple problems from a textbook chapter. These questions were obviously created to limit the instructor time needed to correct them. A typical problem would have students take an existing spreadsheet, follow step by step instructions to change a few cell values and then answer a question based on their changes with a single word or number. Between five and ten of these problems were completed by every student during every class meeting. While these questions often cover useful skills, they require little thought from the students and for that reason can be difficult to retain. Since the best students could complete these problems in a few minutes, instructors often felt compelled to withhold the assignment of specific problems until the end of a lecture to ensure that they were more than a handful of seats filled at the end of class.

The most important change in the move to problem-based learning is the intrinsic motivation that comes from dealing with real world problems (see Barrows, 1992). Instructors feel this motivation as they help the students solve an interesting problem for which they have no simple answer. Students are motivated by their own drive and that of their teammates to try to solve a realistic problem. Over the course of the last year, Business Computer Applications students have developed solutions for the following problems:

- Design a strategy for Apple Computer ...
- Should RIT require incoming students to have a computer? If so, what kind?
- Choose an existing company involved with digital imaging. Develop a strategy for your company to beat the competition in the future.
- Develop a business proposal for a profitable Internet business. Include a demo website to show what it might look like.

In solving these problems, students are learning computer skills while instructing, debating, learning, and compromising. In fact, individual students frequently take it on themselves to learn specific application features *because they want to use them*. In addition to the computer skills that were being taught before, the submitted work now includes writing, analysis and presentation skills. In fact, the student's submissions are now very professional in appearance, including color diagrams, internet sources and some advanced thinking. So much more has been asked, and in response so much more delivered by the students that many instructors have been overwhelmed by the advanced and professional nature of the students' work.

Perhaps not surprising in light of the obvious improvements in the submitted work and learning are a large number of positive student comments:

- "I liked the way I was able to learn the programs without boring instruction, but with the professors support"
- "I liked problem based learning better than using a book...the only class I didn't skip this quarter!"
- "I had very little knowledge of computers before this class; now I am ready to conquer the world."
- "From what I hear I was learning a lot more than previous classes. Taught me how to work better with others."

- "I feel that I have learned more by working on projects and having to figure things out for myself than I would have just doing book work."
- "I have learned more in this course than any other course that I have taken at RIT ... Hands on problem based learning is a great program that should be continued."

Despite these and many other positive evaluations over the course of the past year, the overall student evaluations for the first full quarter of problem-based learning showed a statistically significant drop in most categories. The second quarter reflected an improvement, so that the student ratings were returned to the level where they were before the implementation of problem-based learning. The evaluations in subsequent quarters have also been at approximately the same level as before problem-based learning. So, why have the overall evaluations been so different from individual evaluations?

3.1 Remaining Challenges

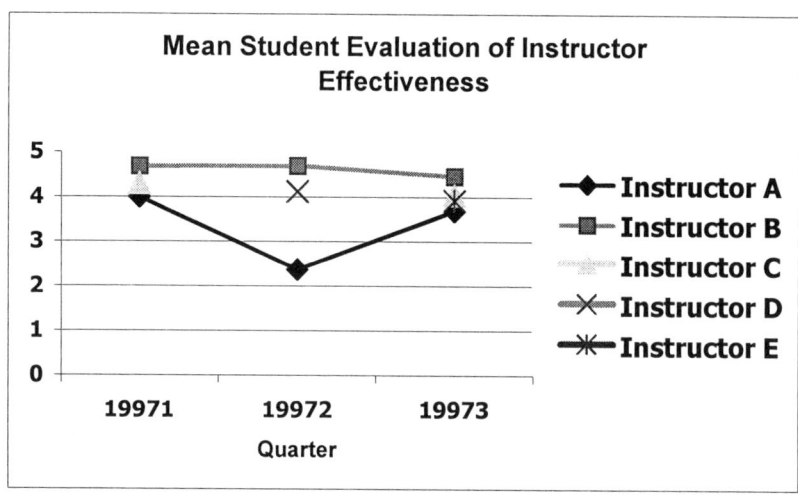

Figure 1. Mean Student Evaluation of Instructor Effectiveness.

The most likely answer to this question is that the course was taught very differently in different sections. Our transition to problem-based learning was greatly limited by the instructors' experience with this style of class. In fact, only one of the six Business Computer Applications instructors had any familiarity with problem-based learning. Figure 1 shows the mean ratings for instructor effectiveness during the transition to problem-based learning. As can be seen in the figure, one instructor's evaluations plummeted for the first quarter that problem-based learning was implemented, and recovered slightly for the following quarter. If this instructor is excluded, most of the student evaluation questions involving perceived instructor effectiveness actually improved significantly over the previous year. The evaluations for this instructor, and for all of the instructors have remained relatively stable at these latter levels in all subsequent quarters. Given the great differences in the instructor evaluations it is clear that a key challenge for the continued success of the course is how to effectively communicate the methodology of problem-based learning to all of the course's instructors. This problem is compounded for our team because the demand for the Business Computer Applications course necessitates the use of several adjunct or visiting faculty members. These part-time and temporary instructors can be different every quarter, and often work on schedules that are unlike those of the full-time faculty. Our first attempt to deal with this problem is to schedule occasional meetings to discuss strategies for the course. These have been haphazardly scheduled, but are usually informative for everyone who attends.

A second challenge for the future stems not from the diversity of the faculty, but rather from the diversity of the students. Because of our recently implemented MIS certificate programs, the number of adult and professional students in MIS courses is increasing every quarter. On the one hand, these mature individuals bring to the course a wealth of experience and usually a very high motivation to do a good job. On the other hand, adult students can be problematic because their daily lives and reasons for being in the course are often very different from the typical undergraduate. One problem is that the work and family schedules of adult students make scheduling team meetings outside of class especially challenging. Also, it can appear very unfair to tie the grades of these students to the performance of their freshmen teammates, since adult students have had years to get used to "real world" responsibility, while the majority of the people in the course are experiencing it for the first time. Furthermore, many adult students feel that they already know how to handle realistic problems, and would prefer a course where only hands-on computer skills are learned. A final issue arises because a fair number of the older students are employees of the Institute, who may have positions of influence over the undergraduates who make up the remainder of the class. The close teamwork required for the course has made some RIT staff members uncomfortable when working with undergraduates under their supervision. To avoid any problems, whether perceived or otherwise, two COB staff members have withdrawn from the course during the past year. As a potential solution to all of these problems, the MIS team is considering a "skills-only" evening section of the class that does not employ problem based learning at all.

Another challenge that is especially salient to untenured faculty is the growing fear of **grade inflation**. This fear can be particularly dangerous to problem-based courses, although there are several reasons why the grades <u>should</u> be higher in this methodology. First and foremost, the dramatic improvement in the submitted work really *merits* higher grades. How can an instructor not give a higher score to a realistic business proposal than to a half-page of single word answers? Second, the inherent motivation that stems from the problems means better attendance, and more attention brought to bear on the course. Clearly the additional effort the students put forward should yield higher grades. Finally, many instructors utilize **iteration**, allowing students to resubmit their work until it is of high quality. Unless the instructor is not behaving consistently, improvements made to the deliverables deserve a higher mark. Unfortunately, there is no obvious solution to concerns about grade inflation, although examples of the student work can be effective tools for convincing others of the merits of the problem-based approach.

4. CONCLUSION

As of this writing, we have just completed our first full year of problem-based learning in the Business Computer Applications class. The continuing evolution of the course has brought both some new challenges as well as some accolades. A particularly difficult problem that is common to many hands-on computer classes is how to deal with very advanced students who are required to take the course, but are already well prepared with software skills. On the one hand, these individuals could be a real asset as part of a team of students in a course. On the other hand, it may be unfair to force a student to sit through a class whose outcomes she/he can already accomplish. As an attempt at a solution, a credit-by-examination option is being developed so that these students can fulfill their requirement, but would not have to sit through a full quarter of instruction. However, the nature of problem-based learning can make this a real challenge. One problem is that much of the learning that goes on during the problem-based experience is not easily assessed with a simple exam. For example, how does one assess a student's ability to do original business research with an exam that lasts only a few hours? A second difficulty arises because the problem-based students end up learning fewer low level software features than with lecture-based instruction. If we are not going to assess the high level skills emphasized in problem-based learning, would it be appropriate to put low level skills on an examination for course credit?

We are also considering a second alternative for dealing with highly advanced students in Business Computer Applications: a self-paced, distance learning offering. Theoretically, advanced students could breeze through the problems very quickly, without the need to spend a lot of their time teaching other students in the course. Other students, particularly adult students, might further benefit in the freedom to do the learning at times that are convenient for them.

Despite the continuing challenges, the overall feedback from students, instructors and RIT as a whole has remained very positive. In particular, the Business Computer Applications course was awarded a 1998 Provost's Instructional Grant to help to complete the implementation, and to disseminate these ideas to others at RIT. Furthermore, the instructors of our problem-based class have been nominated for three Institute wide teaching awards by their students and others. Perhaps because of this highly visible success, more and more faculty members are starting to show interest in this methodology. For instance, problem-based learning has been incorporated into at least three other Management Information Systems courses since the transition of the Business Computer Applications course. Also, two new Provost's grants involving implementations of problem-based learning have been proposed for 1999. Given this initial success, we shall continue to explore this methodology in order to contribute to the international efforts currently improving computer skills and Business education as a whole.

REFERENCES

Barrows, H.S. (1992). *The tutorial process.* Springfield, IL: Southern Illinois University School of Medicine.

Savery, J., & Duffy, T. (1994). Problem based learning: An instructional model and its constructivist framework. *Educational Technology, August,* 1.

Stinson, J., & Milter, R. (1996). Problem-based learning in business and education. *New Directions for Teaching and Learning, no. 68,* 33-42.

Some Evidence on the Use of Writing Intensive Methods in the Principles of Macroeconomics Courses

Martin Milkman[1], Edwin Childers, Jr.[2] & William Payne[1]
[1]*Department of Economics and Finance,* [2]*Department of English, Murray State University, Murray, KY, USA*

1. INTRODUCTION

If, as John E. Maher (1969) asserts in *What is Economics*, it is not what economics deals with that makes it a distinctive science but the fact that economics is a particular way that problems are viewed and analyzed, then students of economics must be able to evaluate situations and draw conclusions based upon the application of theories which are appropriate in an increasingly complex and constantly-changing environment. Yet, the Committee on Graduate Education in Economics and the Committee of College Faculty have examined the economics curricula of select liberal arts colleges in the United States and have found that insufficient emphasis is placed on the development of problem-solving and critical thinking skills, or creativity (Kruger, et al. 1991). Additionally, Cohen and Spencer (1993, p. 219) have found that less emphasis has been placed on writing, even though writing "... can be a powerful tool of teaching students to think like economists." Toby Fulweiler (1987) observed the results of this lack of emphasis when he asked teachers across the nation to identify the student writing problems that concern them most. While spelling, grammar, or punctuation was mentioned, the greatest problems related to flawed thinking. Faculty complained of students' inability to focus, organize, write a thesis statement, or use supporting evidence.

Benzing and Christ (1997) report that lecture with support of chalkboard, textbook, and classroom discussion is still the dominant method of teaching undergraduate economics. Only seven instructors out of 72 respondents reported using research papers, term papers, short papers, or reports. Therefore, it is not surprising that students have difficulty with problem-solving, creative thinking, applications, and writing. While the survey did indicate that 56 percent of the faculty respondents had recently changed their teaching methods, most of the change was toward an increased use of questions, discussion, in-class worksheets, and other active learning techniques. These changes may create a more interesting learning environment, but they do not adequately treat the central issue of perceived student weaknesses in the ability to write, to make economic arguments, and to think critically.

Cotter (1998) suggests that we spend too much effort in higher education on our separate specialties and that we lose sight of how all work comes together to achieve a desired outcome. Students are often independently faced with the critical job of creating connections and finding coherence between various disciplines, yet all disciplines rely heavily upon information and abilities learned in supporting academic areas. Economics faculty cannot prepare students for an increasingly complex world with traditional one-right answer approaches to teaching. It is critically important that economists possess the writing skills necessary to clearly explain their particular approach to problems and reach conclusions which can be understood by the general public.

This paper presents a qualitative analysis of a pilot project which introduced a writing component in the Principles of Macroeconomics class at Murray State University in an effort to address the need for improving both the critical thinking and communication skills of undergraduates.

This pilot project was conducted during the Spring Semester of 1998 in all four sections of the class. Each section had initial enrollments of between forty and fifty students. The paper begins with a discussion of issues raised in the literature related to using writing intensive methods in various business courses and then describes how the writing component was integrated into the Principles of Macroeconomics class. This discussion is followed by an examination of the impact of incorporating the writing component in the class. The paper then concludes with a discussion of changes which have been made in the writing component as a result of our analysis of the pilot project.

2. WRITING IN ECONOMICS EDUCATION: A BRIEF REVIEW OF THE LITERATURE

The use of writing across the curriculum is an effort to encourage faculty in all the disciplines, including economics, to use writing to further provide their students "... opportunities to learn to use the particular patterns of inquiry of a discipline, whether they be processes of observation and generalization or a problem-solving process of applying a general principle to specific situations" (Herrington, 1981, p. 381).

Above all, the use of writing across the curriculum serves to enhance the learning environment of any given discipline, since " ...writing is ... a process of discovery. As a means of communication, it is more than a one step act of writing a finished copy; and as an intellectual process, it is more than merely putting down on paper what is already known" (Herrington, 1981, p. 386). Writing is a process that requires defining one's task, formulating one's ideas, acquiring and evaluating information to further develop and support those ideas, shaping and re-shaping those ideas through review and revision, and presenting those ideas clearly and concisely to the general public. Regardless of the discipline, "[w]riting has an integral role to play in any course as a medium for learning and for teaching how to learn" (Herrington, 1981, p. 387).

Comprehensive writing across the curriculum programs have been underway for a number of years at several institutions of higher learning. These programs have been designed to improve both student writing and learning skills. One example is at Indiana University's School of Business. In a project involving a "write to learn" collaboration between a business professor and a writing teacher, students learn their subject matter as well as employ critical and analytical skills and develop their knowledge and skills through a recursive writing process. The instructors concluded that both student writing skills and knowledge of international economic policy issues improved (Davidson & Gumnior, 1988). Similar conclusions were reached by Cohen and Spencer (1993) in an article on using writing across the curriculum in economics, who found that a collaboration between an economist and a writing instructor yielded much improved student papers and students who were better able to think like economists.

A slightly different approach was employed at the University of Wisconsin--Madison where faculty in the College of Letters and Science were asked to give more and explicit attention to student writing at the undergraduate level. Formal assistance was not provided by the English faculty; however, all writing assignments were developed and evaluated by the faculty of the College and several supplementary writing texts were used. A conclusion reached by one of the faculty participants indicated that writing-intensive courses seem to more clearly meet the goals of the economics major than many of the conventionally organized courses that are typically taught (Hansen, 1993). Similarly, Peart (1994) proposes advanced topic courses at the undergraduate level designed to help students understand how advanced economic theory may be used in a wide range of applications and to treat the deficiencies in problem solving, creativity, applications, and writing. The writing intensive nature of the proposed course is intended to help students develop their writing skills, to make economic arguments, and to think critically.

All of these approaches are based on the research-supported premise that writing is a complex intellectual-linguistic process which involves a wide range of thinking skills and language abilities applicable and, indeed, crucial to all disciplines. Writers move through three stages in the writing process, the first of which involves activities before writing begins. These prewriting experiences are primarily involved with recording ideas, collecting data, and seeing if the data fit in a meaningful way. Second is the act of writing a first draft, where the writer takes those ideas and data and converts them into coherent written thought. The third activity involves revision in response to outside readers and to the writer's own rethinking. Unfortunately, most courses that do incorporate a writing component tend to do so in the form of one mid-term and one final essay and fail to include any mechanism for revision. In these cases, the writing process stops at the second stage, before the evolution of the written product is complete.

The general characteristics of a well-designed course incorporating writing involve writing assignments that place emphasis on the student as an original thinker and on the development of his or her thoughts from the inception of an idea to its final communication. It is important to provide guidance at all phases of the process, from prewriting through revision and editing to the receiving of a response from a readership. Herrington (1981, p. 382) argues that "[t]his point is especially crucial in an introductory course where a student is being exposed to the particular methodologies and jargon of a discipline for the first time."

While college instructors readily support these characteristics, most are not trained to effectively guide a student writer through the entire process. Most instructors feel confident in providing discipline-based information and in helping students identify topics appropriate to their specific course; however, very few instructors outside English departments have received instruction in appropriate ways to guide students through the three broad types of activities discussed earlier. Though some faculty may feel comfortable implementing a writing intensive course with no outside help, it seems clear that a much more effective approach will involve the assistance of a well-trained individual to help instructors with the development of effective assignments and with assessment and to help students at all phases of the writing process.

3. THE WRITING COMPONENT IN PRINCIPLES OF MACROECONOMICS

The College of Business and Public Affairs at Murray State University conducts surveys of both alumni and the employers of our alumni. Data from these surveys indicate that improving the oral and written communications skills of Murray State University business graduates is vitally important. The majority of alumni rank improving their communication skills first out of an extensive list of possible needs. Employers also indicate a desire for improved oral and written communication skills. As a response to these survey results, a pilot writing project was initiated in the Principles of Macroeconomics classes. This class is normally the first economics class in which students enroll at Murray State and it is a required class for all Business and Economics students as well as some Education and Industrial Technology students. This made it ideal for the addition of a writing component to the curriculum since most students enroll in the class during their sophomore or the first semester of their junior year. By this time students have completed basic English composition requirements. As Principles of Macroeconomics is both a requirement and a foundation course, a greater number of students would be exposed to the additional writing experience than would happen in upper-division or elective courses. Furthermore, students would have greater difficulty avoiding the sections with the writing component in favor of those without it since, as Hansen (1993: pp. 213, 214) found in his experience at the University of Wisconsin – Madison, students tend to be "... deterred ... from enrolling in or completing." courses including additional writing.

The pilot project involved matching each instructor of the class with a graduate assistant from the English Department in order to facilitate the experience by providing an individual trained in both guiding students completely through the writing process and in composition assessment. Prior to the beginning of the pilot semester, all instructors of the classes and the English graduate assistants met to coordinate this project. The writing component was introduced to the students on the first class day. This presentation was made jointly by the instructor and the graduate teaching assistant, primarily to ensure that, from the beginning, students completely understood the roles that the instructor and the graduate teaching assistant would fill as far as the writing assignments were concerned.

In each class three writing assignments were required. The assignments involved writing a persuasive essay in response to an assigned question such as "Should the U.S. government relax or restrict current immigration policy?" At least three references were required for each essay. Students were encouraged to include references from various sources including the Internet, newspapers and magazines, and the textbook.

The students were given approximately ten days to complete a draft of the essay. The drafts were graded by the graduate assistant. Each student then met individually for approximately fifteen minutes with the graduate assistant to discuss the rough draft. Approximately one week later the final essays were due. The final essays were also graded by the graduate assistant. A number of handouts relating to the writing component of the class were prepared and distributed in the class. These handouts attempted to convince students that good writing skills are important, and to explain why a writing component was included in the Principles of Macroeconomics course requirements. They also clearly stated the requirements of the assignments regarding style, length, number of references and content. Handouts were also used to clearly outline grading criteria and to point out common errors that students tend to make in both grammar, argument, and style.

The coordination of the writing component portion of the class was critical. The idea was to integrate the writing component of the class with the class material. Essay topics related directly to issues discussed in the class. Class time was devoted to discussing the essay questions and student progress on their research and drafts, and to motivating students to do a good job on the assignments. Students were constantly reminded that communication skills were related to success in the job market.

Another critical area was communication between the instructor and the graduate assistant. The two graduate assistants that were involved in this project did not have training in economics. Therefore it was critical that the essay assignments be discussed before the assignments were given in class. This involved a discussion of the types of economic issues which were likely to be involved in answering the essay questions. Also involved was some discussion of common mistakes in economic reasoning or logic that the instructor expected some students to make (e.g., confusing movements along supply or demand curves with shifts of the curves.) Additionally, an "open door-easy access" policy was critical. When grading the essays, if any question regarding the economic content of an essay question needed to be resolved it was understood that the graduate assistant should not hesitate to ask the instructor or any other economics department faculty member for help.

4. IMPACTS OF THE WRITING COMPONENT

There were several noticeable impacts of including a writing component in the class. First, the student withdrawal rates in the Principles of Macroeconomics sections were twenty percent higher than they had been in the past. However, it seems that withdrawal rates were higher because this program was a pilot project and students thought that if they waited a semester to enroll in the class, perhaps the writing component would disappear. This seems to be consistent with the findings of Hansen (1993). Evidence of Fall Semester 1998 and Spring 1999 enrollment patterns supports this viewpoint. Currently the writing component is viewed as a standard part of the course and the withdrawal rates have returned to their previous level.

Second, students did not like the writing component portion of the course. In the course evaluation forms students were given the opportunity to make open-ended written comments. Thirty-seven of the 127 students completing the evaluation chose to write a comment relating to the writing component. Only two out of the thirty-seven comments were favorable. Most of the students commented that this was not an English course and therefore their grade should not be determined in-part by their writing ability. Clearly, the efforts to convince students that improving their writing skills was a worthwhile goal were not successful.

On a more positive note the writing abilities of the students did improve! This was especially noticeable in comparing the first essay assignment to the third essay assignment. The rough graphs were graded on a thirty-point scale. The average score for the rough drafts increased by over 10 percent. The difference was calculated using only those students who completed both the first and third rough draft assignments. However 17.5 percent of the students who completed the first assignment withdrew from the class before the third assignment was due. There is no statistically significant difference between the average scores on the first rough draft between the students who completed the third rough draft and those who did not complete the third rough draft. This finding lends support to the conclusion that the inclusion of the writing component in the Principles of Macroeconomics class did improve the writing ability of the students.

In addition, the average student performance on the final exam was better than previous semesters, suggesting that students learned more economics; however, this may be due to a sample selection problem affected by the high withdraw rates which occurred early in the semester. It may be more accurate to say that, as Hansen (1993, p. 217) notes, "... students learned what they always learned but learned it in a different way." It seems logical to assume that weaker students were more likely to drop the class in an effort to escape the writing requirement.

5. CONCLUSIONS

This paper has presented a qualitative analysis of a pilot project which introduced a writing component in the Principles of Macroeconomics class. The introduction of the writing component did result in an increase in students' writing abilities as measured by the increased score on the rough drafts. The pilot project was viewed as a success and the College of Business and Public Affairs continues to include a writing component in the Principles of Macroeconomics. Several changes have been made in the format. The number of essay assignments has been reduced to two per semester. This was due to a resource constraint. Given the time necessary for grading the rough draft, meeting with the students to review the draft, and grading the final draft, it was decided that funding could only be secured to support two paper assignments. One challenge is to get students to work harder on their first draft. Many students commented that since it was "only a draft" they should not be expected to put so much effort into the first draft. The goal is that students will treat the first draft as if it is the final paper and increase the time and effort they put into the first draft. To encourage this, the percentage of the grade which is based on the first draft has been increased to forty percent.

An additional challenge is to convey high expectations to the students. In order to communicate to our students that we have high expectations, the graduate assistants, along with the instructors, have prepared sample essays which will be distributed to students. Many students will find these essays to be acceptable; however, the essays do not meet the expectations of the faculty. The faculty and graduate assistants now explain why these essays do not meet our expectations. This takes place before the first essay is assigned and hopefully will result in the students striving to meet our expectations.

One of the keys to sustaining a writing intensive class is to develop a format that meets two criteria. The first criteria is that the format does not require additional work for faculty who are already working to full capacity. The second criteria is that the format will not reduce the amount of discipline specific learning (in this case economics). The pilot program described and analyzed in this paper meets both of these criteria. This innovative approach has now been used for four semesters and is a standard part of the Principles of Macroeconomics course. This is in sharp contrast to many writing across the curriculum programs which start with a large amount of enthusiasm and funding, but quickly die out as funding and enthusiasm decrease.

REFERENCES

Benzing, C., & Christ, P. (1997). A survey of teaching methods among economics faculty. *Journal of Economic Education, 28, No.2*, 183-188.

Cohen, A.J., & Spencer, J. (1993). Using writing across the curriculum in economics: Is taking the plunge worth it? *Journal of Economic Education, 24, No.3*, 219-229.

Cotter, M. (1998). Using systems thinking to improve education. *Quality in student services, 3*, 6-7.

Davidson, L.S., & Gumnior, E.C. (1988). *Teaching business students to learn about global issues through writing*. Paper presented at the Conference on Languages and Communication for World Business and the Professions (pp.1-12). Ypsilanti, MI: ERIC Document 337078.

Fulwiler, T. (1987). *Teaching with writing*. Portsmouth: Boynton/ Cook.

Hansen, W.L. (1993). Teaching a writing intensive course in economics. *Journal of Economic Education, 24, No.3*, 213-217.

Herrington, A. (1981). Writing to learn: Writing across the disciplines. *College English, 43, No.4*, 379-387.

Krueger, A.O., Arrow, K.J., Blanchard, O.J., Blinder, A.S., Goldin, C., Leamer, R., Lucas, R., Panzar, J., Penner, R.G., Schultz, R.P., Stiglitz, J.E., & Summers, L.H. (1991). Report of the Commission on Graduate Education in Economics. *Journal of Economic Literature, 29, September*, 1035-53.

Maher, J.E. (1969). *What is economics?* New York: Wiley.

Peart, S.J. (1994). The education of economists: Teaching what economists do. *Journal of Economic Education, 25, No.1*, 81-92.

Designing Assignments and Classroom Discussions to Foster Critical Thinking at Different Levels in the Curriculum

Susan K. Wolcott
School of Accountancy, Daniels College of Business, University of Denver, Denver CO, USA

1. DESIGNING ASSIGNMENTS AND CLASSROOM DISCUSSIONS TO FOSTER CRITICAL THINKING AT DIFFERENT LEVELS IN THE CURRICULUM

In recent years, business accounting educators have increasingly asked their students to address assignments such as cases that contain open-ended problems for which an absolutely correct answer cannot be known. A major assumption made by faculty is that students' critical thinking skills will be developed through exposure to "real-life" problems in which students must use judgment to resolve ambiguous problems.

There are three major reasons why many students perform poorly and fail to develop critical thinking skills when they are exposed to such assignments. First, students often lack the cognitive complexity to adequately resolve open-ended problems. In fact, their critical thinking skills can be inhibited when assignments are too far beyond their current abilities (e.g., Gainen, 1992; Francis et. al., 1995; Wolcott & Lynch, 1997; Wolcott,

1998a). Second, many students think that all courses should consist of well-defined material that only requires memorization. This causes them to misunderstand or to resist assignments that involve ambiguity. Third, professors are faced with pressures to "cover" substantial quantities of highly defined subject matter, and they tend to reserve insufficient classroom time for teaching critical thinking skills.

In this paper, I provide guidance for professors about how to design assignments and related classroom discussions that will enhance critical thinking development. First, I provide a framework for understanding critical thinking development. Second, I briefly explain how students' beliefs might hinder their critical thinking efforts, and I offer suggestions to improve the design and sequence of assignments and related classroom discussions. Third, I provide an illustrative case with sets of questions designed for courses at different levels of the curriculum. Finally, I offer comments and suggestions for future research on critical thinking development.

2. SEQUENTIAL DEVELOPMENT OF CRITICAL THINKING SKILLS

Although there is no clear consensus about what is meant by the term "critical thinking", most educators would agree that college graduates should be able to apply the following general types of skills (adapted from Lynch, 1996) to open-ended problems such as case assignments:

1. Applies knowledge of subject matter and well-defined problem solving skills;
2. Recognizes the uncertainties in a problem that might prevent a single "correct" solution;
3. Adequately frames a problem (organizes and analyzes information, understands alternative viewpoints, and recognizes and controls for initial biases);
4. Reaches, articulates, and defends a solution as most reasonable;
5. Recognizes the limitations of a solution and considers possible re-evaluations as new information becomes available; identifies problems in on-going situations.

This set of skills is consistent with that called for by employers of business graduates. For example, the chairmen of the largest public accounting firms cited the following as desirable skills (Arthur Andersen & Co. et. al., 1989, p. 6):

> Individuals seeking to be successful in the diverse world of public accounting must be able to ... solve diverse and unstructured problems in

unfamiliar settings. They must be able to comprehend an unfocused set of facts; identify and, if possible, anticipate problems; and find acceptable solutions.

Recently, Lynch, Wolcott and Huber (1998) organized the above set of critical thinking skills into a problem solving process. They developed the process from the perspective of two well-validated developmental psychology theories — the reflective judgment model (King & Kitchener, 1994) and dynamic skill theory (Fischer & Bidell, 1997). Those theories help educators understand that students must learn less complex skills before they can successfully learn more complex skills — specifically, in the sequence listed above. For example, if students are unable to recognize the significant uncertainties related to a problem, they are unlikely to adequately frame the problem. This, in turn, will cause them to have little support for their solution, and they will not be motivated to consider limitations.

Figure 1 (adapted from Lynch, et. al., 1998) presents a summary of the problem solving process and illustrates the sequential nature of the critical thinking skills. Students and faculty find the stair step (or building block) illustration in figure 1 helpful because it represents the idea that each step in the process lays a foundation for the next step. Of course, the way we actually address open-ended problems is much messier and less linear than simple stair steps. Nevertheless, the stair step model is useful because it illustrates that students need to receive sufficient training and support to build their skills beginning at the bottom of figure 1 and proceeding up the steps through the more complex skills. In addition, the stair step model can be useful in providing students with a "roadmap" for future expectations. As discussed more fully below, it is also helpful for students to be exposed to higher level skills even while developing lower level skills.

3. DESIRED CRITICAL THINKING SKILL PERFORMANCE, STUDENT BELIEFS THAT MAY HINDER PERFORMANCE, AND SUGGESTED COURSEWORK ACTIVITIES AND QUESTIONS

Das (1994, p. 335) argues that "most of our business school instructors suffer from a false sense of adequacy in their competence to help students in developing critical thinking skills." This type of overconfidence might result from a failure to recognize the limitations of students' cognitive complexity. To address this problem, this paper discusses how cognitive complexity impacts student performance and how professors can adapt their coursework accordingly. The following brief discussion is based on Lynch, et. al. (1998), who extended the work of Kitchener and Fischer (1990) and Kitchener, Lynch, Fischer and Wood (1993).

> **Re-Addressing** an open-ended problem involves coordinating identifying, framing, and resolving skills in an on-going process. As conditions change and new information becomes available, reconsidering the problem will help students move toward better resolutions or more confidence over time.

⇑

> **Resolving** an open-ended problem is more likely to be successful if students have conducted a thorough and objective analysis. The conclusion should be based on well-founded justifications that explain adequately how various options were weighed.

⇑

> **Framing** an open-ended problem has three major purposes: (a) to understand and analyze important information (including evidence and alternative points of view), (b) to recognize and control for biases in addressing the problem, and (c) to ensure an organized and thorough analysis. Framing can be a very time consuming part of the process as students explore connections between different pieces of information.

⇑

Start Here

> **Identifying** the nature of the problem serves two major purposes: (a) to determine whether the problem is open-ended, and, assuming the problem is open-ended, (b) to gain an understanding of why there is no single "correct" solution. This phase of the problem solving process sets the stage for further analysis (i.e., framing).

⇑

> **Gaining** prerequisite skills is very important because it provides the information and tools needed to analyze the problem. This knowledge typically includes data search methods, expert's opinions, rules and regulations, formulas, and strategies for correctly solving highly structured tasks such as numerical calculations.

Figure 1. Process for Addressing an Open-ended Problem

Adapted from Lynch, Wolcott and Huber (1998).

Lynch, et al. (1998) described how students' assumptions about knowledge and their critical thinking skills are embedded in the scoring rules for the reflective judgment model of adult cognitive development (King & Kitchener, 1994). King and Kitchener (1994, p. 19) argue that students' assumptions "not only affect how [they] will approach the task of defending a judgment but also how they will respond in learning environments..." Given this connection, plus the sequence of skill development described by dynamic skill theory (Fischer & Bidell, 1997), Lynch et al. (1998) provided recommendations about coursework activities and questions that professors can use to promote critical thinking skill development. The following discussion and recommendations are adapted from Lynch, et al. (1998) and from my own classroom experiences.

3.1 Identifying the Nature of Open-Ended Problems

As indicated in Table 1, some students may have difficulty recognizing the existence of and/or the enduring nature of uncertainties related to open-ended problems. For example, students may believe that financial accounting uncertainties will cease to exist as soon as the Financial Accounting Standards Board adopts appropriate accounting rules. If students fail to realistically perceive ambiguities, they will be unable to adequately frame, resolve, or re-address such problems. Such students tend to reach and justify their opinion based on their prior beliefs, their "feelings," or on whim, and they may readily change it. They sometimes assert that their opinion is "logical," but their arguments are often illogical.

Professors may be frustrated by the apparent illogic of these students' arguments and by their ineptitude in addressing complex problems. They may perceive students as being lazy or as having poor reading comprehension. At the same time, these students do not understand why they should make a judgment, and they are easily overwhelmed by the complexity of issues in open-ended problems. Some students are likely to expect the professor to provide them with the "right" answer; a few may believe that the professor is intentionally hiding information from them.

The most important growth opportunity for these students is to learn that true ambiguity exists. Unfortunately, this aspect of critical thinking is often overlooked in educational settings. As suggested in Table 1, professors can help their students understand why some problems will never have a single correct answer. For example, the case illustrated below demonstrates that financial analysts disagreed about an appropriate goodwill amortization life for Blockbuster Entertainment Corp. Professors can also ask students to explore the open-ended aspects of problems. For example, students could be asked to describe the risks and uncertainties surrounding a company's decision to extend credit or to explain why it is not possible to fully know the impact of a human resource decision.

Table 1. Identifying the Nature of an Open-Ended Problem

Core critical thinking skills	• Distinguishes highly-structured problems that have "correct" answers from open-ended problems that are fraught with significant uncertainties. • Identifies the major factors or limitations that prohibit certainty about the best solution.
Reflective judgment level 3 beliefs that may hinder performance	• Uncertainty either does not exist or is merely temporary. • Knowledgeable persons or experts know or will find correct answers to all problems. • Until experts can agree, opinions are equally correct or equally biased guesses. • It is sufficient to view problems holistically without attention to realistic complexities.
Examples of classroom activities to develop skills	• Use cases or readings to confront students with evidence that experts disagree about the best solution to a problem. • Use small group or class discussion to generate a list of the aspects of the problem in which uncertainty is a significant factor. • Ask students to consult experts or explore literature to investigate the range of possible solutions to the problem at hand. • Discuss students' concerns about expecting the professor to provide the "right" answer.
Discussion or assignment questions	• What are the potentially viable opinions or solutions to the problem? • Do knowledgeable persons have different opinions or disagree about the best solution to this problem? • If not, look for more information. • If so, why might they disagree? • Do you think knowledgeable persons can ever be certain about the best solution to this problem? • If so, how do you know which one is correct? • If not, why not? • What factors contribute to the uncertainties surrounding the problem?

Adapted from Lynch, Wolcott & Huber (1998). Beliefs that may hinder performance are based in part on information from Kitchener & King (1985/1996), and some of the coursework activities are drawn from King & Kitchener (1994).

3.2 Framing an Open-Ended Problem

As described in Table 2, students may be able to recognize that some problems involve enduring uncertainties, but they simplistically attribute uncertainties to a superficially narrow set of limitations. Although students may acknowledge the role of evidence, they may not have developed an adequate framework for obtaining, organizing or understanding it. This leads to several observable weaknesses in their approach to open-ended problems. For example, they may disregard evidence and use whim or prior beliefs to reach and justify a conclusion. They are also likely to "stack up" evidence in a quantitative way and ignore contrary information or alternative interpretations. This type of problem solving approach is often promoted by coursework assignments where students are asked to support a given resolution without adequate consideration of alternative points of view.

In the classroom, many students tend to sound very democratic, arguing that "everyone is equal." What they often fail to understand is that individual opinions are not necessarily equal even when human beings are viewed as equals. It is these students' democratic tendencies, driven by their inability to recognize qualitative differences among arguments or to objectively evaluate their own opinions, that sometimes leads them to view professors as "unfair" or "opinionated."

As suggested in Table 2, students need to work on developing complex cognitive tools for framing open-ended problems. Professors can initially help students understand that evaluating an argument is not the same as making a judgment about a person. Students should then be given assignments requiring them to address various aspects of framing open-ended problems and to recognize and compensate for their own initial biases (which can cause them to ignore interpretations of information that is contrary to their own point of view). A good exercise is to organize information on the board as it unfolds during class discussion. Appropriate topics for this type of exercise might include alternative interpretations of financial statement ratios, analysis of various points of view regarding a company's environmental policies, or identification of the pros and cons of a marketing strategy. Special attention should be given to helping these students learn why some evidence is more reliable than other evidence.

Table 2. Framing an Open-Ended Problem

Core critical thinking skills	• Identifies evidence-based processes for examining the problem and potential solutions from a variety of perspectives. • Organizes concepts and information into an objective, balanced picture of the problem and the larger context within which different perspectives fit. • Makes legitimate, qualitative interpretations of evidence from different perspectives.
Reflective judgment level 4 beliefs that may hinder performance	• It is sufficient to simply stack up evidence that supports one's opinion. • Conflicting points of view for which evidence can be provided are equally valid. • Uncertainty is due only to specific limitations such as lost or incorrect reporting of data, limited resources, or inability to correctly predict the future. • Criticizing an argument is the same as criticizing the person who makes the argument. • Experts are biased persons who are simply promoting their own agenda.
Examples of classroom activities to develop skills	• Show students how you identify factors that should be considered when framing an open-ended problem (such as a case). • Have students interpret and evaluate the quality of different kinds of evidence. • In small groups, ask students to take different roles and practice evaluating the same evidence from different perspectives. • Discuss the difference between evaluating arguments and judging people. • Show students and have them practice developing frameworks or concept maps for organizing information and exploring the complexities and the context surrounding a problem. • Have students talk with people who hold views that are different from their own, and then have them articulate how their own assumptions and biases are the same and different from the assumptions and biases of others.

Discussion or assignment questions	• Do you have any initial preferences for one alternative? If so:
	  • What has influenced your preferences or your bias?
	  • How might you set your preferences aside while you conduct your analyses?
	• What connections do you see between the present problem and other problems with which you are familiar?
	• For the various pieces of information related to the problem:
	  • What are the strengths and weaknesses of the pieces of information?
	  • How might the same pieces of evidence be used to support different points of view?
	• For the various points of view:
	  • What are the general arguments for and against each point of view?
	  • What are the assumptions and biases related to each point of view?
	  • How might specific factors in the setting of your problem impact those arguments and assumptions?
	• How might you organize the above information to help you reach a conclusion?

Adapted from Lynch, Wolcott & Huber (1998). Beliefs that may hinder performance are based in part on information from Kitchener & King (1985/1996), and some of the coursework activities are drawn from King & Kitchener (1994).

3.3 Resolving an Open-Ended Problem

As indicated in Table 3, students may be able to adequately identify and frame open-ended problems, but unable to use overarching guidelines to adjudicate across perspectives. This often causes them to be reluctant to select and defend a single overall solution as most viable, or they may select a solution but be unable to express adequate support for its superiority over other solutions. Such students are also likely to fail to recognize the need to re-address a problem.

When students have adequate framing skills, professors may observe them jeopardizing class discussions that involve resolving open-ended problems because they tend to get "hung-up" on the framing phase. For example, students might argue that the class shouldn't discuss the solution to a problem until everyone agrees on definitions.

As suggested in Table 3, professors should model the process of utilizing overarching criteria to select among viable alternatives and then help students develop the principles and frameworks that will help them do this on their own. For example, professors can use cases derived from actual business scenarios to help students recognize trade-offs across perspectives in real-world decision making.

Table 3. Resolving an Open-ended Problem

Core critical thinking skills	• Uses principles that apply across perspectives to choose rationally among potential solutions or opinions. • Uses persuasive reasons and evidence to support assumptions and conclusions about most viable solution, and makes objective and substantial arguments to counter arguments that support other viable solutions.
Reflective judgment level 5 beliefs that may hinder performance	• Endorsing one alternative denies the legitimacy of other alternatives. • Problem solutions may be justified only within a given context or from a given perspective, making it very difficult to endorse and justify a solution as the best alternative. • There are no overarching criteria by which to choose among competing evidence-based interpretations or solutions.
Examples of classroom activities to develop skills	• Show students how you use principles and frameworks to evaluate across potential solutions. • Ask students to articulate how they use principles and frameworks for evaluating across potential solutions. • Require students to choose a solution as most viable and have them articulate and justify their opinion. • Ask students to write an essay in which they examine their reasoning in light of their initial biases and discuss how they have compensated for those biases. • Have students explain how they would respond to arguments that support other viable solutions. • Have students practice communicating their solution to different types of audiences.
Discussion or assignment questions	• How have you compensated for any initial biases you might have had? Are those strategies adequate? • What principles did you use to decide on the best solution? • How did you prioritize the strengths and weaknesses of alternative solutions? • Explain how your values influenced your conclusion. • Given your setting and audience, what is the best way to explain your solution? • How would you respond to arguments that support other solutions?

Adapted from Lynch, Wolcott & Huber (1998). Beliefs that may hinder performance are based in part on information from Kitchener & King (1985/1996), and some of the coursework activities are drawn from King & Kitchener (1994).

3.4 Re-Addressing an Open-Ended Problem

As summarized in Table 4, students may have the ability to adequately identify, frame, and resolve open-ended problems, but fail to re-address open-ended problems because they see resolution as the ending point of the process. Coursework assignments often reinforce this notion by focusing on justifying a solution without asking students to articulate limitations. This view can cause students to fail to consider crucial new information or to establish plans for responding to changing conditions.

Professors often give little attention to students who have relatively strong critical thinking skills through the resolving phase. Nevertheless, as recommended in Table 4, such students can benefit from exercises that require them to articulate limitations as well as justifications for a particular solution and that ask them to establish plans for monitoring decisions under changing circumstances.

Table 4. Re-addressing an Open-ended Problem

Core critical thinking skills	• Recognizes most important limitations of the endorsed solution and their implications. • Systematically employs processes of inquiry (problem solving) that lead to better solutions or greater confidence in the endorsed solution.
Reflective judgment level 6 beliefs that may hinder performance	• Points of view about specific situations may be judged as better than others only in a very tentative way based on one's evaluations of experts' positions or the pragmatics of the situation at hand. • There are no generalized principles and procedures that can be used to further investigate one's tentative resolution to the problem.
Examples of classroom activities to develop skills	• Have students describe the limitations of their solutions and the implications of those limitations. • Introduce new information and have students reassess their solution. • Have students describe conditions under which they would reconsider the solution. • Have students devise or implement strategies for gathering new information that would necessitate a reconsideration of the problem.
Discussion or assignment questions	• What are the limitations, weaknesses, or unknown aspects related to the implementation of your proposed solution? • What are the implications of those limitations in your problem setting? • What new information or changes in conditions might lead you to re-address the problem? • What strategies could be implemented to monitor the results of your proposed course of action and help you revise your approach as needed?

Adapted from Lynch, Wolcott & Huber (1998). Beliefs that may hinder performance are based in part on information from Kitchener & King (1985/1996), and some of the coursework activities are drawn from King & Kitchener (1994).

4. IMPROVING THE DESIGN OF ASSIGNMENTS AND CLASSROOM DISCUSSIONS ACROSS THE CURRICULUM

Any given classroom is likely to be populated by students operating at several different levels of cognitive complexity (e.g., Wolcott & Lynch, 1997). Given this diversity, how can professors design assignments and discussions to provide their students with appropriate levels of challenge? To foster development, professors should attempt to do the following (adapted from Lynch, Wolcott & Huber, 1998):

- Consider the characteristics of students:
  - Utilize classroom assessment techniques to understand students' current ways of thinking (Wolcott & Lynch, 1997; Wolcott, 1998b);
  - Appropriately sequence and structure assignments to take into account the range of students' current abilities (discussed more fully below).
- Help students understand critical thinking as a process:
  - Explicitly talk with students about the process of addressing open-ended problems and provide them with handouts such as figure 1;
  - Model open-ended problem analysis methods and approaches;
  - Legitimize students' discomfort by letting them know that the critical thinking process is complex and messy and that experts (including the professor) struggle.
- Allow time and numerous developmental opportunities:
  - Remember that students' critical thinking skills develop slowly and that individual students undergo periodic plateaus (Kitchener, et. al., 1993);
  - Provide many opportunities for practice and specific feedback;
  - Challenge students one step at a time rather than attempt too much in one course;
  - Begin critical thinking efforts in introductory courses (Wolcott, 1998a).
- Foster students' interest by asking them to grapple with interesting and practical problems.
- Structure classroom discussions to address the diverse developmental needs of students:
  - Design questions to address the entire range of skills in the class;
  - Begin discussions with the least complex aspects of the problem, and then work to progressively more complex critical thinking skills (as depicted in figure 1);
  - Allow students who have not yet developed the more complex sets of skills to "drop out" of the discussion as it becomes more complex.

When addressing the needs of students exhibiting different abilities, the best approach is to focus students' attention first on the prerequisite knowledge related to a problem, then on the ambiguities related to the problem, and so on to the most complex skills. In this way, students having the weakest skills will not be lost too soon in the process, while students having stronger skills will have opportunities to be challenged. It is also important to keep in mind that the most complex critical thinking skills should be addressed at least briefly, even with students having the weakest skills, because this exposure provides students with a "roadmap" for future expectations. To illustrate this process, a case assignment adapted for courses at different levels of the curriculum is described below.

5. ILLUSTRATIVE CASE WITH QUESTIONS APPROPRIATE FOR DIFFERENT COURSE LEVELS

In this section, I illustrate the way in which a case assignment can be designed to challenge students having different abilities and at the same time add to, rather than detract from, the learning of highly structured material. The Appendix provides an illustrative case with alternative sets of questions (homework and/or discussion) recommended for three different courses across the curriculum: introductory financial accounting, intermediate financial accounting, and advanced financial or accounting theory.

5.1 Questions Appropriate for an Introductory Financial Accounting Course

When students are given a case assignment such as the one contained in the Appendix, many professors would simply ask questions such as the following: "What is your opinion about the amortization life for goodwill resulting from Blockbuster's acquisition of other video businesses? What is the basis for your opinion?" However, data indicate that many sophomore-level students do not understand that the uncertainties inherent in cases such as this are enduring and that experts are likely to disagree about the best answer (Wolcott & Lynch, 1997; Wolcott, 1998a). These students need substantial exposure to ambiguity before they can adequately address more complex questions.

The sequence of questions presented in the Appendix for an introductory accounting course starts with five questions about highly structured material (e.g., calculations with single correct answers). Once the professor is satisfied that most students understand the definitions and mechanical aspects of the case, the professor should then move to the next five questions, which will help students acknowledge and accept the ambiguity contained in the case. In a typical undergraduate course, most students will be capable of participating actively in a discussion of these questions. On the other hand, questions 11, 12 and 13 are designed to expose students who have primitive skills to more complex thinking and to challenge students who are already developing the more complex skills. Professors should not expect most introductory students to perform well on these questions; their responses are likely to be simplistic and lacking in appropriate use of evidence. However, exposure to such questions will help set the stage for further development in higher level courses and provide appropriate challenges for students having stronger skills.

5.2 Questions Appropriate for an Intermediate Financial Accounting Course

Many students in an intermediate financial accounting course may already be able to appropriately identify the open-ended nature of problems such as the Blockbuster case. Such students will benefit most from developing an understanding of alternative perspectives and the process of interpreting information. However, because of the diversity of students found in most classes, professors should expect that many intermediate accounting students still require substantial exposure to ambiguities. Compared to the questions recommended for an introductory accounting course, the questions described in the Appendix for an intermediate accounting class contains a smaller number of questions about highly-structured material (three), followed by the same five questions that will help students acknowledge and accept the ambiguity contained in the case. The number of questions that address various aspects of framing has been increased to five, to focus student learning in the intermediate course on these skills. The purpose of the last two questions is the same as in the introductory course.

5.3 Questions Appropriate for an Advanced Financial or Theory Course

Students in an advanced financial or theory course typically understand ambiguities and may have some skill in framing open-ended problems. Such students benefit most from developing more complex aspects of framing and from being asked to adjudicate across perspectives. Compared to the questions recommended for an intermediate accounting course, the sequence of questions for an advanced or theory class contains no questions about highly structured material and only two questions about ambiguities. There are still five questions regarding ways in which students frame the problem; however, the five questions recommended for this course require a higher level of sophistication than those suggested for the intermediate course. For example, students are no longer "hand-held" by specific questions about the perspectives of managers and auditors. In addition, they are asked to identify and compensate for their own initial biases. The number of questions about resolving the case is expanded to four, guiding students into various aspects of resolving the problem. A final question is added to introduce these students to the idea of re-addressing open-ended problems.

5.4 Selecting Appropriate Types of Questions for Students in Different Settings

The preceding recommendations are based on levels of student cognitive complexity typically found in sophomore, junior and senior college students based on the extensive data reported by King and Kitchener (1994, p. 161). However, levels of student cognitive complexity may differ across educational institutions or even across different sections of the same course. To identify the needs of students in a given setting, Wolcott and Lynch (1997) and Wolcott (1998b) described classroom assessment techniques that can be used for this purpose. Given assessment results, faculty may find that even students in an advanced level course may need to focus primarily on ambiguities. For example, I have found that large proportions of my introductory MBA students require this type of focus.

When designing assignments and discussions in their own courses, professors should also be aware that the illustrative case provided in this paper does not require knowledge of complicated but highly structured accounting material. It is generally not difficult for students to understand the mechanics of goodwill amortization, and the illustrative questions were designed under the assumption that advanced or theory students would be competent with this material. If a case contains highly structured material that is very difficult or that is first taught in an advanced or theory course, then questions about the highly structured material should be included in the case discussion. The same is true for ambiguities. For example, students in an advanced accounting course may be unfamiliar with the ambiguities surrounding foreign currency translation. A detailed discussion of these ambiguities would then be important.

6. CONCLUSION

The purpose of this paper is to help professors understand how to do a better job of designing assignments and discussions to help their students develop critical thinking skills. A major contribution of this paper is that it describes a methodical process that can be used to improve the structure of case discussions or other classroom activities. The process depicts the increasingly complex skills students must master to appropriately address open-ended problems: identifying, framing, resolving and re-addressing.

The paper also provided a number of tools and techniques to help professors modify their coursework to explicitly consider the developmental needs of students. In particular, the paper provided an illustrative case with sets of questions that would be appropriate for three different levels of accounting courses. The illustrative case provides a model for faculty to design their own assignments and discussions. It also demonstrates how relatively simple cases can be used to help students learn highly structured material while they develop critical thinking skills.

Much additional research is needed to further specify educational practices that will promote student critical thinking development. In recent years, considerable attention has been given to the development of models and ideas for improved coursework design. Although progress is being made, much research is still needed. In particular, Hofer and Pintrich (1997) argued that we need more classroom-level studies of the effectiveness of various recommendations (p. 124) and within-subjects studies to determine how individuals respond to problems in different domains or as they develop expertise (p. 127). This paper provides a theoretically grounded starting point for strategies that can be implemented in conjunction with future empirical investigations.

APPENDIX: ILLUSTRATIVE CASE
BLOCKBUSTER ENTERTAINMENT CORP.

In May 1989 Lee Seidler, a senior analyst with Bear, Stearns & Co., issued a report challenging the accounting practices at Blockbuster Entertainment Corp. Seidler argued that the company had used "fancy accounting" to inflate its stock prices. Among the accounting practices he criticized were the accounting lives assigned to video tapes and goodwill. During 1988, the company had increased its depreciation life for hit videos from nine months to three years. In addition, Blockbuster had grown rapidly, acquiring numerous other video businesses. The company's management had chosen to amortize the goodwill resulting from its acquisitions over a 40-year life. Seidler asserted that the company's management was too aggressive in its accounting policies and that shorter, more realistic lives would have reduced Blockbuster's earnings by $0.25 per share (1988 earnings amounted to $0.57 per share).

Seidler asked, "Have you ever seen a 40-year-old video store?" He argued for a five-year goodwill amortization life, consistent with that used by high-technology companies.

H. Wayne Huizenga, Blockbuster's chairman, countered that the company's accounting practices had been approved by Arthur Andersen, the company's auditor, and by the Securities and Exchange Commission. He pointed out during the company's annual meeting that Blockbuster would continue to grow rapidly.

Other financial analysts supported Blockbuster's accounting practices. Gary Jacobson, an analyst with Kidder Peabody, argued that Seidler was using "overly conservative accounting" in evaluating Blockbuster's practices. Timothy Rice, a Johnson Rice analyst, stated, "The business is a growth business and Blockbuster totally dwarfs the competition. It's not like these guys are in the business of faking their numbers."

Blockbuster's stock prices had increased by 354% during 1988 and an additional 69% during the first part of 1989. On the day Seidler's report was released, the company's stock price dropped by 10%.

Sources of information and quotes:
- Lowenstein, Roger, May 10, 1989, "Analyst's Bashing Rocks Blockbuster Entertainment," *Wall Street Journal*, pp. C1-C2.
- DeGeorge, Gail, January 22, 1990, "The Video King Who Won't Hit Pause," *Business Week*, pp. 47-48.

Illustrative Discussion Questions for Introductory Financial Accounting

Questions Addressing Skills with Prerequisite Accounting Knowledge:

- Suppose Blockbuster's goodwill amounted to $___. Calculate the company's annual amortization expense assuming: (a) 40-year life, and (b) 5-year life.
- Given the same information as above, calculate the book value of goodwill at the end of the first and second years assuming: (a) 40-year life, and (b) 5-year life.
- Describe the impact on Blockbuster's balance sheet and income statement from use of a 40-year life as compared to a 5-year life. Which life would result in the higher or lower book value in the first year? In the tenth year? Which life would result in the higher or lower net income in the first year? In the tenth year? Support your answer.
- Suppose you agree with Lee Seidler than Blockbuster should have used a 5-year life instead of a 40-year life for goodwill amortization. Given this assumption, were Blockbuster's total assets overstated or understated in 1989? Was Blockbuster's net income overstated or understated in 1989? Support your answer.
- Would Blockbuster's taxable income be affected by use of a 40-year versus a 5-year life for financial statement goodwill amortization? Explain.

Questions Addressing Skills for Identifying the Nature of the Problem:

- Explain why there is uncertainty about an appropriate amortization life for goodwill resulting from Blockbuster's acquisitions of other video businesses.
- Describe the possible economic sources of Blockbuster's goodwill and explain why there is uncertainty about the useful life related to those sources.

- Identify other alternative lives (besides 5 years and 40 years) that could be used for Blockbuster's goodwill.
- GAAP requires that goodwill be amortized over a period not exceeding 40 years. Explain why many companies use lives shorter than 40-years.
- Explain why different financial analysts could have different opinions about the appropriateness of a 40-year amortization life for Blockbuster.

Questions Addressing Skills for Framing the Problem:

- What are the advantages and disadvantages of using a 40-year life? What are the advantages and disadvantages of using a 5-year life?
- In general, identify the various stakeholders who might be interested in the amortization life of a company's goodwill. What might be the preferences of each stakeholder group? How are different stakeholder groups' preferences likely to be similar/dissimilar?

Questions Addressing Skills for Resolving the Problem:

- What is your opinion about how long Blockbuster should amortize its goodwill? What is the basis for your opinion?

Illustrative Discussion Questions for Intermediate Financial Accounting

Questions Addressing Skills with Prerequisite Accounting Knowledge:

- Describe the impact on Blockbuster's balance sheet and income statement from use of a 40-year life as compared to a 5-year life. Which life would result in the higher or lower book value in the first year? In the tenth year? Which life would result in the higher or lower net income in the first year? In the tenth year? Support your answer.
- Suppose you agree with Lee Seidler than Blockbuster should have used a 5-year life instead of a 40-year life for goodwill amortization. Given this assumption, were Blockbuster's total assets overstated or understated in 1989? Was Blockbuster's net income overstated or understated in 1989? Support your answer.
- Would Blockbuster's taxable income be affected by use of a 40-year versus a 5-year life for financial statement goodwill amortization? Explain.

Questions Addressing Skills for Identifying the Nature of the Problem:

- Explain why there is uncertainty about an appropriate amortization life for goodwill resulting from Blockbuster's acquisitions of other video businesses.
- Describe the possible economic sources of Blockbuster's goodwill, and explain why there is uncertainty about the useful life related to those sources.

Fostering Critical Thinking

- Identify other alternative lives (besides 5 years and 40 years) that could be used for Blockbuster's goodwill.
- GAAP requires that goodwill be amortized over a period not exceeding 40 years. Explain why many companies use lives shorter than 40 years.
- Explain why different financial analysts could have different opinions about the appropriateness of a 40-year amortization life for Blockbuster.

Questions Addressing Skills for Framing the Problem:

- Describe possible reasons why Blockbuster's management chose a 40-year life.
- Describe possible reasons why Blockbuster's audit firm approved of its 40-year life.
- What types of factors might affect the economic value of Blockbuster's goodwill?
- What are the advantages and disadvantages of using a 40-year life? What are the advantages and disadvantages of using a 5-year life?
- In general, identify the various stakeholders who might be interested in the amortization life of a company's goodwill. What might be the preferences of each stakeholder group? How are different stakeholder groups' preferences likely to be similar/dissimilar?

Questions Addressing Skills for Resolving the Problem:

- What is your opinion about how long Blockbuster should amortize its goodwill? What is the basis for your opinion?
- In cases such as this, is it best to choose the conservative option (i.e., a 5-year life)? Why or why not?

Illustrative Discussion Questions for Advanced Financial or Theory

Questions Addressing Skills for Identifying the Nature of the Problem:

- Explain why different financial analysts could have different opinions about the appropriateness of a 40-year amortization life for Blockbuster.
- Describe the possible economic sources of Blockbuster's goodwill, and explain why there is uncertainty about the useful life related to those sources.

Questions Addressing Skills for Framing the Problem:

- Do you have any biases about an appropriate amortization life for goodwill? If so, how might you compensate for those biases?
- What types of factors might affect the economic value of Blockbuster's goodwill?
- In general, identify the various stakeholders who might be interested in the amortization life of a company's goodwill. What might be the preferences of each stakeholder group? How are different stakeholder groups' preferences likely to be similar/dissimilar?
- What are the advantages and disadvantages of using a 40-year life versus a 5-year life from various perspectives, including: (a) management, (b) auditors, (c) financial analysts, and (d) shareholders.

- Overall, what are the advantages and disadvantages of a 40-year life? A 5-year life?

Questions Addressing Skills for Resolving the Problem:

- How might you prioritize the preferences of different stakeholder groups in deciding an appropriate goodwill amortization life for Blockbuster?
- In cases such as this, is it best to choose the conservative option (i.e., a 5-year life)? Why or why not?
- What is your opinion about how long Blockbuster should amortize its goodwill? What is the basis for your opinion?
- Did you objectively evaluate all available and relevant information in your interpretation? Explain.

Questions Addressing Skills for Re-Addressing the Problem:

- Under what conditions would you need to reconsider your opinion?

REFERENCES

Arthur Andersen & Co., Arthur Young, Coopers & Lybrand, Deloitte Haskins & Sells, Ernst & Whinney, Peat Marwick Main & Co., Price Waterhouse, & Touche Ross. (1989). *Perspectives on education: Capabilities for success in the accounting profession.* New York: Authors.

Das, T.K. (1994). Educating tomorrow's managers: The role of critical thinking. *International Journal of Organizational Analysis*, 2, 333-360.

Fischer, K.W., & Bidell, T.R. (1997). Dynamic development of psychological structures in action and thought. In R.M. Lerner, & W. Damon (Series Ed.), *Handbook of child psychology. Vol. 1: Theoretical models of human development* (5th ed., pp. 467-561). New York: Wiley.

Francis, M.C., Mulder, T.C., & Stark, J.S. (1995). *Intentional learning: A process for learning to learn in the accounting curriculum.* Accounting Education Series, Vol. 12. Sarasota, FL: Accounting Education Change Commission and American Accounting Association.

Gainen, J. (1992). Developing intellectual skills in accounting education. In T.J. Frecka (Ed.), *Critical thinking, interactive learning, and technology: Reaching for excellence in business education* (pp. 136-157). Chicago, IL: Arthur Andersen & Co.

Hofer, B.K. (1997). The development of epistemological theories: Beliefs about knowledge and knowing and their relation to learning. *Review of Educational Research, 67 (1)*, 88-140.

King, P.M., & Kitchener K.S. (1994). *Developing reflective judgment: Understanding and promoting intellectual growth and critical thinking in adolescents and adults.* San Francisco, CA: Jossey-Bass.

Kitchener, K.S., & Fischer, K.W. (1990). A skill approach to the development of reflective thinking. In D. Kuhn (Ed.), *Contributions to human development: Vol. 21. Developmental perspectives on teaching and learning* (pp. 48-62). Basel, Switzerland: Karger.

Kitchener, K.S., & King, P.M. (1985, reprinted 1996). *Reflective judgment scoring manual with examples*. New Concord, KY: Reflective Judgment Associates.

Kitchener, K.S., Lynch, C.L., Fischer, K.W., & Wood, P.K. (1993). Developmental range of reflective judgment: The effect of contextual support and practice on developmental stage. *Developmental Psychology*, 29, 893-906.

Lynch, C.L. (1996). Facilitating and assessing unstructured problem solving. *Journal of College Reading and Learning*, 27, 16-27.

Lynch, C.L., Wolcott, S.K., & Huber, G.E. (July, 1998). *A developmental guide to assessing and optimizing professional problem solving*. Work in progress available on the internet: <http://www.du.edu/~swolcott>.

Wolcott, S.K. (1998a). Critical thinking development in the accounting curriculum: Focusing on ambiguity in introductory accounting courses. In D.F. Fetyko (Ed.), *Changes in accounting education: Implementation in specific accounting courses and subject areas* (pp. 1-16). St. Louis: Federation of Schools of Accountancy.

Wolcott, S.K. (1998b). *Developing and assessing critical thinking and life-long learning skills through student self-evaluations*. Working paper under journal review.

Wolcott, S.K., & Lynch, C.L. (1997). Critical thinking in the accounting classroom: A reflective judgment developmental process perspective. *Accounting Education: A Journal of Theory, Practice and Research*, 2, 59-78.

PART IV

CURRICULUM ISSUES

Distance Learning: Paradigm Shift or Pedagogical Drift?

Thomas A. Creahan & Betty Hoge
Morehead State University, Morehead Kentucky, USA

1. INTRODUCTION

Distance learning (DL) is not new, but it has evolved dramatically in recent years. Its nature has changed with advances in technology, and its importance in higher education has grown as improved access has spurred demand. The authors suggest that we are on the verge of a paradigm shift in educational delivery-or is it just pedagogical drift, doing the same things with new technology?

Distance learning has been defined as "that educational process that occurs when instruction is delivered to students physically remote from the main campus, the location or campus of program origin, or the primary resources that support instruction" (Southern Association of Colleges and Schools, 1998). Many institutions of higher learning, particularly land-grant schools, have had individual-oriented programs for over a century. Correspondence courses relied on the mail to deliver standardized courses on individualized schedules. Student-teacher interaction was individualized but slow and infrequent. In recent decades television broadcasts allowed schools to reach more students at a time, with some sacrifice of flexibility for the student. Broadcasts were often handled by public TV stations or closed circuit networks; later satellites expanded those capabilities. Videotape allowed rebroadcast of the same lesson or time shifting by the student. However, the concept was still individual oriented, with students working alone, having limited interaction with the instructor. Another technique to reach remote students was the extended campus, where colleges offer occasional sections of their courses at local community colleges or high schools, using adjuncts or itinerant instructors from the campus.

More recent developments, and the media we address in this paper, are two-way interactive video, using compressed video signals carried over telephone lines, and the Internet. Interactive video allows distance learning classes to more closely resemble the traditional classroom. It is group oriented, with all participants interacting simultaneously. Interactive video instruction increases the capital /labor ratio of the classroom, but it allows more locations, more variety of courses, and a smaller number of students necessary for the class to make at each site. The fixed costs are high, but once the infrastructure is in place the marginal cost of providing instruction at an additional site is low.

While interactive video is capital intensive and the hardware imposes a constraint on course scheduling, Internet delivery of classes avoids both these problems. They make use of hardware that is already in place, although some expansion of server hardware and software may be advisable. Students provide their own hardware and work at their own schedules. Courses delivered over the Internet make use of e-mail, web pages, and the exchange of digital information including video, sound, documents and files from virtually any software application. Internet classes can be highly interactive and flexible, but they can also be very labor intensive.

Interactive video and Internet technologies make distance learning possible, but there are related technological developments that give DL a pedagogical advantage over traditional classes. Graphical browsers and course presentation software facilitate presentation of material. E-mail, chat rooms, and conferencing make interactive discussions feasible. Problem analysis, presentations, and papers can all be handled electronically. The hardware needed for the new technology is inherent in the new DL media, but is not available in most traditional classrooms. New technology in classroom courses tends to be supply driven; some technologically enterprising instructors provide their own resources or find a way to successfully press the university for presentation hardware for on-site classrooms. In DL courses the new technology is demand driven; the hardware is in place and the needs of the student dictate its use in virtual classrooms.

2. POPULAR MYTHS ABOUT DISTANCE LEARNING

"There go our jobs!" Distance learning is not a threat to faculty jobs, any more than large lecture halls are. What makes the new media more promising than older DL media (e.g., one-way video lectures delivered over the airwaves or via videotape) is faculty-student interaction. If faculty/student ratios are important in the classroom, they are critical in the delivery of classes over the Internet or via interactive video. Effective technology-mediated learning is less likely to use one-way, one-time delivery methods, such as lecturing, and more likely to encourage collaborative discussions and team projects, with faculty providing individualized instruction and feedback through interactions well beyond the scope of traditional class "time periods." Most, though not all, high-tech distance learning programs utilize e-mail, real-time (live) Internet chats, asynchronous threaded discussion boards, and online advising to supplement the delivery of factual information and assist in the students' active learning activities (Phillips, 1998; Vasarhelyi & Graham, 1997).

Another counterpoint to the argument that faculty positions might be in jeopardy with distance learning is the fact that distance learning makes it more possible to gain sufficient enrollments to offer elective courses as well as courses which may have limited demand within a finite student community. Being able to reach a larger audience with more specialized courses, allowing students to supplement their institution's curriculum with distance learning courses from other accredited schools, and other forms of sharing courses across sites is most likely to mean additional, not fewer, faculty jobs.

"This is going to save the university a lot of money!" If DL doesn't allow faculty to teach bigger classes, it's not going to reduce faculty payrolls. Interactive video classrooms are very expensive, so the full cost per student may be higher than in a regular classroom. The two major factors impacting the cost effectiveness of distance learning courses are student enrollments and student support. Increasing enrollments can lower per-student costs; however, the reverse is true when considering the rise in per-student costs which results from increased student support services to serve the increased enrollments (Potashnik & Capper, 1998). Markel (1999) argues that faculty productivity will decline due to 1) the need for smaller class sizes to accommodate the vastly increased time the instructor must spend with students individually, and 2) the adjustments in reward systems including tenure, promotion, and release-time policies that are imperative to provide incentives for instructors to create a distance course or even convert an existing course to a distance offering. He points out the time to create a distance course must be measured in months, not in days or weeks. Internet classes do have the potential to save in facility costs, but careful analysis should be undertaken before justifying their introduction on that basis.

The real cost saving resulting from the new DL media is to the student. Travel time and other opportunity costs are reduced significantly for some segment of the potential market, increasing the quantity of education demanded. So universities should not look at DL as a way to save money but as a way to reach students who would not take courses under more traditional arrangements.

Demographic and political forces may put pressure on universities to offer DL courses. High schools in the U.S. will graduate 20% more students in 2005 than in 1996, and many more of those students are going to college (Green, 1997). College enrollments among nontraditional students are also growing. Political fiscal restraint limits new campus growth. Much of the new demand may be accommodated by classes using the new DL media. Furthermore, many schools are participating in a growing number of networks and consortia combining DL courses in virtual universities. It seems likely that much of the response to the increase in demand due to demographics will involve renovation of existing facilities into high-tech classrooms that will facilitate the growth of multi-site interactive video courses.

"Instructional quality will suffer and we'll lose (never get) accreditation!" The quality of education in America is under greater scrutiny than ever before. Carnegie Foundation and other nationally commissioned studies on the status of contemporary higher education have been extremely critical of an over-emphasis on large-group lectures, little contact with professors, and students simply being required to repeat what they've read, and an under-emphasis on developing students with a relevant body of knowledge, critical thinking, and problem-solving skills (Alavi, You & Vogel, 1997; Kenny, 1998). As of mid 1998, 80% of all major companies were using web-based training, and over 50% of universities offered web-enhanced courses (Shrivastava, 1998). This explosion of technology-mediated training has alerted accrediting bodies, particularly in the fields of business, social work, and engineering, to scrutinize distance learning programs and require appropriate program design and assessment (Rahm & Reed, 1997). On the positive side, although accreditation standards will need to change to reflect the changes in delivery methodologies, there is sufficient evidence emerging that technology will eventually lead to the enrichment, rather the replacement, of the student-professor relationship. When implemented appropriately, the growth of computerized delivery of information allows the professor to enhance his or her traditional role as mentor, guide, source of knowledge, and authority, and to do so while all the while introducing students to the tools necessary for learning new skills and performing future work (Young, 1998).

3. THE ADOPTION OF DISTANCE LEARNING AT MSU

Morehead State University has a 22-county service region in Eastern Kentucky. Most of the region is mountainous and is not served by the interstate highway system or other high-speed highways. Travel times are longer than for similar distances elsewhere. Family traditions are strong, so many people settle and work in their home counties. The university has a commitment to serve its place-bound students throughout the service region. Morehead State University has long offered correspondence courses and has also served its service region by offering extended campus classes. The extension campuses offered traditional classroom settings for a limited number of courses. In 1995 the university made a major commitment of resources to a new era of distance learning and began offering interactive video and Internet courses. "Compressed video delivery will enable the University to offer classes at more locations simultaneously, absorb small class enrollments at some locations, and generate more diversity in the mix of students who typically enroll in off-campus classes" (Eaglin, 1995).

With help from a federal Star Schools grant to cover capital costs, MSU has equipped over 20 classrooms in the region with interactive video equipment. About a third of these are on campus, and the rest are in extended campuses, high schools and other locations throughout the region. Each of these sites is fully interactive and can serve as send or receive sites for classes. Faculty who offer their courses over interactive video undergo intensive training, and the number of qualified faculty has increased in pace with the facilities. The number of courses has grown rapidly as shown in Table 1. (Interactive video courses may include one or two courses originating on other campuses.) For comparison, the number of courses offered at off-campus sites in a traditional classroom setting is also shown in Table 1.

The number of interactive video courses has leveled off, not so much because of the lack of demand or physical space, but because of the limited number of feasible time slots. The MBA and graduate education programs offer the most courses. Both programs appeal to working adults. These students can attend classes that meet once a week only in the evenings or on weekends. Because of the overlap in the sites that generate most of the demand for their courses, they have to share the limited time slots available. Education courses are typically offered from 4:00-6:40 and MBA courses from 7:00-9:40 PM. Because of this limitation, the MBA program can only offer six interactive video courses each semester. Internet courses are not subject to that limit, so they expand the total course offerings each term.

Table 1. Distance Learning at MSU

	CV Sites (including on-campus sites)	Interactive Video Courses	Internet Courses	Extended Campus On-site Classes
Fall 1995	7	1	0	NA
Spring 1996	7	11	1	164
Fall 1996	11	19	2	120
Spring 1997	19	26	3	118
Fall 1997	21	24	5	143
Spring 1998	21	23	6	154
Fall 1998	21	20	9	165
Spring 1999	22	26	10	155

The primary reason for offering the MBA Program over the Internet is to make it accessible to potential students who do not have ready access to a traditional MBA program. These include students who are geographically remote from such a program, or whose schedules do not permit attendance at regularly scheduled classes. In the MSU service region there are many students who cannot access our scheduled classes despite our efforts to reach the region through interactive video. Many students have to drive an hour or more to reach even the closest site. The Internet option allows them to complete their work from their desk at work or at home on a schedule that suits them, their employers, and their families.

Throughout the implementation of its distance learning curriculum, MSU has placed a high priority on insuring the quality of its interactive video instructional delivery. However, this is no simple task in light of much that has been written about the special needs of distance learning students and the differences between typical residence or on-site students and typical distance learning students. Students tend to self-select for distance learning classes, basing their choice on convenience or necessity, not preference for a particular mode of delivery or technology. Distance learning students are more likely to be nontraditional , and they do not have the same access to the instructor and other resources as on-campus students. Stoffel (1987) has observed that adult (nontraditional) distance learners have needs and preferences in the way a course is structured that are different from those of traditional, younger, students. The distance learning students have stronger preferences for autonomy. The quality of learning materials is of greater importance, and the knowledge or skill of the instructor less important, for the distance learning student than for the traditional student. Distance learning students' first concerns were for prompt, helpful feedback and availability of the instructor for support when needed. Nevertheless, they seem more willing to work on their own as long as feedback and support is available. These characteristics are probably related more to their maturity and experience than to the fact that they are distance learners.

Another real advantage of these distance learning technologies, asynchronous timing, and active learning assignments is that students never really have to miss class. The non-traditional men and women with responsible, demanding jobs who make up most of MSU's MBA student population frequently must take business trips that conflict with a scheduled class meeting, or last minute business problems prevent the student from getting away from work and to class at a pre-designated time. With CV, students can review a videotape of the missed class session and work with their professor to develop an activity that will substitute for what they missed. With Internet, much of students' work can be done at their convenience anyway, but even when a "live" chat has been scheduled, laptops and other arrangements can be utilized to be part of the class even when out of town.

Less face-to-face access with the instructor may lead to additional student collaboration. Schutte (1997) performed an experiment to test for differences between an Internet class and a traditional class with students randomly assigned to the two media, and found that the distance learning group performed significantly better. He argues that "a lack of face-to-face interaction with the professor leads to greater interaction between students and that this collaboration results in higher student test results." (Schutte, 1)

Does lack of contact with the instructor hurt student achievement? Or do the other advantages of DL, in particular the inherent opportunity to integrate new technologies into the course, more than make up for lack of face-to-face contact?

4. ANECDOTAL EXPERIENCES OF TWO PROFESSORS

Both authors of this paper have been teaching courses via technology-mediated instructional methods since Morehead State University implemented its DL program in the fall of 1996. In the MBA Program, Tom Creahan has taught Managerial Economics, the core (required) economics course. Betty Hoge has taught the capstone course, Business Policy and Strategy. Both authors first taught these courses via interactive video, but have since taught them over the Internet. As is the case in all our core MBA courses, enrollments were high because demand for the program has grown faster than we can expand our course offerings.

MSU's interactive video courses are taught in specially equipped classrooms with video cameras and several monitors at the front and rear of the rooms. The instructor's podium has a control panel (operated by the instructor or a facilitator), a computer, and a document camera. The instructor or facilitator controls the cameras, using preset camera positions or by manually zooming and panning, and chooses whether to display the document camera, the computer screen, or the instructor on one monitor. All of the IV classrooms are similarly equipped, so the instructor can teach, and students can make presentations, from any site.

The student desks are equipped with voice-activated microphones. One monitor always shows the students at the site where a microphone was last activated. Since the microphones are activated by sound, they pick up extraneous noises. Not only does this switch the on-camera site to the one that made the noise, but the noise itself is distracting. So we usually have remote sites muted, which deactivates the mikes. This requires the student or facilitator to unmute the site before anyone at the site can ask or respond to a question. We recommend, and will eventually convert to, trigger-activated mikes that are activated by students grabbing or pressing a button on the mike.

Both authors now teach their courses largely over the Internet, supplemented with some IV sessions and other media. Internet courses are offered using email and the World Wide Web. MSU has invested in proprietary web-based course management software and installed a dedicated server to support it. The software we use is CourseInfo by Blackboard, Inc. Several similar packages are available commercially. CourseInfo provides an easy way to post announcements, lecture notes, and assignments, allows the instructor to assign students to groups with their own threaded discussion boards, maintains a gradebook, and offers many other features.

Below are the authors' personal experiences with the technologies and their evaluations of its effectiveness and applicability.

4.1 Tom Creahan's Reflections

My first experience teaching Managerial Economics at MSU was in the Fall, 1997 semester. The course was offered over interactive video with five sites. The class was modeled on a traditional lecture and problem-solving class; my course content was essentially the same as it would have been in a regular classroom. The course involves a lot of problem solving, so a fair amount of time was spent in each class using the document camera much as I use the blackboard in a regular classroom. I also used spreadsheets for appropriate material such as regression analysis. Students submitted homework by e-mail. Exams were sent as e-mail attachments to the site facilitators who printed them out and made copies for their sites. Completed exams were mailed back to me.

The Managerial Economics course had five sites with an initial enrollment of about 50. A total of 42 students completed the course. With our interactive video setup, one remote site is on camera at all times. With two remote sites it is not difficult to remember to call on each of the sites regularly to bring them on screen so everyone sees everyone else frequently. With five sites it is much more difficult. To make matters worse, I could see the students at the remote sites only through the monitor at the back of the room, which makes them seem especially far away. So I was not able to get to know each of the students as well as I would have liked.

Thanks to the training provided by the university I was able to compensate for the drawbacks by using techniques that I would not have used in a traditional classroom. During class students are looking at a video monitor; this makes it extremely convenient to incorporate computer-assisted instructional technology. We are not blessed with an abundance of presentation hardware in our regular classrooms, so there is little incentive to experiment with these unless we teach a DL class. But in the interactive video classrooms we are already using the equipment, so instructional needs provide the incentive to learn new tricks. I used PowerPoint to prepare and deliver my lectures, and posted the notes on my web page. Some problems were solved using spreadsheets. I used a mathematical rendering program to draw three-dimensional graphs to show relationships that I have struggled to explain or represent in two dimensions. And instantaneous access to the Internet makes it possible to bring real examples into the discussion.

In addition to using these techniques during class, I used the Internet to communicate with students, and to help them communicate with each other, between classes. We had a class e-mail distribution list and students had each other's addresses. All students used and submitted homework by e-mail.

In the Spring I agreed to offer a section of the course during the summer over the Internet. I relied heavily on the course management software, CourseInfo, to post material I had previously put on my own web page. I was pleased with the flexibility, convenience, and organization of the package. I think such programs will become an essential tool of DL because they are so easy to use that even DL novices can use an abundance of features immediately.

Because I was not entirely comfortable with Internet course delivery, I arranged to meet with the class via interactive video on four sessions. Two of them were devoted to review and problem sessions; the other two were for the midterm and final exams. In order to maintain the flexibility promised by the Internet medium, these sessions were not mandatory. (The exams could be made up later.) A large majority of the students attended each session. This was a luxury that would not be available for more widely dispersed classes or for any institution without an interactive video network. However, it seemed to be appreciated by this class. Because of the nature of this course, I'm not sure I'm willing to give up proctored exams, although for many courses this would not be necessary.

The biggest perceived drawback of Internet classes (and DL in general) is the lack of contact or interaction between student and faculty. But this is more the result of class size than of the medium. Instructors must be willing to spend considerable time interacting with students.

The possibilities for computer-assisted presentations and exchange of information among students and instructor are limitless. I've barely scratched the surface, and I'm certain that new applications and opportunities will increase faster than I can learn them. The point is that with DL the infrastructure to use these new technologies is already in place and their use is driven by the needs of the course. We are more likely to use them than in traditional classes. As we learn the new tricks we will find some of them to be so useful that we will insist on having the equipment more available for regular classes.

4.2   Betty Hoge's Reflections

My first experience teaching via distance learning was with Morehead State University's capstone course for its MBA program, Business Policy and Strategy, in the Spring semester, 1997. I had gone through the training MSU had offered for all faculty who would be teaching via the new interactive video technology. I also had the benefit of some extra mentoring sessions by faculty who taught the initial round of interactive video courses. Through each of these, I had been armed with a list of "do's and don'ts" and was fully indoctrinated into the philosophy of "letting the pedagogy drive the use of the technology and not vice versa."

Business Policy and Strategy comprises a variety of case analyses and role play scenarios, making it far less appropriate to use PowerPoint presentations and more appropriate for point-by-point discussions among individuals. Although I was tempted to delete the computer simulation I had planned for the course I was determined "to let the pedagogy drive the technology." That first semester, students mailed diskettes to me to process decisions, enter new data, and mail them back to students for their next sets of decisions. As it turned out, the logistics required to pull all this off were horrendous.

My first couple of interactive video classes reinforced that traditional methods were not only clumsy in this environment, they were very time consuming. Sensitivity of microphones and voice-activated camera operations resulted in sites remaining muted except when students wished to speak. This required a student wishing to join in the discussion to first signal his facilitator to unmute their site. In order to give the camera a chance to focus on that student, and in order to allow the rest of us to gain a mental focus, we also utilized a protocol of each student first identifying himself with his name and site location. In addition, I found that the logistics of tasks such as distributing a syllabus, receiving assignments from students, and returning graded assignments, was no longer simple. In spite of my preparedness, those first few class sessions were painfully slow and tedious.

This early experience with distance learning technology convinced me that technology was going to have to influence the pedagogy at least somewhat if the pedagogy was ever going to get accomplished. This revised philosophy rang especially true to me because I had discovered so many instances when I could actually add to the students' learning effectiveness as I, myself, learned some teaching strategies I hadn't previously imagined possible through some of the new technologies. I became very selfish with the way I used our "on camera" time. Utilizing e-mail messages to a distribution list of students and site facilitators became my method for handling class assignments, logistical instructions, feedback to students, and follow-up case discussions.

One incident revealed even greater opportunities for incorporating the Internet as a supplement to the interactive video classes. I had tripped and sprained an ankle on the morning prior to my class. I telephoned one of the better students in the class to arrange for her to facilitate the class discussion. Preparation questions had already been distributed by e-mail. I sent another e-mail to the entire class advising them what to expect. Class went on as scheduled. My class plan was executed as planned, except for my presence. The next day, the student who had facilitated dropped off a copy of the videotape from the class. I reviewed the tape, critiquing the amount and quality of discussion. For some of the discussions, there had been no clear solution, and this seemed to generate even more debate, along with a few laments about my not being there to resolve the issue for them. Had I been there, I hate to admit there is every possibility I would have jumped in and "solved" the problem for them. As it was, I believe their abilities grew dramatically that night as they exercised their own critical thinking and problem-solving skills. After I reviewed the tape, I prepared a written response to their discussions—what they had done well, corrections to some misguided thinking, and particularly some encouragement to a couple of students who actively participated in class discussions for the first time that term.

My distance learning classes have come a long way since that first one. Admittedly, they will evolve even more in the future. At this point, I teach the capstone course as a combination of interactive video and Internet, utilizing only about half the previous amount of interactive video air time. The interactive video meetings I do use concentrate on getting the students indoctrinated into the simulation, demonstrations, complex and spontaneous group discussions, and student presentations. The simulation's authors have improved its technology, and with guidance from their technical support people, I have developed a method for transferring decisions and results via CourseInfo. In lieu of some of the more tedious class discussions, I substitute more outside written projects, some of which require collaborative team debates while others promote individual reflection and expression. I base these outside assignments on a combination of theoretical textbook material and real-time, real-world events in order to avoid plagiarism from former students. I also use CourseInfo to post information about the course and assignments, manage test taking and grading, handle course discussions, facilitate student projects (particularly those done in teams), and to provide Internet links for students' use. I still use the U.S. Mail to receive professional-quality reports. I also take advantage of access to the interactive video media to require students to make multimedia presentations, enhancing their preparation for future corporate teleconferencing they may encounter.

Compared to the teaching technologies we're using at MSU today our distance learning methods of only two years ago seem almost "stone age." So does my original attitude toward the delivery method. My original outlook, mildly described as "how can I make the technology accommodate what I need to have happen in this class?" has evolved to "what else is available and how can I use the technology in a way that fosters student learning and that also makes my life more manageable?"

5. EARLY RESULTS FOR MSU'S DISTANCE LEARNING PROGRAM

Enrollment in the MBA program at MSU has increased dramatically in the three years since the program was restructured and offered through distance learning. In addition to making all courses available via interactive video or Internet, the program was changed from 30 to 36 hours and the prerequisites for nonbusiness majors were streamlined by offering a set of four foundation courses. Total enrollment in all courses (double counting students enrolled in more than one course) increased from fewer than one hundred in the Fall of 1995 to almost four hundred in the Fall of 1998.

Little research exists to date reflecting the effectiveness of distance learning. Early studies suggest, however, that no significant differences exist between the performance of students at remote sites compared to face-to-face instruction or between students who learned in traditional classrooms compared to those who learned via technology-mediated methods (Vollmers, Hoge, & Vollmers, 1998). As additional studies related to the effectiveness of distance learning technologies emerge, a greater number of factors influencing student learning outcomes are being identified, including the quality and reliability of the technology itself, the instructor's and the students' attitudes toward and comfort level with the technology used, the instructor's style of teaching (interactive or not interactive), and classmates' attitudes (Webster & Hackley, 1997). In two separate studies, Ahern and Repman (1994) found that instructional design had a greater impact than the choice of technology in impacting the quality of student-teacher interaction and, subsequently on student learning outcomes. Perhaps even more important in comparing the effectiveness of distance learning technologies to traditional classroom delivery methods is the recognition that the evaluation methods themselves must change. The greatest student benefits from use of distance technologies seem to be based on a shift away from an emphasis on instructors "teaching" content to an emphasis on student learning material through critical thinking and by applying knowledge to real or simulated situations. Such enriched outcomes are not assessed adequately (if at all) with traditional objective exams designed only to measure content knowledge (Ciglaric & Vidmar, 1998).

Beginning in the first year of MSU's distance learning program, graduating MBA students were surveyed to determine their perception of their distance learning experiences. Students were asked questions about both of the primary delivery methods utilized: interactive video and Internet. All of the students surveyed had taken an interactive video course, while 71% had taken an Internet course. Relevant results are shown in Table 2.

5.1 Interactive Video

Students were asked to judge the quality of instruction of an interactive video class compared to traditional classroom instruction. A majority of students (65%) felt that instruction quality in the interactive video class was equal to the instruction of a traditional classroom. A small percentage of students (6%) perceived that interactive video offered better quality instruction than a traditional classroom. Twenty-nine percent of students rated the quality of instruction for an interactive video class lower than in a traditional classroom.

Table 2. Assessments of Interactive Video and Internet Classes

Quality of Instruction	Interactive Video Class	Internet Class
Better quality instruction than in traditional classroom	6%	11%
Quality of instruction equal to traditional classroom	65%	62%
Lower quality instruction than in traditional classroom	29%	27%
Amount of Class Discussion	**Interactive Video Class**	**Internet Class**
Greater class discussion than in traditional classroom	12%	14%
Class discussion equal to traditional classroom	72%	51%
Less class discussion than in traditional classroom	16%	35%
Amount Learned	**Interactive Video Class**	**Internet Class**
Learned more than in traditional classroom	4%	14%
Learned equal amount as in traditional classroom	80%	65%
Learned less than in traditional classroom	16%	21%
Convenience	**Interactive Video Class**	**Internet Class**
More convenient than taking a traditional class	53%	79%
Equally convenient to taking a traditional class	41%	16%
Less convenient than taking a traditional class	6%	5%
Overall Experience	**Interactive Video Class**	**Internet Class**
Very Positive	22%	43%
Positive	53%	32%
Neutral	17%	14%
Negative or Very Negative	8%	11%

A majority of students (72%) felt that class discussion in an interactive video class was equal to that of a traditional classroom setting. In addition, eighty percent of students perceived the amount learned in an interactive video class was equal to that of a traditional classroom.

The interactive video class was rated as more convenient than a traditional class by fifty-three percent of respondents, while forty-one percent found it equally convenient. Overall, students reported that they had a positive or very positive (75%) experience with interactive video. Only eight percent of students reported having a negative or very negative experience with the interactive video class.

5.2 Internet Courses

Students were asked to judge the quality of instruction of an Internet class compared to traditional classroom instruction. Sixty-two percent of students felt that instructional quality of the Internet class was equal to the instruction of a traditional classroom. Some students (11%) perceived that the Internet class was characterized by better quality instruction than a traditional class. Twenty-seven percent of students rated the quality of instruction for an Internet class lower than a traditional classroom.

Fourteen percent of students felt there was more class discussion in the Internet class than in a traditional classroom. Fifty-one percent felt the amount of class discussion was equal to a traditional classroom.

A majority of students (65%) thought they learned an equal amount in an Internet class compared to a traditional class. Fourteen percent of Internet students thought they learned more than in a traditional classroom. Twenty-one percent of students felt they learned less in an Internet class than in a traditional class.

The Internet course was rated as more convenient than a traditional class by seventy-nine percent of respondents, while sixteen percent found it equally convenient. Overall, students reported that they had a positive or very positive (75%) experience with an Internet course. Only eleven percent of students reported having a negative or very negative experience with the Internet class.

6. CONCLUSIONS

Technology-mediated distance learning is becoming an important option within education because it facilitates the sharing of costs, information, and expertise across a broader spectrum of stakeholders, while also providing previously unavailable educational opportunities for distant or disadvantaged students. The number of four-year colleges and universities listing "cybercourses" increased 8-fold between 1993 and 1997, with about one million or 7% of the total college class enrollment in virtual college classrooms at that time (Vasarhelyi & Graham, 1997). Vasarhelyi and Graham (1997) predict that the number of cyberstudents will more than triple by the end of this century.

Business schools particularly are under ever-increasing pressure to graduate students experienced in using emerging technologies (Markel, 1999). As new electronic technologies continue to be developed and become more widely available, educators use progressively advanced methods, and combinations of methods, to offer more courses to more students with increasing levels in quality of learning outcomes (Ciglaric & Vidmar, 1998; DeSanctis & Sheppard, 1999).

Distance learning offers real benefits in addition to some cost efficiencies for a variety of constituencies. It is a means for universities to increase enrollments and better reach underserved populations. Employers, including businesses, government bodies, and nonprofits alike, find distance learning training and education useful in developing workers' skills and filling the growing number of positions demanding well-educated workers. Individuals find it possible to fit education into their already busy lifestyles in order to enhance their career opportunities and professional development. The demand for distance learning programs is resulting in an explosion of offerings. The Internet Age is accelerating acceptance of distance learning. Accrediting bodies worldwide are developing standards for distance education as well as on-site, technology enhanced educational methods. Advancing technologies and educator-experience curves are increasing the quality of course offerings in established and emerging programs. These factors can be expected to continue the rapid growth of technology in education in general and in distance learning environments specifically. There is much economic and social pressure forcing universities to change. The use of distance learning can only continue to grow exponentially. We believe it is truly part of an even larger paradigm shift in higher education. The dangers of pedagogical drift lie in educators and administrators who either treat it with too little respect (as though it is only a fad and will go away) or as too much of a panacea (as a means of increasing revenues without increasing costs as well).

Over the coming years, universities will continue to face many challenges to the one-course, one-semester, one-instructor, one-site traditions of contemporary educational settings. Along with more emphasis on creative education methodologies and distance relationships, educators and educational administrators will need to shift the way we deal with texts and other resource materials, academic calendars, transcripts, faculty workload composition, and student support services. Trends suggest we may even need to re-examine the label we have placed on distance learning, since the paradigm shift may be reflecting something quite different than mere physical distance between teacher and student. Changing instructional design and philosophy for these remote personal relationships may actually be creating less distance between the student and the actual learning activity, sometimes placing it as close as a computer screen only inches away, and a keyboard at their fingertips. Our summarized recommendations for those administrators and instructors who have not yet made the plunge into "the new" distance learning are presented in the Appendix to this paper.

APPENDIX:

Thinking of Starting a DL Program?
1. Consider Internet, interactive video, and hybrids of these: Think multimedia.
2. Don't do it to save money.
3. Consider DL as a way to extend the reach of current programs, decrease cost to students, and increase demand.
4. Don't do it alone.
5. Get administrative commitment and support.
6. Utilize administrative support such as IT people and site facilitators, and bring them into the planning and development process.
7. Don't limit participation to techies and nerds by making each faculty member learn on their own.
8. Offer training and support and offer incentives for the best teachers to use it.
9. Consider adopting some course-administration software on a university-wide basis to help develop large pools of users for mutual support among faculty and students.
10. Network with other schools to cross-list classes and arrange proctoring sites for exams for Internet courses.

Internet Courses
1. Provide students with the e-mail address of the instructor and the start date when they register for the course. Require them to initiate contact by that date.
2. Use web pages to post information, or even better, some course-management software.
3. Require students to have basic hardware, software, and computer skills as a prerequisite. Don't let them hold back the class if they don't.
4. Have some form of class mailing list or central e-mail discussion group.
5. Require discussion among students through group projects, evaluation of each other's work, team discussion, etc.
6. Maximize flexibility by allowing students broad time frames for their participation. Don't expect or require them to be on-line at the same time.
7. Include Internet research skills as a course objective, and require some research from the web.
8. Plan for exams and let the students know in advance what will be expected of them. Make arrangements for proctored exam sites if they are to be used.

Interactive Video Courses
1. Use big monitors (at least 35")
2. Use big typefaces on presentations (36 point or greater recommended on a 35" monitor)
3. Use button-activated student microphones at each student desk so they can be available at all times without picking up extraneous noise.
4. Plan seating arrangements and use camera presets to maximize student visibility at other sites. Resist student preferences to sit in the far corner!
5. Use e-mail and the web extensively, especially for instructor communication with students, but also for handing in assignments, group work and discussion, even exams.
6. Make sure site facilitators have the same software that you use and that they can receive attachments. Send exams as attachments and have them print them out (unless you are well enough organized to trust the mail).

7. Have facilitators fax all completed exams to you (immediately, if possible) before mailing them. They may be hard to read, but it's critical if originals get lost or delayed in the mail.
8. Plan backups every class in case of equipment failure.
9. Work with your facilitators to get most efficient camera coverage and free you to move around the room.
10. Visit and teach from each site at least once, early in the course, if at all possible.
11. Have the students at every site make presentations from the podium, on camera, every week if numbers allow, so students at all sites will get to know each other.
12. Have students use the other technology as well, so they feel more comfortable in the DL setting. Have them use the document camera, make PowerPoint presentations, etc.
13. Call on every student regularly, and have them identify themselves on camera.
14. Vary your presentations; put the technology to its best uses.
15. Use active learning techniques.

REFERENCES

Alavi, M., You, Y., & Vogel, D.R. (1997). Using information technology to add value to management education. *Academy of Management Journal*, 40 (6), 1310-1333.

Ciglaric, M., & Vidmar, T. (1998). Use of Internet technologies for teaching purposes. *European Journal of Engineering Education*, 23 (4), 497-502.

DeSanctis, G., & Sheppard, B. (1999). Bridging distance, time, and culture in executive MBA education. *Journal of Education for Business*, 74 (3), 157-160.

Eaglin, R.G. (1995). Letter from MSU president to SACS.

Greene, K.C. (1997). Money, technology, and distance education. *On the Horizon*, 5 (6), November/December, 2.

Kenny, S.S. (1998). What's wrong with college? *Lexington Herald-Leader*, May 31, 1998, F2.

Markel, M. (1999). Distance education and the myth of the new pedagogy. *Journal of Business and Technical Communication*, 13 (2), 208.

Phillips, V. (1998). Online universities teach knowledge beyond the books. *HR Magazine*, 43 (8), 120-128.

Potashnik, M., & Capper, J. (1998). Distance education: Growth and diversity. *Finance and Development*, 35 (1), 42-45.

Rahm, D., & Reed, B.J. (1997). Going remote: The use of distance learning, the World Wide Web, and the Internet in graduate programs of public affairs and administration. *Public Productivity and Management Review*, 20 (4), 459-474.

Schutte, J.G. (1997). Virtual teaching in Higher Education: The New Intellectual Superhighway or just another traffic jam? *http://www.csun.edu/sociology/virexp.htm.*, California State University, Northridge.

Shrivastava, P. (1998). Web site for YOUR courses for the fall, [contribution to Academy of Management's Management Education & Development listserv June 16, 1998] *MG-ED-DV Digest*, MG-ED-DV@maelstrom.stjohns.edu

Soper, J.C., & Walstad, W.B. (1983). On measuring attitudes. *Journal of Economic Education*, 14 (4), 4-17.

Southern Association of Colleges and Schools, Commission on Colleges. (1998). *Criteria for Accreditation*. Decatur, GA.

Stoffel, J.A. (1987). Meeting the needs of distance students: Feedback, support, and promptness. *Lifelong Learning,* 11 (3), 25-28.

Vasarhelyi, M.A., & Graham, L. (1997). Cybersmart: Education and the Internet. *Management Accounting,* (Aug), 32-36.

Vollmers, S.M., Hoge, B., & Vollmers, A.C. (1998). The use of technology-mediated distance learning in education. *Proceedings for 40th Mountain Plains Management Conference*, (in press).

Webster, J., & Hackley, P. (1997). Teaching effectiveness in technology-mediated distance learning. *Academy of Management Journal*, 40 (6), 1282-1309.

Young, J. (1998). Computers and teaching: Evolution of a cyberclass. *PS*, 31 (3), 568-572.

The Integration Of Service Management Principles In A Business School Curriculum

Klaes Eringa & Hans Otting
Christelijke Hogeschool Noord-Nederland, Leeuwarden, the Netherlands

1. INTRODUCTION

Management education has been subject to critique since the start of the first school of finance and commerce at the University of Pennsylvania in 1881. A school of commerce was said to be too vocational and its place in a university was questionable (Cheit, 1985). From the beginning of the 20th century the opposition in universities to business education gradually decreased. As the number of students and schools increased and the quality of the business schools grew, they became a more or less respected part of the university establishment.

Due to the economic decline in the eighties business schools were blamed for not delivering the right quality of graduates. Porter and McKibbin (1988) distinguish two major types of general criticism: shortcomings in generating vision in students and unsatisfactory emphasis on i tegration across functional areas. Criticism is further directed at the emphasis on quantitative analytical techniques and lack of attention to managing people, communication skills, the external environment, the international dimension of business, entrepreneurism, and ethics. Graduates have high and unrealistic expectations about their first jobs and have an insufficient knowledge base for the challenges in management practice (Boyatzis et al., 1994).

Cheit (1985) argues that business schools have to maintain a balance between academic and professional interests. Business schools are more or less variations on two basic models: the academic model, stressing theory and a discipline directed scientific approach, and the professional model emphasizing the manager's activities and responsibilities in a complex business environment and focusing on the application of theory and techniques.

Knowing what the problems of business education are does not mean that the solutions are readily available. Management education does not change overnight. Most of the solutions to the insufficiencies of management education focus on a change in objectives and content, a technocratic approach to curriculum reform. However, the change of the curriculum and the implementation process are far more complicated. An integrated approach focusing on the content, pedagogy, and the organization of management education is needed to bring about a fundamental change in the business school curriculum.

We will first review the demands of the service industry and describe the specific character of services in paragraph 2. These demands have a high impact on the content of management education and the way education is organized and executed. In paragraph 3 follows a brief introduction to constructivist principles of learning. Paragraph 4 provides an integration of service management concepts with learning theory. We will focus on three interrelated levels of analysis: content level, pedagogical level, and organizational level. The content level refers to the knowledge the student needs to gain. The pedagogical level refers to how students learn and learn how to learn. The organizational level refers to the context in which the learning processes are facilitated. In the final paragraph, we will present two examples from the program at the Christelijke Hogeschool Noord-Nederland (CHN).

1.1 Serving the Service Market

The nature of the business world is changing rapidly. De Geus (1997, p. 36) describes it as "continuous, fundamental changes in the external world - a turbulent business environment - require continuous management for change in the company. This means making continuous fundamental changes in the internal structures of the company." In the past few decades we have seen a shift from an industrial society to a knowledge intensive service society (Grönroos, 1990).

Most management literature on services assumes an integrated, cross-functional approach. The service trinity with the integration of marketing, operations and human resources often functions as a basis (Love-lock, 1992). Service management is a total organizational approach in which the quality of services as perceived by the customers is the number one driving force for the operation of the business (Albrecht, 1990). Services are characterized by "a high degree of intangibility, simultaneity of production and consumption and active customer participation in service production, which is typical entrepreneurial or non-standard, especially in the early stages" (Zeithaml, 1981, p. 190). Alternatively, as Gummesson (1993, p. 22) puts it: "a service is something that can be bought or sold, but which you cannot drop on your foot." This element of intangibility is often regarded as most obvious. It is important because customers often have a hard time evaluating the service before they purchase or use it. Even after consumption, it may be difficult to judge how successful the experience was.

The elements of customer participation and interaction are even more relevant. Both elements refer to the process character of services, and both imply that the value for the customer is as much process as outcome related. It means that service quality is largely created in the service delivery process. This makes it difficult to control the quality of services, but it also creates opportunities to customize and personalize the service. In order to reduce the risk of failures and to optimize the opportunities, it is necessary to take a process perspective on services.

Schneider and Bowen (1995, p. ix) list five critical principles that service firms must follow to deliver service quality:
1. Never divorce the customer from thoughts about what a service business really is or how it should be managed. Customers are *part* of your firm.
2. Select, train, and reward employees for delivering service quality - as your *customers define your own market research.*
3. Pay as much attention to the backroom people and operational details as to the front-line people and procedures. Service is in the details - and if service quality is poor, your customers will not care from whom that service comes.
4. In trying to meet customer expectations and needs, integrate internally across functions, to ensure that all functions present the same *seamless* quality orientation to the customer.
5. *Coordinate* 1-4 above to promote a "service culture" as your service guarantees. You can really only manage service quality through culture because you cannot be there during every transaction.

A customer driven company will adopt service logic; it creates value for both the customer and the company in a service profit chain. Kingman-Brundage et al. (1996) developed a service logic model (figure 1) in which they distinguish service concept, organizational culture, and three forms of logic: customer logic, employee logic, and technical logic.

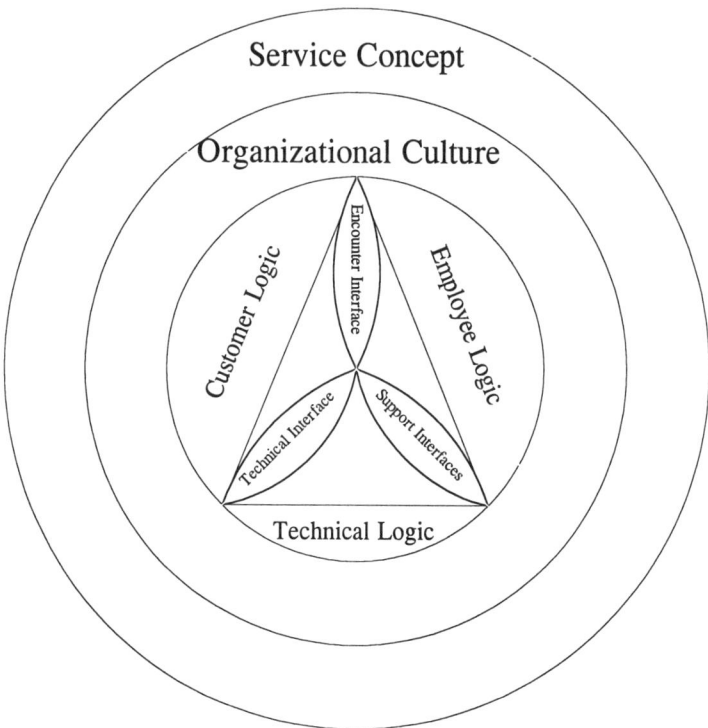

Figure 1. Service Logic Model (Kingman-Brundage & George, 1996, p. 109).

A service concept may be seen as an umbrella concept that should state "which core service, facilitating, and supporting services are to be used, how the basic package could be made accessible, how the interactions are to be developed, and how customers should be prepared to participate in the process" (Grönroos, 1990, p. 80). Organizational culture is here seen as the norms and values the company adheres to.

The three forms of logic represent the primary elements in the service process, observed from the perspective of the customer, the employee, and the operational system. Customer logic explains what the customer does and why. It is driven by their needs, expectations, and perceived risks. Customer needs are often deep and unconscious. They tend to reflect feelings of security, esteem, and justice (Schneider & Bowen, 1995). Customer expectations reflect promises made by the company and past experiences of the customers involved. Risks as perceived by customers typically regard "value for money." Employee logic is driven by needs for security, esteem, and respect, from both the customers and the company. Efficiency and reliability typically drive technical logic.

The interfaces between the three logics reflect the interactions that take place between different participants in a service process. These interfaces are the encounter interface between customer and employee, the technical interface between customer and the firm's technical system, and the support interface between employee and technical logic. Quality in this model means that the drivers of the three logic's are identified and put into balance and that the interfaces between them are managed in such a way that "service breakthroughs" can be realized (Heskett et al., 1990). Interaction is one of the most important factors in services and hence quality can be established at these "moments of truth" (Normann, 1991).

2. A CONSTRUCTIVIST APPROACH TO MANAGEMENT EDUCATION

Traditional models of learning "assume that knowledge is external to the learner and can be objectively specified" (Knuth & Cunningham, 1993, p. 164). Knowledge is regarded as stable, complete and correctly structured. Students systematically use rules, draw logical conclusions and gain objective knowledge. Learning is the transfer of external knowledge into some form of internal representation. Lecturers transmit information, that they consider as relevant, to students who passively receive and store this information until they are required to reproduce it in a formal, pencil and paper test. In this perspective quality of education is seen as an output measure.

Since the late 1980s, constructivist theories of learning have grown out of cognitive theories. Constructivism is a viewpoint in learning theory founded on the premise that we construct our own understanding of the world. "Learning in constructivist terms is

- both the process and the result of questioning, interpreting, and analyzing information;
- using this information and thinking process to develop, build, and alter our meaning and understanding of concepts and ideas; and
- integrating current experiences with our past experiences and what we already know about a given subject" (Marlowe & Page, 1998, p. 10).

Constructivism is a theory of learning that focuses on in-depth understanding, critical reflection, and thinking processes. Quality in this perspective is a measure of both the process and the outcome of the learning activities. A constructivist view of learning emphasizes a learning process in which students actively construct knowledge for themselves. Learning is a search for meaning, an active construction process. The contexts of learning, social and authentic frameworks offering real life experiences, are essential elements of the learning process. Learning takes place in interaction with the environment.

Radical constructivists reject the possibility of instructional design, because they believe it is not possible to predict student behavior and learning outcomes (Knuth & Cunningham, 1993). Moderate constructivists still value authentic learning environments and flexible curricula. Savery and Duffy (1995) describe eight educational principles based on constructivism:
1. relate all specific learning activities to a larger task complex;
2. support the student in gaining ownership for his learning objectives;
3. design authentic tasks;
4. design the task and the learning environment to reflect the complexity of the future work environment;
5. give the student ownership of the learning process;
6. design the learning environment to support and challenge the student's thinking;
7. encourage the generation of alternative ideas, views and contexts;
8. support reflective thinking throughout the learning process.

Constructivism provides a context for experimentation with a range of learning environments and learning methods. Problem-based learning offers the students a rich diversity of learning opportunities. Savery and Duffy (1995) consider problem-based learning as the almost ideally capture of the constructivist principles. Other practices of teaching and learning that fit in the constructivist framework like project work, case-based learning, and action learning can enrich the learning situation. All of these views assume a learning environment in which students can deploy authentic learning activities. An authentic learning environment enables students to develop new ideas and in-depth understanding of the real world. The cultivation of imagination and resourcefulness, the entrepreneurial spirit, leads to an "intellectual entrepreneurship", a conscious and deliberate attempt to explore a world of ideas (Chia, 1996).

3. FROM A TEACHING ORGANIZATION TO A LEARNING COMMUNITY

In recent years, one of the main topics in business debates seems to be the shift to a knowledge society (Hamel & Prahalad, 1994; de Geus, 1997). This means that learning in organizations rapidly gains importance and that knowledge, in particular specialized knowledge, plays a crucial role in creating competitive advantage. The demand for education is growing, not only for regular university programs, but also for specialized courses. A whole range of people simply has to learn in order to stay employable and to maintain their earning power (Davis & Botkin, 1994).

Universities have always been involved in the creation and dissemination of knowledge; it is their core business. However, the market for education and training is changing and competition is getting fierce. "Scientific and technological knowledge production are now pursued not only in universities but also in industry and government laboratories, in think-tanks, research institutions and consultancies, etc" (Gibbons et al, 1994, p. 11). Therefore, universities are involved in a strategic re-orientation. They have to find a new balance between their classical function, fundamental research, and the advancement of theory, and the societal demands for applied research and the development of practical knowledge and competencies.

University programs for the service industry have a dual perspective, because they are part of the same complex they train their students for. This calls for a parallel between developments in the service industry and educational institutes on the three levels mentioned in the introduction: the content, pedagogical and organizational level. Universities have to start preaching what is being practiced, and talk the walk.

3.1 Maintaining the Balance

A business school curriculum has to reflect the dynamics in the business environment, a change from a modern to a post-modern society and a change from an industrial to a service society. The specific characteristics of the service industry and the rapid changes in the business environment have a strong influence on the content of management education. However, a review of content alone is insufficient. In order to meet the changing demands of the service industry a complete update of the curriculum is needed. Not only the objectives of education have to be revised; a thorough redesign of the learning environment and a review of the educational philosophy are necessary. Innovation in a business school involves an integrated reform of the content, pedagogy and organization of the curriculum.

The scientization of the field of management education with its focus on factual knowledge, quantitative methods, analytical and problem solving skills in a variety of disciplines like business administration, operations research, organizational and behavioral sciences has been associated with the success of management education. However, this 'tangible' orientation towards managerial subject matter is an insufficient answer to a constantly changing business environment. It tends to regard "the manager's job as one of clear, practical, tangible results which can be quantified and assessed accurately" (Van Baalen, 1995, p. 3).

A new orientation towards management education is needed that pays more attention to the "intangible" aspects of management. This 'intangible' orientation "emphasizes the socio-political context of managerial decision making, it stresses the importance of ethical aspects in management education, it pays attention to the context of application and cross-functional training (Gibbons, 1994), it stimulates creativity and entrepreneurship, and it promotes an actionist approach to science and learning" (Van Baalen, 1995, p. 3). On the one hand, there is a call for specialization; on the other hand, attention for the 'intangible' aspects of management is required. The leaders of successful entrepreneurial universities respond adequately to changes in the market and seek a dynamic balance between the "tangible" and "intangible" aspects of management education.

3.2　Focus on the Student

Students need to be confronted with the "tangible" and "intangible" aspects of management. This calls for an alteration of the curricula for management education. The pedagogy of management education has to change from teacher led knowledge transfer to student initiated learning activities, from an emphasis on teaching to an emphasis on learning.

Where the service industry asks for self-managing employees, the curriculum of a business school program should invite self-directed learning. The program should only be prescriptive on a general level, and allow the students to formulate their own learning objectives based on their personal learning needs. The traditional "teacher centered" educational program has to change towards a "student centered" study program (Wijnen & Wolfhagen, 1993). The consequences of this change are illustrated in table 1.

The objectives of management education focus on the integration of the general aspects of management with the service management and marketing principles. The interdisciplinary nature of service management and the way service management is integrated in the programs reflect the significance we attribute to the proliferation of ideas of delivering optimal service and value for our internal and external customers. Just as the service industry requires a holistic, integrated and cross-functional approach, the innovation of educational programs must be consistent and coherent. The discipline based curriculum structure has to be altered to a thematic, interdisciplinary approach. A focus on an integrated curriculum organized around the unifying concept, service management, provides a significant contribution to new and innovative ways of management learning.

Table 1. Educational program and study program (Wijnen & Wolfhagen, 1993, p. 25)

Educational program	Study program
Focus on teaching	Focus on learning
The teacher as an expert	The teacher as a facilitator
Passive learning	Active learning
Transfer of knowledge	Acquisition and application of knowledge
Teaching hours and teaching tasks	Study hours an study tasks
Context independent	Context dependent
Supply by teachers	Demand by students

3.3 Towards a Learning Community

Students have a diversity of demands on the university. They want flexible programs, possibilities for specialization, quality of education and value for money. Not only, a shift of the educational focus is needed, but also a change of the organizational perspective. The traditional organizational pyramid has to be turned upside down. Students are the primary customers of the university, and the performance of staff in interaction with the students determines whether the organization will be successful or not (Grönroos, 1990). The emphasis on interaction and integration can only be successfully accomplished by teamwork. The formation of interdisciplinary and self-managed teams can make a significant contribution to innovation in education. Empowered self-managed work teams are enabled to plan, execute and evaluate the educational processes, thus reflecting the collective entrepreneurial culture of the university (Clark, 1998).

Entrepreneurial universities should become learning organizations. Leadership in learning organizations is an important factor for innovation. "Leaders in learning organizations are responsible for *building organizations* where people are continually expanding their capabilities to shape their future – that is, leaders are responsible for learning" (Senge, 1990, p. 9). The way management behaves and supports the innovation, not only by well-intentioned statements, but also with a change in their actual behavior, is a determining factor in the innovation process. It takes a major effort to change from a teacher-centered approach to a learning oriented approach. The mental model of education, the beliefs, and conceptions of management and lecturers may be resistant to change (Tillema, 1995; Kember, 1997). In observing, the actual behavior of managers and lecturers one can notice the contradiction between their espoused theory of education and their theory-in-use, between the way they think they are acting and the way they really act. Sometimes managers and lecturers are both convinced of the benefits of student centered learning and at the same time act from a teacher centered perspective. They are consistently inconsistent in the way they act (Argyris, 1994).

A constructivist approach to education also focuses on how lecturers themselves learn and construct knowledge. An essential factor in innovation is the lecturer's actual teaching behavior. Opportunities for learning and experimenting with new teacher behavior are essential elements in the process of transforming schools. Lecturers have frequent and diverse contacts with students, they are responsible for the interaction in the classroom, and they implement a new approach to learning and teaching. In a supportive learning community, lecturers, students, and staff are able to discuss and express their view on constructivist principles of learning and are offered room for experimentation with new teaching and learning behavior.

4. EXAMPLES FROM THE EDUCATIONAL PROGRAM AT THE CHN

The Christelijke Hogeschool Noord-Nederland (CHN) is a university for professional education with 5,000 students. Started as a teacher training institute for primary education the CHN has now one of the world's largest hotel management programs, a tourism and leisure program, a retail management and small business program, and programs for art therapy and social studies. The CHN works with a system of problem-based learning (PBL). PBL is an educational philosophy for designing curricula and an instructional method that uses problems as a context for students to acquire and apply knowledge (Gijselaers, 1995). PBL is an integrated system for student learning. At the CHN, it is characterized by a modular, thematic, and interdisciplinary approach.

We will give two examples of developments at the CHN that reflect the change in focus described in the previous paragraphs. In the first example, a six week interdisciplinary module *"Learning in Context"*, the focus is on the improvement of the learning process and learning context. In the second example, the flexibility in the specialization phase, the main line of argument is taken from an organizational perspective bearing in mind the pedagogical and content perspective.

4.1 "Learning in Context"

The first example concerns the development of the module *"Learning in Context."* After a tryout in the Retail Management and Small Business programs in the study year 1998-1999, this module will be the first module in the programs of the business departments. We are even discussing the introduction of this module with the necessary adaptations in every CHN program.

The reasons for developing this module are:
- the necessity to improve the way we introduce all students to problem-based learning;
- the enhancement of students' capacity to learn how to learn;
- the development of a variety of study skills;
- the introduction of the student to the general context of the service industry;
- the discussion of the relevance of the CHN mission statement for social and ethical issues.

Students do not just learn facts or digest pre-given information, but are actively involved in the search for information. In group discussions, they evaluate the use and relevance of the information. Specific attention is given to the interaction between the normative and value-driven aspects of knowledge, and the students' preconceived notions and ideas. The pedagogical responsibility of management education includes moral, social, political and philosophical issues. Students have to critically reflect upon themselves and the world of management, and investigate their assumptions and opinions about man and society. The articulation of the student's norms and values plays an important role in the learning process. Consequently, the normative, social and ethical aspects of learning and working in the service industry are addressed in an open discussion.

The general theme of the module *"Learning in Context"* is divided in three interrelated sub-themes:
- learning to learn;
- specific attention is paid to the development of study skills relevant for problem-based learning;
- learning in a community of learners;
- students learn how to live, learn and work together in a postmodern society;
- learning about the environment;
- students are introduced to the context of service management in general and retail management and small business in particular.

The thematic nature of the module is reflected in the focus on integration of the various disciplines. Specific disciplinary approaches are made subservient to the thematic approach of the module. The learning environment invites students to develop and express their learning needs, to cooperate with each other, to interact actively with staff, and to make use of different sources of information. Thus, the student is introduced to problem-based learning as a new way of learning. *"Learning in Context"* may be considered as an initiation in the basic elements of a lifelong learning process.

4.2 Flexibility in the Specialization Phase of the Curriculum

The last three semesters of the eight-semester curriculum are reserved for a choice semester, an industrial placement, and a dissertation. After an evaluation of this specialization phase with specific attention to the learning opportunities of the students, the organization and the content of the programs, we came to the conclusion that we had to redesign the choice semester. In the redesign of this phase we had to balance the specific demands of the stakeholders involved, the service industry, the government, the students, the lecturers and the institute, all with specific and sometimes conflicting needs and wishes.

We first created more options for the choice semester:
1. The student makes a free choice out of all the available modules in the FEM.
2. The student can also choose an integrated track of three interrelated modules. These tracks were designed based on research in the different segments of the service industry (hospitality, retail, small business, leisure, and tourism).
3. The student can take part in the internationalization program. We have international exchange programs with over 25 universities in and outside Europe, so there are many options available.
4. A group of students can make a project proposal. The proposal has to be accepted by the exam committee. If the proposal is accepted a lecturer is appointed to guide the project and the students can devote all the available time to the project.
5. The student makes a combination of the options 1,3 and/or 4.

Except for beforehand stated capacity reasons, there are no limitations to the choice.

Secondly, the fixed duration of the three elements in the specialization phase, choice semester, industrial placement, and dissertation was abolished and a flexible schedule was introduced. Each element of the specialization phase obtained a minimum and a maximum in duration with learning objectives varying accordingly and appropriately. The choice semester is no longer a semester, but varies between one module and six modules. The dissertation can take from one to three modules and the industrial placement can vary between three and six modules. The student has to balance the options, set his priorities, and design his own learning program. The flexibility that is created in the specialization phase reflects our main ideas of optimization the service for our customers. The choice semester thus demonstrates the interrelations between the changes in the content, pedagogy, and organization of our educational program.

5. CONCLUSIONS

Management education is relatively slow in adapting to the changes in the business environment. Therefore, management education has been under extensive and fundamental criticism from the business community. Most of the criticism focuses on the content of the curriculum. The development from an industrial society to a service and knowledge based society is hardly reflected in the content of the curriculum. In our view, it is essential to explore the nature of and the specific demands from the service industry and use the concepts of service management and marketing as indispensable elements for a business school curriculum. The development of a more flexible curriculum, based on the needs of the students and the service industry is necessary. The service logic model (Kingman–Brundage & George, 1996) is used as the basic model for developing a new curriculum.

In the previous paragraphs, we have argued that an integrated approach to educational innovation not only involves adjustments at the content level of the curriculum. Transformations at the content level are interdependent with fundamental changes at the pedagogical and organizational levels.

The pedagogical approach to management education we use has its roots in a constructivist view on learning emphasizing the student's active acquisition of knowledge, his in-depth understanding of subject matter, and his abilities for critical reflection. Consequently, the learning environments that foster active learning processes have to be designed around authentic tasks and problems. Methods like problem-based learning and action learning can successfully be used to enhance the student's learning opportunities. The context and the authenticity of the learning situation are the basic constructivist values reflected in the example that is given of the module "*Learning in Context.*"

On the organizational level, an entrepreneurial focus for universities is needed. Universities have to behave more businesslike and have to focus on the customers, both the students and the service industry. Therefore, the university's organizational pyramid has to be turned upside down enabling lecturers to contribute in self-managed teams to significant innovations of education. Flexible responses to demands from students and business communities are reflected in our example of the design of the specialization phase of the curriculum.

In this paper, we have demonstrated that a university, as an entrepreneurial and knowledge-intensive service organization, has to integrate educational and service management principles so that optimal quality for customers, both students and industry, can be created.

REFERENCES

Albrecht, K. (1990). Total quality service: An applied organization change model. *QUIS 2*, 81-90. International Service Quality Association: New York.

Argyris, C. (1994). Good communication that blocks learning. *Harvard Business Review*, July-August, 77-85.

Baalen, P.J. van. (1995). Facing the challenges: An introduction. In P.J. Baalen, van (Ed.), *New challenges for the business schools* (pp. 1-6). Erasmus University Rotterdam: Rotterdam.

Boyatzis, R.E., Cowen, S.S., & Kolb, D.A. (1994). *Innovation in professional education*. San Francisco: Jossey-Bass Publishers.

Cheit, E.F. (1985). Business schools and their critics. *California Management Review*, XXVII, 43-62.

Chia, R. (1996). Teaching paradigm shifting in management education: university business schools and the entrepreneurial imagination. *Journal of Management Studies*, 33 (4), July, 409-428.

Clark, B.R. (1998). *Creating entrepreneurial universities: Organizational pathways of transformation*. Pergamon.

Davis, S.M., & Botkin, J.W. (1994). *The monster under the bed; how business is mastering the opportunity of knowledge for profit*. London: Simon & Schuster.

Davis, S.M., & Botkin, J.W. (1994). The coming of knowledge-based business. *Harvard Business Review*, September-October, 165-170

Geus, A.P. de. (1997). *The living company*. London: Nicholas Brealey Publishing.

Gibbons, M., Limoges, C., Nowotny, H., Schwartzman, S., Scott, P., & Trow, M. (1994). *The new production of knowledge*. London: Sage Publications.

Gijselaers, W.H. (1995). Perspectives on problem-based learning. In W.H. Gijselaers, D.T. Tempelaar, P.K. Keizer, J.M. Blommaert, E.M. Bernard, & H. Kasper (Eds.), *Educational Innovation in Economics and Business Administration, The Case of Problem-Based Learning* (pp. 39-52). Dordrecht: Kluwer Academic Publishers.

Grönroos, C. (1990). *Service management and marketing, managing the moments of truth in service competition*. Massachusetts: Lexington Books.

Gummesson, E. (1993). *Quality management in service organizations*. New York: International Service Quality Association.

Hamel, G., & Prahalad, C.K. (1994). *Competing for the future*. Boston: Harvard Business School Press.

Heskett, J.L., Sasser, W.E. Jr., & Hart, C.W.L. (1990). *Service break-throughs*. New York: The Free Press.

Kember, D. (1997). A reconceptualization of the research into university academics' conceptions of teaching. *Learning and Instruction*, 7, no 3, 255-275.

Kingman-Brundage, J., & George, W. (1996). Using service logic to achieve optimal team functioning. In B. Edvardsson, S.W. Brown, R. Johnston, & E.E. Scheuing (Eds.), *Advancing Service Quality: A global perspective* (pp. 101-110). New York: ISQA.

Knuth, R.A., & Cunningham, D.J. (1993). Tools for constructivism. In T.M. Duffy, J. Lowyck, & D.H. Jonassen (Eds.), *Designing Environments for Constructive Learning*. Berlin: Springer-Verlag, 163-188.

Lovelock, C.H. (1992). A basic toolkit for service managers. In C.H. Lovelock (Ed.), *Managing Services*. Englewood Cliffs, NJ: Prentice Hall.

Marlowe, B.C., & Page, M.L. (1998). *Creating and sustaining the constructivist classroom*. Thousand Oaks: Corwin Press.

Normann, R. (1991). *Service management: Strategy and leadership in service business*. Chichester, UK: John Wiley & Sons.

Porter, L.W., & McKibbin, L.E. (1988). *Management education and development: Drift or thrust into the 21st Century*. New York: McGraw-Hill.

Savery, J.R., & Duffy, T.M. (1995). Problem Based Learning: An instructional model and its constructivist framework. *Educational Technology*, September-October, 31-38

Schneider, B., & Bowen, D.E. (1995). *Winning the service game*. Boston: Harvard Business School Press.

Senge, P.M. (1990). The leader's new work: Building learning organizations. *Sloan Management Review*, *32* (1), 7-23.

Tillema, H.H. (1995). Changing the professional knowledge and beliefs of teachers: A training study. *Learning and Instruction*, *5* (4), 291-318.

Wijnen, W.H.F.W., & Wolfhagen, H.A.P. (1993). Stimulating study progress in the Netherlands. In T.M. Joosten, G.W.H. Heynen, & A.J. Heevel (Eds.), *Doability of Curricula* (pp. 23-28). Lisse: Swets & Zeitlinger.

Zeithaml, V.A. (1981). How consumer evaluation processes differ between goods and services. In *Marketing of services, Proceedings of the 1981 Conference on Services Marketing* (pp. 186-190). Chicago: American Marketing Association.

Promoting the Human Element in Resource Based Learning for Undergraduate Business Education Programs

Neil Harris[1], Roger Ottewill[2] & Adam Palmer[3]
[1]*Southampton Business School, Southampton Institute,* [2]*School of Business and Management, Sheffield Hallam University,* [3]*Southampton Business School, Southampton Institute, United Kingdom*

1. INTRODUCTION

Increasingly, higher education institutions (HEIs) in the UK are resorting to variations on a theme of resource-based learning (RBL). Arguably, however, in so doing they are motivated more by the need to find a means of reconciling the inevitable tension between increases in participation rates, on the one hand, and the reducing unit of funding, on the other, than by pedagogic considerations. Consequently, there is a grave danger that they will damage irreparably the learning experience of undergraduates. This is mainly because, in applying the principles of RBL, managers have often given far less attention to human, than to other, often electronically based and technologically sophisticated, resources. In other words, RBL is seen primarily as a means of curtailing rather than enhancing the human element in the learning and teaching process.

For undergraduate business education programs, given their overtly vocational orientation, such a trend is extremely worrying and should not go unquestioned. As Harvey et al (1997) have found, when recruiting graduates employers attach particular importance to interactive attributes such as interpersonal skills, team working and communication skills, (since) these are pivotal for delayered project focused organizations. Likewise, a scan of job advertisements for posts at graduate level, particularly in the sphere of business and management, confirms the high priority given by employers to transferable personal skills, with similar considerations applying to the provision of work experience attachments. Consequently, it would seem perverse to devalue the human dimension in education which makes a significant contribution to the development of such skills and attributes.

Another concern is that students attend HEIs to engage in discourse with tutors, information specialists and peers, not simply to access and utilize paper and computer and information technology (CIT) based learning resources which they could do elsewhere. It is the quality of this engagement with others, especially tutors, which can be said to constitute the unique selling proposition of what HEIs offer. Thus, before it is too late, careful attention needs to be given to the human element in RBL, especially in the context of undergraduate business education programs. This does not mean rehearsing, yet again, the arguments for the retention of, or the return to, traditional methods of learning and teaching. Rather, it requires a more sensitive approach to the development and implementation of RBL and one which does not neglect or undervalue the human dimension. Indeed, RBL does have a great deal to offer tutors and students as well as managers. In short, it can be a liberating experience for tutors and students alike.

It also has the potential to facilitate the acquisition of skills needed in the changing workplace. This is unlike some traditional methods of learning and teaching which, arguably, do little to enhance employability and bear little relation to the realities of organizational life in most business enterprises. In this respect, the following comments of Ramsden are particularly apposite:

> "Studies of graduate satisfaction with courses and reported development of generic employment skills show that powerful links exist between emphasis on student independence, learning outcomes such as team work and problem solving ability, and course satisfaction" (Ramsden 1998, p.159).

If used with care and due regard to the motivation of all concerned, RBL can undoubtedly foster the independence of students and strengthen the relationship between learning outcomes and learning activities. In addition, where CIT is involved, it can contribute to the development of the information retrieval, processing and management skills and competencies that business graduates need in the late 1990s. At the same time, however, there is a need to resist the temptation to rely exclusively on RBL and to

Resource Based Learning

ensure that the interpersonal requirements of group work, problem solving and other aspects of learning and teaching are fully acknowledged and adequately resourced. In short, it has to be recognized that RBL is not a panacea for the problems of HEIs as they seek to cope with rapidly growing areas, such as business and management.

In this paper, it is intended to:
- outline the nature of RBL, particularly communication and information technology (CIT) led versions, within higher education;
- examine the implications of RBL for tutors and other staff and for students; and
- consider the way forward for management in adopting what can be described as a more humane approach to RBL.

This paper draws on experiences of business and management tutors at Southampton Institute and Sheffield Hallam University, as well as the literature, with a view to encouraging debate and setting an agenda for institutional policy making.

2. RESOURCE-BASED LEARNING

Although RBL has been defined in many different ways, it is generally seen as an umbrella term "encompassing a wide range of means by which students are able to learn in ways that are on a scale from those that are mediated by tutors to those where students are learning independently." (Brown & Smith, 1996, p.1). On business courses within higher education, RBL tends to be characterized by:
- a requirement that students access, and utilize, the rapidly expanding range of learning resources, particularly computer based (e.g. CD-ROMs, Internet, CAL packages) as a supplement to, and in its purest form a replacement for, lectures and, to a lesser extent, seminars;
- reduced contact between tutors and students; on the assumption that the quality of the contact which does take place will be enhanced as a result of more attention being given to the range and variety of uses to which this time can be put and more effective preparation by the students (Jennings & Ottewill, 1996); and
- a proliferation of, often specially prepared, learning support materials, both paper based and electronic, to compensate for the reduction in contact time and to guide students in their use of learning resources.

While these features can be said to foster independent and student centered learning, and thereby lay the foundations for lifelong learning, one of the current objectives of education policy in the UK, and for reflective practice, they are by no means unproblematic. Nonetheless, in the present climate, it is very unlikely that there will be any significant shift away from RBL, at least for the foreseeable future, despite the issues to which its adoption gives rise. Thus, there is a need to seek ways of ensuring that RBL enriches rather than debases learning and teaching.

It is, of course, understandable that HEIs should seek to embrace the principles of RBL and associated CIT to help them solve the problem of teaching more students, with proportionately fewer staff. Indeed the proceedings of recent EDINEB conferences are illustrative of this trend, with many papers being devoted to technology based learning systems. Likewise, in the UK, the Dearing Report on Higher Education (1997) has emphasized the importance of every HEI exploring ways of producing and utilizing good computer based learning materials and using CIT for the organization and delivery of courses, within a clearly articulated institutional strategy and an adequate infrastructure. More specifically it has recommended that:

> "All students should have open access to a network desk top computer by 2001, by 2005/6 they should have access to their own portable computer" (recommendation 46).

Underlying these developments is the assumption that investment in CIT will lead to reduced costs and greater efficiencies. However, such claims should be viewed with a degree of caution especially when the investment needed in human resource development and various hidden costs are taken into account (Gamble, 1998). As the authors have argued elsewhere, in order to maintain quality while increasing the use of RBL teaching, staff need greater support. The roles of all staff in higher education also need to be redefined and students require better preparation (Harris & Palmer, 1996; Jennings & Ottewill, 1996). Such a view is very much in line with that of the Dearing Report (1997) which recommended that:

> "All institutions should, over the medium term, review the changing role of staff as result of Communication and Information Technology, and ensure that staff and students receive appropriate training and support to enable them to realize its full potential" (recommendation 9).

Unfortunately, however, the human requirements of RBL seldom receive the attention they deserve especially when technology is driving the moves towards RBL. It would appear that many HEIs, as illustrated by their strategic plans (HEFCE, 1998), embrace the technologically determinist version of RBL unquestioningly. There is little evidence that they have a strategy for RBL that considers appropriateness to staff and student needs. Thus, too often... they (teaching staff) are thrown in at the deep end and are required to produce learning resources with little help, guidance or money to do it. In some cases this results in the re-hashing of lecture notes into dull, dreary packages which lack any kind of student interaction or visual interests (Rust & Wisdom, in Brown & Smith 1996, p.38). In the case of students, the problem is reported to be that they came to university expecting to be taught ... (Mapp, in Brown & Smith 1996, p.65) not to spend all their time engaging with impersonal learning resources. These human factors, particularly the impact on tutors and students, acquire even greater significance if the inevitability of the technology driven RBL mode of business education is accepted.

3. IMPLICATIONS FOR TUTORS AND STUDENTS

Despite a belief in the efficacy of RBL, HEIs do not appear to have fully explored the implications, for staff and for students, of moving away from traditional approaches to teaching and learning. In other words, insufficient attention has been given to the human dimension on both sides of the educational equation. On business courses this could be critical since, as mentioned earlier, one of their principal functions is to develop the interactive attributes identified by Harvey et al (1997). Their role is also to prepare students for professional life in general. An important reminder of what it means to behave professionally is provided by Cox (1992, p.218).

> "As professionals we are not told what to do; we have to work it out for ourselves. If we do not want to do it we are likely to be inefficient. We need to know how to do it and so need to know what we need to learn and how to learn it and to actually put it into practice. Having done it we need to be able to make a balanced and critical judgement about how efficient and how effective our work has been, and finally we must know how to improve it in the future."

Clearly this presents business and management tutors with a considerable challenge, if they are to continue providing high quality, vocationally oriented business education in the current climate of significant reductions in the amount of staff-student contact. In using RBL as a response to this challenge, tutors must ensure that the contact which does take place is geared towards the interactive attributes and professional behavior to which employers attach great importance. This would include the development of presentational and negotiating skills and the ability to engage in debate and discussion. In the process, tutors must shift from being primarily teachers to being essentially managers or facilitators of learning. What this means in practice can be presented in terms of a number of new and redefined roles and responsibilities. These are set out in Table 1.

Table 1. Tutor Roles and Responsibilities in a Resource Based Learning Environment

Role	Responsibilities
exemplar	demonstrating workplace skills accessing and utilizing learning resources being a reflective practitioner/lifelong learner critical thinking behaving professionally
motivator	shaping learner expectations designing and applying a coherent framework for learning enhancing learner capability providing reassurance and, where necessary, guidance for individual learners by means of feedback on performance
expediter	contributing to decisions on the availability of learning resources acting as gatekeeper to learning resources collaborator with information specialists and technical staff to facilitate the learning process
counselor	supporting learners as they adjust to the personal demands of RBL helping learners deal with personal problems by finding a solution for themselves
interlocutor	establishing and maintaining an academic dialogue with learners stimulating and guiding discussions by posing questions and drawing out and summarizing key points
mentor	coaching • facilitating reflection on behavior and outcomes • developing interactive attributes

If performed effectively, these roles provide tutors with the means of contributing to the personal, as well as the academic, development of their students. They do, however, change the nature of the relationship with students, and as a result, tutors have to confront a number of key questions concerning the engagement of students with RBL.

First, there are questions concerning learner competence. What skills must students have to cope with the demands of RBL, and to what extent do they possess them when they enter higher education? Many come from educational environments where the emphasis is very much on face-to-face tutor centered learning rather than RBL. Thus, at the very least, ways need to be found of facilitating the transition process.

A second set of questions relate to learner commitment. These include the steps to be taken to ensure that students are as committed to the principles of RBL as the HEI applying them. Also, who should be responsible for ensuring that students sustain the high level of motivation and self-discipline needed to cope with the demands of RBL, and what are the best methods for achieving this objective?

Thirdly, questions arise as to the implications of what can be described as 'learner compliance'. Of critical importance, in this respect, is the extent to which students should be required to comply with tutor initiated guidance regarding pathways through the resources at their disposal, or should be permitted and encouraged to undertake personal 'voyages of discovery' through them. Related to this are questions concerning the degree of compliance and assessment requirements.

Finally, there are various questions about learner comprehension. What forms of guidance and support are most appropriate and effective for ensuring that students understand what is required from them regarding resource utilization? Who should take responsibility for the provision of guidance and support?

As with other aspects of teaching and learning, there are no easy or universally applicable answers to these questions. In the field of business education, responses are likely to be different from those in, say, engineering or history. What is important is that course or unit teams acknowledge them and keep them constantly under review. Such a process needs to be encouraged and supported by institutional managers as part of a coherent and sympathetic strategy for the adoption of RBL. The form and content of such a strategy serves as the theme for the next section of the paper.

4. THE WAY FORWARD FOR PROVIDERS OF UNDERGRADUATE BUSINESS EDUCATION

The role of management in creating an environment where RBL can be successfully implemented and make a significant contribution to the provision of vocational higher education, particularly in the field of business and management, is critical. In short, by their actions, managers can either harness or dampen the enthusiasm of tutors and students alike.

In the present climate, any consideration of management's role must start with the positioning of the institution concerned within the higher education 'market'. In his analysis of the market Finn (1998) predicts that 'brand name' (i.e. high status, well established, elite) institutions, will sustain a high level of demand for their services. They will continue to provide relatively expensive higher education because either they have substantial revenues from a variety of sources to subsidize undergraduate education and/or people will be prepared to pay higher fees on the basis of the perceived value of its qualifications. At the other end of the market, cheaper 'convenience' institutions will offer an 'any time, any place, any where' study package delivered with the aid of advanced educational technologies. He concludes that institutions that are unable to offer either, in other words the middle of the road mass HEIs, will be increasingly unattractive to students. This analysis, however, is based on the situation in the USA and does not recognize that, in the UK, a number of these middle of the road HEIs have a vocational mission, with respect to business and management and other fields, which requires them to synthesize some of the features of both 'convenience' and 'brand name' institutions. In other words, their goal is the application of RBL with a 'human face' which should enable them to maintain a niche within the HE market.

Once the market position is clear, management is faced with a significant challenge. This involves changes in working practices and academic staff roles. The purpose of this is to use human resources in a way which achieves synergy between the deployment of new RBL mechanisms and the expertise of tutors. This will ensure the development of students' interactive skills and prepare them for professional life. Movement on this scale, involving the development and implementation of new delivery systems and formats for teaching students, calls for the application of considerable skill and sensitivity on the part of managers. In tackling the issues involved the early work of the socio-technical systems school has relevance in that it is a reminder of the pitfalls of not achieving the right balance between soft systems and hard systems. Further, in the context of academic institutions, the more recent work of Middlehurst (1993) and Ramsden (1998) offer a way forward.

Drawing on the work of McNay (1995), Ramsden (1998) shows how none of the collegial, bureaucratic or corporate models of academic management are appropriate for a challenge of the kind envisaged here. The preferred approach to leading change, argues Ramsden, is entrepreneurial, visionary, supportive and professional, developed through critical reflection on experience. This 'enterprise culture model' of leadership fits well with the goals of many middle of the road, vocational HEIs. In offering services to students and business their distinctive contribution is the value added by staff to the other learning resources available. Thus, managers need to harness the critical and innovative attributes of academic staff in ensuring that the unique selling point of the 'non virtual' university is the more effective preparation of students for the workplace.

Another strand of Ramsden's (1998) work offers a framework for managing change which can accommodate the human dimension and adapts well to issues surrounding the adoption of RBL. Based on Kotter's (1990) four management and leadership task areas, the first requirement is the creation of an agenda for change.

With respect to the application of RBL within undergraduate business education, one of the purposes of this paper is to contribute to the agenda setting process. It is acknowledged, however, that for many academics the past is more attractive and comfortable than the future and encouraging tutors to change, particularly their working practices, is extremely difficult. One possible reason for this is that many academics are more interested in their subject discipline than in learning and teaching issues. Nonetheless, academics are often characterized by their ability to think critically and to solve problems. Thus, the agenda for change needs to be couched in terms that inspire academics to generate imaginative solutions to the pedagogic challenges they, and their institutions, face. In addition, it should take account of the suspicion of many academic staff towards corporate style goals.

For example, at one business school an agenda was set to move to a more resource based approach to delivering a first year economics module. This involved introducing WinEcon, an inter-active computer package, which has been developed in the UK in recent years. There were two reasons for this. Firstly, WinEcon helps students to learn more effectively by providing access to interactive learning resources outside formal classes. Secondly, there is a wider business school strategy to limit class contact to quality learning as indicated in Table 1. This enables academics to focus on their 'classical' teaching role of intellectual development while WinEcon undertakes part of the knowledge provision.

This leads on to applying the second area of Ramsden's framework, the development of a human network. Once the overall agenda is accepted, no matter how grudgingly, academic staff have the intellectual abilities to develop new systems which they can test critically in liaison with colleagues both internally and externally, through networks such as EDINEB. For this to occur, however, managers need to engender a culture within which it is normal practice for tutors, formally and informally, to share their experiences and ideas with respect to the delivery of vocational higher education.

In the business school where WinEcon was being introduced Year 1 economics results were good and student feedback was very positive. Academics were concerned that changing their traditional approach to delivery would have an adverse effect on student performance in the module. Therefore attempts to recommend the use of WinEcon to students had proved unsuccessful while academics themselves rarely accessed the package on the staff intranet. In part, this was because the package had been provided by a central service rather than the Business School, and there was, therefore, a lack of ownership by academic staff.

To generate such ownership two economics tutors were targeted. Not only were these delivering the two biggest economics courses, they were also innovators in the Marketing sense of the word. Reduced class contact was given to each of them to permit greater involvement and ownership. An agenda was agreed which included gathering information on other HEIs which had used WinEcon, visits to other HEIs where it had been used (and in one case abandoned), and the running of a pilot scheme with a sample group of business school students. Additionally, staff from the University of Bristol, who had undertaken much of the early development work, ran a half day workshop for full-time and part-time economics tutors.

Ramsden's third area is the execution of the agenda. Here it is recognized that cynicism and lack of trust can be barriers to progress, with many academics being skeptical of, and hostile towards, RBL and the motives of management in promoting such changes. To overcome these hurdles a strong lead is needed to satisfy internal and external stakeholders thereby ensuring that the institution remains competitive. If academic staff can see the continued importance of their role in a resource based system, and are empowered to meet the new challenges of the environment, their independence and self management are real strengths in effecting the changes that will be required.

To address staff suspicion and distrust of change the business school plan, which contained proposals to move to more resource based learning, was widely disseminated and debated within the business school and at institutional level. By creating ownership of the agenda, the need to improve continuously the quality of student learning and to make courses more attractive was accepted.

A fourth and final area of Ramsden's framework is impact. The WinEcon initiative is part of a wider business school strategy for academic development which seeks to improve the quality of the student learning experience. Learning and teaching initiatives form a integral part of the business school plan to maintain its competitive edge. It was also the pilot study which led the way for a wholesale review of program delivery, and the implementation of other initiatives. An important element in the offer to students is the approach to program delivery in addition to program content. Sensitive application of technology in resource based learning enhances the staff and student experience. In evaluating the case outlined above the authors were mindful of some of the possibilities and problems concerning further application of 'humanized' versions of RBL on a wider scale.

One possibility is Brighton Business School's model (see Bourner & Flowers, 1997) which exploits the varying strengths of teaching staff. Based on the assumption that there will be no more resources for teaching than already exist, and further increases in participation rates, the approach outlined combines the expertise of a typical new university with the potential of RBL for teaching large numbers. In this model, the emphasis is very much on quality.

It is argued that any face-to-face encounter with students must be 100% worthwhile both from a student point of view and from ensuring the proper deployment of resources in the most effective manner. Hence those who excel at teaching large numbers in innovative ways are encouraged to specialize in that activity. There is a threshold suggested for minimum class size for a face-to-face encounter to be justified. Other teaching staff engage in designing high quality learning materials and identifying sources of information for students, to support the intensive face to face encounters. Although not mentioned in the paper, it is likely that a third group of academic staff would engage primarily in program management and personal support and guidance. Thus, the tutor roles outlined in Table 1 are shared rather than all being performed by the same person. In this model the savings in contact hours are used to resource the preparation of high quality materials and the more finely tuned guidance given by tutors to students pursuing the program.

A variant of this model is one which in reality reinvents the traditional tutorial based system particularly associated with 'brand name' HEIs. Here RBL would be used to provide the bulk of the program for students supported by academic staff who would guide large numbers of students but at much less frequent intervals. One approach to resourcing this would be for institutions to allocate to teaching teams the equivalent of the resources they would have received for traditional teaching activities (e.g. lectures, seminars, tutorials) but provide support and incentives to convert these contact hours into new configurations and ways of dealing with learner competence, commitment, compliance and comprehension. As argued in Harris and Palmer (1997), this requires the development of considerable trust between institutional managers and teaching staff based upon an assurance that efficiency gains are not used as a vehicle for further increasing the work load of teaching staff, thereby undermining teaching quality and morale.

Both models need to be underpinned by carefully managed change in developing staff and student capability and to wean students off their alleged appetite for 'convenience' HE. The first approach is based on an industrial model of economic specialization whereas the second is more organic, relying on multi-skilled academics and would certainly require substantial investment in staff development.

There are many examples of significant investment on the material infrastructure for RBL, such as the Adsetts Centre at Sheffield Hallam University. There is also an array of good practice examples of innovation in business education that have combined the enthusiasm of staff with the increasing availability of CIT (see Eastcott, Farmer & Gibbs, 1994) and Committee for the Advancement of University Teaching (1995)). However these are the exception. Arguably, unless due attention is given to agenda setting, the creation of a human network and the execution of a well designed program of staff and student development, learning and teaching in HEIs will go on much as before. At the very least, a number of unevenly developed RBL programs will co-exist incongruously with traditionally structured teaching programs thereby undermining the credibility of vocationally based business education. In other words, the impact of the changes in delivery methods will be diminished.

Hence, a strong case can be made for mobilizing the resources of educational development centers to facilitate change. Over the past 10 years these have been the predominant vehicle for promoting innovation and critical reflection on learning and teaching within HEIs (Gosling, 1996). Despite having a variety of titles (for example, at Sheffield Hallam University it is the Learning and Teaching Institute) they are all principally concerned with providing a range of opportunities for staff development for tutors. Typically, this would be in the form of qualifications for those new to higher education teaching and schemes for developing new approaches to student learning through funded project work. In some cases, secondments are offered to develop research into pedagogy and to assist full-time staff developers with promoting new approaches to learning across institutions through workshops and in-house conferences.

Links between these centers and new CITs have not always been strong and this can be a problem in integrating expertise in pedagogy with available expertise in, for example, multimedia systems. Increasingly, this is being recognized. For instance, at Sheffield Hallam University, the Adsetts Centre brings together information sources, information technology and educational development expertise in a single location. However, even with these moves to greater integration there are still issues of perception on the part of academic staff who are actually teaching the students on the ground. There is a view that the educational technologists in particular have little practical experience of the challenges of teaching large numbers of students and designing acceptable programs for them which allow students sufficient levels of human 'support'.

To date, pedagogic innovation in many HEIs with respect to CIT based RBL is quite small scale and represents the work of a minority of learning and teaching enthusiasts. Further, as stated by Gosling (1996), centralized units to stimulate innovation in learning and teaching are often seen as tools of management to effect greater efficiency and further exploitation of a diminishing unit of resource. Hence, the importance of developing human networks is to ensure that the problem is shared by all tutors and that there is a pay-off in terms of the quality of their working lives and enhancement of the quality of the student experience.

If it is to be effective, RBL cannot be a minority activity. In the authors' experience, partial embrace of RBL can lead to confusion and conflicting objectives amongst students and staff. For example, students may well be prepared to become more independent learners and then encounter significant vestiges of a more dependent regime promulgated by other staff teaching them. Alternatively, staff who champion RBL may discover student resistance when other modules provide what is perceived as greater student support through more traditional tutor led activities.

The moves to RBL must, therefore, be something that is owned by as many tutors, support staff and managers as possible. An institution's particular approach to RBL must be accepted, be total in its nature and drive all aspects of policy. For example, staff recruitment and selection strategies must be geared towards securing staff who are committed to the institution's approach. Course documentation and quality manuals need to be re-written to reflect the methodologies that will be used and a comprehensive staff development program has to be implemented to cover all staff who are involved in the teaching and learning process, thereby enabling them to perform the roles identified in Table 1 in a confident and competent manner. Students need to be prepared to benefit from the approach taken to RBL and be informed of the implications of the HEIs philosophy. Publicity material relating to the institution needs to explain to prospective students and other stakeholders the particular rationale for RBL and its benefits. The strategy for the use of the HEIs estates needs to embrace the aims of the approach to RBL in, for instance, the design of learning and teaching areas and student study bedrooms.

With sensitive handling by visionary and supportive managers of the kind envisaged by Ramsden (1998), it should be possible to implement the changes needed to apply RBL in such a way that it facilitates the vocational mission of HEIs engaged in the provision of undergraduate business education programs. For most academic staff, the credibility of such changes will be greatly strengthened if full cognizance is taken of their concerns, and those of students, regarding the impact on the learning and teaching experience. In short, the human dimension of the educational enterprise must be given top priority.

5. CONCLUSION

Many HEIs are moving in the direction of the 'convenience' market discussed previously to remain solvent. Very often this means investing heavily in CIT based RBL systems. Institutions with a large stake in business and management education are by no means exempt from this trend. However, to meet the needs of employers, they must not lose sight of their vocational mission. In other words, there is still a vitally important role for the human element in the educational process. Indeed, since the strength of new CIT systems is their contribution to expanding access to information, the niche that such institutions can fill is helping students prepare for careers in 'information rich' organizations, as well as equipping them with the requisite interactive attributes.

Thus, the future of undergraduate business education envisaged here is not that of the 'doomsday scenario' presented by Bourner and Flowers (1997) or the 'training camp' analogy eluded to by Laurillard (1993) in which technology reigns supreme. These predictions are only plausible if it is accepted that the primary role of tutors is simply to offer a diet of information presented to large groups of students, supported by reading lists and traditional examinations. Undoubtedly, there are fears that HEIs are being pushed in this direction by the diminishing unit of funding per student and will seek to deploy their largest expense, human resources, in the most cost effective way. Ironically, the unimaginative but international response of building larger and larger lecture theatres in order to teach more students at lower cost, has made it easier to argue that this form of 'live' information presentation can be replicated by technology. Clearly, CIT will play a major role in information delivery and access but there is an opportunity to use the expertise of staff in far more meaningful ways than simply information disseminators.

The agenda for the future of vocational higher education should be based on the following principles. For staff there needs to be greater flexibility and, at the same time. an improvement in the quality of their working lives. The effective delivery of RBL based business programs requires a much higher value to be placed on collaborative working practices both within and across disciplinary boundaries. The scarce and precious resource of staff contact time with students needs to be completely rethought. Ideally, priority should be given to activities which develop the critical faculties of students and the tools and attributes they need to recognize and exploit the learning opportunities available to them. These two way 'close encounters of the human kind' are very much the key to success in a system increasingly dominated by RBL, particularly in undergraduate business education where vocationality is to the fore.

The hurdles that need to be surmounted if these principles are to be applied are, as with most management of change issues, dominated by human considerations. At present, the resourcing of undergraduate business programs is inflexible and based on standard outmoded formats which are not suited to the adoption of RBL. In many instances, investment in CIT has been separated from consideration of the capability of staff and students to realize its potential. These first two hurdles, in turn, create problems of commitment and ownership amongst staff in engaging with RBL because of their perception that it is technologically determinist in its orientation.

As documented elsewhere (Harris & Palmer 1997), staff need space ☐to execute the agenda' and grapple with the questions of learner competence, commitment, compliance and comprehension, and issues surrounding the transition to new systems of learning. For the students' part, their expectations need to be suitably shaped and then met in ways that are appropriate to vocationally oriented higher education.

For most HEIs a strategy for overcoming these hurdles is to negotiate a far more flexible approach to workload planning, perhaps embracing a new model of student caseload rather than class contact hours. Focused staff development needs to be planned which concentrates on the collaboration and problem solving required to move to new modes of delivery and support for students. Where business and management tutors are not heavily involved in subject based research, resources should be targeted towards encouraging increased activity in pedagogic research and development. Increasingly, in preparing undergraduates for the challenges of the changing workplace, tutors will need to concentrate far more on the processes of development and socialization. Thus, the primacy of content will need to diminish in order to release scarce human resources to equip undergraduates with the competencies they need to cope with the transition from role of student to that of employee. It is envisaged that by moving away from traditional delivery systems, and tempering the potential of CIT with a targeted approach to the development of students' 'interactive attributes' vocationally oriented business and management programs can continue to add value by enhancing employability of undergraduates.

REFERENCES

Bourner, T., & Flowers, S. (1997). Teaching and learning methods in higher education: A glimpse of the future. *Reflections of Higher Education, 9*, 77-101.
Brown, R. (1998). The post Dearing agenda for quality and standards in higher education. *Perspectives on Education Policy*. Institute of Education: University of London.
Brown, R., & Smith, B. (Eds.). (1996). *Resource-based learning*. London: Kogan Page.
Cooper, J. (1993). The management of resource-based learning. *Mendip Papers*. The Staff College Bristol.
Committee for the Advancement of University Teaching (1995). *Improving University Teaching*. Canberra Australia: Department of Employment, Education and Training.

Cox, R. (1992). Learning theory and professional life. *Media Technology for Human Development, 4 (4)*, 217-232.

Daniel, J.S. (1996). *Mega - universities and knowledge media, technology strategies for higher education*. London: Kogan Page.

Dearing Report (1997). *Higher Education in a learning society*. Report of the National Committee of Enquiry in Higher Education. London: HMSO.

Eastcott, R. Farmer, B., & Gibbs, G. (1994). *Course design for resource based learning: Business*. Oxford Centre for Staff Development.

Finn, C.E. Jr. (1998). Today's academic market requires a new taxonomy of colleges. *The Chronicle of Higher Education (USA)*, 9th January.

Gamble, P.R. (1998). Low cost multimedia for distance learning. In R.G. Milter, J.E. Stinson, & W.H. Gijselaers (Eds.), *Educational Innovation in Business and Economics III* (pp. 315-330). Dordrecht, Netherlands: Kluwer Academic Publishers.

Gosling, D. (1996). What do UK educational development units do? *International Journal for Staff Development, Vol. 1*, 75-83.

Harris, N., & Palmer, A. (1995). Doing more with less: improving the quality of the first year experience on business undergraduate courses within the context of a diminishing resource base. *Journal of Further and Higher Education, 19 (3)*, 63-73.

Harris, N., & Palmer, A. (1996). Preparing students for the honours challenge. *Journal of Further and Higher Education, 20 (3)*, 31-44.

Harris, N., & Palmer, A. (1997). *A review of strategies for professional development in higher education*. Paper delivered at 4th EDINEB conference, Edinburgh UK.

Harris, N., Lawson, D., & Palmer, A. (1998). A collaborative approach to improving students critical thinking on business undergraduate courses in the UK and US. In R.G. Milter, J.E. Stinson, & W.H. Gijselaers (Eds.), *Educational Innovation in Business and Economics III* (pp.229-245). Dordrecht, Netherlands: Kluwer Academic Publishers.

Harvey L, Moon, S., & Geall, V. (1997). Graduate's work: Organizational change and students' attributes. Centre for Research into Quality. The University of Central England in Birmingham.

Higher Education Funding Council England (1998). *Analysis of 1997 strategic plans*. HEFCE Report 98/07.

Jennings, P.L., & Ottewill, R. (1996). Integrating open learning with face-to-face tuition. *Open Learning, 11 (2)*, 13-19.

Kotter, J.P. (1990). *A force for change: How leadership differs from management*. New York: Free Press.

Laurillard, D. (1993). *Rethinking university teaching*. London: Routledge.

McNay, I. (1995). From the collegial academy to the corporate enterprise: The changing cultures of universities. In T. Schuller (Ed.), *The changing university?* Buckingham: SRHE and Open University Press.

Mapp, L. (1996). Implementing computer-supported resource-based learning. In S. Brown, & B. Smith (Eds.), *Resource-based learning* (pp. 58-69). London: Kogan Page.

Middlehurst, R. (1993). *Leading academics*. Buckingham: SRHE and Open University Press.

Ramsden, P. (1998). *Learning to lead in higher education*. London: Routledge.

Rust, C., & Wisdom, J. (1996). Helping individual staff to develop resource-based learning materials. In S. Brown, & B. Smith (Eds.), *Resource-based learning* (pp.38-48). London: Kogan Page.

Non-Prescriptive Guidelines For More Effective Learning About High Quality Leadership, In Management Education And Development

Erwin Rausch[1] & John B. Washbush[2]
[1]Didactic Systems, USA, [2]University of Wisconsin, USA

1. INTRODUCTION

More has been published on leadership than on any other single topic in the behavioral sciences. There is a large number of perceptions of who a leader is, or what distinguishes a leader from other people. Leadership has been studied from all possible perspectives and contexts, from good and bad, in anthropology, in social psychology, in human relations/resources, in sociology, in education, in political science, in theology, and in business. According to Rost (1991), "By far, most leadership scholars are in schools of business and write for corporate executives and business students... Stogdill (1974) and Bass (1990) collected and analyzed some 4,725 studies of leadership." Stogdill concluded that "the endless accumulation of empirical data has not produced an integrated understanding of leadership."

Klenke (1996) quotes Bennis and Nanus (1985) as expressing little optimism about arriving at a clear understanding of Leadership: "Decades of academic analysis have given us more than 350 definitions of leadership ... no clear and unequivocal understanding exists as to what distinguishes leaders from non-leaders and, perhaps, more important, what distinguishes effective leaders from ineffective leaders, and effective from ineffective organizations."

We believe that the inability to generate a consensus is largely due to the fact that the word leadership is just that, a word. Every writer and researcher has been free to define it as he or she saw fit. As a result we can teach ABOUT "leadership", but not how one can BECOME a leader. No one can learn how to become a Lincoln, Joan of Arc, Billy Graham, Martin Luther King, Jack Welch, Mother Theresa, Napoleon, Hitler, or Saddam Hussein. Still, the literature has taught us many things about what distinguishes competent leaders from others. It is therefore possible to help everyone, and especially managers, become MORE effective leaders than they are, and better managers at the same time. That is what the Guidelines Concept attempts to do.

Some people associate the word "guidelines" with specific directions for what to do. They even see guidelines as possibly limiting one's thinking. These perceptions do not apply to the guidelines discussed here, because they are non-prescriptive. It is probably best to think of these guidelines as REMINDERS of some, or possibly most, of the issues that should come to mind and that MIGHT be considered when making a management/leadership decision. Managers/leaders who find the idea of thinking with guidelines to be beneficial, will probably use the ones suggested here only as a springboard to the creation of personal guidelines that help them consider ALL the issues they believe to be important when making a decision or developing a plan.

This paper briefly presents a model of the leadership component in management decisions and a possible set of non-prescriptive guideline questions that can provide a bridge between leadership and motivation theories and their practical application in critical and day-to-day decisions of managers at all levels. These guidelines, though worded very simply in their basic form, involve the processes that are used to set goals at all levels of the organization, to achieve coordination and cooperation, to establish and maintain appropriate norms and standards, and to determine communications policies and practices. They concern the need to consider competence of stakeholders, conflict prevention and resolution, performance evaluation policies, and the tangible and psychological reward systems. They help the user think beyond the immediate challenge and consider the long-range implications.

2. THE TWO COMPONENTS OF MANAGERIAL DECISIONS

All managerial decisions, and many in avocational and family affairs, require simultaneous consideration of 1) functional aspects (those pertaining to technical issues, the specific occupation or function), and 2) leadership/managerial aspects (those that apply in all occupations, including education and avocations, and even some activities in private life). These decision considerations pertain to the 3Cs: effective CONTROL, not top down or bottom up but appropriate for the situation, COMPETENCE for all functions, by all stakeholders, and an achievement oriented, yet satisfying, CLIMATE).

Education, interest, and short term success of managers, all favor emphasis on functional considerations. As a result, the leadership component of decisions frequently does not receive the level of emphasis, which it deserves, and which is essential for high quality planning, and implementation decisions. Management education heavily favors explanations of theories and few bridges to practical use of the theories are usually provided. Students are often frustrated by this seeming lack of relevance to their needs.

The frustration with inadequate bridges between theory and practical application, especially in the Organizational Behavior courses and others where leadership and motivation theories are covered, is articulated exceptionally well in this passage (Bowditch & Buono, 1994):

> ... the initial idea (for this book) came early in our teaching careers. Following class discussion of motivation, perception, communication, and group dynamics, a bright student questioned "where the course was going." Even though we had initially devoted a few sessions to introducing the various topics in organizational behavior, the student - and subsequent discussion revealed many others like him - did not have a good sense of the interrelatedness or utility of the topic areas ...

Missing are effective bridges between conceptual learning, and practical use. Case studies, simulations and field assignments can provide a portion of such bridges. However, appropriate, comprehensive, non-prescriptive guideline questions can provide structure, with and without experiential learning, for coping with the complexity and ambiguity that faces learners when they attempt to apply what they have learned, to practical situations.

A similar situation exists in management development, where programs frequently concentrate on sharpening narrow interpersonal skills. There is often little that bridges to the vastly more complex and important determinants of effective leadership - creating environments in which people strive to achieve challenging goals, are continuously enhancing their competence, and find satisfaction and appropriate rewards.

In functional courses, i.e. operations, marketing, finance, MIS, etc. the need to consider the management/leadership aspects of decisions is given low priority. If architectural education were to follow the same practice by teaching only mathematics, and expect students to derive formulae for beams and columns by themselves, or consider people needs, there would be many unsafe structures, and few would be people-friendly.

For the management/leadership considerations, the specific type of (prescriptive) guidelines used in the technical/functional subjects, such as the formulae, tables or databases, are not appropriate because effective actions depend on the many complex aspects of the situation. Here, guidance can best be gained from non-prescriptive guidelines - questions that raise the critical issues. The more knowledgeable users of such guidelines are about the issues, the better they can apply them. Often, however, with just common sense and knowledge based on experience, even the simplest, most basic form of such guidelines can improve decision quality. At the same time, in this abbreviated form, they stimulate the desire to know more about what will make for even better answers to the questions.

A set of three fairly basic, non-prescriptive guideline questions (the 3Cs guidelines) can immediately be used by educators, learners, and managers, by interpreting the questions on the basis of past learning and experience. They can serve as starting points for the development of guidelines that are more comprehensive and appropriate to the individual's style and situation.

3. THE 3CS MODEL

The guidelines are based on a model, The 3Cs Model, also called the Linking Elements Concept (Rausch, 1978) that builds from a widely accepted statement that <u>it is the manager's/leader's responsibility to lead the team, the organizational unit or the organization toward doing the right things right</u>.

That requires involving people and/or affects people. When people are involved, it is necessary to consider their reaction. In effect, managers/leaders must <u>bring alignment between the characteristics and needs of the organizational unit, or of the task, with the characteristics and needs of the people involved and/or affected (the 'stakeholders')</u>.

As the figure below shows, to achieve this alignment three sets of characteristics and needs must be considered. They are depicted in figure 1.

- The Control needs of the organizational unit or of the task, and the attitudes of the staff members with respect to the methods used to achieve and exercise control.
- The Competence needs of the organizational unit or of the task, and the knowledge, skills and abilities of the stakeholders (the staff members and others who are affected by a decision).
- The Climate offered by the organization and the psychological and tangible needs of staff members.

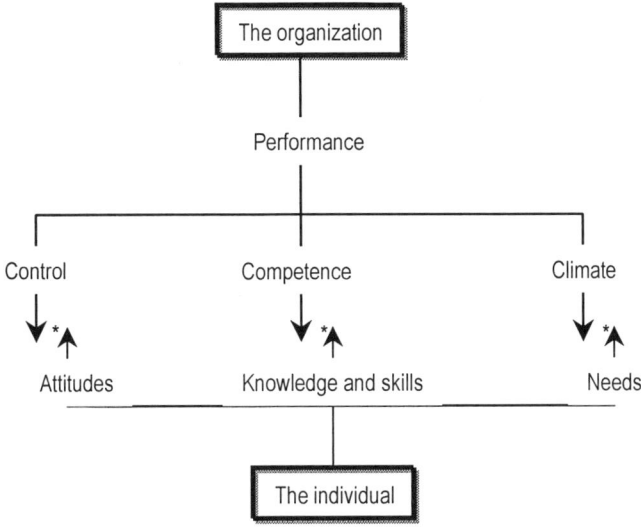

Figure 1. The basic diagram of the 3Cs (courtesy of ASQ Quality Press Rausch and Washbush, 1998)[13]

For these conditions to be satisfied, there should be:
1. Appropriate goals, and norms, participatively arrived at and effectively communicated so that the end result of the task or activity is known, specified, or at least understood. There should be adequate awareness of the steps toward completion of the task, or goal, to broadly clarify when progress is satisfactory and when corrective action is indicated. When leading toward setting and achieving goals, there is a need for coordination procedures, leadership toward cooperation, with levels of participation in decisions that consider the situation, and the

---

[13] High quality leadership: practical guidelines to becoming a more effective manager, by Erwin Rausch and John B. Washbush; ASQ Quality Press, Milwaukee, WI. Reprinted with permission, by Didactic Systems, INC. PO BOX 457, Cranford, NJ 07016; TEL: +1 908.789.2194; FAX: +1 908.789.0038; E-MAIL: DIDACTICRA@AOL.COM

characteristics, competence, personality, and professional maturity, of the individuals who will be involved. To achieve appropriate control, managers also apply their respective professional expertise, and many of the functional managerial knowledge and skills that are taught in universities and professional seminars, such as strategic planning.
2. Human resource development policies and procedures, including encouragement and psychological incentives, backed by necessary support to stimulate staff members to accept responsibility for their own learning.
3. Psychological and tangible rewards that will ensure that staff members and other stakeholders will be satisfied with what is happening, or at least not be so unhappy that they will present obstacles. For most rapid/efficient and effective progress, they should be very satisfied with their respective roles. Such a climate, assures best possible acceptance and implementation of the decisions or plans, by anticipating and adjusting for their impact on people. In an appropriate climate, members of the organizational unit feel committed to the best interest of the organization and motivated to do their best. The other stakeholders who are affected by the decision or plan will have positive rather than negative reactions.

Figure 2 shows an expanded picture of the diagram in figure 1, with these needs and characteristics of the organization and of individuals in greater detail.

4. THE 3CS GUIDELINE QUESTIONS

The model provides the foundation for the guideline questions. At first, before most managers have a thorough grasp of the full meaning of each one of the requirements, no more may be needed than that they ask three questions of themselves and of other staff members involved in a decision or plan, before making it final:

- What needs to be done to ensure effective CONTROL, so that the decision or plan alternative, which we are considering, will lead us toward the outcome we wish to achieve?
- What needs to be done so that all those who will be involved in implementing the decision, and those who will otherwise be affected, have the necessary COMPETENCIES to ensure effective progress and use of the product or service, if they do not have them already and,

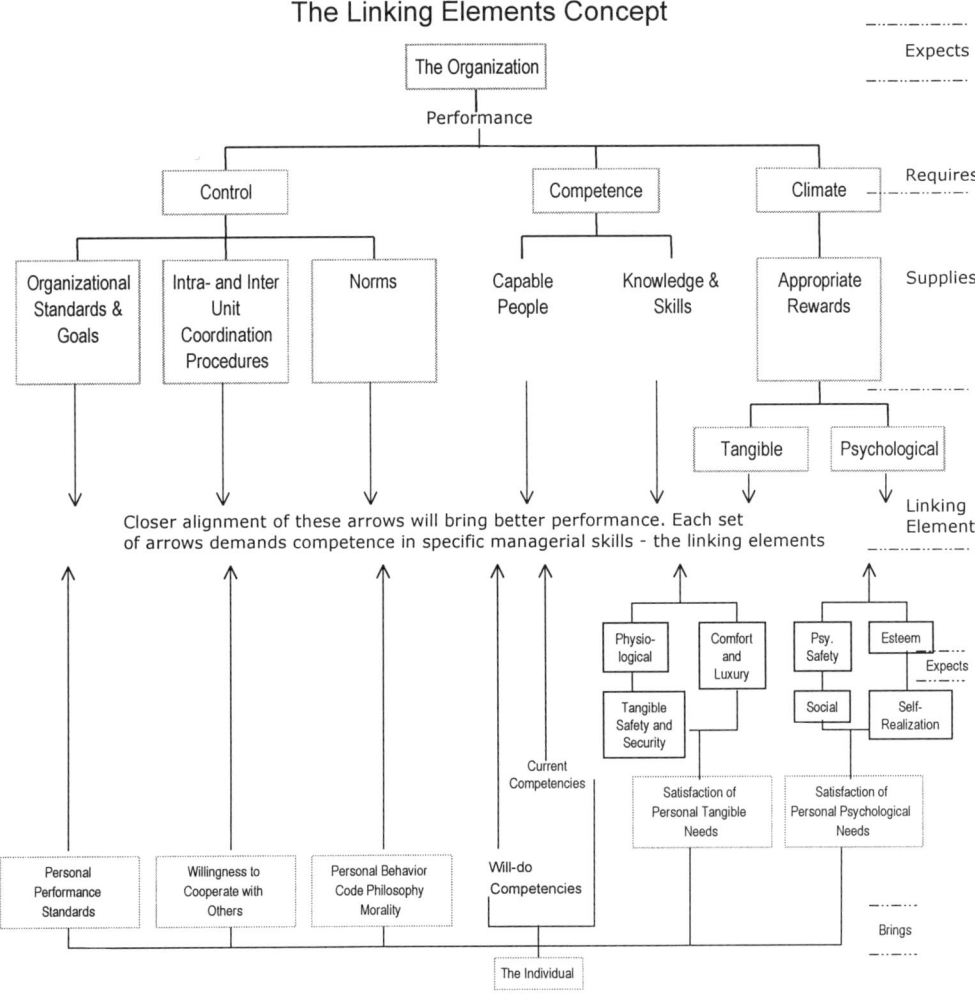

Figure 2. The expanded diagram of the 3Cs (courtesy of ASQ Quality Press. Rausch and Washbush, 1998)[14]

- What needs to done, if anything, so that the reaction of the various groups and individuals who have to implement the decision/plan of this alternative, and those who will be affected by it, will be in favor of it or at least have as positive a view as possible - so there will be a favorable CLIMATE?

---

[14] High quality leadership: practical guidelines to becoming a more effective manager, by Erwin Rausch and John B. Washbush; ASQ Quality Press, Milwaukee, WI. Reprinted with permission, by Didactic Systems, INC. PO BOX 457, Cranford, NJ 07016; TEL: +1 908.789.2194; FAX: +1 908.789.0038; E-MAIL: DIDACTICRA@AOL.COM

Even at this simplest level, the questions have proven their value in more than one hundred management development seminars and consulting assignments. Managers were asked to think of decisions they had made recently or that they were about to implement. They were then asked to review those decisions in light of the three questions. Almost without exception, they made some change, or wished they had made a change in their approach to the opportunity or challenge. Obviously, the more comprehensive a manager's understanding of concepts behind these three INITIAL guideline questions, of the factors that bring effective control, including the management of conflict, of techniques for managing learning, and of the influences on climate, the more meaningful the three questions become.

5. PEDAGOGICAL CONSIDERATIONS

Making a subject relevant, and providing expanding foundations for material to which the learners will be exposed later on, can make absorption of new information, and even discovery, more effective, and efficient. Organization of material can thus provide neural receptors and prepare pathways for storing new information (Bloom, 1956; Bass, 1966; Lefrancois, 1995).

A conceptual model and guidelines based on it, can give learners such a structure for learning. (Bruner, 1966; Gagne, 1977). At the same time as foundation for vicarious and practical application, this structure adds further to the effectiveness with which new information is absorbed, and prepared for use. Such a model, and the guidelines, should emphasize the critical distinction between the two aspects: the functional, and the management/leadership considerations, as the 3Cs model does.

6. BENEFITS OF NON-PRESCRIPTIVE GUIDELINES FOR LEARNERS, EDUCATORS AND COACHES

Sound, comprehensive and well-integrated guidelines bring many benefits for learners in colleges, universities, and management development programs, and even for self-study. They include:
1. A foundation on which to build new learning (neural receptors for better retention):

- Initial, yet comprehensive and integrated, non-prescriptive guidelines present learners with a few key issues which they can use immediately for classroom or practical decisions, based on their existing knowledge and experience.
- New knowledge can enrich this skeleton of simple questions with more structure and background, so that answers to the questions become more thorough and effective.
- Initial guidelines subtly challenge learners to find more comprehensive answers; they create neural receptors and exert a motivational pull that stimulates inquiry and discovery.
- When new information that is presented to learners, is organized along guidelines that become increasingly comprehensive, learners can better integrate the information into their existing store of knowledge - because they can see how and where it is related to what they have previously learned.

2. Seeing where the course or program is going, with immediate evidence of practical use of what will be learned. Learners can see from the initial explanation of the guidelines that they will gain deeper understanding of sound decision making.

3. Satisfaction of the need for structure with which to face the complex world and for understanding how to deal with the bewildering demands of managerial/leadership decisions:
   - Non-prescriptive guidelines, (those suggested in this paper whether accepted as stated, modified to better fit the individual user's style, or entirely different comprehensive and integrated ones), bring structure to the definition and selection of alternatives for decisions in complex and unpredictable environments, as well as in more routine situations.

4. Applicability of the guidelines to improve decisions in personal life:
   - In many situations, one, two, or all three, of the guideline questions (which will be outlined later) can apply to family situations, to career decisions and to decisions in avocational pursuits.

5. While learners often question or challenge concepts presented by authorities, there is little to prevent acceptance of guidelines that are primarily questions and which learners are encouraged to modify, if they wish, to fit their individual needs.

There are also significant benefits for **educators**, **coaches**, and **mentors** who use non-prescriptive, comprehensive and integrated guidelines in instruction, simulations and cases, other assignments, test construction, and grading:

1. Appropriate guidelines provide useful structure to many presentations and ensure consistency from sub-topic to sub-topic.

2. Following the lead of guidelines can bring more consistent instructions and evaluation of performance in many case analyses, simulations, and other assignments.
   - The guidelines can make it easier to explain to learners how they can effectively analyze cases, perform simulations and complete other assignments.
   - The guidelines can help the instructor bring more consistency to evaluation of learner performance in simulations, cases and other assignments.
   - Satisfaction of educators, coaches and mentors is increased by the ease and extent of learning, and the satisfaction of learners.

7. BENEFITS FOR ORGANIZATIONS, MANAGERS AND LEADERS

There can be very substantial benefits for managers and leaders and their organizations when the habits are formed to use guidelines. It is, of course, desirable for the managers/ leaders in an organization to use guidelines that are as similar as possible. The benefits include:

1. Better decisions, greater effectiveness, (greater efficiency, higher quality of product or service, and fewer errors).
2. By creating a structure for appropriate participation in decision making, guidelines can ensure that the special knowledge and the views of several people can be used to enhance any decision. With the spreading use of PC networks, these insights and views can be focused on a specific decision or plan without the need for lengthy meetings or the emergence of conflicts.
3. By providing a framework for easily recording the use of the guidelines, a record and audit trail can allow review of decisions or plans just prior to implementation.
4. Decisions of new managers/leaders can be reviewed for coaching purposes.
5. If an organization decided on encouraging the regular use of guidelines, it could make that a requirement for consideration in promotion decisions. That would signal to all staff members that it would be in their interest to develop their decision-making competence with the use of the organization's guideline questions or similar ones of their own.
6. Guideline questions lead to inquiries about the causes of problems and a deeper understanding of the issues that need to be addressed so that the current challenge and similar challenges are met thoroughly, not only for now, but also as well as possible, for the future.

7. Guideline questions bring more thorough analysis of issues, and thereby improve critical thinking, and continuing learning.

8. A REPORT ON RELATED RESEARCH

Recently, a survey research project, focused on the pedagogical potential of the 3C concept was conducted by faculty at eleven institutions widely dispersed in the US. The student participants were in a variety of courses, from basic management and Organizational Behavior to Public administration. Class sizes ranged from six to more than 20. Most were undergraduates, with some in graduate school. There were two classes from an HBU (Historic Black University). A large proportion of the students had previously been exposed to leadership or motivation theories, though none had heard of the guidelines before. A significant minority, including some full-time students, had some supervisory responsibilities.

The survey assessed their views with respect to the teaching of management subjects, specifically those that pertain to management/leadership aspects of decisions. The specific hypothesis being tested was that students would support the use of 3C guidelines in their management courses. The survey protocol was simple. It required only these steps:

- Handing out background reading consisting of two and one-half pages of brief synopses of leadership and motivation theories and an equal amount of reading on management/ leadership guidelines, and a questionnaire.
- Asking learners to provide 'Learner Information' that asked primarily educational and work profile questions.
- Asking learners to read the background material.
- Asking learners to answer questions on learner views with respect to whether the guidelines should supplement instruction on theory, and which should be explained first.

There was no class discussion of guidelines, or of the purpose of the survey, prior to its administration. The survey was conducted at different times in the various courses. Despite the great differences in schools, geography, and student background, results showed that they were exceedingly uniform in confirming the hypothesis. A synopsis of the result is provided below:

- There was overwhelming interest in guidelines. Every question mentioning guidelines showed strong student interest for learning them.
- A huge majority (approximately 90%) showed by their responses, that they would want theories explained together with immediate bridges.

- With an even larger percentage, students felt that guidelines should be explained. There was a small preference for explanation occurring after (rather than before) theory presentation.

These results should be seen in light of the fact that the guidelines were not explained at all. Nor was time allowed for answering questions. Based on the brief written descriptions in the handouts, students saw the value of the guidelines, in conjunction with the theories.

9. CONCLUSIONS

There are two conclusions that can be drawn from the study and from the reactions of managers to the use of the guideline questions.
- The results of the survey study have strongly confirmed the hypothesis that students would welcome it if guidelines became part of the syllabi in their management courses.
- The power of three guideline questions lies in their role as gates to better immediate decisions and to still better decisions later, as their deeper meaning becomes clearer and clearer. Obviously, the more comprehensive a leader's understanding of concepts behind these three initial questions, the more likely that decisions will be of the highest quality.

REFERENCES

Bass, B.M., & Vaughan, J.A. (1966). *Training in industry; The management of learning.* Belmont, CA: Wadsworth.

Bass, B.M., & Stogdill, R.M. (1990). *Bass and Stodgill's handbook of leadership theory, research, and managerial application.* New York: Free Press.

Bennis, W., & Nanus B. (1985). *Leadership: Strategies for taking charge.* New York: Harper & Row.

Bloom, B.S. (Ed.) (1956). *Taxonomy of educational objectives, the classification of educational goals, handbook I: Cognitive domain.* New York: David McKay.

Bowditch, J.L., & Buono, A.F. (1994). *A primer on organizational behavior.* (3rd ed.). New York: Wiley.

Bruner, J.S. (1966). *Toward a theory of instruction.* Cambridge, MA: Harvard University Press.

Gagne, R.M. (1977). *The conditions of learning* (3rd ed.). NY: Holt, Rinehart and Winston.

Klenke, K. (1996.) *Women and leadership: A contextual perspective.* NY: Springer.

Lefrancois, G.R. (1995). *Theories of human learning.* (3rd.ed.). Pacific Grove, CA: Brooks/Cole Publishing.

Rausch, E. (1978). *Balancing needs of people and organizations - The linking elements concept*. Washington, D.C.: Bureau of National Affairs. (Cranford, NJ: Didactic Systems, 1985).

Rausch, E., & Washbush, J.B. (1998). *High quality leadership: Practical guidelines to becoming a more effective manager*. Milwaukee, WI:ASQ Quality Press.

Rost, J. (1991). *Leadership for the 21st Century*. Greenwood: Prager.

Stogdill, R.M. (1974). *Handbook of leadership: A survey of theory and research*. New York: Free Press.

Cross-cultural Learning Practices for Business Education

Karina R. Jensen
International Communication & Development, ENPC Graduate School of International Business, Paris, France

1. GLOBAL BUSINESS AND HUMAN RESOURCE NEEDS

1.1 The Global Business Environment

The current strategic business framework is mostly based upon industry and competition within existing markets. However, emerging management theory seeks innovation through collaboration in order to create new markets (Moore, 1996). A success formula normally defined strategic fit as "consistent with a firm's goals and values, with its external environment, with its resources and capabilities, and with its organizations and systems" (Grant, 1995). Companies are pre-occupied with the strategic fit of existing resources and capabilities. However, management experts are now calling upon business leaders to seek a strategic "misfit" between resources and aspirations in order to discover future opportunities (Hamel & Prahalad, 1994). Time has come for management to consider the creative tension found within core competencies and functionalities in striving for human value in business. While traditional management models clearly paved the way for strategic thinking and structural frameworks in business, they rarely addressed the dynamics of human interaction in the global marketplace. The intersection of global strategy and culture has also demanded increased attention to international organizational behavior and global human resource systems. This highlights the importance of cross-cultural learning to effect positive global change and innovation.

1.2 Towards Collaborative Systems in an International Environment

The promise of new market creation, industry transformation or opportunity environments is largely based upon the organizational development of human value for employees, customers, and partners. The new paradigm in strategy-making means thinking in terms of whole systems where the individual and the company is part of a wider economic ecosystem and environment (Moore, 1996). Economic co-evolution aims to link cooperation with competition for improved human value and business productivity. The new strategic architecture looks beyond existing market capabilities and resources and identifies broad competencies that will capture future opportunities. Knowledge acquisition for continued development and growth becomes a key requirement. Thus the global organization requires renewed commitment to expanding relationships - strengthening internal communication as well as achieving external learning. The appreciation of cultural diversity and the development of shared values require common company-wide disciplines and perspectives for increased communication and teamwork (HBR, 1994).

Cultural diversity plays an integral role in developing vision and imagination for future opportunities in the global business environment. Gary Hamel and C.K. Prahalad emphasize that companies with impressive industry foresight benefit from "rich cross-currents of interfunctional and international dialogue and debate" (Hamel & Prahalad, 1994). A cross-section of ideas can only be created through diverse multifunctional and multinational teams. A multidimensional organization can also leverage cultural diversity in creating flexibility and responsiveness within its strategic and environmental framework. As the new conceptual frameworks evolve into the creation and management of diverse, distributed, and cross-functional teams, the old business models of individual initiative and hierarchical structure will be replaced by new competencies in global teamwork and leadership (O'Hara-Deveraux & Johansen, 1994). When researching and evaluating the strategic value of cultural differences for the EIU, author Lisa Hoecklin noted that organizations are becoming

Cross-cultural Learning Practices 323

increasingly aware of the competitive advantages of international diversity (Hoecklin, 1995). Where synergy and reconciliation are important business skills, Fons Trompenaars emphasizes that the best integrated diversity helps a corporation excel (Trompenaars, 1998). Thus, a key business challenge is to create a collaborative learning environment where cultural diversity shapes and strengthens the organizational knowledge pool.

1.3 Building Value and Commitment for Global Teamwork

Although many multinational corporations today recognize the need for a global vision, they are still struggling with the question of how to change traditional managerial mind-sets and assess cross-cultural training needs. Management training and development programs may succeed in developing a strategic vision, however managers are still consumed by their immediate operating responsibilities while influenced by parochial behavior when facing global issues (Bartlett & Ghoshal, 1994). Enlarging managerial frames and cultivating a learning or unlearning behavior demands selection, development, and integration of human resources. Global leaders are best developed through participation in global teams where action learning is employed to solve global issues (Marquardt, 1998). This places additional responsibility and emphasis on the global human resource management function for recruitment, development, and training of global business managers. The opportunity for business success is the development of a holistic strategy involving new managerial mindsets and new organizational capabilities (HBR, 1996).

1.4 Developing Cultural Learning in a Knowledge Economy

Although the potential learning benefits are numerous, the challenge and complexity of cross-cultural management demand a cultural orientation and commitment to continuous learning by today's managers. The value of cross-cultural collaboration needs to be recognized and appreciated before a true global culture and vision can be created within the organization. Individual and team learning thus requires a new collaborative space where new approaches and solutions can be created and defined (O'Hara-Deveraux & Johansen, 1994). The first step is to develop cultural self-knowledge where personal responsibility is accepted for one's own learning needs. This is an evolutionary process which starts from a recognition of cultural differences and moves towards an understanding of cultural values and behavior. The successful identification and interpretation of these two stages leads to the third stage or collaborative phase where cultural learning can take place. The mindset and commitment required to evolve through these learning stages demands cultural exposure from personal, professional, or educational experiences.

Although professionals who have developed a particular country or regional expertise have a considerable advantage, the scale and intensity of global teamwork require further cross-cultural competencies that go beyond country or regional knowledge (O'Hara-Deveraux & Johansen, 1994). The emerging global learning organization again demands that managers adapt their cultural understanding and apply cross-cultural management skills within a multi-faceted environment. In a 1997 study identifying 40 global leaders in fifty firms across Europe, North America, and Asia, the top strategies for developing the mind-sets of global leaders were identified as international travel, multicultural teams, global training programs, and transfer assignments overseas (Gregersen, Morrison, & Black, 1997). The RAND study found that cross-cultural teamwork was often introduced as a key component to strengthen a company's global strategy and to ensure successful results for international projects (RAND, 1994). Leading companies worldwide such as General Electric, ABB, Hewlett-Packard, Motorola, Unilever, and Procter & Gamble have demonstrated that a focus on cross-cultural team learning through global projects is contributing to increased productivity and performance for their organizations.

Along with cultural self-knowledge comes the necessity for a shared vision and team learning. This creates an opportunity for cultural synergy where management recognizes the role of culture and the potential for cultural diversity in the organizational framework. Rather than adopting an ethnocentric or parochial view of global work, employees view cultural diversity as a competitive advantage and key resource for the global learning organization (Adler, 1997). The application of cultural synergy allows professionals to develop new ideas that incorporate cultural variables and insights for a global solution. Egon Zehnder International, the most profitable executive search firm per capita in the world, attributes its success to its ability to treat its global firm as a single team, where strategic growth relies on networking, relationship-building, and a collective performance drive (Goleman, 1998).

1.5 Key Features of the Global Learning Organization

The new generation of management leaders and researchers speak passionately of vision, innovation, and collaboration in the global economy. Imagination and cooperation are often viewed as the key drivers of these values. Several corporations and organizations worldwide continue to adopt or create new versions of Peter Senge's Five Disciplines: personal mastery, mental models, shared vision, team learning, and systems thinking. According to a 1997 study, top-performing companies worldwide exhibit similar characteristics including initiative, commitment, open communication and trust-building, collaboration, support, innovation, risk-taking, and shared learning (Fitz-Enz, 1997). There is also an increased awareness of the importance of professional development to an organization's economic health. The European Centre for Work and Society (ECWS) defines the learning organization as a new organizational model developed closely with organizational competencies, including four characteristics: interaction with the environment, a managerial approach to learning, building a shared vision, and team learning (ECWS, 1998). From structure to systems to process, learning has become a prime driver of change and innovation.

The challenge of life-long learning can only be realized through a personal commitment to self-development, shared vision, and team learning. Translated into global business language, the critical skills for the new paradigm become cultural self-awareness, global vision, and cross-cultural team learning. Cross-cultural, cross-functional, and multilingual knowledge will be among the most highly valued assets in the global management arena (O'Hara-Deveraux & Johansen, 1994). Cross-cultural learning becomes a key resource for the global knowledge economy. Multinational corporations are currently creating posts for Chief Learning Officers and Chief Knowledge Officers. Companies like ABB, Procter & Gamble, Coca Cola, Hewlett-Packard, and Royal Dutch Shell are applying global strategies at various levels including international best practices meetings, multicultural teams or task forces, management assignments worldwide, and an increasing number of foreigners in headquarters (Hoecklin, 1995). It is the transfer of individual and team learning to organizational learning that empowers employees within all levels, disciplines and nationalities.

1.6 The Global Business Professional

The hiring needs for creative, culturally aware, and globally trained managers places critical importance on the self-development, education and experience of professionals. Competencies such as cultural self-awareness, global perspectives, multilingual competence, tolerance for ambiguity and differences, cultural flexibility and strong communication skills are considered as key attributes for global business professionals (Marquardt, 1998). An awareness of their own cultural biases and perspectives, the ability to capture a shared global vision, and the cross-cultural competence for team learning are inherent in the management process. When cultural diversity is used as a resource rather than a liability, managers have the opportunity to discover and create the opportunities of cultural learning. Cross-cultural competence and process facilitation become the key management skills for global teamwork (O'Hara-Deveraux & Johansen, 1994).

However, managers must first and foremost become culturally aware of the biases and influences of their own culture. This requires an openness and adaptability to cultural differences in organizational structure, management styles, communication, and teamwork. In a 1997 study where US Fortune 500 firms were surveyed, 85 percent did not believe that they have an adequate number of global leaders. The study further identified that effective training programs for global leadership development should include participants from the companies worldwide operations, topics such as international strategy and vision, worldwide organizational structure and design, change management, cross-cultural communication, international business ethics, multicultural team leadership, new market entry, dynamics of developing countries and markets, managing in uncertainty, and action learning components such as a field-based business project (Gregersen, Morrison, & Black, 1997). On one hand, the global manager needs to recognize the sources of local and global strengths within structure, resources, and knowledge; on the other hand, the global manager must possess the cultural knowledge and communication skills to identify and motivate the employees that will develop organizational capabilities (see figure 1).

Global Business Skills
Structures, Resources & Knowledge

Knowledge Management Skills
Technology, Information & Communication

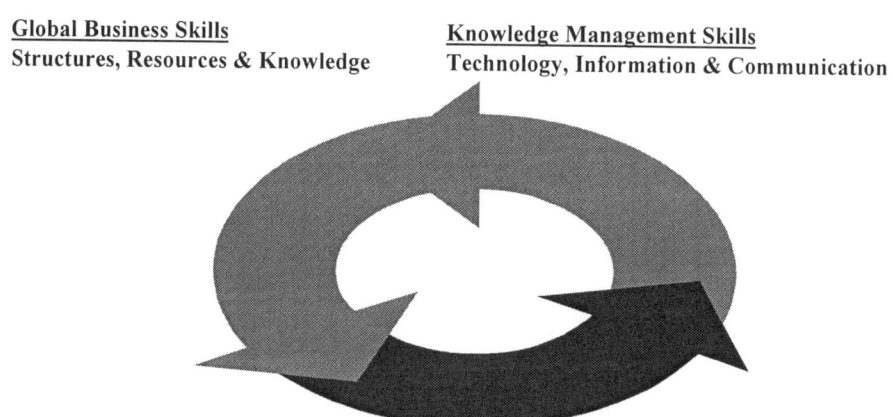

Cross-cultural Learning Skills
Global Vision, Self-Awareness, Team Learning

Figure 1. Global Management Development Model.

2. CHANGES IN GLOBAL BUSINESS EDUCATION

2.1 The Growth of International MBA Programs

Since worldwide learning has become a priority for today's business organization, it is important to examine the role of cross-cultural learning practices in international business schools. How are international business schools teaching students to build learning organizations within the global marketplace? Business schools play an increasingly important role in shaping the learning process for global teamwork. An educational knowledge network that incorporates a global vision, cultural self-knowledge, and cross-cultural team learning is essential to business professionals. As organizations continue to face a changing global economy, the educational learning model must adapt to the needs of culture, technology, innovation, and leadership.

In response to the growing demand for global and entrepreneurial management skills, business schools are facing the need for programs that incorporate a global focus, international business curriculum, innovative learning methods, communication and teamwork skills. Accreditation bodies such as AMBA in Europe and the AACSB in the US are also playing active roles in the development and growth of international MBA programs. Top-ranking guides such as Which MBA by the Economist Intelligence Unit and the US publication BusinessWeek focus on international competencies in the ranking of a business school, including a global view, teamwork, and internationalism. Prominent business schools along with young and innovative business schools worldwide are playing influential roles through academic leadership and closer cooperation with the business community.

US business schools have traditionally served as strong and progressive leaders in providing core business education, whereas European business schools have led the way for international and innovative business education. In view of globalization trends, many US schools have set aggressive goals and are catching up to some of their European counterparts in various areas of international business education. Although the US and European MBA programs have historically differed in structure and content, the leading business schools are presently borrowing from best demonstrated practices in the US, Europe and other world regions. While providing a longer, more in-depth program that largely appeals to a younger student body with some work experience, American business schools are also introducing flexible and more intensive programs to appeal to a larger audience. In terms of international business education, the European schools tend to appeal to professionals who seek a shorter, more intensive program involving a more experienced student body in a multicultural environment.

According to an MBA Career Guide survey of 1000 MBA recruiters worldwide (approx. 50% US corporations, 40% European corporations, 5% Asian/Australian corporations, 5% Latin American corporations), MBA recruitment has steadily increased during the 1990s (Quacquarelli, 1996). As a result of worldwide GDP growth, trends for MBA recruitment have steadily grown in North America and Europe, along with increased growth in the Asia-Pacific region and promising growth opportunities in Central Europe and Latin America. The Asia-Pacific region has particularly experienced a dramatic increase in the demand for MBAs. In terms of MBA employers, management consulting firms (26%) and financial services (28%) were the major recruiters, whereas industry represented 26%. An overwhelming 68% of the companies surveyed were found to be recruiting MBAs for their worldwide sites. With the growing need for a global management cadre, business schools are increasingly facing the demands and challenges of meeting the critical new human resource requirements.

2.2 The Cross-cultural Learning Gap

While globalization and entrepreneurship continue to pave the way for MBA curriculum, there is also a growing focus on communication. A 1995 survey of 215 business schools in the US (53 percent AACSB-accredited) revealed that few programs included communication courses in their programs. Whereas many business schools recognize that a problem exists, survey administrator Dr. J. David Pincus of the University of Arkansas notes that the results uncovered an absence of required communication training in most business schools (Pincus, 1996). Although attitudes towards the value of business communication training has improved, most of the educational emphasis is on technical communication skills rather than interpersonal communication skills. Technical communication skills focused on personal competencies and one-way communication such as writing, visual aids and presentation skills. On the other hand, there was a lack of training in interpersonal skills that focused on social competencies and two-way communication such as negotiation and teamwork. Moreover, the surveyed communication topics did not include any references to intercultural communication skills. The conclusions of the survey point towards the increasing recognition and value of communication in business curriculum, yet the lack of direction and applications for integrating communication disciplines into MBA programs.

While business schools consider the need for communication skills, corporate criticism of business school curriculum in the area of communication continues to grow. Companies emphasize the global nature of business and the need to manage an increasingly diverse work force make it essential for managers to have significant communication and learning skills. The 1994 RAND study on Global Preparedness and Human Resources found deficiencies between university preparation and corporate needs and expectations in Europe and the US. Most of the global respondents believed that academia cannot keep up with new learning practices in corporations (RAND, 1994). Cognitive, interpersonal, social and communication skills are receiving greater attention from employers. Thus, the ability to successfully apply domain knowledge appears to rely on the concurrent and effective use of generic skills. Since cross-cultural competence has appeared as the critical new human resource requirement, global business strategy must further incorporate cognitive, social, and interpersonal skills for performance measures.

It is important to note that the attitudinal and cognitive elements play a crucial role in developing global professionals. Personal traits of flexibility, adaptability, openness, cultural empathy, commitment, innovation, and entrepreneurialism are viewed as key success factors in the emerging business environment. Yet the corporations in this study did not believe that universities could fulfill these skill requirements for learning content and processes of the cognitive, social, interpersonal, and cross-cultural dimensions. A global survey on international business education in the 1990s further corroborates the view that most business schools seek to provide only an awareness of the international dimension of business, rather than competence or expertise (Arpan, 1993). Although there is formal commitment to internationalization in mission statements and strategic plans, there are still several challenges concerning internationalization of faculty, international course content, and experiential learning. Compared to US institutions, European institutions showed higher levels of internationalization in terms of faculty and curriculum. However, there is an absence of information on the contribution of the cross-cultural knowledge process to institutional learning models worldwide.

2.3   The Need for a New Institutional Learning Model

The historical development of the learning process in university education demonstrates a separation between science and humanities. Science, the driving force of the industrial age, clearly dominated intellectual achievements in university education throughout the 20th century. The focus on science and technical knowledge completely replaced the leading educational philosophy of the 19th century, where knowledge was driven by an education in the liberal arts and humanities. Students were dedicated to the pursuit of knowledge for its own sake (The Economist, 1997). Heading into the 21st century, science and humanities represent an educational crossroads for the knowledge economy. As a generator of knowledge and ideas, the role of the business school as a developer of human value becomes increasingly important. The challenge rests on the university's preparedness for educating professionals in a global knowledge economy.

Life-long learning joins personal responsibility with institutional responsibility. As noted by Charles Handy, education needs to be re-invented in order to promote continued learning where change is an opportunity (Handy, 1989). Learning encompasses many different types of intelligence for which knowledge acquisition is but one component. Peter Vaill further develops the idea of life-long learning where he contends that learning as an institutional activity needs to be replaced by qualities and behavioral skills for personal learning practices (Vaill, 1996). New ways of thinking need to be devised beyond the traditional learning model in order to achieve life-long learning. The criteria of efficiency, speed, and volume with the philosophical principles of goal directedness, learners' responsibility to value the goals, and learners' lack of responsibility for originating goals is a traditional framework that hampers the new learning needs of conscious, reflective, and collaborative learning (Vaill, 1996).

Life-long learning thus replaces institutional learning as the basis for human learning philosophy and practice. Managerial leadership is no longer a set of technical skills, rather one of learning skills. MBA graduates can no longer survive with data-crunching abilities alone. The main learning challenge is the ability to recognize the interrelationships between the technical, the purposeful and relational in creating a meaningful and rewarding learning process (Vaill, 1996). As the growing importance of learning cannot be shouldered by the business school alone, it requires a learning partnership between the academic institution and the business community.

2.4 The Emerging International Learning Environment

As the globalization process continues for business schools, the immediate concerns center on pedagogical needs in course content, teaching approach, learning approach, and student evaluation. When examining the scope of internationalization, schools need to consider changes in business curriculum, faculty training, the reward system, the research emphasis, student recruitment, and service requirement (Akhter & Ahmed, 1996). Most of the attention has been focused on internationalization of the business curriculum which can be categorized into several stages, from the lowest requirement of course infusion to the highest requirement of a dedicated college of international business. In defining internationalism, three levels of international knowledge most effectively describe the learning process:

global awareness, global understanding, and global competence (Kedia & Cornwall, 1994). In order to achieve an optimal level, the internationalization effort must involve faculty development, curriculum enhancements, cross-cultural training, and international linkages with partner universities (May & May, 1996).

The culturally diverse groups that frame the institutional learning environment play a crucial role in developing and achieving global competency. The remaining challenge for business schools is to leverage this cultural diversity for in-depth learning of intercultural communication and teamwork. An ability to accept and integrate different cultural beliefs and values requires a new attitude and behavior. This also involves the basic recognition and understanding of one's own philosophical beliefs and value system. Globalization is creating an intense and diverse learning environment that can no longer be addressed with the old institutional learning methods of monocultural learning such as cultural models or country research. Although helpful in the learning process, it is only a supplement to learning the real interactions that take place in a changing and culturally different business environment. Cultural learning involves knowledge of oneself in relation to other cultural contexts (Vaill, 1996). Not only developing awareness of our own cultural perceptions but applying the self-developed qualities of life-long learning within the context of a situation (see Table 1). The open and adaptive mind-set required of cross-cultural learning is essential in developing effective work situations; learning about specific mentalities and styles of different cultures will follow.

Table 1: A New Institutional Learning Process

The Cross-cultural Learning Model	
FROM	**TO**
Parochial View	Global View
Sciences	Humanities & Sciences
Teaching	Learning Partnership
Learning Content	Cultural Learning Process
Goal-directed, Structured & Individual Learning	Conscious, Reflective & Collaborative Learning
Personal Development	Cultural Self-knowledge
Teamwork	Cross-cultural Teamwork
Monocultural Approach	Multicultural Approach
Country-specific Education & Training	Life-long Learning of Cultural Contexts

Cross-cultural learning practices that aim to achieve interpersonal and cultural awareness are being applied within experiential contexts at a few leading business schools worldwide, however there is a larger number of schools that lack such practices. The ability to apply cross-cultural learning is becoming more important than traditional learning practices such as language training and overseas study. Openness and adaptability to different cultural perspectives are thus becoming a focus for a growing number of business schools. In response to increasing demand from corporate recruiters, business schools are beginning to provide courses incorporating global content and teamwork processes. The remaining question centers on the ability of business schools to transform themselves into global learning organizations.

2.5 Examples of Learning Practices - Business Schools/US & Europe

International business schools tend to build upon a global vision, awareness, understanding, and competence within their learning environments. It is within the area of global competence that effective cross-cultural learning is examined. In studying best learning practices amongst leading international business schools in Europe and the US, global competencies were evaluated against the global leadership development criteria set forth by the corporate recruitment studies presented in section one of this paper and summarized by the following factors: 1) culturally diverse groups, 2) courses covering international strategy and vision, cross-cultural communication, and multicultural team leadership, and 3) action learning or field-based projects. These criteria are further examined within the framework of the key learning skills presented in this paper: global vision, cross-cultural team learning, and cultural self-awareness.

A sample of sixteen schools in the US and Europe were selected for their reputation and dedication to international business education, where the majority offer a school dedicated to international management studies. The US business schools that were studied for global competencies include Pennsylvania (Wharton); MIT (Sloan); Duke (Fuqua); UC Berkeley (Haas); Babson (Olin); American (Thunderbird); University of South Carolina (Moore); Monterey Institute of International Studies. The selected European business schools include IMD, Switzerland; Insead, France; London Business School, England; IESE, Spain; Rotterdam (Erasmus), Netherlands; Nijenrode, Netherlands; Wirtschaftsuniversitat Wien, Austria; and Theseus, France.

2.6 Global Leadership Development Criteria

The selected business schools share a global focus, integrated course content, innovative learning methods, and a culturally diverse and collaborative learning environment. All of the selected schools require international business courses as part of the core curriculum, a majority have a dedicated school to international business studies, teamwork is applied to coursework, and courses are offered on communication and teamwork and cross-cultural management. Learning innovations are applied through action-learning or field-based projects involving academic and corporate settings. Offering participants an experiential and interactive focus, coursework in the business schools is often cross-disciplinary, modular and theme-based.

After a radical program restructuration in 1994, Babson focused on the need for entrepreneurship and global education. In addition to employing visiting faculty, the school offers creative case methods and an international consulting program. Faculty work in module and stream teams across four modules that address the business development cycle from creative management to growing business in a changing environment. IMD offers an ambitious modular format with eight clusters beginning with an overview of general management and ending with self-development and awareness in a global context. Aside from providing participants with classic topics, personal development, and a consulting project, Theseus has created four thematic clusters including organizational learning and change and the information society. The Theseus MBA program has chosen an innovative philosophy of management education that centers on the need for integrating technology, management, and cross-cultural learning.

It is encouraging to view the growing activity within international research, partnerships, learning practices, and knowledge management for the selected schools. Recruitment policies aimed at increasing cultural diversity further underscore the changing learning environment. In order to strengthen the cross-cultural learning process, schools are seeking participants from different cultures with international perspectives. Although the US business schools are aggressively expanding their international recruitment efforts, the European schools still offer the highest percentage of international students with an average of 83% for Europe compared to an average of 36% for the US of the sixteen selected schools (see Table 2). The initial effectiveness of cross-cultural communication and teamwork thus becomes highly dependent upon the ability to develop and leverage cultural diversity.

2.6.1   Global Vision

A school's ability to develop a global vision or mind-set lies in the ability to exchange ideas and implement activities across intercultural differences and international borders. An international mission statement that points toward leadership, innovation, and a changing global business environment provides the key educational path for these business schools. In strengthening their vision, the business schools have relied primarily on a global network of partnerships to boost international curriculum, research, language studies, and cultural immersion programs. Thunderbird, American Graduate School of International Management, has an impressive global network of cooperative university programs, overseas business centers, business partners, and foreign institutional programs for ensuring a global view and exposure to all participants. The University of South Carolina and Wirtschaftsuniversitat Wien have formed an innovative partnership to offer an international MBA degree that incorporates both European and US business education practices. Participants benefit from study on two continents, international coursework, and multicultural team consulting projects.

A great advantage of a strong global network is the knowledge available to participants. London Business School is employing collaborative learning through the International Teachers Program, organized by nine International Schools of Business Management (ISBM) in Europe and the US, for the development and enhancement of teaching effectiveness. In order to ensure the continued internationalization of faculty, the University of South Carolina's College of Business Administration offers a yearly seminar series on Faculty Development in International Business (FDIB). The professional development seminars show faculty how to further internationalize their knowledge, courses, and research.

Research at several institutions is taking on added importance in the areas of cross-cultural management, teamwork, and business education. University of Pennsylvania's Wharton School of Management is currently focusing on research concerning cultural bridging and managerial incentives, impact of culture on leadership, and rate of innovation in different societies; research at the newly established Center for Leadership and Change Management also includes management of team conflict. Teaching and innovative learning methods are receiving more attention and interest in international schools. MIT has initiated a teaching and learning laboratory dedicated to the visibility and legitimacy of learning. Aside from exploring peer-based learning and new educational technologies, the lab will develop assessment and evaluation, research, and learning skills as core services.

2.6.2 Cross-cultural Team Learning

The ability to recognize, understand, and integrate cultural values and behavior leads to cross-cultural team learning. Cross-cultural teamwork is becoming a standard practice for tapping into the learning advantages of a global MBA program, in the form of course projects, business plans, and consulting projects. Teams are often formed with members of culturally diverse backgrounds and perspectives within a course, a module, or an academic term. Wharton begins the team learning process in the first term through its Foundations of Leadership and Teamwork course where participants receive guidance and feedback from faculty in weekly meetings. Interactive and action learning is applied through peer and team feedback for team and individual development.

Other business schools rely heavily on field-based work through international business projects. At UC Berkeley, an elective course on international business development involves the selection of culturally diverse and cross-disciplinary teams that take on feasibility studies or market entry analyses for companies in developing markets. Aside from preparing students to evaluate overseas market opportunities, the course also addresses cross-cultural, communication, and interpersonal training needs. The Monterey Institute of International Studies requires a year-long project involving cross-cultural teamwork on an international business plan developed for a sponsoring company. In creating learning partnerships with other business schools, IESE participants have the opportunity to participate in a Global Roll Out Workshop (GROW) where multinational teams around the globe develop an international marketing strategy for a company.

2.6.3 Cultural Self-Awareness

The ability to accept personal responsibility for one's own learning needs of cultural perspectives and contexts results in the development of cultural self-awareness. As learning methods incorporate more interactive and experiential applications, cross-cultural communication skills become increasingly important for ensuring a successful learning experience. Although only half of the schools in this study require a course addressing cross-cultural management, most of the schools require a course or workshop on communication and teamwork skills. Nijenrode offers a dedicated stream on competencies and personal development which includes a cross-cultural management workshop, applied communication skills, and managerial competencies. And IMD has introduced cross-cultural management issues within its modules on general management, business functions, and global business management. Courses are thus addressing technical and interpersonal communication skills with references to the global business environment.

Although course content develops awareness of cross-cultural issues, it is even more critical that course processes involve cultural self-knowledge for developing competencies. Self-awareness and self-reliance skills are utilized in very few business schools. In order to teach participants the value of learning skills, MBA programs need to pursue more courses involving self-development, interaction and communication. Fuqua has demonstrated a strong commitment to personal development through a year-long course on individual effectiveness that addresses managerial communication on all levels. Together with a course on managerial effectiveness, participants can link individual learning with group learning. London Business School is encouraging self-directed careers through the Professional Development Initiative where coaching is applied to individual professional development. Emphasizing the importance of personal growth for managerial success, IMD offers a dedicated module "Leading Self" that examines personal needs and practices of life-long learning. In exploring cultural differences, MIT allows participants to serve as cultural guides or advisors through presentations of their culture during the managerial communication course. The importance of teamwork and diversity is stressed throughout the orientation week and discussed in a special forum.

2.7 Toward Cross-cultural Learning Practices

The path to cross-cultural learning is taking on new purpose within international business schools. However, the selected schools represent only a small sample of a larger community of business schools that still lack similar learning practices worldwide. Although several schools offer international faculty, curricula, and research, they rarely require formal training in intercultural communication and teamwork. Cross-cultural teamwork is often applied through course projects, however there is little opportunity for reflection and evaluation of individual and group learning processes. Aside from recognizing and understanding cultural differences, it is also important for students to learn from cultural diversity. However, the educational value of international students in US schools is often ignored (RAND, 1994). European schools are still more advanced than US schools in attracting and developing a multicultural student body. As the importance of a culturally diverse workforce continues to be underscored by executives in leading companies, schools are increasing their recruitment efforts to attract more foreign students. Leveraging cultural diversity for team learning processes is therefore an important focus for the development of international managers.

Table 2. Overview of Business Schools and International Learning Practices

B-schools	Intl Mission	Dedicated IB School	Cult. Diversity	Int. Bus Courses	Teamwork	Com / Tmwk Course	Cross-cultl Mgmt Course	International Learning Innovations
Europe								
IESE	yes	yes	55%	yes/req	yes	yes / not req	yes / not req	GROW - Global Rollout Workshop
IMD	yes	yes	99%	yes/req	yes	yes/req	yes/req	Modular & Cultural courses, Global Knowledge Network
Insead	yes	yes	87%	yes/req	yes	yes/req	yes / not req	Electives on Managing Across Cultures
LBS	yes	yes	75%	yes/req	yes	yes/req	yes / not req	International Teachers Program, Professional Development Initiative
Nijenrode	yes	yes	84%	yes/req	yes	yes/req	yes/req	Competencies & Personal Development Stream
Rotterdam	yes	yes	85%	yes/req	yes	yes/req	yes / not req	Electives in Cross-cultural Management, Organizational Learning
Theseus	yes	yes	85%	yes/req	yes	yes/req	yes/req	Thematic clusters, organization & action learning courses
WU Wien	yes	yes	95%	yes/req	yes	yes/req	yes/req	IMBA w/USC, cross-cultural communication course

B-schools	Intl Mission	Dedicated IB School	Cult. Diversity	Int. Bus Courses	Team-work	Com/T mwk Course	Cross-cult Mgmt Course	International Learning Innovations
US								
Babson/Olin	yes	yes	30%	yes/req	yes	yes/req	yes/req	Thematical clusters, interactive learning streams
Duke Fuqua	yes	yes	27%	yes/req	yes	yes/req	yes / not req	Indvl & Mgrl Effectiveness courses
MIT/Sloan	yes	no / ib dept	40%	yes/req	yes	yes/req	yes / not req	Teaching & Learning Lab, mgrl/cultl communication course
Monterey	yes	yes	51%	yes/req	yes	yes / not req	yes/req	International Business Plan, international organization behavior course
Thunderbird	yes	yes	43%	yes/req	yes	yes / not req	yes/req	Global network
UCB/Haas	yes	no / ib dept	35%	yes/req	yes	yes/req	yes / not req	International Business Development course
UP/Wharton	yes	no / Lauder MBA	30%	yes/req	yes	yes/req	yes / not req	International research, Foundations of Leadership course
USC/Moore	yes	yes	30%	yes/req	yes	yes/req	yes/req	IMBA w/WU Wien, Faculty Development in International Business (FDIB)

Shared Features: Global Focus, Cross-disciplinary Coursework, Innovative Learning, Cultural Diversity, Collaborative Work Environment

3. DEVELOPMENT OF CROSS-CULTURAL TEAM LEARNING

3.1 Cross-cultural Team Learning Process Study

In an effort to determine and assist the team learning needs of MBA students at the ENPC School of International Management, participants were offered additional training and evaluation in cultural resource assessment and intercultural teamwork during academic year 1997/98. The student sample consisted of 50 students with 8 project teams of 5-6 members, 60% male and 40% female, ages 22-52 with an average age of 29. The cultural profile of participants consisted of 27 nationalities with 42% from Europe, 23% from Asia, 17% from Middle East & Africa, 12% from North America, and 6% from Latin America.

Culturally diverse teams were selected at the beginning of every term for the duration of the academic year. Learning methods and tools for evaluating the cross-cultural learning process included a workshop, resource guides, debriefing meetings, and a student learning team. These activities incorporated the conscious, reflective, and collaborative learning necessary for interacting and communicating during multicultural teamwork. In order to provide a holistic view of the team learning process, the following study is presented with the same learning criteria as the previous section on business education: global vision, cross-cultural team learning, and cultural self-awareness.

3.2 International Management School Profile

The learning philosophy at the ENPC School of International Management in Paris is based on values-driven leadership, involving a holistic approach to business education. Much like the profiled business schools, the ENPC international MBA program offers a global focus, cross-disciplinary coursework, innovative teaching and learning methods, and a multicultural student body. However, the mission of the ENPC MBA program is uniquely focused on the development of values-driven leadership, where professionals learn to operate with vision, innovation, and collaboration in a changing global environment. The ENPC MBA learning philosophy is dedicated to individual and collaborative learning through self-assessment, decision-making, and personal development. The program is self-designed according to each participant's business vision, which enhances personal risk-taking and decision-making skills through inner knowledge and reflective learning.

3.2.1 Global Vision

The student body mostly consists of foreign students (85%) from a variety of backgrounds. The rich diversity in age, education, professional disciplines, culture, and language has succeeded in creating a dynamic and stimulating learning environment. The international courses are mainly taught by visiting faculty from top universities in Europe, the US, and Asia. The class size is limited to 60 students in order to create more involvement and exchange between faculty and students. Finally, participants have the opportunity to participate in study trips or exchange programs with universities and partnership programs within the school's global network

The multicultural learning environment of the ENPC MBA program provides faculty, staff, and students with a unique opportunity for reflection and collaboration. Through a learning partnership between faculty and participants, there is continuous dialogue and evaluation concerning the personal and professional needs of participants. The program structure and the learning approach require a great deal of self-awareness, initiative and flexibility. Although the participants find the learning environment educational and rewarding, it has also become evident that additional support systems and tools are required to ensure effective cross-cultural learning.

3.2.2 Cross-cultural Team Learning

In order to track the learning process for the first two terms of the academic year, a self-assessment survey and group discussion was employed with team members during the de-briefing meetings at the end of each term. The responses provide some insights to the actual team learning process that MBA students face in multicultural teamwork situations. This information will prove helpful to the development of intercultural communication and teamwork training and coursework at ENPC. Overall response rate for the survey in Term 1 was 100% and overall response rate for the survey during Term 2 was 90% due to a few absences during the de-briefing meeting.

In evaluating the teamwork process, members were asked to determine the easiest and most difficult steps of groupwork during the academic term. The easiest activity during groupwork involved task assignments or delegation of work for both Term 1 (20%) and Term 2 (29%). However, the most difficult aspects of teamwork involved management of the time-line during Term 1 (23%), also involving the creation of a common learning objective and framework (16%) and definition of group roles (15%). Discussion and agreement upon common work values during Term 2 (24%), followed by assessment of group resources (19%) and definition of group roles (19%) proved more challenging. It is apparent that the learning process in Term 1 focused on a task-focused and time-driven agenda where organization and coordination become the primary skill-building priorities. As students had strengthened their cultural awareness and understanding by Term 2, the focus shifted to cultural learning skills such as resource assessment and exploration of work values. However, it is clear that students often replaced cultural learning with task delegation due to time pressures during group work.

3.2.3 Cultural Self-awareness

Aside from recognizing and understanding cultural differences, it is also important for students to learn from cultural diversity. When asked if a particular cultural approach dominated during groupwork, a majority of the respondents (61%) felt that the American and Western culture dominated during Term 1, due to the influence of American and Western faculty, literature, and classmates. Achieving a more collaborative environment during Term 2, only 18% of participants felt that a cultural approach dominated during Term 2, giving references to American, Western, and Asian cultures. When applying conscious and reflective learning skills, a majority of the participants in both terms recognized cultural differences, understood their own cultural assumptions, and viewed cultural differences as opportunities rather than barriers.

On the other hand, it was more difficult for participants to consider why different cultural approaches may benefit groupwork and how cultural differences could be communicated. When participants were asked to identify teamwork skills for personal improvement, a majority listed strategic questioning/communication, resource assessment, and organization for both Term 1 and Term 2. Reflections upon improvements for cross-cultural teamwork centered on the need for more time, commitment, communication, socialization, and cultural resource assessment. The participants also valued the cultural self-knowledge they gained in terms of team commitment, cultural awareness, diversity of thinking, organization, and team synergy.

3.3 Cross-cultural Learning Practices for Business Education

In view of the growing needs of employers, business schools, and students, it is clear that cultural synergy during teamwork should be further examined and practiced for the development of future global business professionals. The ability to leverage cultural diversity within a collaborative space is an important practice for international business education. However, cultural learning is often challenged by the time pressure and task focus created by course projects. More time needs to be spent on the process of learning. It is interesting to note the time to market pressure that companies face with global business development projects. The competitive focus on immediate output in existing markets often creates enhanced versions of old solutions rather than the collaborative development of innovative and new market solutions. In much the same way, the traditional academic learning structure and individual task focus of assignments train students to focus on project content rather than the team learning processes necessary for producing innovative results.

Institutional missions and strategies need to be more focused on the development needs of the changing global economy and the link between individual and institutional learning. In order to develop life-long learning skills, business schools need to consider the importance of a global network and educational framework with experiential and interactive learning methods and tools. The structures are emerging, however the systems and processes need to follow. The development of an open mind-set is the key to a global vision, cultural self-knowledge, and cross-cultural team learning. As reported by Jonathan Winter, Managing Director of Whiteway Research International, a successful MBA graduate will be able to manage a life-long relationship with work and learning. In preparation for a 21st century career, he recommends that graduates obtain skills such as self-awareness, reflective learning, cross-cultural sensitivity, teamwork, foreign languages, and international experience (Winter, 1997). The development of reflective, conscious, and collaborative learning skills will thus allow business professionals to effectively manage the culturally diverse learning environment of a global economy.

REFERENCES

Adler, N.J. (1997). *International dimensions of organizational behavior*. Ohio, USA: South Western College Publishing.

Akhter, S.H., & Ahmed, Z.U. (1996). Internationalizing business curriculum. In Z.U. Ahmed, *International Business Education Development* (pp. 1-4). New York: International Business Press.

Arpan, J.S., Folks Jr., W.S., & Kwok, C. *International business education in the 1990s: A global survey*. US: Academy of International Business .C.Y. (1993).

Bartlett, C.A., & Ghoshal, S. (1991). *Managing across borders*. Massachusetts: HBS Press.

Fitz-Enz, J. (1997). *The 8 practices of exceptional companies*. New York: Amacom.

Grant, R.M. (1995). *Contemporary strategy analysis*. Massachusetts: Blackwell Publishers.

Gregersen, H.B., Morrison, A.J., & Black, J.S. (1998). Developing leaders for the global frontier. *MIT Sloan Management Review*, Fall 1998, 21-31

Hamel, G., & Prahalad, C.K. (1994). *Competing for the future*. Massachusetts: HBS Press.

Handy, C. (1989). *The age of unreason.* Massachusetts: HBS Press.
Harvard Business Review. (1994). *Global strategies.* Massachusetts: HBS Press.
Hoecklin, L. (1995). *Managing cultural differences.* England: Addison-Wesley Publishing & The Economist Intelligence Unit.
RAND Institute on Education and Training. (1994). *Global preparedness and human resources.* California: RAND.
Kedia, B.L., & Cornwell, B.T. (1994). Mission based strategies for internationalizing US business schools. *Journal of Teaching in International Business, 5* (3), 11-25.
Marquardt, M. (1998). *The global advantage.* Texas: Gulf Publishing
May, B.H., & May, D.R. (1996). Implementing internationalization. In Z.U. Ahmed, *International Business Education Development* (pp. 35-40). New York: International Business Press.
Moore, J.F. (1996) *The death of competition.* New York: Harper Business Publishing
O'Hara-Deveraux, M., & Johansen, R. (1994). *Global work.* California: Jossey-Bass Publishers
Pincus, J.D. (1996). Progress in communication classes limited. *The MBA Newsletter. 5* (10), 1-9
Quacquarelli, N. (1996). Recruitment trends for MBAs. *MBA Career Guide.*
Trompenaars, F., & Hampden-Turner, C. (1998) *Riding the Waves of Culture.* New York: McGraw-Hill.
Vaill, P.B. (1996). *Learning as a way of being.* California: Jossey-Bass Publishers
Winter, J. (1997). Skills for graduates in the 21st Century. *EMDS International Careers.* 26.
A Survey of universities: The knowledge factory. (1997). *The Economist.* 3-4

Lessons Learned: The Implementation of an Innovative Core Curriculum in Business

Valerie S. Perotti
College of Business, Ohio University, Athens, Ohio, USA

An exciting and challenging program of curricular transformation is under way at Ohio University's College of Business. Placing the Ohio case in the context of change theory, this paper reviews the process leading to the program's development, design and implementation. Through structured reflection, the paper synthesizes and explores suggestions for future curricular change agents.

1. WHAT DO WE KNOW ABOUT CHANGE?

Rosabeth Moss Kanter (1983) defines change simply: "Change involves the crystallization of new action possibilities (new policies, new behaviors, new patterns, new methodologies, new products, or new market ideas) based on reconceptualized patterns in the organization" (p. 279). Kanter, upon completion of an exhaustive multi-organization-based research study, summarizes her view that change may be internally or externally driven and responses to change vary widely with the prevailing *perceptions* of the meanings attached to the precipitating forces and attendant organizational responses.

In her view, "Organizational change consists in part of a series of emerging constructions of reality, including revision of the past, to correspond to the requisites of new players and new demands" (p. 287). Her recognition of the "symbolic, conceptual, cultural side of change" (p. 281) creates a meaningful context for the reflections contained in this paper.

Kanter provides additional insight as to failed change attempts. "The primary set of roadblocks to innovation result from segmentation: a structure finely divided into departments and levels, each with a tall fence around it and communication in and out restricted--indeed, carefully guarded ... Preexisting routines set the terms for action and interaction, and measurement systems are used to guard against deviations" (p. 76).

2. CHANGE IN BUSINESS EDUCATION

The American Assembly of Collegiate Schools of Business (AACSB), charged with assessing and documenting the quality of accredited schools of business in the United States, commissioned a landmark study to answer the question: "Given that the future seems certain to bring about major and fundamental changes affecting society, organizations, and managers, what do we, as management educators, *do* about it? (Porter & McKibben, 1988, p. 7)."

Through an exhaustive and lengthy study reviewing literature, interviewing corporate and higher education leaders, and surveying AACSB members schools, non-member schools and corporate managers, the results, published as <u>Management Education and Development</u>, emerged. It identified numerous areas for attention and development among business educators, but two major criticisms overrode the others:

1. *Insufficient emphasis on generating "vision" in students ...*
2. *Insufficient emphasis on integration across functional areas...*This issue ... is, does the typical business school curriculum--particularly at the undergraduate level--provide sufficient knowledge in an integrated approach to the increasingly complex, fast-changing, and multi-dimensional problems of contemporary business? (pp. 64-65)

Thus, Porter and McKibben have challenged educational institutions to renew their sensitivity to stakeholder concerns through--in part--functional integration. This challenge, however, rises exactly in opposition to many traditions and values of higher educational institutions.

2.1 Obstacles to Needed Change

With the first university's founding in Paris, in 1240 AD, protections for academic freedom and sanctuary began their evolution. This worthy emphasis upon classroom-based freedom of speech and performance has, over time, led to academic structures such as promotion hierarchies and tenure. While in 1240, the embattled cleric may have had to (literally) fight to win the right to say what he knew to be true, today's cynic might suggest that the untenured professor must contain herself or himself until tenuring is complete and one is safe in the system.

If this is true, then those young, newly minted Ph.D.s who strive for tenure are least likely to risk contributing new ideas for change. Innovation in curriculum is, one might infer, entrusted to those senior, well-experienced, tenured folk who are least likely to seek or accept it. We know, for example, that "Much resistance to change occurs because recipients bring their own interests, goals, and group memberships to the change table" (Kanter, Stein & Jick, 1992, pp. 16-17).

Some faculty object to curricular innovation on the grounds of academic freedom, apparently believing that accommodating colleagues in course interaction somehow limits "the free search for truth and its free exposition" (AAUP, 1940). Academic freedom, articulated formally for the first time by the American Association of University Professors (AAUP) in 1940, protected faculty from arbitrary intervention on the part of politicians charged with the burgeoning growth of public higher education institutions. A review of the AAUP document offers no objection to innovative approaches, but rather a grave concern for the protection of responsible professionals in the carrying out their duties. The emphasis on academic freedom, however, illustrates well the inertial forces (Hannan & Freeman, 1989) which inhibit curricular change.

3. SPECIFIC PROBLEMS OF BUSINESS EDUCATION

Interestingly, Boyatzis and his colleagues (1993), on attempting to address this challenge by building an integrated approach to the functional curricular areas at Case Western University, found major obstacles:

> Since the structure of most schools is geared toward specialization and compartmentalization, the maintenance of integrating mechanisms is difficult. This is particularly true during the early stages of implementation--the point of maximum vulnerability.... Integrative devices are unnatural in academia. Even if a similar sort of structure were already present, the usual forms of collaboration across departments, disciplinary units, and staff groups would not be sufficient for the needs of the new program. Many aspects of organizational life in a university

are counter to the ongoing use of such integrative mechanisms as accounting for faculty time and effort, rewarding and recognizing collaboration on design, and team teaching (p. 8).

Existing power structures and reward systems restrict institutional flexibility, thus creating an environment which inhibits faculty collaboration in the classroom. Where tenure, promotion and compensation systems are based upon conventional definitions of teaching, research and service, exploring innovative approaches to curriculum not only violates cultural norms of the academy but also places the careers of courageous young innovators in jeopardy.

4. WHAT IS THE OHIO UNIVERSITY CONTEXT?

In 1994 Ohio University's College of Business participated in an evaluative visit by a team representing the American Assembly of Collegiate Schools of Business (AACSB). AACSB is viewed by many as the premier accrediting body for business programs in the United States. Ohio University's College of Business has been accredited since shortly after its inception in the 1950's.

The accreditation visit yielded a status of "provisional reaccreditation" for Ohio--the college would work to address certain shortcomings for the period of a year at which time it would host a "focused visit" by evaluators. If sufficient progress were not made in the interim, the possibility of losing accreditation was very real. One of the targeted areas was curriculum.

In response, the Dean of the college established "Continuous Improvement Teams" targeted at the questionable areas. Thus, an Undergraduate Curriculum Continuous Improvement Team (UGCCIT) was formed. Responding to AACSB concerns that there was no systematic review and development of curricular initiatives, the Dean challenged the team to create "the best possible curriculum for our graduates, paying no attention to current limitations or structures" (Kelley, 1994).

Recognizing that one of the two key issues AACSB research suggests are of primary importance to the corporate community is functional integration-- structured interaction across academic disciplinary lines which demonstrates the ambiguity and fuzziness of work world decision making. The CIT challenged itself to develop an innovative approach to the college's core curriculum demonstrating such functional integration.

Months into the process of academic dialogue, the CIT determined to attempt a pilot project, called "Business 20/20." Borrowing pedagogical methodology and a faculty mentor from the problem-based MBA program at the college, four faculty linked their respective courses' core learning outcomes together using a series of five authentic business problems. "Business 20/20" became the name of the program--an identifier that would reflect the future-oriented, clear-eyed view that the approach hoped to provide.

Faculty and administrators alike registered surprise when the response to the program emerged. Students demanded other course work in the same format. Parents wrote letters to the dean. Company recruiters prioritized "20/20 veterans" for job interviews. The response led to a series of three pilot offerings, testing and refining the model over a nine month period. With the encouragement of the Dean, the Curriculum CIT proposed that all students be required to complete at least one quarter of fully integrated core course work in order to graduate from the college. In 1995 the faculty as a whole adopted the proposal and thus the implementation of a massive change began.

Shortly thereafter, AACSB fully accredited the College of Business. The curricular initiative was but one of several directed to areas of concern which, in the period of one year, were addressed with leadership and initiative on the part of the college's faculty and administration leading to the positive outcome.

5. THE CURRENT SITUATION

At present, every student in the College of Business must complete at least one full-time, fully integrated quarter of work in the action learning format. Two "clusters" of courses are available: Business Analysis Cluster (Business Law, Management, Management Information Systems, Marketing and Professional Communication) and Strategy Cluster (Business Policy, Finance, Operations, and Professional Communication II). At this writing, approximately 160 alumni and 600 undergraduates have completed at least one cluster with approximately 400 moving through the system each year. 26 of the 74 faculty currently devoted to undergraduate teaching at the college have participated.

As the program evolves, logistic obstacles are eroding. In its pilot phase, the program required students to compete for the limited spaces by being first to arrive for a manual registration process conducted by a college official. With the official recognition of the program through university curricular review, university registration processes have been modified to allow students to register for the clusters exactly as they register for other classes. Room scheduling (securing a single classroom for sixteen hours per week) has been adjusted to accommodate the clusters.

The process of building acceptance and support among faculty continues. Recognition with an award for curricular innovation from AACSB and a grant from the Procter and Gamble Foundation have aided in providing faculty with external validation of the efforts they have undertaken.

The success of future evolution and improvement depends largely upon the ability of the college community to reflect upon the experiences gained and use such reflection for learning to build for the future. *What follows is a distillation of lessons learned from what has gone before.*

6. WHAT LESSONS MAY BE LEARNED FROM OHIO'S CURRICULAR CHANGE PROCESS?

Through a faculty, executive and employer review process, a cross-disciplinary curriculum team (known as the Undergraduate Curriculum Continuous Improvement Team or CIT) was charged with a complete overhaul of the core curriculum. The CIT consisted of representatives of each college discipline along with representatives of departments outside the College of Business providing courses to business students. External representatives came from the English, Mathematics, Interpersonal Communication and Economics departments.

6.1 Lesson One

Team members addressing major redrafting of curriculum must be both knowledgeable and senior in their departments.

Why? In Ohio's situation, two department chairs appointed either part-time or adjunct faculty to serve as their representatives to the team. While part-time or adjunct status protects the individual from undue pressure on tenure or promotion, he or she may not fully understand the will of the full-time, tenured persons in their respective departments. Nor are they positioned to exert influence on peers.

The team determined early that its first challenge was to answer the question, "What knowledge and skills must mark the competent Ohio University College of Business graduate?" The answers to this question came in two forms: first, the faculty adopted a list of seven learning outcomes for the college as a whole:
- Solve problems.
- Formulate an integrated business strategy.
- Exercise initiative.

- Manage oneself effectively.
- Communicate effectively.
- Network and collaborate effectively.
- Think with a global perspective. (Curriculum Overview, 1995)

This list was developed through a paper survey and executive review process, eventually returning to the faculty as a whole and receiving a vote of endorsement.

The second step (which took months to achieve), and one that was far more difficult, was to determine the mission of the core curriculum in the context of the college program.

6.2 Lesson Two

Never undertake to revise curriculum until this question has been answered to the satisfaction of the faculty charged with its delivery: "Is the core curriculum designed to introduce, attract and prepare students for the disciplines from which they will choose their majors OR does the core curriculum have a mission of its own? If so, what is that mission?"

Why ? Extended debates using hours of CIT meeting time were fruitless at Ohio because of partisans who actively represented strong and dramatically different positions. What we failed to see was that these advocates were operating on assumptions about core mission that were not shared or understood. Once the answer to the question was decided, it became a litmus test for all future decisions about the core.

The answer the CIT chose was the latter. "The core curriculum is designed to prepare students with the knowledge and skills for the lifetime career; the major curriculum is designed to prepare students with the knowledge and skills for the first professional position" (Curriculum Overview, 1995). With this framework in place, the Team began the debate leading to selection of disciplines, hours and non-business course work which would constitute the core program.

6.3 Lesson Three

Never assume that departmental or disciplinary representatives are, in any way, sharing information with or seeking guidance from their departmental leaders or colleagues. Decisions to support or oppose proposals at a meeting, we now understand, are often made unilaterally and without consultation. Thus, the decisions reached at the conference table may appear well debated and well resolved to the team but actually do not represent the will of the department or disciplinary group.

Why? The approval process (for core curriculum) at Ohio University requires a three step process: 1) Curriculum Team Action; 2) College Faculty Approval—by vote; 3) University Curriculum Council Approval—by vote. While the Curriculum Team may have quelled resistance from one member or endorsed a team member's view which was not consistent with departmental priorities, when the proposal was brought before the faculty as a whole, the most common objection was "I never heard of this before." Indeed, we found team members denying they had voted for the proposed action when faced with the ire of the departmental peers.

Perhaps more disturbing is the chance that individuals, disgruntled with the process or its outcomes, prefer not to deal with the issue at the departmental level, but go directly to the university level body to voice objections.

7. WHAT DIFFERENTIATES THIS CURRICULUM FROM OHIO'S PAST?

Graduates in the year 2001 from Ohio's College of Business will complete the following learning activities—different from graduates in the past.

7.1 Changes in Non-Business Requirements

- A sequence of at least three courses of a modern language beyond entry level OR three courses devoted to a specific region of the world outside the US, such as the History of Modern Chile, Anthropology of Chile and Latin-American Politics (This step was repeatedly and aggressively advocated by the executives advising the college).
- At least eight hours of course work in performance-based communication (beyond the basic speech class) such as Group Process, Interviewing, Interpersonal Communication.
- Targeted General Education courses selected by the CIT to require performance beyond basic "Introduction to—" level. (This step was designed to address perceptions that students, left to their own devices, most often chose General Education courses rumored to lead to the easy "A.")

Implementation of an Innovative Core Curriculum

7.2　Lesson Four

Incorporating team challenges which suggest the us (College of Business) vs. them (Non-College of Business) syndrome may provide moments of high productivity and morale lifting for the team. Making sweeping and dramatic changes in requirements delivered OUTSIDE the College is a unifying action and readily accomplished, given the interdisciplinary nature of the CIT. Members of the team coalesce as they discuss AACSB accreditation requirements and are called upon to persuade other units of the university of needs in those areas.

Why? In our case, personal and professional barriers to change seemed to diminish when individual stakeholders were focused on resources which they themselves were not called upon to surrender or deliver. Even teammates who refused to "give" on an issue in committee would readily cooperate when people or systems OUTSIDE the College were unable or unwilling to deliver. In hindsight, a more strategic thinker would have paced and planned such elements in the process to relieve tensions which sprang up over resources and "turf" within the College.

7.3　Changes in Business Requirements

- Core business courses undertaken as early as first quarter of freshman year (Introduction to Business and Accounting) coupled with a general tendency to move core course work into the second and third year, reserving the fourth year for heavy concentration in the major.
- At least one quarter's experience in a fully integrated learning community (known on our campus as "Business 20/20"), where faculty and students address core disciplinary learning through action learning methods.
- All core disciplines integrated to some degree in "clusters" referred to as "harmonized."

7.4　Lesson Five

Proposing change in the manner or mode of instructional delivery appears to be the single most stressful and challenging step in the curricular process—both to curriculum team members and to the faculty as a whole. Where individuals might readily see the benefits of reasonable increases or decreases of hours in a discipline, or even removing a course altogether, the process of integrating core disciplines through collaborative faculty interaction, planning and delivery threatens a fundamental value of the academic—autonomy in the classroom.

Why? Competing explanations have been offered in our team over time. Here are a few: 1) Some faculty have never shared a classroom with other faculty. The process is intimidating and raises issues of self-doubt and vulnerability. 2) Academic freedom pertains equally to WHAT is said and HOW it is said—the team has no right to suggest instructional methods. 3) "I learned it this way; if it was good enough to bring me to an advanced degree and tenure, it is good enough for my students." 4) "Covering all the material is the most important outcome in my classroom; I can't cover the material if I have to share time with others." 5) This approach takes too much time. If our reward system is based on research, then I need to devote my time to research.

7.5 Lesson Six

Piloting new projects in order to field test their relevance and applicability is a major asset. Piloting with skeptical faculty on the team is a plus, not only in hopes of converting critics, but also helping advocates to see more objectively.

- **Informing** the faculty community that the pilot is undertaken and inviting participation and observation builds internal awareness.
- **Informing** the student pilot project participants of their status as "pioneers" and urgently requesting and recording reflection and feedback throughout the pilot process helps students to understand their roles in the future of the program while providing documentation of successes and failures. If our experience holds true, they will continue to provide feedback on program usefulness even after graduating and beginning their professional careers.
- **Involving** key figures throughout the university in major activities associated with the pilot helps gain visibility and public acknowledgements of the efforts under way—despite their being in the pilot stage. This endorsement supports the will of open-minded faculty to attempt to participate. (At Ohio, the University President, two deans and several executive advisors did attend sessions and debrief students.)
- **Writing and Researching** about the pilot helps participants develop a sense of reality—the project really does exist. Acceptance of articles and presentations by academically viable outlets suggests to the skeptical that there may be some validity to the approach. In other

words, the greatest success comes from making the abstract idea into some form of reality through documentation.
- **Structured Reflection** and adjustment of the program throughout the pilot period begins the building of an ethic of continuous improvement.

Why? Well documented pilot trials of new formats (provided they are well researched and assessed) offer a wealth of information, experience, testimonials and data from which to draw in dialogue with faculty who must approve the curricular delivery change.

In our case, a pilot program of the fully integrated quarter brought unsolicited letters from parents, employers and excited students who eagerly urged the dean to continue the program. The pilot project won first place in a competition sponsored by the AACSB Midwest Council of Deans for "Leadership in Curricular Innovation." Publicity about the award brought congratulatory letters to college leaders and a rich source of subject matter for alumni meetings and development efforts. The small financial award was assigned to help fund a series of faculty development seminars aimed at building awareness of the theoretical foundations of the new approach—thus the faculty could explore—without risk—the new format, while benefiting from its recognition.

Perhaps more importantly, the pilot trials brought a new sense of participating faculty competence, confidence and comfort with the format. Essentially, the cadre of future program experts was initiated and trained through the pilot program.

8. HOW WAS THE PROGRAM IMPLEMENTED?

The curricular approval process as described above is designed to demonstrate the support of college faculty and, subsequently, the university as a whole, for the curriculum which is, in fact, the purview of the faculty body. Once developed, designed and approved by the CIT, the program, therefore, would require the scrutiny and approval of the faculty as a whole, since the core curriculum is "owned" by them.

The team, therefore, circulated copies of the proposed curriculum in writing to all department chairs as well as to all faculty, and scheduled informational meetings to discuss proposed changes. Further, the team met with and received feedback from the college's Executive Advisory Board. The team received few suggestions from the Executive Advisory Board; informational meetings were attended by approximately 10% of the faculty.

Having incorporated suggestions as appropriate, the team requested time before the Faculty Organization for a vote.

The session opened with an introduction by the team Chair, explaining the context for the changes, AACSB guidelines for core curriculum and the process by which the program had been developed. She then moved the adoption of the new core curriculum. The discussion which followed was volatile, emotional and marked by sophisticated tactical efforts on the part of groups of faculty unified by discipline or by other stakes in the existing system. Whole departments had met in advance to marshal their forces, develop a position and lobby other departments (or specific individuals known to be supportive) to join them. Tacticians in the group had votes counted and moved about the room continuing to assess support and solicit votes during the discussions. Several individuals denied having received informational materials, denied being invited to informational meetings, and, indeed, suggested that the Dean had initiated and conducted the core curriculum change process in secret. It was not academe's finest hour.

Ultimately, after numerous amendments and adjustments, the faculty did adopt the program.

8.1 Lesson Seven

Circulating paper-based information and providing public meeting times does not, in the view of many, constitute sufficient advance information. Subsequent review and reflection suggests that the faculty would have felt better prepared for the debate were an initial discussion held during a regular faculty meeting or in formally scheduled departmental meetings.

Why? While partisans for and against the change proposal may be passionate and unwilling to adapt, there remains a group of individuals, uncommitted to a single view and willing to learn. For the sake of these individuals, a period of open discussion (before a vote is called for) would be productive.

Armed with the endorsement of the faculty, the team set out to complete the many-layered process of program approval at the University level. Having kept the chair of the University Curriculum Committee informed throughout the program development process, the CIT drew her into the discussions as to forms, course titling and numbering and the like. Her assistance was invaluable.

8.2 Lesson Eight

When moving through the curricular process outside the unit, work to create a warm and receptive relationship with faculty leaders (and their support systems) of the process. Resolve logistical details either with them or after hearing their suggestions carefully.

Why? Calling upon such leaders to help with the bureaucracy builds mutual respect and can convert a rule-maker into an advocate. Waiting for logistic decisions (such as course numbering and catalogue entry decisions) would have saved our team at least three steps which we eventually had to re-do after meeting with the University leaders.

With the eventual approval of the University Curriculum Council, the team began developing an implementation plan for the new core. The Assistant Dean for Student Services joined the curriculum team at this point and has become a permanent member. Through his experiences with counseling students about curriculum, he was able to provide considerable insight to the group not only about the mechanics of the new curriculum but also about the means by which students would be advised—one of the team's greatest concerns.

His solutions included several initiatives: 1) the development of a comprehensive advising website where basic information for each student in every major is included; 2) the development and implementation of advisor training workshops which have proven invaluable though not well attended; 3) the development of comprehensive written information which is placed in the hands of each student and each faculty member; 4) the initiation of an "Ask the Advisor" email slot on the college web page. Students both inside and outside the college receive personalized responses to emailed questions within 24 hours.

8.3 Lesson Nine

Involve individuals who must implement curricular policy in the process.

Why? Though the academic tradition awards "ownership" of curriculum to the faculty, advice from people who daily face the challenges of dealing with students and their parents over curricular matters can prevent unanticipated errors before they occur.

9. THE FIRST CLASS

In 1997, the entering freshmen of the Ohio University College of Business received a <u>Catalogue</u> describing the new core curriculum and related requirements. This monumental achievement was greeted with quiet celebration in the CIT meeting. Commitment by the university and the College at this level required the team to undertake the next challenges in the process: faculty development and program assessment. The team determined that no cluster would be delivered without a pilot version for existing, volunteer students. Thus, faculty would continue to refine systems and build faculty competence for the future.

9.1 Lesson Ten

The core curriculum development process is never finished. Continuous review, assessment and cycling of feedback into curriculum development would have prevented the wrenching period Ohio has just lived through.

Why? The massive and almost self-defeating size of the changes at Ohio in the last four years resulted from years of "satisfaction with the status quo" as Lyman Porter (GMAC, 1997) characterized the state of affairs when he and McKibben undertook the AACSB study, <u>Management Education and Development</u>, published in 1988.

Faced with a genuine and deep-seated desire across the faculty to retain AACSB accreditation, the college community proved ready to accept and struggle with enormous change. We were very lucky. A structure aimed at continuously gathering and cycling information for continuous curricular refreshment is the only way to sustain a relevant and viable curriculum in an environment chaotic with change.

Even as the class of 2001 enters its second year in the program, fine tuning of the clusters and methods continues. Departmental proposals for a shift in level (Marketing moves from third to second year, for example) are taken for faculty vote and implemented accordingly. Indeed, assessment results may, at some future time, lead to a rethinking of the integrated clusters and a new model of delivery. We are certain, however, that the process will continue and change will be its hallmark.

10. REFLECTIONS FROM A MORE PERSONAL POINT OF VIEW

Stewardship of the curriculum of a college of business is an awesome responsibility and an amazing opportunity for professional growth. The four years of curricular transformation at Ohio have been, without a doubt, among the most challenging of a thirty year career in higher education. Here are a few of the personal lessons I have learned:

10.1 Lesson Eleven

Commitment to the process of curricular revitalization is best enacted through openness to the approaches of all stakeholders. The leader of the curriculum committee or team must balance the interests of all—even those who do not participate openly or fairly.

Why? The curriculum is the means by which faculty and students prepare for and prepare to advance their professions in the world today. The curriculum is the responsibility of the faculty—all faculty share that burden, even difficult individuals or individuals whose motives might be questioned. The team leader is but a medium—organizing and channeling information across the system to accomplish curricular goals.

10.2 Lesson Twelve

The hard working curriculum team must be noticed, praised and rewarded. The hard working curriculum team must be noticed, praised and rewarded.

Why? Few "service" tasks in the department or college today are less noticed and less appreciated. While a year devoted to publication of a paper is likely to gain recognition, whether public praise or salary increment, four years of service on the curriculum team have gained our teammates little but the satisfaction of the accomplishment itself. When time committed to curricular matters prevents an untenured faculty member from gaining tenure or a young Assistant from moving to Associate, the value system of the institution must be reassessed.

Team members who have allied themselves with the team in getting things done, might well have risked the ire of senior departmental members who play a role in evaluation, tenure and promotion. College leaders must take the steps necessary to protect and reward those people who are guiding and protecting the mission of the college.

10.3 Lesson Thirteen

Cultivate the support and intervention of individuals higher in the academic order. Seek and heed their counsel.

Why? While, in some instances, the endorsement of academic proposals by a dean can bring the so-called "kiss of death," these individuals do carry the power of resource allocation and the wisdom of considerable political experience. Most importantly, however, if significant change is not supported at the very top of the organization, it will never come to pass.

10.4 Lesson Fourteen

Have courage. Take no offense. Look back only to learn how to move forward.

11. CHANGE THEORY IN THE CONTEXT OF LESSONS LEARNED

Clearly, the innovations enacted at Ohio offer an interesting "laboratory" for the exploration of the validity of change theories.

11.1 A Precipitating Event

One might observe that, without the impetus of AACSB's "provisional accreditation" and concomitant threat of loss of accreditation no effort for major curricular change would have taken place. Thus, a precipitating event occurred which created the perception among organization members that AACSB would not be satisfied with "the same old response" suggesting that "grass roots experiments or local innovations must be grabbed" Kanter, p. 293).

11.2 Constructions of Reality

As noted earlier, resistance to change is often a function of *perceptions* of reality. The Ohio experience suggests that the single most difficult step in its process had to do with recommended changes in the teaching and learning environment in the classroom. This resistance, Kanter would suggest, stemmed from the *perception* that classroom autonomy was being violated in the process. Had the team designed and implemented a means for affecting the perceptions of its proposal, it may well have been met with less resistance.

11.3   Openness to Naysayers

It may be a unique characteristic of the academy that challenging dialogue and strenuous debate are appreciated and can facilitate positive change. Few theorists would endorse the notion that naysayers be welcomed into the change design process as has been suggested above.

11.4   A Vehicle for Action

The use of a pilot project to test the proposed change and to disseminate information about it suggest that Ohio's College of Business capitalized on an "action vehicle." "Productive change involves making sure there are mechanisms that allow the new action possibilities to be expressed" (Kanter, p. 298). Thus, members of the organization may see the change in a concrete way, rather than attempting to grasp the reality through abstract or symbolic means. This, too explains the poor result of paper announcements and information sheets describing proposed changes.

11.5   Individual Resistance to Change

That disparate groups of faculty attempted to coalesce to oppose the change should have been expected. The behavior of people in organizations is shaped by their place in structures and by the patterns and power those structures imply. Proposing change in the daily activity patterns of the largest number of organizational members threatened the comfort of "place."

12.   IN CONCLUSION

The single, complex instance of Ohio's College of Business curricular transformation has provided an opportunity for reflection upon both theories of change and lessons that may be learned from practical experience. Perhaps the most telling conclusion to the tale comes from Charles Fishman (1997): "In the real world of change, leaders desert you, your staunchest allies cut and run, opposition comes from the places you least expect, and your fiercest opponent can turn out to be your most vital supporter. In other words, when emotions are running high and the stakes are even higher, people act like people" (p. 71).

The people of Ohio's College of Business have determined to embrace the challenge of curricular change and to move forward. The positive outcome will be not only an improved learning experience for students, but an environment in which continuous review and innovation become the cultural norm.

REFERENCES

1940 Statement on Academic Freedom and Tenure. *The American Association of University Professors.* http://www.aaup.org.

Boyatzis, R.E., Cowen, S.S., & Kolb, D.A. (1993). Implementing curricular innovation in higher education: Year One of the New Weatherhead MBA Program. *Selections, (Spring),* 1-9.

Curriculum Overview (1995). *Documentation of progress toward reaccreditation submitted by Ohio University College of Business to the American Assembly of Collegiate Schools of Business.*

Fishman, C. (1997). Change. *Fast Company, (April),* 64-74)

Hannan, M., & Freeman, J. (1989). Structural inertia and organizational change. *American Sociological Review, 49,* 149-64.

Kanter, R.M. (1983). *The change masters: Innovation for productivity in the American corporation.* New York: Simon and Schuster.

Kanter, R.M., Stein, B.A., & Jick, T.D. (1992). *The challenge of organizational change: How companies experience it and leaders guide it.* New York: MacMillan.

Kelley, A. (1994). Dean's charge founding the curriculum continuous improvement team. *College of Business.* Ohio University.

Perotti, V., Gunn, P., Coombs, G., & Day, J. (1998). The Business Core Curriculum at Ohio University. In R. Milter, J. Stinson, & W.H. Gijselaers (Eds.), *Educational innovation in economics and business III: Innovative practice in business education.* Dordrecht, London, Boston: Kluwer Academic Publishers.

Porter, L.W. (1997). A decade of change in the business school: From complacency to tomorrow. *Graduate Management Admissions Council. (http://DJInteractive.com)*

Porter, L.W., & McKibben, L.E. (1988). *Management education and development: Drift or thrust into the 21st century?* New York: McGraw-Hill.

PART V

NEW ASSESSMENT PROCEDURES

Who Am I, What Do I Want, What Can I Do? An Assessment Centre as Part of the HBO Curriculum

Veronica Bruijns & Elisabeth Pieké
Hogeschool van Amsterdam, Co-op HEAO, Amsterdam, the Netherlands

1. BACKGROUND OF CO-OP[15] HEAO ASSESSMENT CENTRE

1.1 Link Education/employment Market

The optimum link of higher education programs to the employment market is a matter of constant concern and attention; the employment market is so heterogeneous and subject to change that linking education to this is a complicated process.

Consequently, the qualifications a higher education graduate should have are also subject to change. Knowledge quickly becomes out of date; thus, it is necessary for every employee to acquire new knowledge and to be able to apply it. Not only does knowledge quickly become out-dated, labor processes are becoming increasingly complex. Employees must be able to quickly comprehend complex material and make use of this in carrying out their job responsibilities. Companies and organizations must always be on

---

[15] The term cooperative education is also used for different forms of collaborative education. In this article it is used in the meaning of alternating study and work periods.

the alert to respond to quickly changing circumstances. Organizational structures are constantly subject to change, and employment contracts are becoming more and more flexible. This demands flexibility on the part of employees as well. Finally, increasing efficiency and effectiveness requires a business-like and result-oriented attitude from employees. These developments in the employment market must be reflected in higher education. Students in a higher professional education program must not only have an higher education knowledge level, but also a personal approach that is characterized by flexibility, creativity, curiosity and dynamism. They must learn to acquire new knowledge and be able to reflect on their learning process. A graduate must also have excellent communication skills because a great deal of work is done in teams or in changing groups of employees on a project basis.

To achieve the best possible link between higher education and the employment market and to respond to the changing situation in the employment market, educational forms are sought in which study programs and practical experience can be integrated. The system of cooperative education was introduced in the Netherlands in 1992 as an experiment; it was one of the dual learning paths that attempted to optimize the link between educational programs and the employment market.

2. ALTERNATING WORK AND STUDY

The Co-op HEAO of the Hogeschool van Amsterdam has been structured according to the cooperative education model. This means that after a common one-year preparatory phase, students alternate between a half-year of work and a half-year of study. The program is completed with a full year of study. The total duration of the program is 4½ years.

The program was initiated in 1993 and the first students graduated in the spring of 1998. The Co-op HEAO has six programs: Business Economics, Business Administration, Business Information Technology, Commercial Economics, Communication, Management, Economics & Law, and Accountancy. A number of underlying principles were established at the foundation of the institute:
- a strict alternation of six months work and six months study;
- the student is granted permission to work after gaining a number of credits (study points) as established by the program;
- work consists of paid work and is not a matter of internships; the student is a full-fledged employee of the company/organization with all the rights and responsibilities that this entails;

- the three work periods have an increasing level of difficulty and the positions must be approved by the program;
- the program sees to sufficient job openings;
- the student is responsible for acquiring a position that fits in his[16] phase of the study program and chosen specialty;
- open programs, which are not tied to a specific branch or set of branches.

The objective the institute has set for itself is: to train young adults and give them an advantage when they make their actual entrance into the employment market as a result of their 1½ years of work experience. They will be able to function more quickly in a position at the level to which they have been trained because they have relevant work experience.

In addition to alternating work and study, another unifying theme is the concept of "learning to learn." This educational concept emphasizes that the student should be allowed to study independently and actively, and in this manner initiate a process in which he gains more and more self-guidance of his own learning process. One of the educational reasons for implementing "learning to learn" is to respond to the demands made of educational programs by the employment market: motivating individuals to work independently and prepare them for a given professional attitude. The rapid social changes mean that employees are required to keep up with developments themselves and to quickly conquer new knowledge and skills. "Learning to learn" demands an active attitude on the part of the student, namely being able to learn independently.

The program should provide varied learning situations which are as complete as possible for professionalisation. These situations offer sufficient profession-relevant learning experiences. They are geared to individual needs, possibilities, styles of thinking and learning, and they make use of a large range of learning means. The learning situations also require varying forms of working together with other people. In other words, it is a matter of providing adequate circumstances to teach the student to reflect on his own actions in a professional context.

There are two aspects to making the "learning to learn" approach operational in Co-op HEAO: learning objectives and learning issues. Learning objectives concern the following questions: what do I want to learn, what do I need to work on, on what should I concentrate in this phase of my study? Learning issues are the concrete actions, which a student believes he can use as a means to achieve his learning objectives. During the initial first year, the learning objectives and learning issues are fixed, and it is primarily a matter of becoming acquainted with the "learning to learn" concept. In the rest of the study program and during the work periods,

---

[16] Wherever 'he' or 'his' is used, 'she' or 'her' may also be read.

students gradually learn to determine their own learning objectives and learning issues within the context of the learning outcomes established by the program.

Table 1. Blueprint Co-op HEAO (source: Co-op HEAO

	Personal development	Study career guidance	Learning to learn	Contents
Application phase	Starting point for self reflection	Written application and preliminary interview		
1st propedeutical Year	Strategic self-management, making applications	Initial interviews and discussions of study progress, personal file opened	Learning objectives are fixed, learning issues are fixed, reflection on one's own learning style	Basis, by means of becoming acquainted with concepts
1st Work period	Learning objectives work period	Return evenings	Theory applied in practice	MBO+ level
1st Year main phase	Self-reflection by means of work report, employer's assessment of intermediate terms	Study progress discussion Group meetings	Learning objectives are fixed, learning issues formulated by student	Instruments and application
2nd Work period	Learning objectives work period	Return evenings	Theory applied in practice	Work activities with content
2nd Year main phase	Self reflection by means of work report, employer's assessment of intermediate terms Self-assessment, assessment center, plan of approach	Group meetings: supervision	Learning objectives in consultation, learning issues formulated by student	Strategic aspects and analysis
3rd Work period	Learning objectives work period	Return evenings	Theory applied in practice	Final HEAO level
3rd Year main phase 4th Year main phase	Employer's assessment of intermediate terms	Group meetings: supervision / intervision Individual talks with supervisor	Learning objectives and learning issues formulated by student	Integration and independent knowledge acquisition

Table 1 shows how the various aspects of Co-op HEAO fit together horizontally and vertically. The horizontal axis gives five aspects of the program and the vertical axis the structure of the study program. The logical composition and development is shown vertically in each column. The horizontal axis shows how the five aspects fit together, in other words, how the activities and developments form a consistent whole. Table 1 represents a situation that has been partially put into place and is partially still to be effectuated.

3. WHY A DIFFERENT ASSESSMENT METHOD?

The first reason for using another assessment method emerged from the co-op concept. A characteristic of the co-op concept is that part of the learning process takes place during the three successive work periods. This learning process is removed from the direct supervision of the program. It is important not only for the student, but also for the institution of education to be able to chart this learning process, so as to have an idea of students' development. One of the hypotheses is that the alternation of learning and working has a synergetic effect. Another hypothesis is that the progress of development during the work periods can vary considerably from student to student. There is also the question of whether the student has made enough progress during his work period.

The second reason is the educational concept of "learning to learn." Theories about learning emphasize that effective learning is more than knowing and reproducing. For learning to be effective is should include being able, willing and daring to put knowledge an abilities into practice. Because traditional assessment methods mainly focus on knowledge and reproduction, an assessment center is an adequate instrument to assess the performance of students. Besides, methods for testing knowledge acquired in a learning context are not sufficient for testing learning gained from experience. The assessment center is extremely well suited for testing experience-based learning because it is focussed on integration of knowledge and skills. Next to this, an assessment method was required that would reveal the progress of a student's learning process and at the same time would be structured in such a way as to fit into self-guided and self-responsible learning. An assessment center is made up of professionally relevant situations which are as realistic as possible; these are used to observe how the student functions. An assessment center allows the student to gain a perspective of his own functioning and to steer his own learning process. An assessment method not only offers a perspective on the student's learning process during the work periods, but also one that responds to the learning concept of "learning to learn."

To the institution an assessment center approach reveals the effectiveness (structure, doability, consistency) of the curriculum and provide information about the study progress and learning needs of students in relation to the curriculum. Gaps and bottlenecks in the curriculum will also become visible.

Thirdly, a link was sought with existing assessment methods in business and industry. The assessment method decided upon by Co-op HEAO was an assessment center, based on the reasons given above. This method systematically examines the progress of the student at a given moment in terms of the formulated learning outcomes of the program. Before going into the development and actual content of the Co-op HEAO assessment center, we look in the next paragraph at assessment centers, which we will define both in its general sense and in that of the education assessment center used by Co-op HEAO.

4. ASSESSMENT CENTRE: POSSIBLE APPLICATIONS

'Assessment' means consideration, appraisal or evaluation. The starting point for this is the supposition that "Behavior predicts Behavior" (Jansen & De Jongh, 1993). It is assumed that human behavior is consistent and that observations provide a reliable prediction for behavior in similar, future situations; they have a predictive value (Dochy & De Rijke, 1995). This does not mean that behavior is fixed, Behavior tends to be repetitive but this does not mean that it cannot change.

An assessment center gathers information about Behavior in a standardized and controllable manner. The behavior is compared to the expected and required Behavior in a future job. The tasks that must be carried out for the assessment center make use of observable behavior and are as close to tasks in the specific professional position as possible; they are intended to be an imitation of this. A candidate's qualities are registered, making use of various techniques. Components of an assessment center may include: an interview, psychological tests or various assignments. They are combined in a meeting in which several candidates carry out assignments on one or more days, either individually or together; they are observed by a number of evaluators while they do so.

Initially, the method was used in the selection and career development of managers. Since that time, its use has been extended to situations in which there is a desire to gain a perspective of the capacities and development possibilities of people, for example to:

- select external and internal candidates for specific positions;
- determine growth possibilities and career development;
- determine education and training needs of individual employees or organizations as a whole;
- further the perception of one's own capacities.

These last three possibilities link to the need formulated above of a different assessment method for Co-op HEAO.

A recent development is the use of the assessment center in the choice of career and school programs (Van Brussel, 1994) and with target groups for whom other methods are insufficient. These include long-time unemployed, recent immigrants, people re-entering the work force and high school pupils (Luken, 1995).

A related development is the use of assessment centers in assessing qualifications acquired outside of regular education programs. This stems from the idea that people can acquire knowledge in various manners. Knowledge based on experience has no official status in a specific organization or in the employment market. The recognition of qualifications acquired in this way offers individuals the chance to let this knowledge or skill be assessed and thus made official, regardless of the manner in which it was acquired (Klarus, 1995).

The developments described above are related to a process that takes place either before or after completion of a learning process. There is also increasing interest within education in an assessment center as an instrument to be used during a learning process. There is a need for a method aside from the testing of knowledge in traditional testing methods to "monitor" the integration of knowledge and skills.

The publication "Assessment centers, new applications in programs, education and HRM" (Nieuwe toepassingen in opleiding, onderwijs en HRM) (1995) edited by F. Dochy and T. de Rijke, goes into the new areas of application of assessment centers, one of which is education. This publication gives the following definition of an education assessment center: "an educational assessment center can be described as an information center for certain programs by which an individual can be 'tested' and which has on hand all the necessary information to help him find the most appropriate educational program (....) or to create a plan of study (....). The purpose of education assessment center, in other words, is the measurement of potential but also the crediting of schooling and training" (Dochy & De Rijke, 1995, 32). This definition focuses primarily on the choice of an educational or training program and has a diagnostic value, which is particularly useful in making career and educational choices.

The Co-op HEAO assessment center is different in nature and therefore does not fit into the definition given above. The Co-op HEAO assessment center is based on two underlying principles. First of all, a relationship is made between the desired qualifications of the student upon graduation and the actual level of knowledge and skills at a given moment. Secondly, we assume the vision of the program: what does the program believe to be the desired final HEAO level in relation to the desires and demands of the employment market.

Because our purpose is different, we choose for the following definition: an education assessment center is an assessment center that focuses on the assessment of a complex of knowledge, personal qualities and skills which is intended to give the student a perspective of his capacities at a given moment during his study program so that he is capable of drawing up a realistic and concrete development plan. Assessment center instruments are used because they offer the opportunity to observe and assess complex behavior in situation-related environments. The result of the assessment center for a student is a realistic self-image of one's own level of knowledge and skills made by the person himself and checked by an assessor. Thus, it is possible to work systematically in the last year of study on any lacking knowledge or skills in a goal-oriented manner.

According to the above definition, the education assessment center is both a component of the curriculum and an instrument in the "learning to learn" process. It is the continuation of an earlier development phase based on reflection and self-knowledge. During the initial first year, students are prepared for their first work period by means of self-management and job application coaching. After the first and second work periods, the students write a work report, which is intended to make them reflect on the previous six months. The assessment center is a logical completion of this process because it takes place before the third work period. In this third work period and the subsequent 4th year of study the results of the assessment center are used to set up a personal development program which students can use to independently formulate their own learning objectives and learning issues and in this way learn on their own. This last year is the rounding off of the "learning to learn" program.

5. DEVELOPMENT AND STRUCTURE OF THE ASSESSMENT CENTRE

In the autumn of 1996 a start was made on the development of the assessment center, and in February of 1997 it was organized for the first group of students. The core of this was the student's own assessment, making use of a self-assessment and an assessment of his knowledge of the field, personal qualities and skills made by an assessor.

This self-assessment and assessment took place making use of criteria from the professional profile of the program. The objective is to use the results of the self-assessment and assessment of an assessor to make a plan of approach with concrete learning objectives for the third work period and the final year of study.

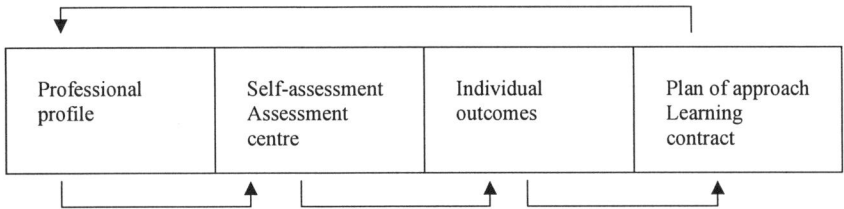

Figure 1. Relationship of the components of a phase of reflection (source: Co-op HEAO)

A number of steps must be taken to carry out an assessment center. A yardstick must be developed. For this, the existing learning outcomes are grouped in four areas. Each outcome is defined and specified in greater detail and then converted into measurable and observable Behavior. This results in a more focused description of the outcome and a 5-point scale in which this outcome is made operational. Next, the appropriate instruments for the assessment center can be chosen to assess these areas.

5.1 Learning Outcomes

On the basis of the formulated learning outcomes of each program four areas have been established for the Co-op assessment center to aid in the choice of measurement instruments: knowledge, personal qualities, cognitive skills and social skills. This provides a profile for each program. These areas are described as follows:

– *Knowledge*

Knowledge in this context has to do with specific knowledge of the professional field and knowledge relevant to the program. For example: communication students should have at their command knowledge about economics that is relevant to their future functioning in communications.

– *Personal qualities*

Personal qualities have to do with internal behavior; such things as creativity, flexibility, result-orientation and empathy.

– *Social skills*

Social skills consist of external Behavior, such as discussion techniques, presentation, working together, providing leadership, negotiating.
— *Cognitive skills*
These include skills such as the ability to express one's self in writing and analytical skills. In contrast to social skills, these are perceived indirectly.

Opinions vary considerably about the possibility of assessing knowledge by means of an assessment center. In this context, it is not so much a matter of an alternative or extra assessment of knowledge as takes place in normal testing. Rather, the objective is to test to what extent a participant is capable of using and applying his specific knowledge in a concrete work situation.

5.2 Making Assessment Center Operational

After determining the four fields, the second step is to make the various outcomes operational in observable and measurable Behavior. A five-point scale has been selected for this with descriptive scales to assess the observed Behavior. These descriptive scales make it possible to indicate the desired level of skills in a given phase of the study.

Table 2. Steps in the operationalization of the outcomes with an example and the translation into assessment center (source: Co-op HEAO)

Development			Assessment center	
Categorizing outcomes of the program in four areas	Specifying and defining in measurable criteria	Concretizing in measurable behavior on a five-point scale	Choice of instruments which make behavior visible, observable and possible to be assessed	Observation and appraisal of behavior
Example: Social skills: - Working together - Negotiating - Etc.	Working together: effective contribution to a group, communicative, multi-disciplinary approach, team player	Capable of ...	Role playing: situation which calls for working together	Assessment of students' behavior during the situation of working together

There are many different ways in which outcomes are made operational. In the case of knowledge criteria, the following method is used to translate them into recognizable and measurable behavior:

Step 1: Knowledge of and insight into the basic concepts/theories and instruments;
Step 2: Application of concepts/theories and instruments in simple situations;
Step 3: Independent effectuation;
Step 4: Integration and implementation;
Step 5: Independent working, development, complex situations.

The five-point scales are set up in such a way that position three or four is the desired level upon graduation. Position five indicates an excellent student.

5.3 Instruments

The next phase in the designing of an assessment center is the choice of instruments for assessment (see below).

Table 3. Components of the Co-op HEAO assessment center (source: Co-op HEAO)

Student	Student and assessor
1. Self-assessment after completion of the third work period	
2. Filling out of the APEX profile	Assessment center: assessment by assessor - in-basket exercise - role playing - feedback
1. Plan of approach and learning contract	

The assessment center developed at Co-op HEAO has three components. First of all, students carry out a self-assessment and make a presentation on this. Next comes the assessment center itself, which is made, up of: an attitude test, an in-basket exercise, role playing, and a final individual interview. The third component is based on the outcomes of the assessment center and consists of the setting up of a plan of approach and a learning contract. The sequence is based on the following arguments: a self-assessment allows students to indicate how they estimate their knowledge and skills. The assessment center examines the extent to which this self-image coincides with the image of an assessor. The plan of approach gives students the opportunity to indicate their learning objectives based on their self-image and the feedback from the assessor. These are made explicit in a learning contract.

Several areas come into play in the diverse components. This yields the following combination:

Table 4. Combination of areas and instruments (source: Co-op HEAO)

	Knowledge	Personal qualities	Social skills	Cognitive skills
Self-assessment	x	x	x	x
Assessment center				
a. APEX		x		x
b. in-basket	x	x		x
c. one-on-one interview	(x)	x	x	x
- meeting situation	(x)	x	x	x
- working together	(x)	x	x	x
feedback		x	x	x

x = is assessed by this instrument (x) = is assessed implicitly

5.4 Meeting the Criteria

To be able to call a program an assessment center, it must meet quality requirements set out in the Standards and Ethical Considerations for Assessment Centre Operations (Dochy & De Rijke, 1995). The most important quality requirements for an assessment center are:
- the behavior of the candidate is assessed, making use of unequivocal criteria;
- assessment techniques that are used in the assessment center must be developed in such a way that they collect information, which can be used to assess behavior characteristics;
- assessors should use a systematic procedure to register specific behavioral observations;
- at least two assessors should be used per candidate. This sees to it that one assessor does not determine the assessment of the candidate and thus suffer from subjectivity.

The assessment center as developed by the institute meets to our opinion the first three quality requirements. We have not followed the fourth requirement. Our assessment center is a development assessment center and not a selection assessment center. The assessment center is intended as a learning process for students and the outcome has neither favorable or unfavorable consequences. No decisions are made based on the outcome of the assessment center. Assessors have no interest in the outcome, unlike managers acting as assessors to assessment employees' performance. In many cases, assessors do not know the students and have no preconceived idea about them.

Given the specific situation of an educational assessment center, we believe that in spite of this variance from the quality requirements, we can guarantee validity and reliability. The descriptive five-point scale assures consistency in observation. There is also sufficient time available for checking and discussing with colleague-assessors. The decision and its advantages and disadvantages are discussed with the assessors beforehand. The evaluations have shown that the assessors see the one-on-one situation as very positive.

6. EVALUATION

The evaluation of the use of the Co-op HEAO assessment center, based research, had two purposes: to determine whether the assessment center has met the objective and whether modifications should take place. Student evaluations have indicated that the objective, achieving an insight into the knowledge and skills of students and of creating a clear self-image, is achieved with this instrument.

Both the students' and assessors' evaluations as well as interviews with them indicated a number of topics needing further study or modification. The main points are:
− specific characteristics of the age group;
− translation of results into a plan of approach;
− place in the curriculum.

6.1 Specific Characteristics of the Age Group

One of the underlying principles of an assessment center is that "behavior predicts behavior": the behavior of a candidate during the assessment center has a predictive value. The assessment center carried out by Co-op HEAO concerns young adults who are in a phase of life in which they do not always display consistent behavior. At the end of the assessment center, it was noted that an "adult behavior" was displayed during the exercises as was expected of them, but that outside of the exercise students often showed "immature" Behavior. This phenomenon can be placed in the larger context of the Co-op concept. During the work periods, the students are called upon to display "adult" behavior. The work period, however, does not have such an influence on behavior to alter it significantly during the study periods. Back in their school program, many participants behave again as students. "Student" behavior and group processes again play a dominant role. The question remains whether this is inherent to the alternation between working and studying or whether the program allows this behavior and even contributes to the double situation by not addressing students in an "adult" manner.

A more general question is: how does this age group deal with the experience of an assessment center? It is striking that students are enthusiastic about the assessment center; they appreciate it very much and are pleased with this individual method of assessment. They are also content with the assessment of their skills as a whole. Generally they recognize themselves in the image that is presented to them during feedback, but it is remarkable that they almost never exchange their experiences with other fellow students and instructors.

6.2   Converting Results into a Plan of Approach

Another striking point which is related to the above is that students find it very difficult to convert the results of the assessment center, including self-assessment, into concrete actions and results to be achieved in their plan of approach. The results differ in terms of level of concreteness and reference to the professional profile. This may be caused by the fact that this first group of Co-op students is not sufficiently trained to formulate learning objectives and learning issues for themselves. Another possible cause may be that the feedback from the assessors during the final interview does not offer sufficient concrete links to formulate learning objectives. It may be concluded that the program must support this process more than it has so far. Having the assessor formulate recommendations or make suggestions might do this. Another point deserving attention is the transition from the assessment center to the subsequent phase.

The actual starting up of a the development phase based on the assessment center is problematic. This has to do with the problems of the age group as we discussed above. A number of students experience the final report of the assessor as similar to an examination. A positive report leads to the attitude that no more work is necessary on further development. The other extreme is a dependent attitude in which the student asks the program the open question: "what now?" One of the improvements that will be made, consequently, is a clearer presentation of the possible concrete actions that can be taken and the offering of help in this.

6.3   Place in the Curriculum

The assessment center was conducted after the third work period. During the evaluation, students and assessors were asked if they found this to be a logical moment within the program. When the assessment center was being set up, the question also arose as to the most effective place for the assessment center in the curriculum. Prior to the third work period has the advantage that students are given the opportunity during the third work period to devote attention to achieving the objectives of their plan of approach.

The working environment offers a variety of concrete situations in which the student can practice his social and cognitive skills. The effectiveness of this is greater than in the relatively safe and familiar situation of the institution where the student practices these skills with fellow students whom he has come to know quite well. These were the considerations used to make the decision to place the assessment center before the third work period.

7. CONCLUSIONS

The objective of Co-op HEAO was to find a different assessment method to fit the combination Co-op concept and "learning to learn." We believe that we have found this new assessment method in the assessment center. The assessment center, which has been developed and implemented by Co-op HEAO, has in our opinion, brought out new aspects both in the area of the assessment center and in education. In the area of the assessment center method, we can speak of a new target group: higher education students and a new application in higher education programs. Progress is assessed during the program, the objective of which is to steer the development and training phase of students making use of systematic and methodical measurement on a broad spectrum of criteria related to learning outcomes.

The assessment center is a method, which also assesses skills and personal qualities. As we have remarked above, companies and organizations attach more and more importance to such skills and qualities as communication skills, initiative, flexibility, etc. Education has been traditionally geared to the assessment of specific knowledge. The acquisition of social skills has been recognized more recently as an important and essential addition to the acquisition of knowledge. Thus, business has developed other instruments as well as the assessment center such as functioning and assessment interviews. Traditional forms of testing in education are insufficient for the assessment of a complex of knowledge, skills and personal qualities. The assessment of social skills and personal qualities is an underdeveloped area in educational situations.

In the area of education, the assessment center is an innovation that gives the student the opportunity to study more effectively because it offers him a concrete view of what is and what is not desirable in his future job. There is also a direct relationship between the results of the assessment center and personal learning issues. A year before the student graduates, he gains insight into his own abilities in relationship to the learning outcomes. The student sets down concrete learning objectives making use of a learning contract. This provides the opportunity to learn in a self-guided and result-oriented manner, which is one of the underlying principles of the "learning to learn" concept. Next to this important self-guiding purpose an assessment center is also a new way of assessing students' capabilities to act. As we stated earlier being able to act on basis of one's knowledge and skills is an important issue in recent theories about effective learning.

A number of other advantages also arise. First of all, the assessment center not only affords the student an insight on the individual level, it also provides the organization with opportunities to gain information about the effectiveness of the curriculum. The program can make implicit ideas explicit and thus provide better structure to the didactic forms of work and content of the curriculum. In this way, the assessment center provides input for the institution of education as learning organization.

Secondly, instructors gain experience with a different aspect of their profession through the process of setting up and implementing assessment centers. The "learning to learn" concept requires a different role of instructors than the one-sided transfer of knowledge. This is a task that is geared more to the individual student and has more of a guidance function. Carrying out an assessment center offers the instructor the opportunity to gain experience in the role of an assessor. In the subsequent phase of the assessment center, the instructor is coach and counselor of the supervision/intervision phase. Making the learning outcomes of the program operational requires instructors to look at the curriculum from a different point of view.

A third and important aspect is a new form of contact with the business community. Good contacts with the "field of customers" is important for every higher education institution. By involving assessors from business community, these contacts are strengthened and increased. The external assessors come to know the program extensively and intensively. In a short period of time, they form a good idea of the level of the student and thus of the program.

REFERENCES

Bie, D., Blom, S., Hoekstra, K., Inklaar, Y., Ramaekers, S., & Steenbergen, G. (1996). *Leren leren als middel en doel*. Amsterdam: Hogeschool van Amsterdam.
Brussel, G.J.J. van (1994). De assessment center methode: perspectiefvolle aanpak in het onderwijs? *Dekanoloog, 8*, 432-435.

Dochy, F.J.T.C., & Rijke, T.R. de (Eds.). (1995). *Assessement centers: nieuwe toepassingen in opleiding, onderwijs en HRM.* Utrecht: Lemma.

Inspectie van het hoger onderwijs (1991). *De aansluiting onderwijs-arbeidsmarkt: een inventarisatie op zeven hogescholen.* Den Haag: Ministerie van Onderwijs, Cultuur en Wetenschappen, nr. 1991-6.

Jansen, P.G.W., & Jongh, F. de (1993). *Assessment centers: een open boek.* Utrecht: Het Spectrum.

Klarus, R. (1995). Ervaring telt op de arbeidsmarkt en in het onderwijs. In F.J.T.C Dochy, & de Rijke T.R. (Eds.). *Assessement centers: nieuwe toepassingen in opleiding, onderwijs en HRM* (p. 151-186). Utrecht: Lemma.

Luken, T. (1995). Het assessment raadsel: het werkt maar hoe. *Conferentie Assessment voor laagopgeleiden.* Tilburg.

Roe, R.A., & Daniels, M.J.M. (1984). *Personeel beoordeling: achtergrond en toepassing.* Assen: Van Gorcum.

Rijke, T.R., & Dochy, F.J.R.C. (1995). Assessment centers in bedrijf en onderwijs: stand van zaken. In F.J.T.C. Dochy, & de T.R. Rijke (Eds.), *Assessement centers: nieuwe toepassingen in opleiding, onderwijs en HRM* (p. 17-38). Utrecht: Lemma.

Rijke, T.R. de, & Beemer, C.F.H. (1995). Zelf-assessment. In F.J.T.C. Dochy, & T.R. de Rijke (Eds.) (1995), *Assessement centers: nieuwe toepassingen in opleiding, onderwijs en HRM* (75-92). Utrecht: Lemma.

Tillema, H.H. (Ed.) (1996). *Development centers: ontwikkeling van competenties in organisaties.* Deventer: Kluwer Bedrijfswetenschappen.

The Assessment Center: Global Issues and Local Responses[17]

Michael K. McCuddy, Wendy L. Pirie, Mary York Christ, Larry E. Mainstone, David L. Schroeder & Sandra E. Strasser
College of Business Administration, Valparaiso University, Valparaiso, Indiana, USA

1. INTRODUCTION

Employers and other external stakeholders have become increasingly dissatisfied with the business education provided by universities and colleges. Much of the criticism has focused on the poor interpersonal and communication skills of graduates. Universities have responded by developing innovative programs to provide students with opportunities to develop these skills. For example, Indiana University, the University of Pennsylvania, and the University of Tennessee redesigned their MBA programs to emphasize leadership, communication, and teamwork abilities (Extejt & Forbes, 1996). However, it is not only necessary to redesign the curriculum but to evaluate the success of these changes in delivering the desired outcomes.

---

[17] This paper is based on experiences with and results from an assessment center that is part of a curriculum development project supported by Grant No. 1996-0896-000 from the Lilly Endowment Inc.

In addition, AACSB — The International Association for Management Education has changed its criteria from input measures to outcome-oriented measures to ensure that colleges and universities are achieving their stated missions. Colleges and universities seeking AACSB accreditation or reaffirmation must prove, not assume, they are adding value. This could be done with:

- Affect measures (*e.g.*, alumni surveys to assess the satisfaction of graduates with their education);
- Cognitive measures (*e.g.*, pre- and post-tests of knowledge);
- Outcome measures (*e.g.*, improved job/graduate school placements, research output); or
- Behavioral measures (*e.g.*, assessment centers).

The first three measures have serious deficiencies and offer little assistance in helping business schools either assess or improve the interpersonal and communication skills of students. Self-reported satisfaction measures by either current or former students tell us little about the actual behavioral skills of these students. Similarly, what a person knows about interpersonal skills and how that person behaves could be vastly different. Finally, the placement of graduates can be attributed to many factors other than the quality of the education received. Behavioral measures have received less attention but hold the most promise in appraising whether graduates have the necessary managerial skills. These behavioral skills can be assessed in several ways — internships, projects for real organizations, and assessment centers.

An advantage of the assessment center over alternative means is the control it affords over the assessment process. Assessment centers generally consist of an evaluation of behavioral skills in a series of exercises. These exercises enable assessees to demonstrate skills that are utilized in the real work environment. Observers (assessors) evaluate the assessees' skills in performing these tasks.

1.1   The Need for Assessment Centers

In a review of 108 studies, Cohen (1984) found that life success as defined by a number of variables and school performance as measured by grade-point average were only marginally related. These results would support the hypothesis that while content knowledge is important it is not sufficient for success in business.

In support of behavioral skills development, Mintzberg (1975) said:

The Assessment Center

Management schools will begin the serious training of managers when skill training takes its place next to cognitive learning. Cognitive learning is detached and informational, like reading a book or listening to a lecture. No doubt much important cognitive material must be assimilated by the manager-to-be. But cognitive learning no more makes a manager than it does a swimmer. The latter will drown the first time he jumps into the water if his coach never takes him out of the lecture hall, gets him wet, and gives him feedback on his performance. Our management schools need to identify the skills managers use, select students who show potential in these skills, put the students into situations where these skills can be practiced, and then give them systematic feedback on their performance.

Whetten and Cameron (1983) identified three characteristics of effective managerial skills:
- The skills are behavioral, not personality traits or cognitive skills.
- The skills are paradoxical, being oriented toward teamwork and interpersonal relations as well as towards individualism and entrepreneurship.
- The skills are interrelated and overlapping.

Social learning theory (Bandura, 1977) establishes the link between teaching of behavioral skills, practicing of the taught skills, and feedback on the skills. This method is useful in helping individuals develop management skills. A key component of social learning theory is making individuals aware of their current level of skill competency. This requires the individual to perform the task and receive feedback about their current skill level. To help a person understand which skills to improve and the reasons for improving them, an assessment activity must be performed. This helps the person to become more aware of his/her strengths and developmental needs. Armed with this knowledge, a person may be motivated to develop a plan to improve.

1.2   Overview of Assessment Centers in Industry

An assessment center is an elaborate series of individual and group tasks designed to evaluate a person's strengths and weaknesses. The individual (assessee) performs realistic tasks while being observed by experienced managers (assessors). The assessor compares the assessee's actual performance with desired performance, and provides the assessee with feedback. The three key elements of an assessment center are: (1) identifying the skills to be observed; (2) developing the assessment center exercises and activities; and (3) recruiting assessors with the ability to make accurate observations and provide helpful feedback (Wendel, 1988).

In general, assessment centers tend to be valid predictors of future performance, and are highly accepted (Gaugler et al., 1987). However, assessment centers are not free of criticism. The major criticisms of assessment centers include the following:

- assessment centers are expensive;
- assessment centers rely heavily on the adequate training of the assessors – and assessors are subject to all the biases and inconsistencies of being human; and
- assessment centers are subject to the Hawthorne effect — that is, observation of behavior can change behavior.

In the United States in 1986, about 2,000 public and private organizations were using assessment centers to identify individuals with the ability to manage. Among these organizations were such large firms as IBM Corp., General Electric Co., AT&T, and Standard Oil of Ohio (Waixel, 1986). The concept has been used in many countries worldwide, including Canada (Fisher, 1992), Britain and France (Shackleton & Newell, 1991), Scotland (Dalziel, 1993), Germany (Steuer, 1992), Central and Eastern Europe and the former Soviet Union (Fogel, 1990), Turkey (Woolfenden, 1990), and Japan (Taylor & Frank, 1988).

Large firms often encounter two major problems when implementing an assessment center — high cost and a lack of adequate expertise. For example, recent data indicate that the cost per assessee ranged from $50 to more than $2,000 (Cascio, 1995). Keel et al. (1989) suggest that before launching assessment activities, certain objectives should be accomplished, including the development of criteria for success and the identification of relevant skills. Originally developed in order to select among applicants for management jobs and to assess long-term potential, there is an increasing emphasis on the diagnosis of participant training and development needs (Guerrier & Riley, 1992) and a move toward use by smaller organizations (Keel et al., 1989).

Assessees include such diverse populations as educational administrators (Wendel et al., 1989), sales agents (Wellstead, 1992), pilots (North, 1992), police officers (Coulton & Feild, 1995), firefighters (Yeager, 1986), and fire chiefs (Lowry, 1996). Recently, assessment centers have been used in graduate business education (Bartz & Calabrese, 1991; McMahon, 1992).

Based on what industry has done, we determined there are three reasons for a business school to conduct an assessment center. These reasons are: a desire to improve behavioral skills; external pressure from stakeholders; and the previously demonstrated success of assessment centers. Based on these reasons, it was concluded that an industry-type assessment center would be useful in evaluating and developing behavioral skills in undergraduate students.

In the remainder of this paper, we will discuss general theoretical issues in the design and operation of an assessment center, and describe how these issues were handled in the assessment center run by Valparaiso University's College of Business Administration.

2. GENERAL THEORETICAL ISSUES IN THE DESIGN AND OPERATION OF AN ASSESSMENT CENTER

The design of an assessment center involves five categories of issues:
- determining the skills to assess;
- choosing the assessment exercises and measuring instruments;
- resolving ethical issues in assessment;
- managing the logistics of operating an assessment center; and
- using assessment center results.

The most fundamental category of issues in designing an assessment center involves determining which behavioral skills to assess. Priorities must be established since it would be extremely costly and time consuming to assess all desired behavioral skills. In establishing priorities, the importance of the skills to stakeholders should be considered and whether the skills can be assessed more efficiently and effectively by alternative means. These priorities should be re-examined continuously to take into account the shifting nature of stakeholder expectations.

A second category of issues is the choice of appropriate exercise and measuring instruments for use in the assessment center. These choices include both (a) the tasks to be performed by the assessees, and (b) the rating scales/instruments that the assessors use in evaluating the assessees' behavioral skills. Having reliable and valid measurement tools is absolutely critical to the process. In addition, the costs of the exercises and measuring instruments must be considered. As in most decisions, a cost/benefit analysis is required.

A third category of issues concerns the ethical implications of using an assessment center. An assessment center in many ways can be compared to an experiment using human subjects, with all the ramifications that entails. In this area, it is important to consider how we deal with feedback to the assessees and our right/responsibility to suggest behavioral changes. It is important that one attempts to not impose a personal agenda on the assessment process.

A fourth category of issues revolves around the actual operation of the assessment center. This addresses such questions as where the center will be held, when it will be held, who will be involved (assessors and assessees) and the nature of their involvement, what kind of training will be provided to the assessors, and what type of feedback will be provided to the assessees and the timing of the feedback. For an assessment center to be successful, a substantial amount of time needs to be spent on the logistics of running the assessment center.

The fifth category of issues involves the use of assessment center results. Issues of confidentiality and the appropriate use of the results for assessee development and program development must be addressed prior to actually running the assessment center. If the results are to be available to individuals other than the assessees, appropriate measures must be taken to ensure confidentiality. Further, before making information available to anyone other than assessees, the assessment center administrator should be confident that such information is useful in terms of assessee development or program development. Another issue relates back to the ethical question of behavior modification. To what extent can or should behavioral skills be developed, refined, or modified?

3. DESIGN AND OPERATIONAL ISSUES IN THE CBA ASSESSMENT CENTER

The following sections discuss how we addressed the general theoretical issues in the local environment of the College of Business Administration (CBA) Assessment Center at Valparaiso University.

3.1 Determination of the Skills to Assess

To identify the competencies that employers desire in skilled graduates, we asked seventeen executives, in a focus-group setting, questions such as "What knowledge, skills, and attitudes are you looking for in new hires?" Response identified not only the desired knowledge, skills, attitudes, and experiences but the areas where the business community viewed graduating students as weak.

The desired knowledge, skills, attitudes, and experiences, based on these discussions, were identified as:

- Solid knowledge base for business.
- Flexibility, tolerance for ambiguity, global thinking, ability to continue to learn.
- Self-management skills.
- Integrative perspective on problem solving.
- Ethics and service to the community.
- Communication skills.
- Teamwork skills.
- Computer skills.
- Experience interacting with the business community.

These results confirmed the critical competencies that are described in the literature (Brown, 1992, 1994; Church, 1993; Evers & Rush, 1996; Galagan, 1992; Henkoff, 1993; Kiechel, 1993, 1994; Mathes, 1992), as well as those described earlier in the discussion of the need for an assessment center. Thus, the competencies that VU's business stakeholders desire in our CBA graduates can be generalized to graduates of other institutions as well.

Behavioral skills, communication skills, and integration skills predominated the focus-group discussions of students' skill deficiencies. Thankfully, the general consensus was that the students were not lacking core business knowledge. The business community believed that the lack of the previously mentioned skills would hinder graduates' progress and effectiveness within an organization. This is a theme consistent with observations in and criticism found in non-academic media (e.g., Barr & Harris, 1997). This preliminary definition of referent skills for assessment matches suggestions in academic literature also (Keel et al.,1989). However, as important as they are, behavioral, communication, and integration skills are difficult to teach and equally difficult to assess.

Unfortunately, in most business education it has been assumed that behavioral and communication skills will develop through some process of osmosis. To quote Barr and Harris (1997, p. 39) regarding integration, "Until now we've all acted as if integration will happen by some immaculate conception process." It is all too easy for business professors to assume that these skills are someone else's responsibility. Going to academic conferences, one often hears things such as: "I am a finance professor, not an English professor." "I am too busy teaching content to worry about behavioral skills." "I trained all these years in a specialty, and now you want me to be a generalist." These faculty comments are mirrored by the students. For example, the following observations are all too common: "I'm an accounting student, why do I have to know anything about human behavior?" "Why do you evaluate my presentation skills and not just the content of my report?" "Why do I have to work in a group? I work much better alone!" "You have no right to grade me on how well I work in a group!"

It was in the face of such resistance that some of the CBA initiatives were undertaken. The assessment center was conceived as a tool for monitoring the development of the aforementioned skills over time by each student and for the student body as a whole. Additionally, a pilot project of a team-taught class was developed. This pilot project integrated the introductory finance, management and organizational behavior, management information systems, and marketing courses within one class.

In this type of class, the belief was that the students would better develop their behavioral, communication, and integration skills. With this format, no individual professor could abrogate the responsibilities for those skills by assuming they were developed elsewhere. Also, the students were required to undertake a project for an external client. This project forced students to integrate knowledge across the functional areas, and to develop communications and behavioral skills — particularly, with regard to teamwork, leadership, and followership. The assessment center will be a critical means for evaluating the effectiveness of the pilot integrated class in developing the desired skills.

3.2 The Choice of Assessment Tools

The assessment center lasted three hours and consisted of three exercises. These exercises were purchased from a commercial vendor as part of a larger set of instruments. Once purchased, they may be freely reproduced for use. The decision to use these instruments was based on the fact that they had been pre-tested for reliability and validity. In addition, while the initial fixed cost was high, the subsequent variable cost was and will continue to be low.

One exercise involved a group problem-solving task in which the participants were lost at sea after a fire on their boat. They had a limited set of salvaged items and needed to agree on the relative importance of each. This task was chosen because it was one where the assessees would not be experientially different – that is, there would be a level playing field. This exercise was used to evaluate various teamwork and consensus-building skills, as well as general problem-solving and communication skills.

A second task was an in-basket exercise in which the participants were placed in the role of a company vice-president with a variety of memos and messages on their desk. Each item on the desk had to be prioritized and disposed of in some manner during a constrained time period. This exercise assessed the student's ability to set priorities and delegate, each of which is a component of problem-solving and critical thinking skills.

The final task involved the completion of two instruments that measure different aspects of an individual's decision-making style. First, a cognitive-style inventory measured whether the student is more of a systematic or intuitive decision-maker. Second, an inventory of barriers to creative thought and innovative action provided information on individual characteristics (e.g., lack of self-confidence, a need for conformity) that can impede creative thinking. Using this information should permit the assessees to have a better understanding of their strengths and developmental needs relative to decision-making style.

3.3   Ethical Issues in Assessment

Running an assessment center and conducting research using human subjects are somewhat parallel in nature. At Valparaiso University the assessment center was reviewed and approved by the university's Institutional Review Board – a committee which is charged with the oversight of human subjects used in research. The assessees were required to complete a consent form prior to participation in the assessment center. Also, appropriate precautions were taken to ensure confidentiality of information regarding each of the assessees.

Regarding the issue of behavioral changes, many students were receptive to the assessors' feedback and seemed to benefit from the insights the assessors provided. However, not all students were receptive to the assessors' observations and suggestions. Two contrasting examples provide a rather powerful illustration of this point.

Student A was told by the assessors that he tended to try to dominate groups and to talk an excessive amount with little content. Student A was viewed as being on transmit but not receive. Student A completely rejected the assessment even in the face of professorial endorsement, based on classroom observation, of the assessment. The next term three out of sixteen students responding to the question, "To what extent was the course a learning experience for you?" wrote "Only to the extent that Student A was not talking." or something of a similar nature. Clearly, Student A failed to learn from the assessment center. Subsequent feedback from an internship supervisor provided information confirmatory of this observation. While we felt a moral obligation to identify the consequences of his behavior, there is controversy as to whether it is our right versus obligation to force Student A to modify his behavior. This dilemma remains to be resolved.

Student B was told by the assessors that he failed to take the initiative and did not demonstrate leadership. During the next term, Student B made a conscious effort to be more proactive in classes and groups. In the summer, he took a 'blue collar' job. When his boss gave him instructions, he responded by asking what else he could do, and what was the next step. Over the summer, Student B was assigned more and more responsibility as well as overtime. In two months of summer employment, Student B made $15,000 as a result of his initiative. The following fall term Student B, studying in Japan, was assigned a position of responsibility in the class based on his leadership skills and knowledge of teamwork.

Student A and Student B represent the ends of the spectrum for student response to the assessment. In general, the value to the students of an assessment center is moderated by their own willingness to accept the assessment and to either modify their behavior as necessary or to continue desirable behavior.

3.4 Logistics in Operating an Assessment Center

In November 1997, a pilot assessment center was conducted in the College of Business Administration building at Valparaiso University, using available classrooms and commons areas. Thirty-five junior business students and five assessors participated. Participation was synchronous but feedback was asynchronous.

Of the 35 students, 31 were enrolled at the time in the first pilot of an integrated functional business curriculum (described earlier). The other four were students in a traditional introductory finance course. It was stressed to the students that the assessment center results were confidential and intended to assist them in their personal development. Also stressed was the fact that assessment center performance would have no effect on any course grades. Members of the regional business community were used as assessors in order to provide an independent, unbiased evaluation of the assessees. We feared that professors might be influenced by previous knowledge of the students.

The assessors attended an evening training session three days prior to the assessment center. The assessors were oriented to the activities that would occur during the assessment center and were briefed on the evaluation forms to be used. In future assessment centers, a more formal training in assessment skills will be conducted.

In the pilot version of the assessment center, assessors observed students during the group exercise. The assessors were in the room with an assigned group and observed the group interactions, taking notes on each participant's behaviors. Both the in-basket and the decision-making inventories were completed independently by the participants during designated times of the assessment center. These exercises were evaluated after the students completed all the tasks.

The limited involvement of the external assessors in the pilot run of the center was intentional. This allowed for increased experience in structuring the logistics of the day as well as feedback from the assessors on how to utilize their time in the future. They provided numerous suggestions, most of which will be incorporated into the next assessment center. Subsequent assessment centers will incorporate two or more individual tasks where assessors evaluate students' behavioral skills. Additionally, assessors will continue to observe the group problem-solving sessions. Also, feedback will be provided at the time of the task rather than later. This change is the result of comments made by both assessees and assessors.

In the pilot, the assessees received a packet of feedback information three days following the assessment center. Faculty helped them interpret the results and answered questions. For the in-basket exercise, assessees received an explanation of the "expert" disposition of items along with a summary of their responses and a corresponding numerical score of their performance. For the decision-making inventories, assessees received descriptive results along with background information on how to interpret those results. For the group task, assessees received information on an "expert" ranking (with explanations) of the available items. They were also given a summary of their individual score versus the expert solution, each of their team member's scores (without identifying the team member), and the group score. Finally, each assessee received a typed summary of all comments the assessors had on his/her teamwork, communication, and problem-solving skills. They also received background information on group roles and how various behaviors may enhance or inhibit group decision making.

This provided for a major value added component of the CBA Assessment Center. Namely, the assessees were able to develop a better understanding of their strengths and areas of needed improvement relative to certain behavioral skills.

3.5   The Use of Assessment Center Results

As initial discussions on the concept of an assessment center progressed, several useful purposes became apparent. To catalog the potential benefits of the assessment center, CBA stakeholders were identified. Also identified were the stakeholders' interests in the CBA and how the assessment center might help fulfill those interests. The identified stakeholders were students, professors, parents, potential employers, alumni, administration at the CBA and VU, the CBA Advisory Council, the VU Board of Directors, the VU

Career Center, the community, and the AACSB. Each group has an interest in the CBA but their focus is different.

Parents, students, and employers have a common interest in students acquiring and developing skills necessary for employment in their chosen field and for advancement in that field. The professors are interested in providing students with those skills. The Career Center wants the CBA to meet these goals so that they can attract more employers to campus and better fulfill its objective of helping students gain employment. The Administration and the Board of Directors are interested in meeting the needs of the other stakeholders in a cost effective manner. All stakeholders are interested in the CBA enhancing its reputation so that, in turn, their own prestige and credibility is enhanced by association.

Each CBA stakeholder should benefit from the CBA Assessment Center. The students gain the experience of participating in an assessment center and of being evaluated by executives from the community. The experience should aid their job search by providing local industry contacts and by enhancing their resumes. Receiving executive (non-professorial) feedback gives students an early opportunity to improve their skills before entering the workplace. Having the knowledge of personal strengths and weaknesses can be an advantage in career planning and job interviews (you must know your product to properly promote it). In the long term, students should have greater confidence and ability to advance in their chosen careers.

Parents, who as a whole have been very supportive of the CBA Assessment Center, see their children's improved opportunity for jobs and long-term success. Parents often comment on the benefit of increasing the number of potential employers on campus. The university Career Center would benefit in a similar way. Additionally, parents value the skills-oriented feedback received by their children.

Perhaps the professors benefit the most from the assessment center. Professors are given almost instantaneous feedback on students' behavioral abilities — something that is difficult to effectively assess in the classroom. As a consequence, changes in curricula and/or teaching methods may occur. This feedback permits evaluation of curricula and/or teaching methods. The assessment center provides data for continuous quality improvement. In the long term, as the CBA's reputation is enhanced, the quality of incoming students will improve.

The Board of Directors and the administration at both university and college levels could use the assessment center as a tool to better evaluate the results of changes in resource allocations. They would also be able to use the center as a marketing tool to increase enrollment. In the long term, as word of the center spreads and as alumni advance in their careers, donations to the university and/or College of Business Administration should increase.

The alumni will have a greater opportunity to network and to come back to their college to serve as assessors. As with all stakeholders, the alumni would benefit from the enhanced reputation of the CBA and its students.

The assessment center should benefit employers by providing them with graduates who possess improved behavioral skills. Given the students' greater knowledge of their strengths and weaknesses, both students and employers should make better employment decisions, resulting in a better "job fit."

The local community, anxious to become involved with the university, has been eager to lend support and expertise in this venture. Anything which strengthens the "town and gown" relationship is beneficial. The CBA Advisory Council has also been helpful in giving their advice and support to the project.

And finally, an accrediting team from AACSB – The International Association for Management Education would be better able to assess the college's achievement of its mission. This ties back to AACSB's criterion change from input measures to outcome-oriented measures to ensure that universities are achieving their stated missions.

4. CONCLUDING OBSERVATIONS — VALUE ADDED

Even as a pilot run, the CBA assessment center provided several benefits to various stakeholders. The students were able to develop a better understanding of their strengths and developmental needs relative to specified behavioral skills. The students were encouraged to form an action plan for addressing their skill development needs. Members of the business community who were involved had very positive reactions to the experience. The assessors, in general, were favorably impressed with the students. However, these students were not necessarily representative of the CBA student body as a whole because they were primarily students in the pilot project integrated course. Faculty benefited by developing better insights into current student skills and by having the opportunity to discuss the results with those students.

The CBA curriculum may ultimately be affected. Since the majority of participants in the pilot assessment center were also involved in the pilot curriculum, it was difficult to form any immediate conclusions about the relative effectiveness of the pilot curriculum and the traditional curriculum This was due to the lack of a sufficiently large control group. A more complete pool of students will be assessed at the completion of their senior year. Currently, the CBA assessment center is assessing a mix of juniors who do and do not participate in the pilot integrated curriculum. Once additional data are collected, a more definitive answer may be provided regarding the effectiveness of the CBA's integrated functional core curriculum in developing critical behavioral skills.

Based on observation in the pilot integrated class, the presentations to NCUR,[18] comments from the students, observations of faculty in subsequent courses, and comments of prospective employers, it seems that the pilot project had the desired impact. Of course, this is primarily anecdotal data, and the assessment center will be an integral tool in testing the effectiveness of this type of class. Among the questions that must be addressed are the following: Did the students in the pilot project class actually develop good behavioral, communication, and integration skills? Were the skills superior to those of the students taking the curriculum delivered in the traditional manner? Unfortunately, we cannot answer these questions with only a pilot run of the assessment center. However, these questions can be answered by comparing the pilot assessment results with the results from future runs of the assessment center.

The primary problems encountered in the assessment center concerned the assessors. As the assessment center grows, it becomes increasingly difficult to recruit a sufficient number of assessors and to ensure that they are adequately trained. An interesting possibility was suggested at the 1998

---

[18]The following are abstracts of presentations that students from this class are making to the National Conference on Undergraduate Research:

The Importance of Consultant Sensitivity: Contrasting Perspectives. A consultant's sensitivity to his client's needs determines the effectiveness of an analysis. Business environments are evolving quickly and also are growing more varied. In an environment of widely varied organizational cultures, outside consultants must realize and understand the culture and dynamics of each particular client. The paper discusses a cost/benefit analysis performed for an organization while upholding its mission and goals. Issues covered include: the conflict between profit goals and helping the organization maintain its identity and good rapport with its customers; also, strategies to promote mutual understanding within the client/consultant relationship.

Teamwork Development While Working on an External Client Project. A number of factors (financing, marketing, management, information systems, and inventory controls) were analyzed and considered in the coordination of a semester-long project aimed at assessing the economic efficiency and financial viability of the client's operations and plans. During the project, a great deal of information was received from the client which required interaction among the student group. As a result, the thirty-three students evolved into an effective, efficient, and cohesive team. The evolution of the team will be discussed in the presentation.

EDINEB Conference by the presenters from the Hogeschool Van Amsterdam (this volume). At their institution, a tuition-based program is offered to train assessors for industry. The final test for the trainees is to assess students within the college of business. This has two benefits: (1) it provides the needed assessors, and (2) it raises funds to cover the cost of an assessment center.

In conclusion, we have provided one perspective on how an academic institution can deal with global assessment center issues, including the determination of the skills to assess, the choice of assessment tools, ethical issues in assessment, logistics in operating an assessment center, and the use of assessment center results. This approach is not the only way to resolve these global issues in a college of business. However, we fervently hope that this paper will stimulate others to grapple with these issues in ways which are meaningful for them.

REFERENCES

Bandura, A. (1977). *A social learning theory*. Englewood Cliffs, N.J.: Prentice-Hall.

Barr, S., & Harris, R. (1997). Incomplete education. CFO: *The Magazine for Senior Financial Executives, 13 (4)*, 30-39.

Bartz, D.E., & Calabrese, R.L. (1991). Enhancing graduate business school programs. *Journal of Management Development, 10 (1)*, 26-32.

Brown, A. (1992). TQM: Implications for training. *Industrial & Commercial training, 24 (10)*, 3-9.

Brown A. (1994). TQM as a focus for better general training. *Journal of European Industrial Training, 18 (7)*, 3-4.

Cascio, W.F. (1995). *Managing human resources*. New York: McGraw-Hill.

Church, G.J. (November 22, 1993). Jobs in an age of insecurity. *Time*, 32-39.

Cohen, P.A. (1984). College grades and adult achievement: A research synthesis. *Research in Higher Education, 20*, 281-291.

Coulton, G.F., & Feild, H.S. (1995). Using assessment centers in selecting entry-level police officers: Extravagance or justified expense? *Public Personnel Management, 24 (2)*, 223-254.

Dalziel, S. (1993). Introducing development centers into management education: The way forward? *Management Education and Development, 24 (3)*, 280-292.

Evers, F.T., & Rush, J.C. (1996). The bases of competence: Skill development during the transition from university to work. *Management Learning, 27 (3)*, 275-300.

Extejt, M., & Forbes, J.B. (1996). Evaluation of multi-method undergraduate management skills development program. *Journal of Education for Business, 71 (4)*, 223-231.

Fisher, R. (1992). Screen test. *Canadian Business, 65 (5)*, 62-64.

Fogel, D.S. (1990). Management education in Central and Eastern Europe and the Soviet Union. *Journal of Management Development, 9 (3)*, 14-19.

Galagan, P.A. (1992). On being a beginner. *Training & Development, 46 (11)*, 30-38.

Gaugler, B.B., Rosenthal, D.B., Thornton, G.C., III, & Bentson, C. (1987). Meta-analyses of assessment center validity. *Journal of Applied Psychology, 72 (3)*, 493-511.

Guerrier, Y., & Riley, M. (1992). Management assessment centers as a focus for change. *Personnel Review, 21* (*7*), 24-31.

Henkoff, R. (July 12, 1993). Winning the new career game. *Fortune*, 46-49.

Keel, S.B., Cochran, D.S, Arnett, K., & Arnold, D.R. (1989). ACs are not just for the big guys. *Personnel Administrator, 34* (*5*), 98-101.

Kiechel, W., III. (May 17, 1993). How we will work in the year 2000. *Fortune*, 38-52.

Kiechel, W., III. (April 4, 1994). A manager's career in the new economy. *Fortune*, 68-72.

Lowry, P.E. (1996). A survey of the assessment center process in the public sector. *Public Personnel Management, 25* (*3*), 307-321.

Matthes, K. (1992). Team building: Help employees change from me to we. *HR Focus, 69* (*9*), 6.

McMahon, J.T. (1992). Teaching management to MBA students: The issue of pedagogy. *Journal of Managerial Psychology, 7* (*1*), 21-24.

Mintzberg, H. (1975). The manager's job: Folklore and fact. *Harvard Business Review, 53*, 49-71.

North, D.M. (1992). Airbus pilot training center stresses task-sharing, good communications as key to flying advanced aircraft. *Aviation Week & Space Technology, 136* (*12*), 63-64.

Shackleton, V., & Newell, S. (1991). Management selection: A comparative survey of methods used in top British and French companies. *Journal of Occupational Psychology, 64* (*1*), 23-36.

Steuer, E. (1992). Assessment center simulation: A university training program for business graduates. *Simulation and Gaming, 23* (*3*), 354-369.

Taylor, C., & Frank, F. (1988). Assessment centers in Japan. *Training and Development Journal, 42* (*2*), 54-57.

Waixel, C. (1986). The naturals. *World, 20* (*2*), 24-28.

Wellstead, W.R. (1992). A career track for sales agents. *Training and Development, 46* (*4*), 49-52.

Wendel, F.C. (1988). *An introduction to the assessment center method*. Research/Technical Report: University of Nebraska.

Wendel, F.C., et al. (1989). *Measurement practices used in the certification of educators*. Research/Technical Report: University of Nebraska.

Whetten, D.A., & Cameron, K.S. (1983). Management skill training: A needed addition to the management curriculum. *Organizational Behavior Teaching Journal, 8*, 10-15.

Woolfenden, G.A. (1990). A national hospitality curriculum for Turkey. *Journal of European Industrial Training, 14* (*3*), 24-28.

Yeager, S.J. (1986). Use of assessment centers by metropolitan fire departments in North America. *Public Personnel Management, 15* (*1*), 51-64.

Assessment & Development Centers in a Problem-based Learning Environment
Building interfaces between Business and Education

Wichard Zwaal & Klaes Eringa
Institute for Service Management, CHN, Leeuwarden, The Netherlands

1. INTRODUCTION

Four years ago, in 1995, we started a number of pilots to implement Assessment and Development Centers (ADCs) in our professional university. The reasons underlying this decision were:
- industry signaled that students had acquired enough knowledge, but fell short in the area of skills and attitudes;
- the ADC approach seems particularly well suited for assessment purposes in a problem-based curriculum;
- the ADC approach appears to be a promising device for more flexible and adaptive education;
- the ADC approach has quite a good reputation both among psychometricians and the public at large.

This paper is an account of the experiences with the exploratory application of ADCs in Higher Vocational Education. We will first give a brief characterization of ADCs. Next we will illustrate construction, operation and evaluation of ADCs, using a number of case studies from our professional university, the Christelijke Hogeschool Noord-Nederland (CHN) in Leeuwarden, the Netherlands. They are evaluated on different psychometric and pragmatic criteria. We will close with some final comments on the future of ADCs at the CHN.

2. ASSESSMENT AND DEVELOPMENT CENTERS

2.1 Proliferation of ADCs

The historical roots of the assessment center approach lie in the German, British and American military context. German military psychologists developed early applications of the multiple assessment approach for selection of army, air force, and naval officers in the period of the buildup of the German armed forces after World War I (Thornton & Byham, 1982, p.23). During World War II, the British War Office Selection Boards (WOSB) assessed potential officers in a 3-day or 4-day program. Beginning in 1945, the British Civil Service Selection Board developed assessment center procedures for nonmilitary settings.

During World War II the assessment center technology was also developed in the United States by Murray and the Office of Strategic Services (OSS).

The first industrial application was the American Telephone and Telegraph Company's (AT&T) Management Progress Study by Bray. Companies who followed were: Standard Oil, IBM and General Electric (Seegers, 1997, p.128).

At the outset, the main purpose of assessment centers was selection of persons for higher level managerial positions. During the last two decades an expansion in the application of AC technology has taken place in three directions (Ballantyne & Povah, 1995; Lee & Beard, 1994; Woodruffe, 1993; Dochy & De Rijke, 1995; Tillema, 1996):
a) from high level jobs to all levels of jobs
b) from selection to career development
c) from industry to education.

2.2 Characteristics of ADCs

An assessment center is defined in the "Guidelines and ethical considerations for assessment center operations" as: "a standardized evaluation of behavior based on multiple inputs. Multiple trained observers and techniques are used. Judgments about behavior are made, in major part, from specifically developed assessment simulations. These judgments are pooled in a meeting among the assessors or by a statistical integration

Assessment & Development Centers in PBL 401

process. In an integration discussion, comprehensive accounts of behavior, and often ratings of it, are pooled. The discussion results in evaluations of the performance of the assessees on the dimensions or other variables that the assessment center is designed to measure. Statistical combination methods should be validated in accord with professionally accepted guidelines." (Thornton, 1992; Thornton & Byham, 1982).

Essential features of an assessment center are (Thornton, 1992):
- Job analysis
- Multiple assessment techniques, designed to match the behavioral dimensions
- Situational exercises, eliciting relevant behavior
- Observation and registration of behavioral responses
- Classification and valuation of behavioral observations
- Multiple assessors
- Trained assessors
- Integration of observations

The added value of the ADC method lies in its versatility as a HRM instrument, its appeal to participants as an informative, transparent and acceptable appraisal instrument, and its favorable cost/benefit relation (Seegers, 1997; Lievens & Seegers, 1997; Luken, 1996; Thompson & Carter, 1995; Zaal, 1991; Van der Maessen de Sombreff, 1992). Table 1 contains exercises frequently used in assessment and development centers (Thornton, 1992).

2.3 Behavioral Dimensions

The choice of exercises and behavioral dimensions should be based on a thorough job analysis. The choice of the kind and the number of dimensions is complicated for the following reasons:
- The profession for which the ADC is developed is generally not singularly defined. The jobs attainable for applicants may be at different positions, at different levels, dependent on specific organizational and situational settings. Furthermore, most jobs are changing in contents due to socio-economic, political and technological developments. The necessary vocational requirements will change accordingly and should be organically defined.
- The second reason is a lack of consensus on a taxonomy of management skills. Several authors have tried to classify managerial skills but all came up with a different system. Mintzberg (1973) identified ten managerial roles; Boyatzis (1982) distinguished six competence-clusters; Thornton & Byham (1982) mention 33 dimensions of managerial performance and Quinn (1996) recently published a model with 8

managerial roles and 24 skills. In the Dutch literature you can find lists ranging from 12 (Jansen & De Jongh, 1993), 22 (Dochy & De Rijke, 1995), 39 (Seegers, 1997) to 51 dimensions (Van Minden, 1996).

Table 1. Various widely used assessment exercises

In-basket
All kinds of written material like letters, memos, brochures, etc. have to be processed within a limited amount of time (1-2 hours) and without any assistance from secretaries or colleagues. For each item the candidate has to write down his reaction, comment, or instructions for further processing.
Case analysis
Information is given about the organization and operations of a company. The candidate is asked to write and or present a proposal for performance improvement.
Group discussion
The group of participants is asked to divide a budget between the different units or departments. Each participant is supposed to be the manager of a different department and is expected to optimize its share of the budget.
Interview simulation
Each candidate is assigned the role of manager who has to conduct an appraisal interview with an employee who is causing some troubles in the organization.
Presentation
Every candidate can choose a subject from a list with different topics for a short presentation for a small audience.
Fact finding
Some information about a company is delivered to the candidates, in combination with a problem statement. For example: at which location should we open our next outlet? Candidates can ask questions to a role-player, who will give relevant information, but only if relevant questions are being asked. After a while, the candidate will have to make up his mind and make a decision. Sometimes this decision is being questioned in a follow up session.

- One of the reasons for the lack of consensus is the overlap between different concepts and the different aggregation levels that are being used within and between classifications. For instance, a concept like social skills is not easily marked out in comparison with communicative skills, interpersonal skills or management skills. And even if we limit the analysis to a concept like communicative skills this could be subdivided into many different components: reading, writing, speaking, and listening, each of which could be further unraveled in sub-components and sub-sub-components. The same thing goes for most of the important concepts. Generally there is a continuum ranging from broad behavioral domains to microscopic behavioral details.

Given the indeterminate nature of target jobs, and the lack of consensus about a taxonomy of behavioral dimensions, and the different levels of analytical detail, we prefer to take a pragmatic position. We suggest that behavioral dimensions are derived from an analysis of the essential and frequently performed tasks, which require a few hours work for a competent job holder (see: Onstenk, 1997). An illustrative example of this approach is the development by the National Council for Vocational Qualifications of the National Standards for Managers (Thompson & Carter, 1995; Lee & Beard, 1994).

2.4 ADCs in Higher Vocational Education

The use of ADCs in higher education is a new development. In the Netherlands Luken (1996) reports on the use of ADCs in secondary schools and Bruijns and Pieke (1997) at the undergraduate university level. Particularly in higher vocational education, where relations with the industry are generally strong, it makes sense to make use of ADCs.

ADCs may serve one or more of the following purposes:

- *Selection*
  The ADC can be used for selection purposes, either from an individual point of view (self-selection or realistic job preview) as from an institutional point of view (choosing only the best five- percent of students).
- *Study career coaching and -counseling*
  Students can participate in an ADC voluntarily or compulsory with the aim of getting a better picture of their own strengths and weaknesses. Students and their mentors can use this information for choosing appropriate study-tracks, internships or jobs.
- *Skills assessment*
  It is possible to organize an ADC for grading purposes. Using different 'stations', a sample of the relevant skills could be demonstrated and judged by trained assessors using pre-structured checklists. If the ADC is repeated at different intervals during the program, a skills progression test is born.
- *Determining final terms and passable learning routes*
  The great educative worth of developing an ADC is its appeal to explicate and operationalize the final aims of the educational program. Preferably this is done in terms of a few core-tasks which are recognized by actual job performers. Employing external and internal assessors can promote the discussion between business and education. Both industry and education can benefit from improved assessment skills of the assessors.
  The ADC can also be used as an instrument to determine the entrance level and learning needs of the participants. It is also applicable as a learning device for skills training, comparable with a management game.

Finally, the ADC can be used for measuring the effectiveness of training programs.

3. DEVELOPMENT, APPLICATION AND MAINTENANCE OF ADCS

There are three main stages related to the use of an ADC: development, application and maintenance. Development includes: job analysis; identification of core tasks; choice of behavioral dimensions; construction of instruments; and choice of rating scales and scoring rules. In section 3.1 we will discuss the construction of the ADCs. In particular the choice of exercises and behavioral dimensions will be explained.

The application stage includes the organization and operations management of facilities and rooms; recruiting and training assessors and role-players; and reports and follow-up. The operational management of the ADCs is discussed in section 3.2.

Evaluation and maintenance consist of the following: quality assurance; psychometric analyses; and revising the instruments. Like any other measurement instrument or assessment device the ADC has to conform to standards of reliability, validity, acceptability, transparency and utility. Since psychometric research is the key to quality assurance we devote a section to different kinds of relevant psychometric analyses.

The three stages will be illustrated with examples from case studies that have been conducted at the Christelijke Hogeschool Noord-Nederland (CHN). We will not describe one case study in total, but rather we show examples that best illustrate the principles that underlie each stage. Also, the examples were by no means chosen to present ideal situations. Indeed, the section on evaluation shows how some simple psychometric research falsified our own beliefs about the validity and reliability of our instruments.

The CHN is a medium-sized professional university in the northern part of the Netherlands. In our faculty of economics and management we have four-year programs for hospitality management, leisure management, retail and small business management, and career management. We work with a system of problem-based learning (PBL), characterized by an interdisciplinary, thematic and modular approach with a strong international orientation. We focus on an integration of applied knowledge, attitudes and skills in both our students and our staff members. Since we train our students for fairly well defined markets we felt the need for a means of testing and assessment that does justice to the demands from those markets. We want to deliver students with a service orientation. Given the steering role of testing in the learning process we are looking for assessment methods that will both stimulate desired behavior and measure this behavior in a valid way.

Our main question was: can we use ADCs to improve the assessment practices in our programs by reconciling both the demands from the service industries and the educational need for an adaptive problem-based curriculum?

Since 1995 a large number of pilot ADCs have been conducted at our institution for CHN students, or for unemployed graduates from the CHN and other professional universities in Leeuwarden (for a full list of all the pilots at the CHN, see the appendix). The number of participants per pilot ranged from 5 to 55. One of the programs of our university is the Career & Personnel Management School (CMSL). As part of their learning program students participate in the development and operation of ADCs in our school. In most of the pilots CMSL students had an active role.

3.1 Construction of the ADCs

The development or construction of ADCs involves a number of steps. The first steps include job analysis, identification of core tasks, the choice of behavioral dimensions and the choice of the situational exercises. In this section the last two elements will be illustrated with material from two case studies on the development of ADC exercises for starting entrepreneurs (June 1997; February 1998). The results from these studies were later used in following pilots (see appendix).

To determine the relevant behavioral dimensions and construct the exercises of three sources of information were used:
1. an analysis of the tasks a starting professional could be expected to perform adequately;
2. the educational goals formulated for a particular study program;
3. lists with competencies developed by Mintzberg, Quinn, Boyatzis, Thornton & Byham, etc.

The studies began with a thorough analysis of critical incidents described in the literature. Reasons why some starters failed and others succeed were identified. The information from this desk research was used as a global indication of the critical tasks for starting entrepreneurs. The second input was formed by the educational objectives of the small business management program. The aims had been categorized in terms of key tasks, under headings like: Financial Management related tasks, Marketing & Sales activities, Production and Operations tasks, Information Technology, Legal Duties, Leading & Organizing, Human Resources Management.

The next step was to relate the list of educational objectives to the lists with behavioral dimensions from Byham and Thornton, Seegers Jansen and

De Jongh. The behavioral dimensions that were selected in this stage were intuitively ranked as to their importance for the job at stake. The set of appropriate dimensions was further reduced, since some of them could only be measured in exercises, which we did not plan to use, mainly for practical reasons.

The final set of behavioral dimensions and exercises is more a matter of satisfying than optimizing. Keeping in mind the restrictions mentioned earlier (2.3), we distinguished the following behavioral dimensions for the different exercises (see table 2). To establish the degree of situation specificity, reliability and validity, each dimension is elicited in at least two exercises.

Table 2. Behavioral dimensions measured in the ADC exercises.

Behavioral dimension	In basket	Group discussion	Presentation	Case analysis	Interview simulation	Fact finding
Interpersonal sensitivity		+			+	
Problem analysis	+			+	+	+
Argumentation	+	+	+	+	+	
Speaking		+	+		+	+
Listening					+	+
Writing	+			+		
Physical pose		+	+		+	
Judgment/ Decisiveness				+		+
Flexibility		+			+	
Planning & organizing	+		+			
Leadership	+	+				
Commercial orientation	+				+	
Customer focus	+				+	+

3.2 Operational Management of the ADCs

The pilots or case studies at the CHN have all been conducted under the auspices of the Institute for Service Management, the service and research institute of the CHN. Where possible, students are involved in the construction and operation of ADCS.

During a six-week module about ten students form a project team, responsible for the organization, operation and evaluation of an ADC pilot. During the first two weeks of the module they study relevant literature about assessment, attend some workshops on ADC construction, measurement issues, results, and organization of ADCs. Starting from week three in the module students actually conduct the ADCs. Different members of the project group perform the following functions:
project manager
- assistant project manager
- assessors (2 persons per exercise)
- director (2 persons per session)
- actors (2 x 2 persons)

The ADC would typically take 4 hours. All participants receive feedback on their performance in the ADC in the form of a written report. The report consists of:
- introduction with a clarification of the main concepts
- all the information forms and scales the observers filled in during the ADC
- the exercises used in the ADC
- scores on the dimensions and the sub dimensions
- striking observations that add to the scores

The performance of each participant in each exercise is judged by two assessors. Assessors are trained in using the ORCE (Observe Record Classify Evaluate) approach in rating the subjects on the different behavioral dimensions. Individual ratings were combined in a consensus meeting into a final rating on a five-point scale for each behavioral dimension. Most important are the comments added to the ratings. Table 3 gives an example based on a group discussion exercise.

Due to the exploratory nature of the pilots no interpretations or advice have been added to the results. In the future advice regarding study and career will be included in the reports.

Table 3. Example of feedback on group discussion exercise.

Score	--	-	±	+	++
Dimensions					
Group orientation			X		
Argumentation				X	
Speaking				X	
Physical posture				X	

Comments:

Group orientation:
You listen well to what other people say, but you do not always respect the opinion of others. You are willing to cooperate, but you stick to your own opinion. You take over the role of chairman when you summarize the agreements at the end of the discussion. We have not observed you showing empathy and sensitivity.

3.3 Evaluation of ADCs

The quality of ADCs can be judged from three different perspectives: first the technical perspective incorporated by the psychometrical who will look for professional criteria like validity and reliability. Secondly, the perspective of the participant who expects an acceptable and transparent procedure. Ideally participation in an ADC is also a pleasant and educational experience. We refer to this as the experience quality perspective. A third perspective, not discussed in this paper, is driven by benefits for the organization that instigates the ADC. This economical perspective values criteria like utility and return on investment.

In this section the first two perspectives will be discussed. We analyze the reliability and validity in the case study on Service Jobs, the internal employment agency of the CHN (June 1998). We also present data from evaluations by participants. The case study concerns 11 students and graduates who were registered at Service Jobs. The whole ADC was organized, constructed, operated and evaluated by students of the Career & Personnel Management School Leeuwarden. The duration of this project was six weeks full time. As usual the following functions were distinguished in the project group: project manager, assistant project manager, assessors (2 persons per exercise), director (2 persons per session), actors (2).

The ADC took 4 hours, with an extra 15 minutes of instruction for the participants. The ADC consisted of four exercises: in basket, group discussion, interview, and presentation. In each exercise the participants were rated on three to eight dimensions, which were in their turn divided into three to six sub dimensions.

3.3.1 Validity

Validity, "the ability of the test to achieve its aims and objectives" (Thornton, 1992), may be seen as the proof of the pudding for ADCs. In general the following varieties are recognized.

Face validity means that the ADC and its constituent exercises are perceived to "closely resemble the actual job and the actual organization. This feature means that employees may be more willing to participate in the assessment center and have more confidence in the results and feedback" (Thornton, 1992). As such face validity is no "hard" or quantifiable measure. It is based on the perception and the experiences of the participants. For that reason face validity might better be listed as a part of the experience quality perspective which will be discussed in section 3.3.3.

Content validity will have to be secured by the quality of the job-analysis. Whether the exercises and the behavioral dimensions cover the essential tasks and core competencies will have to be judged by representatives of the occupational area involved.

Predictive validity is reported as one of the assets of the assessment center method. It is a measure of how well the ADC can predict the candidates' future success.

Construct validity is a reflection of how much the different dimensions that are measured are related. When the measured concepts are entered in a relational network, construct validity is indicated by convergence and divergence in the correlation patterns. Comparable concepts should correlate positively; negative correlations indicate different concepts. Construct validity is generally considered one of the weak spots of the assessment center method (Cascio, 1998; Thornton, 1992).

In the case study on Service Jobs the different forms of validity were measured in the following way: face validity was appraised as an outcome of the participant experience (see 3.3.3). Content validity was secured in much the same way as we described in 3.1: "construction of the ADCs." Predictive validity had not been measured at the time this paper was written.[19] Construct validity was measured as the inter-dimension correlation within exercises or stations, and between exercises.

---

[19] None of the CHN projects so far have included a repeated measurement to ascertain the predictive potential of the ADC. There are only weak indications of progression in mastering skills in the dissertation of Snippe (1996).

a) Inter-dimension correlation within exercises

Whether the different behavioral dimensions are independent of each other can be measured by computing the correlation between the scores on different aspects (dimensions) within the same exercise. As an example, the inter-dimension correlations are shown in table 4 for the interview simulation. In this exercise the following dimensions were distinguished: active listening; asking questions; showing empathy; paraphrasing and clarifying; structuring and controlling; giving feedback; showing respect; and gathering information. The dimensions are based on the studies summarized in table 2, but were altered slightly for the purpose of the exercise.

Table 4. Correlations between dimensions in the Interview simulation.

Dimensions	Dim 1	Dim 2	Dim 3	Dim 4	Dim 5	Dim 6	Dim 7	Dim 8
1. Active listening		.64*	.55*	.64*	.53*	.50*	.78*	.28
2. Asking questions	.64*		.72*	.52*	.34	.29	.71*	.29
3. Showing empathy	.55*	.72*		.65*	.40	.35	.79*	.32
4. Paraphrasing and clarifying	.64*	.52*	.65*		.79*	.55*	.61*	.44
5. Structuring and controlling	.53*	.34	.40	.79*		.00	.39	.65*
6. Giving feedback	.50*	.29	.35	.55*	.00		.34	.06
7. Showing respect	.78*	.71*	.79*	.61*	.39	.34		.14
8. Gathering information	.28	.29	.32	.44	.65*	.34	.14	

* p < .05

Correlations between dimensions range from zero (between dimension 5 and 6) to .79 (between dim 4 and 5, and between dim 3 and 7). Dimension 1 and 4 correlate significantly with all other dimensions except dimension 8. All dimensions correlate significantly with one or more other dimensions. A closer look at the correlations suggests a similarity between dimensions 1 and 4; and between 2, 3 and 7. These dimensions also correlate highly with each other.

The conclusion must be that these dimensions are not very independent. It looks as if the exercise only measures two or three different constructs. The same holds for an analysis of the inter-dimension correlation in the other

Assessment & Development Centers in PBL 411

exercises.[20] It appears that exercises that were constructed with great care have low construct validity. Even though this is in concord with findings in literature, it is a concern for the CHN.

b) Inter-dimension correlation between exercises

Whereas inter-dimension correlation within exercises should be absent or low, correlations between the ratings of a same dimension in two or more exercises should preferably be high. It is the main reason that each dimension is elicited in at least two exercises (see section 3.1). This "relationship among various parts of the assessment procedure" (Thornton, 1992) is another measure of construct validity. The correlation between exercises for the case study on Service Jobs was low, the highest measured being .31 for oral communication skills between the group discussion and the presentation. It indicates a low construct validity of the behavioral dimension. This low correlation is generally found in research (Lievens & Seegers, 1997; Luken, 1996), but again, it leaves a lot to be desired.

3.3.2 Reliability

The reliability of a measurement instrument can be determined in different ways. The internal consistency or homogeneity of an instrument indicates the degree to which the individual items in a scale point in the same direction. Since we did not use multi-item scales to measure the behavioral dimensions, but had them rated directly in a final score, we cannot compute internal consistency measures like Cronbach's alpha. The equivalent or parallel forms reliability is computed by using two different instruments which measure the same concept, and computing their correspondence.

In general, the reliability of a measurement instrument can be improved by increasing the number of items, exercises or situations. In fact, the scores on the behavioral dimensions should be generalizable over time, situations and assessors. That is why we preferred to have each dimension measured in at least two different simulations and have each participant rated by at least two assessors.

Another approach to determine the reliability is to compute the inter-rater agreement. Results for the interview simulation in the case study on Service Jobs are shown in table 5. Thornton (1992) states that "for this kind of study, reliability figures of .80 to 1.00 are considered high, .60 to .80 are moderate, and .60 or below are low" (p. 114).

---

[20] The correlation between dimensions in the In-Basket exercise varies from .01 to .70, in the Group discussion from .30 to .57, and in the Presentation exercise from .54 to .78.

The inter-assessor agreement is partly a result of the behavior of the individual judge and the specificity of the observational ratings. In general, the more specific the categories or dimensions to be rated, the higher the inter-assessor agreement. In the interview simulation participants had to find out about four distinct pieces of information. This is fairly easy to score and led to an agreement of .98. Scoring skills in paraphrasing and clarifying objectively, on the other hand, proved to be more difficult.

Scores for the other exercises, in-basket, group discussion and presentation ranged from fair to high. A very low .11 was found for the dimension physical posture in the group discussion. It would seem that this dimension was either not very well defined in the construction phase, or that assessors lacked proper training concerning this element.

Table 5. The inter-assessor agreement

Dimensions	Inter-assessor agreement Interview simulation
Active listening	.73
Asking questions	.78
Showing empathy	.94
Paraphrasing and clarifying	.45
Structuring and controlling	.94
Giving feedback	.92
Showing respect	.92
Gathering information	.98
Overall	.86

3.3.3 Experience by participants

The experience quality of an ADC is a reflection of how useful or pleasant the participants find the ADC. It is a measure of face validity and an important indicator for the acceptability of the ADC. As part of the procedure for ADCs at the CHN both the exercises and the total organization and relevance of the ADC, as experienced by participants, are evaluated. The results of the evaluations in the case study on Service Jobs are shown in table 6.

The numbers are on a scale from one to ten, ten being the highest. The participant ratings are not significantly different from the ratings on other ADCs conducted at the CHN. In general participants' evaluations are favorable. Their positive opinions are in line with other findings in the literature.

Table 6. Ratings on 15 organizational aspects of the ADC

Aspects	Report mark (N = 11)	Sd
1. Recruitment of participants	6.9	.26
2. Prior information	6.3	.16
3. Registration	7.6	.51
4. Planning	7.3	.42
5. Written confirmation	6.6	.60
6. Reception at the ADC	6.9	.47
7. Experiences during ADC	7.1	.38
8. Behavior ADC manager	7.1	.48
9. Behavior of the role-player	7.0	.31
10. Behavior of the assessors	7.4	.28
11. Length of the ADC	7.4	.31
12. Material for the exercises	7.1	.28
13. Location	6.9	.56
14. Working conditions	6.9	.66
15. Catering (coffee, thee)	7.0	.34

4. DISCUSSION

In the introduction we mentioned four reasons for introducing ADCs in a professional university: realistic assessment of skills and attitudes; suitability for assessing problem-based learning; its relevance for flexible and adaptive education; and its good reputation. The first and last points have well been researched and documented. In 2.4 we have argued what the extra added value of ADCs in an educational setting could be. The good reputation is confirmed formally by positive reactions from participants, reflected in high ratings on evaluations. Informally we hear that school administration and employees react favorably.

The use of ADCs does justice to our educational approach of problem-based learning. In assessing competencies rather than facts and knowledge, it is divergent rather than convergent in nature. Thus it mirrors more closely the constructivist learning environment that we try to create at the CHN (see Eringa and Otting in this volume for a more extensive treatment of a constructivist approach in a business school curriculum).

There remain, however quite a few questions to be asked. Predictive validity has not been researched properly. Psychometric research shows that construct validity is low, and content validity problematic in many cases. A close analysis of ADC exercises that seem to be well constructed, based on a proper job analysis, and with a well-motivated choice of behavioral dimensions, demonstrates that these are not so valid after all. Also reliability still leaves a lot to be desired. Dimensions that have been narrowly defined can be observed and scored with high reliability. Behavioral dimensions of a more complex nature show scoring patterns that are a lot less reliable.

These findings, of course, only call for more attention to the evaluation and maintenance stage in the use of ADCs. In general we find that results of this stage are not very well reported, at least not in an educational setting. Future research should therefore follow students and graduates in longitudinal studies to determine predictive validity. Also content validity should be based on a more thorough analysis of the industry and jobs that students are trained for. And the improvement of construct validity should be an ongoing process, not unlike the empirical research cycle, following the process of developing, executing and evaluating the ADCs.

The pilots that we conducted at the CHN are of an exploratory nature. They were started as a result of the efforts of a small group of people, in different parts of our organization and for different purposes. The results are therefore not readily generalizable. It does, however, provide useful information that can help students manage their own study and professional career. And last, but not least, it provides the students of our Career and Personnel Management program with a real life learning environment.

APPENDIX

ADC projects at the CHN: 1995-1998: Construction, application and maintenance.

- July 1995: Feasibility study and inventarisation of the learning goals of the FEM programs by Annegrit Wijkers, Boudina van der Werf and Esmee Kooistra
- October 1995: ADC-HMSL by Marlies Vrielink and Serge Merkelbach.
- May/June 1996: Interest survey in the retail sector by students of the RMSL.
- August 1996: Dissertation about an exercise for social skills by Marieke Snippe.
- January 1997: Construction of an AC exercise for Creative Therapy by Patries van Veldhoven.
- January 1997: Construction and pilot testing of an exercise on administrative organization by Barbara Eikelenboom and Sandra Lunenborg.
- Module period 4 '97: ADC with 60 participants from the FEM.
- Module period 6 '97: ADC with 40 participants from the FEM.
- July 1997: Construction of an exercise for starting entrepreneurs by Manda van der Zwaag.

- August 1997: Dissertation about an In-basket exercise by Antje Visser.
- January 1998: ADC Consultancy for a business school in Arnhem.
- February 1998: Construction of two exercises for starting entrepreneurs by a project team of second year CMSL students.
- February 1998: Construction of three exercises for Management of Welfare Institutions by a group of CMSL students.
- March 1998: ADC at the start of the course "En nu een baan" ("And now a job").
- June 1998: ADC Small Business School Leeuwarden by a group of third year CMSL students.
- June 1998: ADC for Service Jobs, the internal employment agency at the CHN.
- June 1998: Dissertation by Angelique Kuin about the application of the ADC in ISM training activities.

REFERENCES

Ballantyne, I., & Povah, N. (1995). *Assessment & development centers.* London: Gower.

Boyatzis, R.E. (1982). *The competent manager. A model for effective performance.* New York: Wiley.

Bruijns, V., & Pieke, E. (1997). *Wie ben ik, wat wil ik, wat kan ik?* Hogeschool van Amsterdam.

Cascio, W.F. (1991). *Applied psychology in personnel management.* Englewood Cliffs, NJ: Prentice-Hall.

Dochy F.J.R.C., & de Rijke T.R., (Eds.) (1995). *Assessment centers: Nieuwe toepassingen in opleiding, onderwijs en HRM.* Utrecht: Lemma.

Feltham, R.T. (1989). Assessment Centers. In P. Herriot (Ed.), *Assessment & selection in organizations.* London: Wiley.

Fletcher, S. (1992). *Competence-Based assessment techniques.* London: Kogan Page.

Herriot, P. (Ed.) (1994). *Handbook of assessment in Organizations.* London: Wiley.

Jansen, P.G.W., & de Jongh, F. (1993). *Assessment centers; een open boek.* Utrecht: Het Spectrum/Marka.

Lee, G., & Beard, D. (1994). *Development centers.* New York: McGraw-Hill.

Lievens, F., & Seegers, J. (1997). Het verhogen van de begripsvaliditeit van assessment centers. *De Psycholoog, April,* 160-166.

Luken, T. (1996). Het assessment raadsel: het werkt, maar hoe? In A. Breed, & A. Kooreman (Eds.), *Psychologie in arbeid en loopbaan.* Lisse: Swets & Zeitlinger.

Maesen de Sombreff, P.E.A.M. van der (1992). *Het rendement van personeelsselectie.* Unpublished Dissertation, University of Groningen.

Mintzberg, H. (1973). *The nature of managerial work.* New York: Harper and Row.

Nisbett, R., & Ross, L. (1980*). Human inference. Strategies and shortcomings of social judgment.* Englewood Cliffs, NJ: Prentice-Hall.

Onstenk, J. (1997). Beroepspraktijk bouw en verzorging vertaald naar eindtermen en leerplan. *Profiel, 4,* April.

Quinn, R.E., Faerman, S.R., Thompson, M.P., & McGrath, M.R. (1996). *Becoming a master manager. A competency framework.* New York: Wiley.
Seegers, J.J.J.L. (1997). *Assessment centers. Een personeelsinstrument voor de manager.* Deventer: Kluwer.
Segers, M.S.R. (1996). Assessment in a problem-based economics curriculum. In M. Birenbaum & F.J.R.C. Dochy (Eds.), *Alternatives in Assessment of Achievements, Learning Processes and Prior Knowledge.* Dordrecht: Kluwer Academic Publishers.
Snippe, M.D. (1996). *Constructie en evaluatie van een assessment-oefening 'sociale vaardigheden'.* Leeuwarden: Centrum voor Arbeid & Beroep,
Thompson, J.E., & Carter, S. (1995). The development of competence: National standards for managers. In C.S. Mulder (Ed.), *Corporate training for effective performance.* Dordrecht: Kluwer Academic Publishers.
Thornton, G.C. (1992). *Assessment centers in human resource management.* Reading: Addison-Wesley.
Thornton, G.C., & Byham, W.C. (1982). *Assessment centers and managerial performance.* San Diego: Academic Press.
Tillema, H.H. (Ed.). (1996). *Development Centers; ontwikkelen van competenties in organisaties.* Deventer: Kluwer.
Woodruffe, C. (1995). *Assessment centers. Identifying and developing competence.* Oxford: Blackwell.
Zaal, J.N. (1991). Assessment centers at the Dutch central government. In R.K. Hambleton, & J.N. Zaal (Eds.), *Advances in educational and psychological testing.* Dordrecht: Kluwer Academic Publishers.

PART VI

COGNITION AND LEARNING

What Should We Expect to be Different about How Expert Business Economists Solve Problems?

Brendan K. O'Rourke
Faculty of Business, Dublin Institute of Technology, Dublin, Ireland

1. INTRODUCTION

A primary purpose of economics in business education is to allow individuals to tackle economic problems more effectively, to become, in a sense, experts in solving economic problems. Of course there may be other roles of economics in management education and other less worthy reasons for the presence of economics on the business curriculum: Examples might include the ideological influence of economics or attempts to gain academic repute through association. Yet the discipline's claim is that it is a way of thinking that will improve reasoning about economics problems. As Smith (1996; p. 222) puts it, "One can interpret education in economics and game theory as a process of teaching people to overcome their knee-jerk reactions to situations susceptible to economic reasoning."

If economics education in business does help people reason more effectively one would expect this to be apparent in the way business economics experts solve relevant problems compared to non-experts. After all this is what is meant by expertise and has been shown to be detectable in other domains. Another reason for studying economics expertise is to help the conversation in the business faculty and knowing how different experts in business think should help such communication. Thus progress in both understanding each other's insights and in integrating each other's findings might be aided. In addition by looking at how economics education and experience influences reasoning we might move towards understanding what disciplines might be best at developing skills which best handle particular types of business problems.

Whereas there has been much valuable comment on the relationship of economics to the rest of business academics a lot of the debate has been in the nature of isolated comments and only more recently has been made more coherent. While this debate has become more coherent only some aspects of this debate have progressed to empirical investigation. This paper hopes to be a precursor to providing more empirical data on business economics expertise of relevance to the debate on economics and management learning.

The paper begins with a brief overview of the expertise literature followed by an explanation of the focus on business economics. Next the three basic types of problem-solvers in the expertise literature - expert, novice, and naïve - are defined in the context of business economics. Once this is done expected differences between the three types of business economists are discussed. Some implications of the foregoing for empirical work are then sketched before the paper draws to a conclusion.

2. THE EXPERTISE LITERATURE

The modern study of expertise in particular domains began with work on chess experts by researchers such as Chase and Simon (1973), de Groot (1978) and Voss et al. (1983, 1989). The study of expertise has now covered many domains including physics, medicine, chemistry, mathematics, auditing, and political science. Reviews of the literature are provided by Ericsson and Smith (1991), and by Zeit and Glaser (1994). Generally, systematic differences between domain specific expert and naïve problem solvers have been found. Experts have greater knowledge of the domain and it seems that the quantity of knowledge possessed by experts is also constant and very large across domains. Within their domain experts have superior memories probably due to the hierarchical nature of their knowledge organization and due to dense interconnections between branches of that hierarchy. Pattern recognition of domain specific information is also superior for experts. In addition experts have been found to approach problems differently. They perceive problems as being grouped into more abstract categories related to their more hierarchically organized knowledge structure. Experts routinize certain thinking procedures. One of the most important of these routinized thinking procedures is metacognition - a self-knowledge of how the individual experts are tackling a problem. Experts also have different strategies depending on the problem from naïve and novice problem solvers. For example, a medical expert might work forward from the symptoms of a patient towards an appropriate diagnosis whereas a novice in medicine might check the correctness of a presumed diagnosis by working back through the symptoms.

Chess was ideal for the initial study of expertise. Superior performance was easy to detect, chess problems were well-defined and similar conditions could be reliably reproduced. More prevalent problems for many domains are ill-defined problems i.e., they are without a clear goal or lack clearly defined initial conditions. Many of the problems in social sciences in general and more specifically in business tend not only to be more ill-defined: It may also be unclear in which domain of expertise they lie. Indeed the problems may lie in an area of dispute between experts. There has also been work on expertise in this type of ill-structured domain though the work is perhaps not as conclusive. Nevertheless what has been said about expertise in well-structured domains seems to hold true for less well-structured domains. Additionally it has been found in the less well-structured areas that experts tend to impose constraints in order to make such problems tractable. It also seems to be the case that experts in ill-structured domains spend more time justifying their solutions.

It is true that social science expertise poses difficult problems for observing expert problem solving. Economic theory itself would suggest superior profit performance should not be expected in the long term by undergoing some education course that consistently enhances managerial efficiency- the market would compete away any such supernormal profits. This is why the expertise approach is suitable for business economics performance as "...the expertise approach is an attempt to describe the critical performance under standardized conditions, to analyze it, and to identify the components of the performance that make it superior" (Ericsson & Smith, 1991; p. 8). Problems in social science unlike the problems in more studied domains like chess tend to be ill-defined. A greater part of social science expertise may be in skillful problem representation, perhaps especially in the way constraints are chosen. Adding more to their ill-defined nature is the fact that it is often problematic what constitutes a better solution in social science. Nevertheless differences in the problem solving of experts and non-experts in social science has been found.

The Voss, Greene, Post and Penner (1983) study, while explaining difficulties in detecting social science expertise, showed how experts in political science adopted problem solving approaches to tackling the problems of agricultural productivity in the Soviet Union that were different from the approaches of non-experts. Within the area of management considerable work has been done on auditing expertise. For example Vaatstra, Boshuizen and Schmidt (1995) found that expert auditors used more concepts that related both qualitative and quantitative information from more diverse sources than did naïve and novices auditors. Frederick (1991) has looked at how auditing experts but not auditing novices retrieve information about financial controls of a company when it is presented in a schematic rather than a taxonomic organization. Bacdayan (1996) looked at characteristics of expert leaders of quality improvement tasks.

3. THE FOCUS ON BUSINESS ECONOMICS

The particular type of business expertise being studied here is business economics expertise. The business economics being discussed here refers to the narrower meaning of the term as applied to the discipline of economics as one of the disciplines within management learning, crudely characterized by the debate between neoclassical economists and their opponents. The term is not used here in a more general sense as it is in, for example, the translation for term *bedrijfseconomie* used in the Netherlands, which refers to a wider approach to business academics. Though *bedrijfseconomie* is that stream of business academics more dominated by the discipline economics, this wider meaning is not adopted here. This means for instance the expertise of business economics in this paper is not meant to include auditing expertise.

The present study focussed on the effects of the particular discipline of business economics. This may be problematic because as Vernooij's (1995) work suggests it may be the interaction among different mental models that causes difficulties in the application of knowledge to problems. This means that there may be problems in separating the effects of the economics discipline from the effects of training in cognate disciplines. Indeed Boshuizen (1995; p. 100) points out that one of the features of expertise is the integration of different basic sciences. While accepting Boshuizen's (1995) point it is useful to examine expertise in just one business discipline for number of reasons. Firstly, because by examining one discipline a list of expected features of expertise in that particular discipline can be developed and examined. Secondly, it may be that the experts in management may fall into different discipline groupings generating different types of experts. This is suspected because the basic sciences of management often have such different basic approaches and assumptions that there appears to be different and distinctive types of business experts. There even appears to be different academic groupings within management learning that lack mutual understanding (Whitley, 1989). Business students often specialize in options based on a particular discipline or set of closely related disciplines, often within a course of study dominated by a particular discipline. Further the difficulties shown of integrating concepts even within the same disciplines (see Vernooij, 1995) make it seem unwise to expect experts to emerge who actually integrate the different disciplinary streams of the business school. Perhaps it would be wiser to expect different clusters of business experts to emerge. For these reasons this paper explores a particular type of business expertise rather than a generalized business expertise or even more generalized social science one.

A reason to focus on economics is that it makes much of its claim to be a way of thinking. It is a discipline that seems to disdainfully spurn the more informational aspects of knowledge transfer and puts itself forward as a kind of refined common sense. However psychologists have been skeptical of claims that a discipline can improve general reasoning. In questioning this scepticism, Lehman, Lempert and Nisbett (1988) found that graduate training did have a positive effect on a particular type of reasoning performance: Graduate training in law, medicine and psychology meant better performance on reasoning involving confounded variables and statistical considerations than training in chemistry. While the impact of the economics discipline on general reasoning skills is of interest, work must begin at a narrower level. After all the Voss, Blais, Means, Green & Ahwesh (1989) study finds no particular support for the power of economics education, above any general college education, to improve reasoning even with respect to everyday economics problems. Such results would seem to make claims to improve general reasoning rather far fetched.

So economics has yet to prove itself particularly beneficial to reasoning skills at the narrower subject matter level. Yet this narrower level is peculiar: Much of the subject matter of business economics is shared, or perhaps more accurately disputed, with other disciplines. The influence of these disciplines on particular business education courses varies hugely. Voss (1996; p. 466) points out that "One of the most significant questions requiring study is the extent to which reasoning is similar or different in various subject matter domains." The question of the extent of how similar or different reasoning in disciplines is also of interest.

4. EXPERT, NOVICE AND NAÏVE BUSINESS ECONOMISTS

Dividing individuals into naïve, novice and expert types with reference to a particular domain has been the practice in the expertise literature. It of course is not entirely unproblematic and the strategy adopted here for dealing with any such problems is to raise them as they arise in the discussion of the three types.

Generally individuals are considered naïve with respect to a particular domain if they have neither education nor experience in that particular domain. Thus an individual with no expertise or expertise from separate domains may be considered naïve with respect to the particular domains under discussion. There may be hidden overlaps between domains of expertise. After all Lehman et al. (1988) demonstrated that postgraduate training in psychology, medicine, and law shared the effect of improving statistical and methodological reasoning. So it appears that some other domain experts may be less naïve business economists than others. For this study, truly naïve individuals are those who may or may not be experts in other domains but have neither education nor experience in relevant domains. When dealing with the discipline of business economics there is the added difficulty discussed above of the domain being to some extent disputed between disciplines. Given this dispute and the Lehman et al. (1988) findings relevant domains would include other business disciplines, the social sciences and may even stretch as far as law and medicine.

Given the heterogeneous nature of business education provision one has also to be particularly careful in this domain of some apparent naïves being "disguised novices" with perhaps quite a considerable amount of management education behind them.

Between expertise and naïveté lies the novitiate. At least three dimensions are important: education, experience and ability. With education and experience there may quite different qualities at different stages. For example, it may be that in education novices initially become confused by their exposure to a particular discipline. In the author's personal experiences of teaching economics this is particularly true for introductory economics courses. For a discipline that boasts it is replacing the student's way of thinking about everyday events this may not be particularly surprising. In addition individual differences in ability may mean different progression through such stages. It is reasonable therefore that different novices will not only be different with similar time spent in a domain but that increases in time spent may mean, for some stages, reversals in performance level. Indeed novices caught in particular stages may produce worst performances than naïve individuals. Predications about the performance of novices will therefore have to be quite cautious.

Experts are probably the mostly easily described of the three types of business economist. Experts are clearly individuals who have superior knowledge and performance in the domain. It has been suggested (Ericsson, 1996; p. 13) that only exceptional individuals be considered as expert subjects in the studies of expertise. The argument seems to be that these individuals will have most expertise characteristics and it will therefore be easier to identify and describe them. Apart from the difficulty of gaining access to such outstanding individuals there is another problem. By definition these outstanding experts are extraordinary even for experts. If we are trying to study the general effects and effectiveness of business economics training and education it seems more appropriate to study ordinary or competent experts rather than necessarily outstanding ones. This approach avoids the problem of compiling criteria for selecting outstanding performance in a field where there are few agreed upon solutions. Such an approach seems to have been adopted by others studying various types of management expertise (e.g., Vaatstra, Boshuizen, & Schmidt, 1995). The literature does provide necessary if not sufficient conditions for individual to attain the status of expert. These include at least ten years of experience in the domain. To this might be added a requirement that at least 5 years of formal education in economics prior to the years of experience is added for an individual to be defined as an expert.

5. EXPECTED DIFFERENCES BETWEEN EXPERT, NOVICE AND NAÏVE BUSINESS ECONOMISTS

From the expertise literature (especially the work of Voss et. al., 1983, 1989) and from the literature concerning the roles of the economics in management education (e.g., O'Rourke, 1998) learning certain expectations can be developed concerning the differences between expert, novice and naïve business economists. These are of course largely theoretical until empirical work is completed but serve as pointers to the design of problems for such work. The differences are summarized in Table 1 and discussed below. Given what has been said concerning the heterogeneous nature of novices the remarks concerning their problem-solving characteristics are particularly speculative.

Problem representation or problem space is the solver's mental model of the problem and is thought to be a relatively small subset of all the possible aspects of the problem which when described as fully and as objectively as possible constitute the task environment. Problem representation is composed of a description of the initial state, the goal state, the set of operators, and the path constraints. Problem representation is seen as a key component of problem solving as if the solver does not include in her representation of the problem the elements necessary for solving the problem the problem cannot be solved regardless of the efficacy of the other elements of her problem-solving activity.

Table 1. Expected Differences between Expert, Novice, and Naïve Business Economists

Expected Difference in	Expert Economists	Novices	Naïve
Problem Space – illustrated by number of factors considered.	Largest and expands as expert works through problem.	Intermediate.	Least.
Representation as illustrated by statements interpreting the problem.	More careful and extensive with ill-defined & unfamiliar problems. More explicit assumptions.	Quickly placed in economic theory categories familiar to the novice.	Quick & crude. Less explicit assumptions.
Directness of solution.	More direct only where problem type is very familiar.	Same as experts except where problem types is very familiar to expert.	Same as experts except where problem types is very familiar to expert.
Level of abstraction.	Very high. integration of problem details with abstract principles.	High but lacking integration of problem details with abstract principles.	Focussed on details of problem
Problem decomposition.	Used occasionally.	Used frequently.	Most often used.
Problem conversion.	Hierarchical conversion.	Hierarchical conversion.	Deletion & substitution.
Domain specific strategies.	Routinised use.	Might become obstacles in themselves.	None.
Exploration of solution.	Common.	Rare.	Rare.
Opportunistic problem solving.	Common.	Rare.	Rare.
Constraint posting.	Common.	Rare.	Rare.
Argumentation: Amount.	Most.	Intermediate.	Least.
Argumentation: Quality.	Best.	Intermediate.	Worst.
Number of qualifications to arguments.	Most.	Intermediate.	Least.
Number of counter-arguments.	Most.	Intermediate.	Least.

Table 1. Expected Differences between Expert, Novice, and Naïve Business Economists (continued)

Expected Difference in	Expert Economists	Novices	Naïve
Triangulation i.e. different kinds of supports for same claim.	Most.	Intermediate.	Least.
Prevalent types of argument.	Mixture.	Metaphor & logic.	Narrative & fact.
Recovery from unsound arguments.	Greatest.	Intermediate.	Least.
Solutions.	Superior one general solution.	Intermediate - but may be worse than novice.	Inferior partial solutions.
Concepts of fairness.	Efficiency.	Confused.	Distributional.
Metacognition.	Rarely explicit and if so more focussed on relevant economic concepts.	Explicit not routinized. Referring to subject's progress in solving the problem.	Statements about lack of knowledge.
Calibration.	More calibrated.	Over-confident.	Over-confident.
Evaluation.	Generate test evaluation not means-ends evaluation.	Rare.	Rare.

Ericsson and Smith (1991; p. 20) referring to much of the expertise literature report that expert performers tend to see the solution method as part of the immediate comprehension of the task whereas naïve individuals have to construct a deliberate representation of the task and a step by step solution. Yet Voss et al. (1983; p. 210, p. 191) report that "novices went down the list of things to consider and indicated what should be done with respect to each item. Experts, on the other hand, spent considerable time on problem representation" and that "During the initial phases of protocol generation, experts showed no evidence of having a well-developed solution plan." This conflict may be explained by the nature of the problems studied: In the majority of the expertise literature the problems studied are well-defined problems whereas social science problems are generally ill defined. Indeed the Voss et al. (1983; p. 209) experts did not and would "... not develop extensive problem representations when (1) the wording of the problem suggests that this is not necessary, and (2) when the solver already has a solution in mind." The wording of problems and whether or not they are substantially novel to the expert will influence the expectations of how experts will represent problems. It is not surprising that problem representation would be extensive for social science experts. In most real social science problems understanding of the initial state of a problem, what the goal-state should be, the set of operators and the path constraints are almost always ambiguous and usually mutually interdependent. It is only by understanding what operators or policies might be used that constraints become evident and the most desired features of a goal state are clarified. As Kay (1996; p. 87) puts "It is simpler if we can pursue a single clear objective. But that is the world of sportsmen and soldiers, not of business and politics ... Balancing interests and objectives is what people live their lives for and earn their salaries for." In this context Voss et al.'s (1983; p. 209) finding that, "there is some evidence that the problem space may expand as the expert solver advances his or her solution. This occurs when the solver comes to issues that were not part of the original representation," is not surprising.

Since experts have more hierarchical organized knowledge structure it is also not surprising that their verbal reports tend to be more abstract across a variety of domains. Social science problems are no exception as Voss et al.'s (1989; p. 228) data "reflect the tendency for the more educated and, to some the more economically trained groups, to state more abstract factors ..." While novices may also be abstract social science experts in general - and in this case it is expected business economist in particular - distinguish themselves by the way they integrate details about the problem and its context (Zeitz & Glaser, 1994; p. 2197). Naïve individuals are likely to focus on the surface features of the problems. This tendency towards abstraction might be expected to be particularly strong in business economics experts as the discipline is famed for its explicitly abstract nature.

As regards approaches to dealing with problems that do not yield a direct solution it is expected that expert, novice and naïve individuals will differ. One approach is problem decomposition where the problem is broken up into small sub-problems that can be tackled more easily. While this can be an effective general problem solving approach it has the disadvantage of creating a tendency to ignore sub-problem interaction so important in business economics. Additionally social science experts, as we will discuss below, have been found to seek one general solution rather than partial solutions to particular problems. This is has not yet been demonstrated in an expertise study for business economists. However it is likely to be the case in a discipline which prides itself as being different from other functional disciplines in management learning in having a holistic conception of business. Therefore it is expected that business economics experts will use problem decomposition less than either naïve or novice problem solvers.

Another approach to problem solution is problem-conversion. This is simply converting the problem presented into another problem in order to provide a solution. Following Voss et al. (1989; p. 234) we would expect experts to use a different type of problem-conversion from naïves. Deletion or substitution conversions are expected from naïve individuals in the sense that they tend to merely ignore part of the problem by either deleting it from their representation or substituting a preferred concept for an ignored piece of the task. Hierarchical conversion of the problem can be expected from experts who will tend to put the problem into a more general category of problems or take a subset of the category mentioned in the problem as representative of that problem. Voss et al. (1989) noted hierarchical conversions tended to produce high quality solutions whereas deletions and substitutes did not.

Business economists will have their own discipline-specific ways of addressing problems. Searching for the logical implications of self-interest regardless of the context, finding some unifying function such as profit or utility with countering weighing arguments such as cost and revenue and separating the competitive and co-operative elements of the situation might all be common strategies in economics. Some specific core concepts and theories such as opportunity cost and supply and demand analysis might be used. Given the extensive use of logic diagrams in their field it is also expected that expert business economists will more readily use pen and paper in their problem solving.

Another relevant finding of Voss et al. (1983; p. 210) was that "only experts examined implications of their solutions, and therefore had an opportunity to encounter a sub-problem or constraint." We therefore expect business economics experts to engage in opportunistic problem solving and constraint posting. Opportunistic problem solving is solving a sub-problem as it is encountered during the course of addressing the problem in general or examining the implications of the proposed general solution.

Constraint posting occurs in the course of examining the implications of a proposed solution to the overall problem or a sub-problem the solver finds a constraint is blocking the solution the constraint is then dealt with opportunistically as a sub-problem. Since novice and naïve individuals tend not to examine the implications of their solutions opportunistic problem solving and constraint posting is likely to be rare in their case.

It is expected that economics experts will engage in a greater amount of argumentation. An important reason for this is because many aspects of economics problems are not generally agreed upon and economists need to have expertise in justifying their understanding of the problem. This is even more the case for the audience to whom many business economists may address themselves: non-economists working in organizations with their political complexity. This is the reason given by Voss et al. (1983; p. 210) when they report that their social science "experts spend a large amount of time on argumentation." Voss and co-researchers also speculate that argumentation may be a feature of working on a previously unsolved problems, and so as much a feature of constructing a solution for the solver as persuading others of the value of the proposed solution. Argument may thus be a general problem-solving strategy when no definite procedure for solving the problem is known. It may also act as a way of evaluating the solution when other means of evaluation are absent or costly. Thus chemists and engineers may need less expertise in argumentation as their solution is subject to relatively inexpensive tests whereas the expensive nature of conclusive experiments in their domain make economists and cosmologists more argumentative.

If argument serves as an aid in problem solving and as an alternative to some sort of 'objective' tests then one would expect its quality to be quite high. More consideration of counter-arguments, greater qualifications, greater number of supports for each claim, greater scepticism, fewer unsound arguments and greater recovery from unsound argument should distinguish experts from the naïve. Yet in the Voss et al. (1989; Table 7.9) study it was the college educated without either formal economics training or experience who provided the greatest proportion of their arguments with qualifiers, though economics training seems to elicit more counter-arguments and greater recovery from inferential distortion. One might also expect greater triangulation in argument, in other words, that expert economists should support their arguments with a greater diversity of reasons; e.g., both an appeal to some generally accepted principle coupled with some more context-specific information.

So far we have just been considering aspects of argument where the expert economist will give what most would agree is a superior type of argument. There are also expectations about the type of argument offered that are more to do with the implicit habits of economics than with what are explicitly and generally agreed attributes of a good argument. In analyzing their rhetoric, McCloskey (1990) makes the point that economists make more use of metaphor and logic than story and fact. So we might expect that economists would argue more deductively from axiomatic principles, perhaps especially the axiom that all actors are rationally self-interested. Non-economists could be expected to use more soft behavioral assumptions and more specific information and anecdotes.

One would naturally expect experts' solutions to be superior and more in line with economic theory than those of novices and naïves. It is reasonable to expect that novices especially in the early stages will produce as bad if not worse solutions than naïve individuals. After all they are having their cognitive maps overlaid with formal economic ones that do not make sense until they are used. As mentioned above this is certainly the author's experience with students new to economics. Why then do studies of novices in physics not have the same effect? A possible reason for this is that since economics deals with everyday life even naïve individuals have well-developed if unscientific mental models whereas in other domains naïve individuals do not have such models.

Expert solutions will also tend to be more holistic as in the Voss et. al. (1983; p. 193) study: "The nature of the solutions offered by experts, regardless of strategy is to find one general solution ...... Indeed, one expert, E, indicated that he was unable to provide a solution when he could not come up with this type of general solution even though he suggested that the sub-problems could be handled on an individual basis." Again this is likely to more the case with business economics because, as was mentioned above, the discipline tends to see itself as providing global optima rather than the local optima of other business disciplines.

The concepts of fairness embodied in either the solutions or the arguments behind the solutions of experts would be expected to be different from naïves. Aggregate efficiency over all the parties seems to be a dominant theme in economics. This in part betrays a utilitarian inheritance but also a basic belief in the ability of trading to make sure the overall gain is distributed in some at least satisfying way. For example Smith (1996) suggests that economists would have a different idea of fairness with respect to peak demand pricing.

Given the lack of agreed-upon best solution and the novel nature of many business economics problems not only should we expect more argumentation but also a lot more explicit evaluation. Again this was a finding of Voss and his colleagues in their 1983 study. Their political sciences experts tended to use more of generate-test rather than the means-end type of evaluation. Means-ends test evaluates how close the solution or attempts at the solution are to the desired goal-state of the problem. A generate-test evaluation is an evaluation of the solution as to how it meets certain criteria developed by the problem solver. Given the ambiguous nature of goal-states in many business economics type problems as well the influence of positivism in business economics it is to be expected that business economists would use the more explicit generate-test methods quite often.

Experts should be superior in their metacognition or overall control of their own problem-solving activity so that they can adapt their methods to the problems. For economists who in their models gladly sacrifice reality to usefulness this should be doubly true. Indeed the Voss et al. (1989; p. 241) study found that those with economics education made fewer but more relevant meta-statements. The reason for the lower number of meta-statements was probably because metacognition was routinized and therefore not verbalized. Following Voss et al. (1989) we can expect irrelevant statements from non-experts perhaps focussing on the unsuitability of the solver for the problem.

Generally the expertise literature seems to suggest that experts will be better at calibration i.e., economists will be more tentative and less certain. Yet Griffin and Tversky (1992; p. 430) argue that where accurate forecasts are not possible then experts are more overconfident than the naïve. Perhaps overconfident stock market analysts and psychiatrists are not selling the accuracy of their forecasts but rather the illusion of certainty and reassurance. Also there may well a difference between purely academic business economists and commercial business economists. Nevertheless the experience and education of economics should if nothing else warn against overconfidence. It is therefore the author's none-too-certain predication that expert business economists will be less overconfident than novice and naïve individuals.

6. IMPLICATIONS FOR EMPIRICAL WORK

Ultimately the expected differences between expert, naïve and novice business economists should be tested empirically. Indeed part of the author's purpose in writing this work has been to prepare for planned future research in this vein.

Clearly the problems used in empirical work must be related to testing for the expected differences outlined in the last section. This will require a number of different types of problems. In order to test what is expected as regards representation, problem conversion, opportunistic problem solving, constraint posting, argumentation and evaluation solvers would have to be presented with at least some ill-defined, ill-structured problems that possess a degree of novelty even to the experts. Yet in order to see if it is the nature of problems that causes so much argumentation from experts it might be wise to include at least some easily recognizable problems with commonly agreed upon solutions.

Problems would also need to be accessible to at least some sort of solution activity from naïves and novices. This latter point means that it would be best for the problems to have an everyday context while addressing issues of concern to business economists. Given the concerns of business economists this should be a relatively easy task. In order to identify different degrees of abstract, to provide some involvement and motivation with the problem, and to provide opportunities for the inappropriate deletions and substitutions of the problem it might be best if the context of the problem was reasonably well elaborated.

In order to see if the expert economists have a more aggregate efficiency and less distribution focussed concept of fairness than novices and naïves the problems will have to some possible element of a non-zero sum game in their structure.

Problems should have a proposed audience, as the audience is likely to affect the nature of the argumentation used and so interact with the entire problem-solving process. Business economics problems often are of the nature of advancing the interests of some actor or group of actors acting within a larger society as opposed to the public interest perspective of other economists. In the light of this narrower perspective it might be wise to ensure that the problem-solvers have such an audience in mind. Another audience factor worth considering is any perceived politics that might affect the way the problem-solvers express their thinking. Care should be taken therefore to assure the problem-solvers of confidentiality and to get them to imagine the researcher as a trusted individual who will not use data against them in any way. Furthermore the researcher and the problems should be presented in such a way as to encourage the problem-solvers to fully express their thinking. A way to accomplish this in the design of problems would be to present the problems as being those of an absent third party about whom the solver is concerned.

As there are expected differences in how well calibrated the different types of problem solvers are, at least some of the problems used need to have objectively testable outcomes. While this is problematic given what has been said above the about the nature of the business economics domain there should opportunities in quantitative guesses concerning price differences or changes.

The above concerns also suggest that the kind of data needed is extensive verbal and perhaps paper-based – for example to capture any diagrammatic problem-solving approaches used – data. Given the need to assess the quality and heterogeneity of the data all analysis would initially have to be qualitative, although subsequently much of it might be summarized quantitatively. Voss et al.'s (1989) method seems an appropriate method of analysis for such data.

7. CONCLUSIONS

This paper has drawn on the expertise and reasoning literature most especially the work of Voss et al. (1983, 1989) and of Lehman, Lempert, and Nisbett (1988) and on writings about the nature of economics discipline in general and on its role in management in particular (e.g., O'Rourke, 1998). Though theoretical in nature this work is more empirically orientated than much of economics literature examining the role of the discipline. Unlike much of the previous expertise and reasoning research this paper has focussed on a particular discipline expertise within social science and further confined itself to a particular expertise within management learning – business economics. A number of expected differences in the performance of experts, novices and naïve in the discipline have put forward and the implications of these arguments for empirical have been sketched.

REFERENCES

Bacdayan, P. (1996). Characterizing expert leaders of quality improvement task forces: towards applying research on expertise to training design. Conference paper presented at *3rd Annual International Conference of Educational Innovation in Economics and Business Education*. December 4-7, Orlando, Florida.

Boshuizen, H.P.A. (1995). Teaching expertise. In W.H. Gijselaers, D.T. Tempelaar, P.K. Keizer, J.M. Blommaert, E.M. Bernard, & H. Kasper (Eds.), *Educational Innovation in Economics and Business Administration: The Case of Problem-Based Learning* (pp. 99-105). Dordrecht: Kluwer.

Chase, W.G., & Simon, H.A. (1973). The mind's eye in chess. In W.G. Chase (Ed.), *Visual Information Processing*, (pp. 215-281). New York: Academic Press.

Chi, M.T.H., Feltovich, P., & Glaser, R. (1981). Categorization and representation of physics problems by experts and novices. *Cognitive Science*, 5, 121-152.

De Groot, A. (1978). *Thought and choice in chess*. The Hague: Mouton.

Ericsson, K.A. (1996). The acquisition of expert performance: An introduction to some of the issues. In K.A. Ericsson (Ed.), *The Road to Excellence: The Acquisition of Expert Performance in the Arts and Sciences, Sports and Games* (pp. 1-50). New Jersey: Lawrence Erlbaum Associates.

Ericsson, K.A., & J. Smith (1991). Prospects and limits of the empirical study of expertise: an introduction. In K.A. Ericsson, & J. Smith (Eds.), *Towards a General Theory of Expertise - Prospects and Limits* (pp. 1-38). Cambridge: Cambridge University Press.

Frederick, D.M. (1991). Auditors' representation of internal control knowledge. *The Accounting Review*, 66 (2), 240-258.

Griffin, D., & Tversky, A. (1992). The weighing of evidence and the determinants of confidence. *Cognitive Psychology*, 24, 411-435.

Gijselaers, W.H. (1995). Cognitive science perspectives on learning and instruction. In W.H. Gijselaers, D.T. Tempelaar, P.K. Keizer, J.M. Blommaert, E.M. Bernard, & H. Kasper (Eds.), *Educational Innovation in Economics and Business Administration: The Case of Problem-Based Learning* (p.62). Dordrecht: Kluwer Academic Publishers.

Kay, J. (1996). *The business of economics*. Oxford: Oxford University Press.

Lehman, D.R., Lempert, R.O., & Nisbett, R.E. (1988). The effects of graduate training on reasoning – Formal thinking about everyday-life events. *American Psychologist*, 43, 6, 431-442.

McCloskey, D.N. (1990). *If you're so smart – The narrative of economic expertise*. Chicago: The University of Chicago Press.

O'Rourke, B.K. (1998). Roles of economics in business and management education. In R.G. Milter, J.E. Stinson, & W.H. Gijselaers (Eds.), *Educational Innovation in Economics and*

Business III – Innovative Practices in Business Education (pp.51-63). Dordrecht: Kluwer Academic Publishers.

Smith, V.L. (1996). Puzzle solving: reciprocity, reasoning and behavior. In S.G. Medema, & W.J. Samuels (Eds.), *Foundations of Research in Economics – How Do Economists Do Economics* (pp.216-226). Cheltenham: Edward Elgar.

Vaatstra, R.F., Boshuizen, H.P.A., & H.G. Schmidt (1995). Differences in the Organization and Application of Knowledge Between Novice, Intermediate and Experienced Auditors. In W.H. Gijselaers, D.T. Tempelaar, P.K. Keizer, J.M. Blommaert, E.M. Bernard, & H. Kasper (Eds.), *Educational Innovation in Economics and Business Administration: The Case of Problem-Based Learning* (p.63-68). Dordrecht: Kluwer Academic Publishers.

Vernooij, F. (1995). Problem solving strategies. In W.H. Gijselaers, D.T. Tempelaar, P.K. Keizer, J.M. Blommaert, E.M. Bernard, & H. Kasper (Eds.), *Educational Innovation in Economics and Business Administration: The Case of Problem-Based Learning* (p.69-77). Dordrecht: Kluwer.

Voss, J.F. (1996). Reasoning. In De Corte, E. (Ed.), *The International Encyclopedia of Developmental and Instructional Research Psychology* (pp. 464-467). London: Pergamon.

Voss, J.F., Blais J., Means, M.L., Greene, T.R., & Ahwesh, E. (1989). Informal reasoning and subject matter knowledge in the solving of economics problems by naïve and novice individuals. In L.B. Resnick (Ed.), *Knowing, Learning and Instruction* (p.217-251). New Jersey: Lawrence Erlbaum.

Voss, J.F., Greene, T.R., Post, & Penner, B.C. (1983). Problem solving skills in the social sciences. *The Psychology of Learning and Motivation, 17*, 165-213.

Whitley, R. (1989). On the nature of managerial tasks and skills: Their distinguishing characteristics and organization. *Journal of Management Studies, 26*, 209-224.

Zeitz, C.M., & R. Glaser (1994). Expert level of understanding. In T. Husén, & T.N. Postlethwaite (Eds.), *The International Encyclopaedia of Education* (2nd Edition) (pp. 2194-2199), Volume 8. London: Pergamon.

Tracking Down the Knowledge Structure of Students

Fons Vernooij
University of Amsterdam, ILO, Amsterdam, The Netherlands

1. INTRODUCTION

In this chapter the term "discipline" refers to accounting and economics, which each consist of subdisciplines. In these subdisciplines many terms are used that are either synonyms (different terms relating to the same concept) or homonyms (the same term is used for different concepts). This results in specific jargon for each subdiscipline. In this sense, each subdiscipline can be considered to have a dialect of its own.

A surprising number of basic terms are homonyms. They seem to be simple words, while in fact they are not. Take, for instance, the term "profit." At least two definitions are in common use. In newspapers the *accounting concept of profit* is used in reporting a company's performance, whereas students at school are taught about the *economic concept of profit* as the ultimate way of defining profit.

In the accounting concept of profit the payment of dividends to stockholders, as a payment for the capital used by the company, is not part of the company's costs. A company that does not make any profit at all is for that reason unattractive to stockholders. In the economic concept of profit, however, cost is defined on the basis of opportunity costing. From that perspective cost covers a reasonable financial compensation for all factors of production. Using the economic concept of profit, stockholders may be well-pleased if their company does not make any profit at all for many years, at least if there is no loss either.

Still, many students and even some teachers are not aware of the difference between these two concepts of profit, which result from different definitions of the term "cost." They therefore don't understand how companies can survive in the long run in situations of full competition without making any profit at all.

To switch from the accounting concept of profit to the economic concept of profit is like crossing a boundary between two domains. In the accounting domain the description on the basis of historic cost prevails, whereas in the economics domain the assumed description of optimal situations prevails. These different ways of reasoning in accounting and economics each have their own logic and they lead to many homonyms in the terminology, of which cost and profit are only two examples. Dictionaries are full of homonyms, because many words have different meanings in different situations, but in scientific works, each term is supposed to have just one meaning.

Once students cross the boundary from the accounting domain into the economics domain by learning about opportunity costing, it is difficult for them to return to the accounting domain when they are reading the daily newspaper. They run the risk of applying concepts from the economics domain in the understanding of the accounting domain, which easily leads to a misunderstanding of the situation. Students then build a wrong mental model (Norman, 1983) of the situation they are trying to understand.

As Layton (1991) points out, well-developed scientific concepts allow for cognitive actions (e.g. calculations). But if cognitive actions can take place in different subdisciplines, each having its own dialect, it is essential to be familiar with the dialects. To become expert, students must develop the ability to switch between dialects.

The language problem is mentioned by O'Rourke (1998) as well. He claims that economics is one of the most abstract and impractical of the business disciplines, yet proponents argue that it provides a crucial way of approaching business problems. Theoretical discourse has clarified some differences in use of terms between the various (sub)disciplines, but empirical research still needs to be done. How do students actually deal with new definitions of well-known terms? Do they consider it as switching between different definitions of the same word, as is normally the case with homonyms? Or do they consider it as switching between classification systems?

Research must focus on the way students deal with homonyms. As Chi (1992) points out, a *conceptual change* is required for a student to deal correctly with two different notions behind the same term. A homonym covers two different concepts and the student must shift between these two concepts. To know, for instance, that a whale is not a fish but a mammal is not just a matter of redefining the term whale. It requires the understanding that a whole new system of definitions is needed to classify whales.

Vosniadou (1994) points out the misunderstandings that arise when students assimilate new terms without revising old ways of thinking. To add, for instance, the term profit to the customer concept of cost (as the price one pays for a product), some clarification is required about the way of defining both terms. Therefore, the phenomenon of conceptual change must be studied by teachers in order to understand the mistakes students make in solving problems.

The present article tries to gain insight into the mechanisms that cause students to misunderstand the knowledge offered to them. I reflect upon the way experts handle their terms, and I suggest a new way of teaching where explicit interest is shown in how students build a knowledge structure.

The article starts with an investigation into the nature of misunderstandings. The approach is based upon cognitive psychology and can be of help in developing curricula by shifting attention away from the two usual perspectives in education, namely economic practice and economic theory, towards a third perspective: the knowledge structure students build in their minds.

To complete the article, a simple true-false test is presented which was used to investigate the ability of students to deal with economic terms like cost, payment, and expenditures. With this type of testing, not only can the knowledge structure of students be tracked down, but the test results can be put to use by discussing them afterwards with the students.

2. MISCONCEPTIONS

Many frequently used terms turn out to be homonyms. The same term has different meanings in different situations which are rooted in different subdisciplines of economics and accounting. If the relationship between a term and a subdiscipline is not sufficiently clear in a specific situation, homonyms can cause or reinforce misconceptions, leading to problems in students' understanding of economic processes or accounting procedures.

A misconception is a mini-theory which a person has in mind, but which is scientifically not true. A mini-theory contains a conclusion and an argument to support the conclusion. It can show up long after education should have molded the mini-theory in a different shape. Marton (1988) calls the study of misconceptions "phenomenography." Examples of mini-theories are that the sun shows up in the daytime and the moon shows up at night, because in the daytime light comes from the sun and at night light comes from the moon and the stars. Or, that force is required to keep an object moving at the same speed, because you always have to push a trolley through a supermarket if you want to keep the trolley moving. Or, that cost is what you pay for an object, because the shop assistant names the selling price when a customer asks what a certain product costs.

In physics a lot of research has been done on misconceptions (Gilbert & Watts, 1983). Misconceptions are formally defined as: "The occurrence of utterances (about a class of physics situations) that are (a) deviant from current scientific theories, (b) consistent within groups of age, culture, etc., and (c) stable and hard to modify through education" (Taconis, 1995). Misconceptions can occur even before schooling starts (Marton, 1988) but they can also result from formal education as natural by-products of the process of knowledge acquisition (Driver, Guesne & Tiberghien, 1985). Examples are that the sea level rises when a floating iceberg melts, or that a current of electricity is comparable to a current of water.

In economics little research has been done on misconceptions. Yet there is every reason to do such research, as economics is much more a matter of context-bound cognition than is generally realized. Experts are usually able to decide upon a complex problem very rapidly because of their knowledge structure. Their thinking is triggered by small signals, and in specific situations experts deduce the meaning of the terms from the perspective of the situation involved (Chi, Slotta & De Leeuw, 1994). They have developed an understanding of different meanings related to different (sub)disciplines and they switch between them nearly unconsciously. This skill should be taught in the classroom.

The major issue is to acquire the skill of switching from one context-bound definition to another: *the ability to switch*. How to switch from the accounting concept of profit to the economic concept of profit? And how to switch back? Especially the step backwards is important, because once the switch is made from one concept to another, the student must be able to switch back and accept two different concepts for the same term, each from its own perspective. If he is not able to switch back, misconceptions distort the comprehension of new problems. In terms of cognitive psychology, the student builds in his mind a wrong initial representation of the situation involved (Anderson, 1985).

2.1 Some More Causes For Misconceptions

Besides the use of homonyms, it was found in a study on solving problems in accounting that misconceptions can result as a by-product of education as well (Vernooij, 1995a, 1996). Students who followed a course in accounting and had finished a chapter on bookkeeping were asked to study a chapter on cost accounting. They had to solve problems about computing the cost price of products and the profit an entrepreneur could make with those products (Vernooij, 1995b). Some terms like cost of sales, gross profit and net profit, which students were familiar with from the perspective of bookkeeping, were used again in the chapter on cost accounting. But now they had a slightly different meaning. To track down the knowledge structure these students had developed, some of them were asked to solve some problems thinking aloud. These sessions were taped and transcribed. The transcriptions made clear where misconceptions arose when tackling the problems presented.

One cause of misconceptions was students' assumption that authors always use a term in the way they have defined it. In the book under investigation, the author stresses in the chapter on bookkeeping that students should remember that gross profit equals sales in a period minus the cost of goods sold excluding the purchasing costs. However, the author, as a real expert in his subject, changes in the chapter on cost accounting to another meaning of gross profit, without making this switch clear to the readers. "As we have seen before", he states, "the margin for gross profit of a certain product consists of a percentage of the cost of goods sold including the purchasing costs." The two concepts of gross profit differed, however, in three respects: per period versus per product, real versus normative, and excluding versus including purchasing costs.

Another cause of misconceptions was the lack of ability to understand conceptual change. Some students stuck to the meaning of a term once it had been proven correct in an exam. In the "think aloud" sessions one student said explicitly: "I stick to the meaning we learned before, because that was approved in my bookkeeping test."

A third cause was found in the opposite behavior: some students were not able to switch back to the old knowledge structure once they had learned a new meaning of a homonym. They replaced the old meaning by the new one, instead of accepting two different knowledge structures at the same time. Such students rewrote the past by projecting newly learned meanings onto older terms. "At first we defined the term that way, but then we learned this new meaning, so from now on I use the term in this sense." In fact, these students refuse to accept the existence of homonyms.

Still, the most interesting cause of misconceptions found was the desire to create consistency where it did not exist. Some students recognized the different meanings in different situations and tried to solve the riddle by creating their own definitions. As a matter of fact, they created a knowledge structure based on *a dialect of their own*. They incorporated elements from different subdisciplines and created something new in their minds. They created their own definitions and assumed they did really understand what was meant by the author of the book.

2.2 Cognitive Economy

Some students are really brilliant in creating a world of their own. They create a whole system of interrelated misconceptions to fit different (sub)disciplines at the same time. Or at least they think it fits different (sub)disciplines, whereas in reality it causes them problems wherever they go. As the result of the instruction process, they acquire only part of the knowledge structure the teacher intends. At the same time, they acquire a knowledge structure the teacher does not know about or even imagine.

For instance, once a student reduces the concept of gross profit in a period (measured in $ per month) and gross profit margin per product (measured in $ per product) to "gross profit" (measured in $), a new concept is born. The student does not distinguish anymore between two different concrete concepts but reduces his cognitive load to remembering just one concept that is more abstract. He assumes he will be able to work this one concept out into a particular form as soon as the situation requires him to do so.

In fact students try to reduce complicated knowledge structures to simple models in order to store the knowledge in their long-term memory. Rosch (1978) calls this "cognitive economy": the art of restructuring knowledge in a way that reduces the cognitive load required to remember the body of knowledge.

This process of concept building has been found in many students. It is supported by economists' habit of neglecting to make proper mention of the units in which terms are defined (Vernooij, 1993). Students behave the same way as is done in the Dutch encyclopaedia of business economics. The encyclopaedia defines two different concepts of cost. One is cost as a flow variable measured in (Dutch) guilders per period. The second is cost as a stock variable measured in guilders per product. But the encyclopaedia goes on to say that what these terms have in common is that they are both expressed in guilders, which implies that the general definition of cost is a variable expressed in guilders.

2.3 Different Concepts Behind the Term Cost

One fundamental term in economics is cost. People who have not studied economics or accounting think of cost as the selling price. As customers they often ask for the price of a product by saying "How much does it cost?"

Their perspective is the customer's view and they have the customer's notion of the word cost in mind. In fact, the word cost in this situation has two different meanings: price and expenditures. The unit in which cost is measured in the customer's view is the local currency.

In the customer's view, the words cost, price and expenditures are considered to be synonyms for the same concept. If somebody considers a word to be a synonym of another word, it means that he thinks this word could be substituted for the other word without changing the meaning of the sentence.

When students are introduced to accounting, they usually start with financial accounting. There they are confronted with the term profit, which is defined as the difference between revenues and cost. And as profit is a flow variable, which should be expressed in $ (or any other currency) per period, cost must be understood in the same way. Students are taught that cost reduces profit, and they understand that less cost leads to more profit. They also start to understand that not all expenditures are costs, as only the costs related to the products sold in a certain period can be subtracted from the revenues of the same period.

The development of this new meaning of cost requires a conceptual change (or shift) from cost as "expenditures" (measured in a currency) towards cost as "expenses" (measured in a currency per period). Because of this transformation cost is a quantity that has a negative influence on profit. Especially trading companies use this concept of cost.

A second round of conceptual change occurs as soon as a shift to management accounting is made. Then, the notion is introduced that cost is a valuable asset in the theory of costing. In management accounting, cost is a constituent part of the value of a product. As such, cost is measured in $ (or any other currency) per product. Product cost per unit is not the sum of expenses, but the sum of value added in the production process (Horngren & Foster, 1991). The more cost is required, the higher the price will be. That is to say, the industrial notion of cost implies that not the real cost is part of the production cost but the standard cost, that is the cost required under rational behavior.

Three broad domains of thought have been mentioned up till now: ordinary life, financial accounting and management accounting. Microeconomics can be added as another domain with its own notion of cost. Because of assumptions like *perfect foresight* and *opportunity costing*, a third round of conceptual change would be necessary if the microeconomic meaning of cost was introduced. In microeconomics the difference between real cost and standard cost has disappeared, because an entrepreneur has in advance all the information required to know what the results will be. Cost is reduced to standard cost and consists of the financial compensation for all factors of production, including the capital that stockholders have put into the company.

Experts are able to distinguish between the four different meanings of cost, because they have developed four different concepts behind the term cost. They recognize the nature of the situation at hand, which makes it possible for them to decide upon the proper meaning of the homonym cost at that moment. But they recall as well problem schemata and procedures relevant to the situation involved. In cognitive psychology this phenomenon is called using scripts (or scenarios) (Schank & Abelson, 1977; Anderson, 1985).

The expertness of economists is based upon their ability to switch from one meaning of an economic term to another on the basis of characteristics of the situation. As soon as they notice a switch in situation they automatically switch to a different concept, mostly without being aware of that switch. This expert knowledge should be the central focus of instruction.

2.4 Becoming Expert

In summary, because economics and accounting are based upon a number of subdisciplines each using their own dialect, students must not only learn to handle synonyms (different terms for the same concept) and homonyms (the same term for different concepts) but must also learn different ways of classifying terms. To become expert, students must develop the ability to switch from one meaning of a term to another meaning by identifying the situation in which the term is used.

Besides, students develop mechanisms to store the knowledge in their long-term memory. They assume authors always use terms in the way they define them and they assume consistency even when it does not exist. Instead of accepting different meanings for the same term, students tend to choose between three ways of handling homonyms. They stick to old knowledge that was approved in a test, or they rewrite their old knowledge and stick to the new definition, or they create a world of their own, sometimes far beyond the expectations of the instructor.

A lot more research in economics and accounting is needed to describe the full implications of conceptual change. Such research is necessary to find out more about the way students build their personal knowledge structure. In the second part of this article a simple instrument is presented to investigate the knowledge structure students have already developed. But the test is not only useful for students. Teachers as well have done the test, leading to fierce discussions on the real meaning of fundamental terms like cost, expenditures, expenses and payments in the situations presented in the test.

3. TRACKING DOWN THE KNOWLEDGE STRUCTURE

One way of measuring the ability to switch between different meanings of homonyms is the true-false test (Bacdayan, 1998). One such test is presented in the appendix. This test was developed for tracking the knowledge structure of undergraduate students in accounting. Later on, it turned out to be of value as well for graduate students and even teachers. The test consists of six situations. Each situation is accompanied by six statements with the choice between 'correct' and 'incorrect'. Students are asked to make a choice for each of the six statements. In figure 1 one of the test items is presented.

First task: Choose "correct" or "incorrect" for each of the six statements about the following situation

A factory making wooden doors employs two men for $ 900 per month each. They are paid on the 25th of each month. At the end of the month this cost is entered on the income statement.

1. In this situation cost is synonymous with "payment."
   O correct
   O incorrect
2. In this situation cost has the meaning of "expenses."
   O correct
   O incorrect
3. In this situation cost has the same meaning as "asset."
   O correct
   O incorrect
4. In this situation cost is synonymous with "expenditures."
   O correct
   O incorrect
5. In this situation cost has the same meaning as "added value."
   O correct
   O incorrect
6. In this situation cost is synonymous with "reduction of profit."
   O correct
   O incorrect

Figure 1: A test of conceptual knowledge

Two of the six statements refer to cost as expenditures (measured in $ or any other currency as the unit), two refer to cost as expenses (both measured by the unit $ per period) and two refer to cost as assets (measured by the unit $ per product). In the situation presented in figure 1 there is a check whether students have gone through the conceptual change between everyday language (cost as expenditures) to financial accounting (cost as expenses).

Then there is a second situation as presented in figure 2. In this second situation there is a check on the change from financial accounting (cost as expenses) to management accounting (cost as assets). In a third situation the conceptual change to microeconomics could be measured.

Second task: Choose "correct" or "incorrect" for each of the six statements about the following situation.

A factory making wooden doors employs two men for $ 900 per month each. They are paid on the 25th of each month. In order to compute the right selling price per unit, the cost for labor is considered to be part of the product cost per unit.

1. In this situation cost is synonymous with "payment."
    O correct
    O incorrect
2. In this situation cost has the meaning of "expenses."
    O correct
    O incorrect
3. In this situation cost has the same meaning as "asset."
    O correct
    O incorrect
4. In this situation cost is synonymous with "expenditures."
    O correct
    O incorrect
5. In this situation cost has the same meaning as "added value."
    O correct
    O incorrect
6. In this situation cost is synonymous with "reduction of profit."
    O correct
    O incorrect

Figure 2. Testing a different meaning of cost

These tests are not only useful in giving the teacher an impression of the knowledge structure students have developed up to the moment of testing, they are valuable as well in setting off a discussion between students. To invite students to discuss their concepts, this test on conceptual knowledge can be used in different ways.

The easiest way to do this in class is to give all students a sheet with one situation and six statements and ask them to fill in the form. Then the results are counted in public. Usually students will have different choices on the same statements, and they must be able to justify their choice. Then a discussion can start.

A bit more complicated is an approach where two forms are distributed one after another with two different situations in which cost has two different meanings. Then the results are counted in public on these two

Knowledge Structure of Students

situations. The answers to all 12 statements can be summarized in a matrix as in figure 3.

	Situation 1		Situation 2	
	correct	incorrect	correct	incorrect
statement 1				
statement 2				
statement 3				
statement 4				
statement 5				
statement 6				

Figure 3. Matrix for assembling the results of a test of conceptual

First, the number of students must be counted who think statement 1 is correct. Then the number of students must be counted who disagree in order to be sure everybody has made a choice. Once the matrix is full, all choices are clear to everybody.

As soon as everybody has made a choice, students can be asked to justify their choice. This way the test becomes an important instrument for starting a discussion on the nature of the term "cost."

Some items usually have the remarkable result that half the population agrees and the other half disagrees. As a matter of fact, even among teachers in economics and accounting such evenly divided results have been found. In a workshop at the 5th Edineb Conference the two situations were presented. In the first situation only statements 2 and 6 are correct; in the second situation statements 3 and 5 are correct (see figure 4).

	Situation 1		Situation 2	
	correct	incorrect	correct	incorrect
statement 1	4	2	2	4
statement 2	*4*	2	2	*4*
statement 3	0	6	*2*	4
statement 4	4	2	3	3
statement 5	3	3	*6*	0
statement 6	*2*	4	0	*6*

The right answers are the italicized numbers in each row.

Figure 4. Results of the test of conceptual knowledge as given in a workshop at the 5th EDINEB conference in Cleveland, Ohio

The italicized numbers are the right answers. In situations 1 and 2 a lot of disagreement existed between the participants, resulting in fierce discussions. As a matter of fact the participants lined up in constantly changing groups, disputing each other's choices. Agreement only grew after the units were introduced as criteria for identifying the true meaning of cost in the two given situations.

3.1 Scientific Relevance of the Test

To use a test consisting of true-false items, one must determine that the test is valid and reliable. A test is valid if it measures what it is intended to measure. This can be found out by determining whether all items contribute positively to the final result. A test is reliable if the results cannot be a coincidence. If the same test is done twice, the results should be roughly the same.

To check the validity and the reliability of the test, it was carried out twice in a program in which 100 students participated (Vernooij, 1993). Then it was checked in different ways. The technical results of these checks are mentioned in the appendix.

4. CONCLUSIONS

Conceptual change is closely related to the existence of different subdisciplines in economics and accounting. Each subdiscipline has its own dialect. If students work within a certain subdiscipline they can try to acquire the traditions and reasoning habits of that subdiscipline. Even then, conceptual change may be required if the discussion switches from one type of company (like industrial companies with mass production) to another type of company (like industrial companies with job-order production).

If problem-based learning (or any other kind of project-oriented approach) is introduced, then conceptual change must be part of the curriculum. Students must be introduced not only to the dialects of different subdisciplines but also to the art of switching between dialects. They must be able to absorb ideas from different books, periodicals and newspapers without building misconceptions. The process of assimilating and revising knowledge in order to build a fruitful knowledge structure must be made a conscious part of the educational process.

In collecting information on their own, students bring concepts from different domains together and have to cope with the different meanings of many homonyms. Somehow they must fit all the different meanings of homonyms and synonyms together. Each student develops his or her own knowledge structure while looking for answers to the problem under investigation. Instruments to identify misconceptions can be very valuable in steering that process. In this article one such instrument was presented, but more instruments could be developed. Any teacher can make up more situations, related to the problems students are confronted with.

The real value of this kind of testing, however, is not so much the result itself, as the discussion it sparks between students. The test offered is a simple true-false test to get a discussion going. It offers both the students and the teacher the opportunity to find out whether all members of the group have the same understanding of basic concepts.

APPENDIX: THE SCIENTIFIC RELEVANCE OF THE TEST OF CONCEPTUAL KNOWLEDGE

To check the validity and reliability of the test on understanding the term cost, the test was carried out twice with the same students. Some 100 students from three different schools who had just finished the same chapter in the same textbook participated in the test. They were offered six situations each accompanied by the same six statements. The second round of the test was a week after the first one. Each of the six situations was considered to be one test-item to which a score could be assigned. Every correct answer to a statement gave one point and so the maximum score per situation was 6 points.

The validity of the test was checked by the item-rest correlation and the consistency test. The item-rest correlation can have a value between -1.00 and +1.00. The results for the test-items varied between +0.32 and +0.61. So none of the items had to be discarded.

The second check on validity is the relationship between a high score on one item and a high score on other items (Cronbach's alpha). This statistical quantity can vary between 0.00 and 1.00. A value of more than 0.60 is acceptable for the statistical judgement that the test is valid. The alpha was 0.68 in the first round of the test and 0.75 in the second, so the test can be considered statistically valid.

The reliability can be measured by comparing the results of the two tests. To find out whether the students who scored high on the first test did as well on the second test, the correlation between the two tests was computed. This statistical quantity (the PMC) can vary between -1.00 and +1.00. A correlation of +0.64 was found, which is an acceptable value.

The conclusion is that this test of six items each containing six statements can be considered valid for tracking the knowledge structure of students as far as the measured terms are concerned.

REFERENCES

Anderson, J.R. (1985). *Cognitive psychology and its implications.* New York: W.H. Freeman & Company.

Bacdayan, P. (1998). *Because problems are only the beginning: Practical techniques for measuring and tracking students' knowledge structures.* Paper presentation at the fifth EDINEB conference, Cleveland, Ohio.

Chi, M.T.H. (1992). Conceptual change within and across ontological categories: examples from learning and discovery in science. In R. Giere (Ed.), *Cognitive models in science: Minnesota studies in philosophy of science.* University of Minnesota Press.

Chi, M.T.H., Slotta, J.D., & De Leeuw, N. (1994). From things to processes: a theory of conceptual change for learning science concepts. *Learning and Instruction, Vol. 4, 1*: 27-43.

Driver, R., Guesne, E., & Tiberghien A. (1985). In R. Driver, E. Guesne, & A. Tiberghien (Eds.), *Children's ideas in science*. Milton Keynes, UK: Open University Press.

Gilbert, & Watts. (1983). Concepts, misconceptions and alternative conceptions: changing perspectives in science education. *Science Education, 10*, 61-98.

Horngren, C.T., & Foster, G. (1991). *Cost accounting*. New Jersey: Prentice-Hall.

Layton, D. (1991). Science education and praxis: The relation of school science to practical action. *Studies in science education, 19*, 43-79.

Marton, F. (1988). *Phenomenography and the art of teaching all things to all men*. Göteborgs universitet: Fenomenografiska notiser 8.

Norman, D.A. (1983). Some observations on mental models. In D. Gentner, & A.L. Stevens (Eds.), *Mental Models*. Hillsdale, NJ.: Lawrence Erlbaum Associates.

O'Rourke, B.K. (1998). *Designing problems to differentiate the problem solving approaches of experts, novice and naive business economists*. Paper presentation at the fifth EDINEB conference, Cleveland, Ohio.

Rosch, E. (1978). Principles of categorization. In E. Rosch, & B.B. Lloyd (Eds.), *Cognition and Categorization*. Hillsdale: Lawrence Erlbaum Ass.

Schank, R.C., & Abelson, R. (1977). *Scripts, plans, goals and understanding*. Hillsdale, NJ: Lawrence Erlbaum Association.

Taconis, R. (1995). *Understanding based problem solving. towards qualification-oriented teaching and learning in physics education*. Eindhoven: Ph.D.thesis.

Vernooij, A.T.J. (1993). *Het leren oplossen van bedrijfseconomische problemen. Didactisch onderzoek naar kostprijs- en nettowinstvraagstukken in het voortgezet onderwijs*. Rotterdam: dissertatie (Ph.D.thesis written in Dutch).

Vernooij, A.T.J. (1995a). Problem solving in management accounting, *Economia, The Journal of the Association of European Economics Education* 5, Part 1, Summer 1995.

Vernooij, A.T.J. (1995b). Problem solving strategies. In W.H. Gijselaers et al. (Eds.), *Educational Innovation in Economics and Business Administration: The Case of Problem-Based Learning* (69-77). Dordrecht: Kluwer Academic Publishers.

Vernooij, A.T.J. (1996). Der Einfluss unterschiedlicher fachlicher Strukturen auf die Entwicklung mentaler Repräsentationen. In P. Preiss & T. Tramm (Eds), *Rechnungswesenunterricht und ökonomisches Denken. Didactische Innovationen für die kaufmännische Ausbildung* (139-157). Wiesbaden: Gabler GmbH.

Vosniadou S. 1994. Capturing and modelling the process of conceptual change. *Learning and Instruction 4* (1), 45-69.

Index

AACSB, 150, 327, 328, 346, 348, 349, 350, 353, 355, 356, 358, 360, 384, 394, 395
AAHE, 150, 164
Abelson, R., 444, 450
academic skills, 7
accounting, 72, 73, 76, 77, 78, 79, 81, 83, 235, 243, 244, 247, 248, 250, 251, 273, 353, 434
action-learning, 111, 114, 126, 127, 333
Adams, J., 194, 207
Adler, P.S., 58, 67, 324, 342
Adnett, N., 45, 53
Ahmed, Z.U., 330, 342, 343
Ahwesh, E., 423, 435
Akhter, S.H., 330, 342
Alavi, M., 258, 272
Albrecht, K., 277, 288
Alexander, C., 148
Alexander, S., 74, 84, 139, 141, 142, 143, 147
Algera, J.A., 92, 108
analytic ability, 7
Anderson, J.R., 440, 444, 449
Argyris, C., 81, 284, 288
Aristotle, 75, 84
Armstrong, M., 34, 53
Arnett, K., 398
Arnold, D.R., 398
Arpan, J.S., 329, 342
Arrow, K., 45, 53, 229

Arthur Andersen, 232, 247, 250
Arthur Young, 250
assessment center, 370, 384
assessment method, 369, 370, 371, 380
Atkinson, G.B., 44, 54
Baalen, P.J. van, 282, 288
Bacdayan, P., 422, 434, 445, 449
Ballantyne, I., 400, 415
Bandura, A., 385, 397
Baron, H., 34, 54
Barr, R.B., 149, 164
Barr, S., 389, 397
Barrows, H.S., 215, 219
Bartlett, C.A., 323, 342
Bartz, D.E., 386, 397
Baruch, J.J., 68
Bass, B.M., 29, 164, 186, 208, 250, 288, 307, 314, 318, 343
Bastiaans, N., 169, 186
Bastianutti, 164
Beard, D., 415
Becker, G.S., 104, 106, 108
Beemer, C.F.H., 382
Benbasat, I., 154, 164
Bennis, W., 307, 318
Bentson, C., 397
Benzing, C., 222, 229
Berkely, R.A., 14
Bernard, E.M., 186, 288, 434, 435
Bidell, T.R., 233, 235, 250
Bie, D., 381

Black, J.S., 148, 317, 324, 326, 342
Blanchard, O.J., 229
Blaug, M., 45, 54
Blinder, A.S., 229
Blom, S., 381
Blommaert, J.M., 186, 288, 434, 435
Bloom, B., 76, 84, 314, 318
Borgers, T., 58, 67
Boshuizen, H.P., 422, 425, 434, 435
Bossert, P.J., 129, 145
Botkin, J.W., 281, 288
Boud, D., 188, 207
Bourner, T., 29, 300, 304, 305
Bowditch, J.L., 309, 318
Bowen, D.E., 277, 278, 289
Bower, R., 5, 14
Boyatzis, R., 54, 77, 84, 185, 186, 276, 288, 347, 362, 401, 405, 415
Boydell, T., 54
Brassington, F., 187, 188, 190, 191, 197, 203, 207
Brenda, M., 145
Brennan, J., 5, 14
Briggs, R.O., 160, 164, 165
British Gas, 34, 35, 37, 38, 39, 40, 41, 42, 43, 44, 46, 48, 49, 52, 54
Britt, J., 147
Bromber, H., 141, 145
Brooks, J.M., 139, 140, 145
Brown, A., 389, 397
Brown, C., 39, 54, 293
Brown, K.C., 127
Brown, R., 295, 305
Brown, S., 306
Brown, S.W., 288
Bruce, M., 208
Bruijns, V., 365, 403, 415
Bruner, J.S., 314, 318
Brussel, G.J., 371, 381
Buono, A.F., 318
Burgoyne, J., 54
business administration, 87, 94, 100, 101, 108, 186, 281
business education, 7, 171, 188, 208, 250, 275, 276, 291, 292, 295, 297, 299, 301, 303, 304, 327, 329, 332, 334, 339, 341, 342, 362, 383, 386, 389, 419, 423, 424
business practice, 58, 72, 73, 78, 82, 83

business programs, 71, 73, 304, 348
business school curriculum, 149, 150, 276, 281, 287, 328, 346, 413
business training, 72
Byham, W.C., 416
Calabrese, R.L., 386, 397
Cameron, K.S., 385, 398
Capper, J., 257, 272
Carter, S., 401, 403, 416
Carvalho, G., 208
Carvin, A., 142, 145
Cascio, W.F., 386, 397, 409, 415
Castells, M., 129, 136, 145
CBI, 33, 35, 37, 54
cerebral skills, 4
Chaffee, S.H., 129, 145
Chaharbaghi, K., 188, 190, 208
Chase, W.G., 420, 434
Cheit, E.F., 275, 276, 288
Chepesiuk, R., 145
Chi, M.T., 53, 434, 438, 440, 449
Chia, R.F., 280, 288
Chickering, A.W., 150, 164
Childers, Jr., E., 221
Christ, P., 229
Church, G.J., 389, 397
Ciglaric, M., 267, 269, 272
Clark, B.R., 283, 288
Cochran, D.S., 398
Cochrane, P., 140, 146
cognitive complexity, 231, 233, 242, 245
Cohen, A.J., 221, 223, 229
Cohen, P.A., 384, 397
Cole, R.E., 58, 67
collaborative learning, 139, 141, 152, 323, 330, 332, 334, 339, 342
collaborative student environment, 150, 153, 157
Colling, T., 39, 54
Committee for the Advancement of University Teaching, 302, 305
communication skills, 7, 8, 11, 12, 22, 100, 150, 157, 161, 211, 222, 225, 226, 275, 292, 325, 326, 328, 335, 366, 380, 383, 384, 389, 390, 411
company training, 100, 107
competencies, 4, 6, 19, 31, 34, 35, 41, 44, 47, 59, 72, 74, 76, 77, 81, 82, 151, 171, 281, 292, 305, 321, 322, 324,

325, 327, 328, 332, 335, 388, 389, 405, 409, 413
competitive advantage, 17, 22, 28, 60, 281, 324
comprehension, 76, 113, 235, 297, 301, 305, 427, 440
conceptual change, 438, 439, 441, 443, 444, 445, 446, 448, 449, 450
Conger, J., 22, 29
Conley, M., 139, 148
Connolly, D., 143, 145
construct validity, 409
content validity, 409
Coombs, G., 362
Cooper, 164
Cooper, J., 201, 208, 305
Cooper, R., 208
cooperative education, 365, 366
Coopers & Lybrand, 250
Corbitt, G., 149, 159, 164
Cornwell, B.T., 343
corporate university, 21
Cotter, M., 222, 229
Couger, J.D., 149, 164
Coulton, G.F., 386, 397
Cowen, S.C., 185, 186, 288, 362
Cox, R., 208, 306
Craig, C.J., 14
Craig, I., 146, 148
Creahan, T.A., 255
critical thinking skills, 221, 231, 233, 235, 236, 238, 240, 241, 242, 243, 246, 391
cross-cultural training, 323, 331
cross-functional teams, 322
Csoka, L.S., 22, 29
Cullen, J., 190, 208
cultural change, 17
cultural diversity, 322
Cunningham, D.J., 279, 280, 289
Curcio, R.J., 111
curricular innovation, 347, 350, 362
curricular transformation, 345, 359, 361
curriculum overview, 351, 362
Dalglish, C., 17
Dalziel, S., 386, 397
Dam, G.T., 186
Damon, W., 250
Daniel, J.S., 306

Daniels, M.J., 231, 382
Das, T.K., 233, 250
Davidson, L.S., 223, 229
Davies, L., 6, 14
Davis, S.M., 281, 288
Day, J., 362
De Corte, E., 435
De Groot, A., 434
De Leeuw, N., 440, 449
Dearing Report, 6, 294, 306
Deden, A., 139, 142, 146
Delhoofen, P., 173, 186
Deloitte Haskins & Sells, 250
Denison, E., 136, 146
Denning, P.J., 129, 140, 141, 146
Dennis, 164
Derby, D.R., 14
DeSanctis, G., 269, 272
DFE, 33, 34, 37, 54
Diependaal, R.J., 88, 109
distance learning, 147, 255, 257, 260, 269
Dixon, N., 208
Dochy, F.J., 370, 371, 377, 381, 382, 400, 402, 415, 416
Driver, R., 440, 449
Duffy, T., 190, 191, 196, 207, 208, 219, 280, 289
Dumova, T., 129
Dunning, J.H., 36, 54
Dutton, W.H., 129, 146, 147
Eaglin, R.G., 259, 272
Eastcott, R., 302, 306
economic problems, 419
economic sciences, 87
economics education, 57, 419, 423, 431
economics of learning, 58, 60, 66
Edge, A.G., 7, 14
EDINEB, 36, 54, 294, 299, 306, 397, 447, 449, 450
Edvardsson, B., 288
Eitel, F., 191, 208
Elliott, R., 46, 54
employment market, 4, 22, 365, 366, 367, 371, 372
engineering sciences, 87
Eraut, M., 10, 14
Ericsson, K.A., 420, 421, 424, 427, 434
Eringa, K., 275, 399
Ernst & Whinney, 250

Evers, F.T., 389, 397
expertise, 4, 21, 22, 23, 31, 74, 75, 76, 87, 94, 102, 103, 178, 210, 246, 269, 298, 301, 302, 304, 312, 324, 329, 386, 395, 419, 420, 421, 422, 423, 424, 425, 427, 428, 429, 432, 433, 434
Extejt, M., 383, 397
external learning, 322
face validity, 409
Faerman, S.R., 416
Falconer, S., 3
Farmer, B., 306
Farwell, 165
Feild, H.S., 386, 397
Feletti, G., 188, 207
Feltham, R.T., 415
Feltovich, P., 434
Ferner, A., 39, 54
Field, L., 27, 29, 94
Finn, C.E., 297, 306
Firestone, C.M., 146, 147
Fischer, K.W., 233, 234, 235, 250, 251
Fisher, R., 386, 397
Fishman, C., 361, 362
Fitz-Enz, J., 325, 342
Fitzpatrick, J.A., 14
Fletcher, S., 415
Flowers, S., 300, 304, 305
focus group, 151
Fogel, D.S., 386, 397
Folks Jr., W.S., 342
Forbes, J.B., 383, 397
Foster, D., 141, 146, 242
Foster, G., 443, 450
Foucault, M., 139, 146
Fowler, A., 34, 54
Fox, W.A., 152, 164
Francis, M.C., 231, 250
Frank, F., 398
Frecka, T.J., 250
Frederick, D.M., 422, 434
Frederick, J., 17
Freeman, J., 347, 362
Fulmer, R.M., 21, 29
Fulwiler, T., 229
Gagne, R.M., 314, 318
Gainen, J., 231, 250
Galagan, P.A., 389, 397
Gallupe, R.B., 154, 164

Gamble, P.R., 294, 306, 324, 325, 350
Gamson, 150, 164
Gaugler, B.B., 386, 397
Geall, V., 5, 14, 306
Gell, M., 140, 146
George, 164
George, W., 288
Geus, A.P. de, 276, 280, 288
Gheis, P., 14
Ghoshal, S., 323, 342
Gibbons, M., 281, 282, 288
Gibbs, G., 302, 306
Giere, R., 449
Gijselaers, W.H., 67, 171, 172, 174, 175, 186, 191, 208, 284, 288, 306, 362, 434, 435, 450
Gilbert, 450
Gilbert, D., 208
Glaser, R., 420, 428, 434, 435
Goldin, C., 229
Goodsell, A., 152, 164
Gosling, D., 302, 306
grading criteria, 155, 156, 159, 226
Graham, E., 164
Graham, L., 273
Grandmont, J.M., 61, 67
Grant, R.M., 58, 67, 219, 321, 342, 383
Green, F., 101, 109, 129, 258
Greene, J.F., 423, 435
Greene, K.C., 272, 421, 435
Greenwood, R.G., 7, 14
Gregersen, H.B., 324, 326, 342
Greising, D., 152, 164
Griffin, D., 432, 434
Grönroos, C., 276, 278, 283, 288
groupware, 150, 153, 154, 159, 160, 161, 214
Guerrier, Y., 208, 398
Guesne, E., 440, 449
Guirdham, M., 3, 7, 14
Gummesson, E., 277, 288
Gumnior, E.C., 223, 229
Gunn, P., 362
Gunnarsson, E., 186
Guzdial, M., 189, 190, 208
Habermas, J., 138, 146
Hackley, P., 267, 273
Haeckel, S.H., 133, 134, 135, 136, 146
Hall, L., 55

Hambleton, R.K., 416
Hamel, G., 76, 77, 84, 280, 288, 321, 322, 342
Hamm, S., 5, 14
Hamming, R.W., 146
Hampden-Turner, C., 343
Handy, C., 3, 4, 14, 330, 343
Hannan, M., 347, 362
Hansen, W.L., 224, 225, 227, 229
Hanson, W.L., 10, 14
Harris, N., 294, 301, 305, 306
Harris, R., 389, 397
Hart, C.W., 288
Harvard Business Review, 29, 30, 288, 343, 398
Harvey, L., 3, 4, 5, 7, 14, 292, 295, 306
Hashimoto, M., 106, 109
Haynes, P., 28, 29
Healy, D., 141, 146
Heevel, A.J., 289
Heijke, J.A.M., 85, 86, 107, 109
Henderson, D.R., 147
Henkoff, R., 389, 398
Herrington, A., 223, 224, 229
Herriot, P., 415
Heskett, J.L., 279, 288
Heynen, G.W., 289
Hickson, D.J., 4, 14
Higher Education Funding Council England, 306
higher education institutions, 291, 347
higher vocational education, 399, 403
Hilton, P., 14
Hiltz, S.R., 140, 141, 143, 146, 148
Hodgetts, R.M., 7, 14
Hoecklin, L., 322, 323, 325, 343
Hoekstra, K., 381
Hofer, B.K., 246, 250
Hoge, B., 255, 261, 264, 267, 273
Holland, J., 60, 67
homonyms, 437
Horngren, C.T., 443, 450
Howard, S., 35, 54
Huber, G.E., 233, 234, 236, 238, 240, 241, 242, 251
human capital, 63, 101, 104, 105, 109
human resource management, 73, 323, 416
Hunter, B., 139, 140, 146

Husén, T., 435
Ibbetson, A., 194, 208
IBM, 79, 151, 154, 164, 386, 400
informatics studies, 86, 87, 88, 89
information systems, 71, 72, 149, 151, 164, 165, 208, 210, 219, 349
Inklaar, Y., 381
interactive video, 256, 257, 258, 259, 260, 261, 262, 263, 264, 265, 266, 267, 268, 271
Internet technologies, 256, 272
investment analysis, 111, 113, 127
IS departments, 72, 73, 74, 77
Isselhardt, B., 209
Jansen, P.G., 370, 382, 402, 405, 415
Jarvenpaa, S.L., 146
Jennings, P.L., 293, 294, 306
Jensen, K.R., 321
Jick, T.D., 347, 362
Johansen, R., 322, 323, 324, 325, 326, 343
Johnson, D., 208
Johnson, D.W., 164
Johnson-Laird, P.N., 84
Johnston, R., 288
Jonassen, D.H., 289
Jones, 164
Jones, D., 147
Jongh, F. de, 370, 382, 402, 406, 415
Joosten, T.M., 289
Jordan, J., 68
Kant, 75, 84
Kanter, R.M., 345, 346, 347, 360, 361, 362
Kaplan, D.M., 14
Karpin, D.S., 17, 18, 29
Kasper, H., 186, 288, 434, 435
Kay, J., 428, 434
Kaye, B., 29
Kedia, B.L., 331, 343
Keel, S.B., 386, 389, 398
Keizer, P.K., 186, 288, 434, 435
Kelley, A., 348, 362
Kember, D., 283, 288
Kenneth, W., 67
Kenny, S.S., 258, 272
Kiechel, W., 389, 398
King, P.M., 233, 235, 236, 238, 240, 241, 245, 250, 251

King, S., 41, 54, 308
Kingman-Brundage, J., 277, 278, 288
Kirch D., 208
Kitchener, K.S., 233, 234, 235, 236, 238, 240, 241, 242, 245, 250, 251
Klarus, R., 371, 382
Klenke, K., 307, 318
Knight, P.T., 7, 14
knowledge creation, 130, 131, 140
knowledge hierarchy, 135
knowledge management, 65, 333
knowledge-based organization, 17
Knuth, R.A., 279, 280, 289
Kohn, A., 194, 208
Kolb, D.A., 185, 186, 288, 362
Kollock, P., 141, 146
Kotter, J.P., 298, 306
Krepps, D., 67
Kreps, D., 61, 67
Krueger, A.O., 229
Kulka, 164
Kurshan, B., 135, 146
Kwok, C., 342
labor market, 14, 32, 40, 46, 66, 86, 87, 89, 90, 91, 92, 94, 106, 108, 170, 171, 186
Lane, G., 8, 9, 14
Laurillard, D., 304, 306
Lawson, D., 306
Layton, D., 438, 450
leadership, 307
leadership development, 19, 20, 21, 24, 25, 26, 28, 29, 326, 332
leadership programs, 17, 23, 28
Learner, R., 229
learning algorithm, 62
learning environment, 9, 142, 150, 153, 154, 157, 162, 172, 192, 193, 208, 222, 223, 280, 281, 285, 323, 331, 332, 333, 340, 342, 361, 413, 414
learning experience, 5, 9, 25, 194, 196, 202, 291, 300, 335, 362, 391
learning organizations, 57, 283, 289, 327, 332
learning packages, 31, 32, 50
learning system, 57
learning theory, 113, 306
learning to learn, 250, 285, 367, 369, 372, 380, 381

Lee, G., 415
Lefrancois, G.R., 314, 318
Lehman, D.R., 423, 424, 433, 434
Leidner, D.E., 146
Lempert, R.O., 423, 433, 434
Lenk, C., 135, 146
Lerner, R.M., 250
Lester, R.K., 29
Lievens, F., 401, 411, 415
Light, R., 164
Lim, 154, 164
Limoges, C., 288
Linbeck, A., 54
Little, B., 5, 14, 267
Littlefield, D., 31, 32, 35, 54
Lockard, J., 141, 147
Locke, J., 131, 147
logical argument, 7
Looijen, M., 85, 109
Louis, M.R., 164
Lovelock, C.H., 289
Lowenthal, D., 190, 208
Lowry, P.E., 386, 398
Lowyck, J., 289
Lucas, R., 229
Luken, T., 371, 382, 401, 403, 411, 415
Lumsden, K., 53
Lynch, C.L., 231, 232, 233, 234, 235, 236, 238, 240, 241, 242, 243, 245, 251
Maesen de Sombreff, P.E., 415
Maher, 164
Maher, J.E., 152, 221, 229
Mainstone, L.E., 383
Malek, K.M., 29
management decisions, 308
management education, 26, 164, 190, 272, 275, 276, 281, 282, 285, 287, 288, 289, 304, 309, 333, 362, 397, 419, 424, 425, 434
management skills, 18, 20, 29, 326
managerial skills, 384, 385, 401
Manning, A., 37, 54
Mapp, L., 295, 306
Marien, M., 129, 147
Marimon, R., 58, 61, 67
Markel, M., 257, 269, 272
Marlowe, B.C., 279, 289
Marquardt, M., 323, 325, 343
Marsick, V., 190, 208

Index 457

Martin, 164
Martin, L., 55
Marton, F., 439, 440, 450
Martz, B., 149, 164
Mather, M.A., 140, 147
Matthes, K., 398
May, B.H., 343
May, D.R., 343
MBA programs, 22, 57, 58, 65, 66, 150, 327, 328, 335, 383
McCloskey, D.N., 430, 434
McCormack, C., 141, 142, 147
McCuddy, M.K., 383
McGrath, J.E., 161, 164, 416
McKibben, L.E., 150, 346, 358, 362
McKibbin, 164, 275, 289
McMahon, J.T., 386, 398
McNabb, R., 54
McNay, I., 298, 306
Medema, S.G., 435
Meister, J.C., 21, 29
Melody, W.H., 136, 147
Metcalfe, R.M., 129, 146
methods of instruction, 152
Meyer, M.H., 67
Middlehurst, R., 298, 306
Milkman, M., 221
Milter, R.G., 67, 82, 84, 171, 185, 186, 208, 211, 219, 306, 362, 434
Mincer, J., 101, 104, 109
Mintzberg, H., 384, 398, 401, 405, 415
MMC, 40, 54
models of learning, 57, 58, 61, 62, 67, 140, 279
Money, W.H., 164
Monk, D., 31
Moon, S., 5, 14, 306
Moore, J.F., 321, 322, 332, 338, 343
Morris, N.M., 84
Morrison, A.J., 324, 326, 342
motivation theories, 308, 309, 317
Moust, J.H., 173, 186
Mulder, T.C., 250, 416
multinational teams, 322, 335
Mumford, A., 54
Munn, C., 54
Muth, J.F., 67
Myer, P.J., 133, 136, 146, 147
Nanus, B., 307, 318

Nash, J., 67
NCVQ, 34, 54
Nellis, J.G., 57, 67
Nelson, R., 60, 67
Newell, S., 208, 398
Nguyen, D.T., 141, 142, 143, 147
Nicastro, M.L., 152, 164
Nietzsche, F., 76, 143, 147
Nisbett, R., 415, 423, 433, 434
Nolan, R.L., 133, 134, 135, 136, 146
Nonaka, I., 68
Norman, D., 189, 208, 438, 450
Normann, R., 289
North, D.M., 324, 328, 339, 386, 398
Nowotny, H., 288
Nunamaker, 152, 160, 164, 165, 195, 208
O'Hara-Deveraux, M., 322, 323, 324, 325, 326, 343
O'Rourke, B.K., 419, 425, 433, 434
occupational domain, 86, 94
OECD, 29
OFGAS, 38, 40, 54
Onstenk, J., 403, 415
open-ended problems, 231, 232, 233, 235, 236, 237, 239, 240, 242, 244, 246
organization of learning, 57
organizational values, 17
O'Rourke, B.K, 450
Osborn, A.F., 154, 164
Ottewill, R., 291, 293, 294, 306
Otting, H., 275
Page, M.L., 289
Palmer, A., 291, 294, 301, 305, 306
Panzar, J., 229
Parry, K., 29
partnership, 21, 22, 26, 57, 59, 63, 64, 65, 206, 330, 334, 340
Paul, L., 169
Payne, W., 221
Peart, S.J., 224, 229
Peat Marwick Main, 250
Pedlar, M.I., 29
Pedler, M., 54
peer evaluation, 153, 155
Penner, B.C., 435
Penner, R.G., 229
Penrose, E., 59, 68
Perotti, J., 71
Perotti, V., 209, 345, 362

Perry, W., 208
personal skills, 4, 7, 92, 94, 292
Peters, T., 208
Petersen, M., 84
Pettigrew, M., 3
Pettijohn, J.B., 127
Phillips, V., 141, 147, 257, 272
Pickard, J., 54
Pieke, E., 403, 415
Pieké, E., 365
Pincus, J.D., 328, 343
Pintrich, P.R., 246, 250
Piore, M.J., 29
Pirie, W.L., 383
Pisano, G., 68
Pitcher, J., 15
Popper, K., 131, 132, 133, 137, 147
Porter, D., 146, 147
Porter, L., 141
Porter, L.R., 147
Porter, L.W., 150, 164, 275, 289, 346, 358, 362
portfolio selection, 111, 112, 115, 127
portfolio worker, 3
Post, T.R., 435
Postlethwaite, T.N., 435
Potashnik, M., 257, 272
Povah, N., 400, 415
Prahalad, C.K., 76, 77, 84, 280, 288, 321, 322, 342
predictive validity, 409
Price Waterhouse, 250
problem-based learning, 172, 173, 175, 186, 187, 207, 208, 209, 211, 212, 213, 214, 215, 216, 218, 219, 280, 284, 285, 286, 287, 288, 404, 413, 448
problem-oriented learning, 169, 171, 172, 173, 174, 177, 178, 179
problem-solving, 7, 150, 154, 188, 190, 191, 203, 221, 222, 223, 258, 262, 265, 390, 391, 393, 425, 430, 431, 433
professional practitioners, 72
Pugh, D.S., 4, 14
Purcell, K., 6, 15
Quacquarelli, N., 328, 343
Quinn, J.B., 59, 68, 401
Quinn, R.E., 17, 29, 405, 416
Rahm, D., 258, 272

Ramaekers, G.W.M., 85, 86, 107, 109, 381
Ramsden, P., 292, 298, 299, 300, 303, 306
RAND Institute on Education and Training, 343
Rausch, E., 307, 310, 311, 313, 319
Ray, R., 127
RBL, 291, 292, 293, 294, 295, 296, 297, 298, 299, 300, 301, 302, 303, 304, 305
Reed, B.J., 258, 272
Regan, S., 57
Reilly, F.K., 127
Reinig, B.A., 160, 165
retention, 73, 113, 114, 127, 292, 314
Rheingold, H., 141, 147
Rijke, T.R., 370, 371, 377, 381, 382, 400, 402, 415
Riley, M., 386, 398
Robinson, A., 8, 9, 14, 190
Robinson, G., 208
Roe, R.A., 382
Rogers, E.M., 129, 145
Roget's II the new media thesaurus, 147
Romer, P., 136, 137, 147
Rosch, E., 450
Rosenthal, D.B., 397
Ross, L., 415
Rost, J., 307, 319
Rouse, W.B., 84
Ruelle, D.J., 14
Ruggles III, R.L., 29
Rush, J.C., 389, 397
Rust, C., 295, 306
Rutkowski, A.M., 142, 143, 147
Ryan, P., 54
Saggers, R., 33, 41, 54
Samuels, D., 137, 147, 435
Sapsford, D., 54
Sarin, R., 67
Sasser, W.E., 288
Sattinger, M., 104, 109
Savery, J., 190, 191, 196, 207, 208, 219, 280, 289
Schank, R., 130, 140, 141, 147, 444, 450
Scheuing, E.E., 288
Schmidt, H.G., 422, 425, 435
Schneider, B., 277, 278, 289
Scholtes, P.R., 30

Index 459

Schon, D.A., 190, 208
Schroeder, D.L., 383
Schultz, R.P., 229
Schultz, T.W., 104, 109
Schumpeter, J.A., 59, 68
Schutte, J.G., 261, 272
Schwartzman, S., 288
Scott, P., 288
Seegers, J., 400, 401, 402, 405, 411, 415, 416
Segers, M.S.R., 416
Seiler, M.R., 14
Senge, P.M., 17, 30, 76, 81, 84, 283, 289, 325
Setton, D., 29
Seven-Jump, 173, 174
Shackleton, J.R., 47, 55, 101, 109, 386, 398
Shah, A., 55
Shepherd, M.M., 165
Sheppard, B., 269, 272
Shields, R., 145, 147
Shockley-Zalabak, P., 165
Shrivastava, P., 258, 272
Shuen, A., 68
Simon, H.A., 68, 288, 420, 434
Sloman, M., 55
Slotta, J.D., 440, 449
Small, M., 208
Smith, A., 187, 188, 190, 191, 197, 203, 207
Smith, B., 293, 295, 305, 306
Smith, C., 147
Smith, J., 420, 421, 427, 434
Smith, M., 141, 146
Smith, V.L., 419, 431, 435
Smyth, R., 147
Snippe, M.D., 409, 414, 416
Snower, D., 54
social learning theory, 385
software skills, 209, 218
Soper, J.C., 272
Sorce, P., 209
Souder, W., 201, 207, 208
Southern Association of Colleges and Schools, 255, 272
Spencer, J., 221, 223, 229
Spender, J.C., 58, 67
Sprague, 160, 164

Stark, J.S., 250
Steenbergen, G., 381
Stein, B.A., 347, 362
Steuer, E., 386, 398
Stiglitz, J.E., 229
Stinson, J.E., 67, 82, 84, 171, 185, 186, 208, 211, 219, 306, 362, 434
Stoffel, J.A., 260, 273
Stogdill, R.M., 307, 318, 319
Storey, J., 55
Strasser, S.E., 383
Studiegids, 88, 109
Summers, L.H., 229
Sunal, C.S., 142, 147
Sunal, D.W., 147
Taconis, R., 440, 450
Tagg, 149, 164
Takeuchi, H., 68
Tapscott, D., 129, 136, 147
Taylor, C., 55, 386, 398
Taylor, M., 55
Teal, T., 30
team work, 7, 161, 292
Teece, D., 60, 68
Tempelaar, D.T., 173, 186, 288, 434, 435
Tepper, M., 141, 147
Terlouw, C., 186
Thompson, J.E., 403, 416
Thompson, M.P., 401, 416
Thorne, P., 55
Thornton, G.C., 397, 400, 401, 405, 409, 411, 416
Tiberghien, A., 440, 449
Tillema, H.H., 283, 289, 382, 400, 416
Tinto, 164
Today's news, 148
Torrington, D., 55
Touche Ross, 250
traditional lecture, 209, 262
traditional teaching, 114, 127, 196, 203, 210, 301
training courses, 107
training methods, 31, 32, 33, 34, 35, 36, 37, 38, 39, 41, 42, 44, 45, 46, 47, 48
transferable skills, 4, 6, 7, 8, 9, 13, 64
Trauth, E., 149, 151, 165
Treacy, M., 84
Trompenaars, F., 323, 343
Trow, M., 288

Tsoukas, H., 58, 68
Turoff, M., 143, 148
Tversky, A., 432, 434
Tzannatos, Z., 54
U.S. Labor Secretary's Commission, 165
undergraduate programs, 6
Unison, 55
US Labor Secretary's Commission, 150
Utterback, J.M., 67
Vaatstra, R.F., 422, 425, 435
Vaill, P.B., 330, 331, 343
Valacich, 164
van Hout, J.F., 186
Vasarhelyi, M.A., 257, 269, 273
Vaughan, J.A., 318
Vernooij, A.T.J., 422, 423, 435, 437, 441, 442, 448, 450
Vicere, A.A., 30
Vidmar, T., 267, 269, 272
vocational Universities, 6
Vogel, 164
Vogel, D.R., 258, 272
Vogt, E.E., 131, 132, 135, 148
Vollmers, A.C., 273
Vollmers, S.M., 267, 273
Vosniadou, S., 439, 450
Voss, J.F., 420, 421, 423, 425, 427, 428, 429, 430, 431, 433, 435
Voss, L.A., 14
Waixel, C., 386, 398
Walstad, W.B., 272
Washbush, J.B., 307, 311, 313, 319
Washington State Work Based Learning Resource Center, 8, 15
Watters, C., 139, 148
Watts, 450
Webster, J., 148, 267, 273
Webster's new encyclopedic dictionary, 148
Weele, van der, A., 170, 171, 186
Weibull, J., 68
Weinreich, F., 141, 148
Wellman, B., 140, 141, 146
Wellstead, W.R., 386, 398
Wendel, F.C., 386, 398

Weston, C., 55
Whetten, D.A., 385, 398
Whiteway Research, 55, 342
Whiting, C.S., 154, 165
Whitley, R., 32, 35, 37, 38, 39, 41, 44, 46, 48, 55, 422, 435
Whitley, T., 55
Wick, C., 208
Wiedersheim-Paul, F., 186
Wiersema, F., 84
Wijnen, W.H., 282, 289
Willems, J., 186
Winter, S., 67, 84, 127, 164, 342, 343
Wisdom, J., 295, 306
Woerden, van, W., 172, 173, 186
Wolcott, S.K., 231, 233, 234, 236, 238, 240, 241, 242, 243, 245, 251
Wolfhagen, H.A., 282, 289
Wood, P.K., 234, 251
Woodruffe, C., 400, 416
Woolfenden, G.A., 386, 398
work based learning, 3, 5, 8, 11, 13, 14, 15
work environment, 5, 8, 25, 280, 384
work placement, 4, 5, 9, 11, 12, 13
workforce, 3, 6, 8, 40, 47, 147, 336
working life, 3, 4, 5, 6, 23, 101, 104
workplace, 4, 5, 7, 10, 20, 72, 73, 74, 82, 83, 151, 152, 292, 296, 298, 305, 394
Wright, L., 149, 159, 164
writing problems, 221
writing skills, 93, 94, 96, 97, 98, 99, 106, 222, 223, 224, 226, 227
Yeager, S.J., 386, 398
York Christ, M., 383
You, Y., 258, 272
Young, J., 273
Yu, Q., 14
Zaal, J.N., 401, 416
Zeithaml, V.A., 277, 289
Zeitz, C.M., 428, 435
Zien, K.A., 68
Zuboff, S., 84
Zwaal, W., 399

Educational Innovation in Economics and Business

1. W.H. Gijselaers, D.T. Tempelaar, P.K. Keizer, J.M. Blommaert, E.M. Bernard and H. Kasper (eds.): *Educational Innovation in Economics and Business Administration. The Case of Problem Based Learning.* 1995   ISBN 0-7923-3272-5
2. D.T. Tempelaar, F. Wiedersheim-Paul and E. Gunnarsson (eds.): *Educational Innovation in Economics and Business II. In Search of Quality.* 1998
ISBN 0-7923-4901-6
3. R.G. Milter, J.E. Stinson and W.H. Gijselaers (eds.): *Educational Innovation in Economics and Business III.* Innovative Practices in Business Education. 1998
ISBN 0-7923-5001-4
4. J. Hommes, P.K. Keizer, M. Pettigrew and J. Troy (eds.): *Educational Innovation in Economics and Business IV.* Learning in a Changing Environment. 1999
ISBN 0-7923-5855-4
5. L. Borghans, W.H. Gijselaers, R.G. Milter and J.E. Stinson (eds.): *Educational Innovation in Economics and Business V.* Business Education for the Changing Workplace. 2000   ISBN 0-7923-6550-X

KLUWER ACADEMIC PUBLISHERS – DORDRECHT / BOSTON / LONDON